LETTERS OF DELMORE SCHWARTZ

Photo by Mrs. Forbes Johnson-Storey/Courtesy of the Gotham Book Mart

Letters of
DELMORE
SCHWARTZ

Selected and Edited by
ROBERT PHILLIPS
Foreword by
KARL SHAPIRO

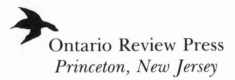

Ontario Review Press
Princeton, New Jersey

Library of Congress Cataloging in Publication Data

Schwartz, Delmore, 1913–1966.
  Letters of Delmore Schwartz.

  Includes index.
  1. Schwartz, Delmore, 1913–1966—Correspondence.
  2. Authors, American—20th century—Correspondence.
  I. Phillips, Robert S.   II. Title.
PS3537.C79Z48   1984   818'.5209 [B]   84-20761

Distributed by **Persea Books, Inc.**
225 Lafayette St.
New York, N.Y. 10012

ACKNOWLEDGMENTS

In the collection, annotation, editing and publication of Delmore Schwartz's correspondence, I have been helped in many ways by individuals and institutions. It is difficult to express adequate appreciation.

My first debt is to the late Dwight Macdonald, formerly Schwartz's literary executor. It was he who enthusiastically gave me permission to pursue and publish the letters—a project he had considered doing himself, had time and health permitted. I deeply regret he did not live to see this volume completed.

Second, my special thanks to James Atlas, for his generosity in opening up his collection of Schwartz letters and memorabilia which he had gathered during the years he was writing *Delmore Schwartz: The Life of an American Poet.* He was of invaluable assistance.

Third, my gratitude to Kenneth Schwartz, the writer's brother and heir, for sanctioning the project and for subsequently naming me Schwartz's literary executor.

Gertrude Buckman and Elizabeth Pollet, Schwartz's two wives, have been cooperative and understanding.

My publishers, Raymond J. Smith and his wife Joyce Carol Oates, were encouraging and helpful from the beginning of this long journey. The editorial attentions of the former have been inestimable.

My wife, Judith, helped decipher many of Schwartz's most illegible letters.

Elizabeth Beardsley of the Katonah Village Library made research facilities available to me. Richard Foerster duplicated the many manuscript pages.

Every owner of Schwartz correspondence I contacted cooperated, with two exceptions: Eleanor Goff did not answer my letters, and Diana Trilling felt Delmore's letters to her husband, Lionel Trilling, could not be accurately represented without publishing the Trilling side of the correspondence as well. This I was not willing to do.

James Laughlin granted partial access to his correspondence, selecting those letters for my use which he felt were not libelous or injurious to others.

Gertrude Buckman and Elizabeth Pollet asked for certain deletions in letters to them. Some of the letters to both at the Beinecke Library, Yale University are restricted.

It is unfortunate that the best letters to Meyer Schapiro, Schwartz's close friend, were borrowed by a scholar who was to write the first book on Delmore and never returned. This was in the days before wide use of duplicating machines. Efforts to locate the scholar have failed. The book never appeared.

I acknowledge the aid of the following individuals and institutions for making letters in their collections available:

Donald Anderle, Associate Director for Special Collections, New York Public Library; The Henry W. and Albert A. Berg Collection, The New York Public Library, Astor, Lenox and Tilden Foundations; Suzanne N.H. Currier, Manuscript Department, The Houghton Library, Harvard University; Amy S. Doherty, University Archivist, George Arents Research Library, Syracuse University; Lillian Doherty, Secretary to Saul Bellow, Committee on Social Thought, University of Chicago; Ellen S. Dunlap, Research Librarian, Humanities Research Center, University of Texas, Thomas B. Greenslade, College Archivist, Chalmers Memorial Library, Kenyon College; Curtis Harnack, Executive Director, Yaddo; Sara S. Hodson, Assistant Curator, Library Manuscripts, The Huntington Library; James H. Hutson, Chief, Manuscript Division, The Library of Congress; Mary Johnson, American Academy and Institute of Arts and Letters; Diane Kent, *The Partisan Review*; Mrs. Mary C. La Fogg, Assistant to the Acting Head, Yale University Library; Alan K. Lathrop, Curator, Manuscript Division, University of Minnesota Libraries; Kenneth A. Lohf, Librarian for Rare Books and Manuscripts, Columbia University; Douglas Macdonald, Research and Manuscript Assistant, Muger Memorial Library, Boston University; John Martin, Black Sparrow Press; Emilie W. Mills, Special Collections Librarian, University of North Carolina at Greensboro; Eleanor C. Nicoles, Special Collections Librarian, Wellesley College Library; Mrs. Mardel Pacheco, Assistant to the Curator of Manuscripts, Princeton University Library; Jean F. Preston, Curator of Manuscripts, Princeton University; Judith A. Schiff, Chief Research Archivist, Yale University Library; David E. Schoonover, Curator, The Beinecke Rare Book and Manuscript Library, Yale University; Elizabeth A. Stege, Manuscript Research Specialist, The Joseph Regenstein Library, University of Chicago; John Sullivan, the Library of Congress; Sem K. Sutter, Manuscripts Research Specialist, Special Collections, Joseph Regenstein Library, University of Chicago; and Brooke Whiting, Curator of Rare Books and Literary Manuscripts, University of California, Los Angeles.

For permission to publish the letters to Ezra Pound and William Carlos Williams, acknowledgements are made to the American Collection of the Beinecke Library, Yale University; to Kenneth Schwartz; to Mrs. Mary de Rachewiltz; and to James Laughlin, acting in behalf of the Estate of William Carlos Williams. The letters to Paul Goodman are published with the permission of Taylor Stoehr, Goodman's literary executor. Letters to R. P. Blackmur belong to the R. P. Blackmur papers at Princeton University, and are published with the permission of Joseph Frank. The letters to Mark Van Doren and F. W. Dupee are published with the permission of the Columbia University Library. The letters to Julian Sawyer are published with the permission of George Minkoff.

For making letters available, for information regarding the location of letters and identification of correspondents, for assistance in annotation, my thanks go to the individuals listed below:

Philip Ahrens, Mary Hoover Aiken, William Arrowsmith, William Barrett, Saul Bellow, Arthur Berger, Frank Bidart, Lady Caroline Blackwood, Philip Booth, Andreas Brown, Gertrude Buckman, Erin Clermont, William Cole, Edward T. Cone, Hope Hale Davis, Robert Gorham Davis, Peter DeVries, Rose Dickson, George Dillon, Sally Daniels Dike, Kate Donahue, Barbara Dupee, Richard Eberhart, Arthur J. Fritz, Jr., Robert Giroux, Sally Goodman, the late Horace Gregory, Elizabeth Hardwick, Gilbert Harrison, Robert Hivnor, Philip Horton, Irving Howe, Mary Jarrell, Gloria Jones, J. M. Kaplan, Alfred Kazin, Richard Kelly, Hilton Kramer, Joseph Langland, James Laughlin, Harry Levin, Robie Macauley, Gloria Macdonald, Nancy Macdonald, William Maxwell, Edward Mendelson, Arthur Mizener, Rosemary Mizener, Mrs. Stanley Monsell, Theodore Morrison, Howard Moss, Mary O'Connor, Marie C. Nelson, Dorothy Norman, Phoebe Palmer, Frank P. Piskor, William Phillips, Elizabeth Pollet, the late Norman Holmes Pearson, Meyer Schapiro, Karl Shapiro, Eileen Simpson, Lawrence Beall Smith, Winn R. Smith, Frances Steloff, Holly Stevens, Taylor Stoehr, Julian Symons, Aileen Ward, Richard Wilbur, the late Marya Zaturenska, Maurice Zolotow, and David H. Zucker.

Every effort has been made to secure permission to publish material. Oversights will be corrected in future printings.

Some of these letters first appeared in *Antaeus*, *Cumberland Poetry Journal*, and *Ontario Review*.

CONTENTS

ILLUSTRATIONS

Frontispiece: Portrait study made in 1938, shortly after publication of first book.

Following page 180:

Another portrait study made in 1943.

On Ellery Street, Cambridge, in the 1940's.

Circa 1949.

With Gertrude Buckman, 1938.

Elizabeth Pollet at the farmhouse in Baptistown, New Jersey, in the 1950's.

R.P. Blackmur in his Princeton office, circa 1951.

With Randall Jarrell at the Library of Congress, 1958.

Letter to R.P. Blackmur, circa 1946.

Circa 1958. "Nobody should look that unhappy."—W.H. Auden

Circa 1961.

Syracuse, October 18, 1965. Perhaps the last photo taken of the poet.

FOREWORD

We were almost exact contemporaries and grew up under the same spheres of influence, Jewish, Depression, intellectual, poetic, but with strongly marked differences in our voyages. He was a literary prodigy; I was not. He was a New Yorker; I was a Baltimorean, a "Southerner." He was well educated; I was educated cosmetically. He was an activist on the attack; I was a spectator without a cause. He fought like a pit bull to avoid the uniform; I accepted conscription with a shrug. He equated literary success with power; I ridiculed literary power. He belonged to the Euro-cultural dispensation; I was a Whitman-Williams isolationist. And so on. He was suspicious of my literary successes, as he was of everybody's, and accepted me as an equal belatedly—"It occurred to me after seeing you again in Chicago that you were just as much an underground character—in Dostoyevsky's sense—as I am, though you handle it with far more grace and tact" [letter of Jan. 20, 1955].

The decade schema is standard in literary commentary today and these letters, a vital part of the Schwartz *oeuvre*, advance from the "dirty Thirties" to the time of his death in the mid-Sixties. Considering the speed with which we lead our accelerated lives this processional is inescapable. We go faster and faster, as if time itself were running out. Schwartz was at the center of the horrors of the Thirties which were barely observed by anyone except the intellectuals. In terms of worldwide cultural significance, events such as the Spanish Civil War, the Moscow Trials and the capitulation to Hitler, the arts were to undergo the most radical surgery, if not death. In the Forties Schwartz was made an editor of the *Partisan Review*, the most ideologically sensitive and outspoken cultural organ in this country. Considered "Trotskyite" by the Communists from whom it had been kidnapped, literally in fact, it provided the proving-ground for poets, fictionists and political and esthetic philosophers, the nexus of the arts, which were being stifled in totalitarian Germany and totalitarian Russia.

By virtue of his youth, explosive talent and critical success, Schwartz

xi

became the touchstone of his generation, which included Wilbur, Viereck, Rukeyser, Roethke, myself, W.T. Scott, Nims, Mayo, Lowell, Jarrell, Holmes, Eberhart, Nemerov, Ciardi, Bishop—to recite from the roster of a Fifties anthology. Among this company only Schwartz was seated at the center of power. This was before the Sixties and the psychological vulgarization of poetry as suicide, the Sylvia Plath syndrome (almost all of this roster was in the military; even Lowell tried to get in but was turned down). Delmore was a point of reference: the *Partisan Review*, which was not partisan except ironically, was a point of reference. Here were the regnant philosophers, Sartre and Camus, Merleau-Ponty, Jaspers and Tillich, here were Orwell and Kafka and Malraux, here was T.S. Eliot, the Samuel Johnson of the age. The *Partisan* had made an end-run around Stalinism. To be published in it was glamorous. To be an editor like Schwartz was awesome.

The poet has a special obligation to disaffiliation, or at least a powerful hankering for it. Schwartz was not and could not be the house canary; he was hawkish to all and to his kind. His swoops kept poets awake. Acceptance in *PR* was acclamation; it conferred a special ideological status on the accepted. Schwartz was in part a byproduct of the intellectual ambitiousness of the real editors, the Rahvs and Macdonalds, and in part a justification of their existence. If this makes too much of a mere magazine, it must be remembered that most American magazines were deliberately anti-intellectual, even unintelligent, stupid, to use one of Schwartz's favorite terms, unable to cope with ideas qua ideas. The superiority of *PR* was "un-American" and of course it was tarred "Jewish." Jewish fulfilled a need for the few important Wasp periodicals, *Kenyon* and *Southern* and *Hudson*. *PR* was the New York conduit to the separated Old World, the crimes of the Red revolution and so on.

Schwartz carried his editorial mission into the academy. It is really here that the story in the letters unfolds. The present generation has forgotten the moral constraints of the academy of the Forties, the monogamic imperative, the lofty anti-Semitism of English professors, the prudishness, the watchfulness, the conformity. Creative writing had not yet invaded the sanctum and Schwartz was something of a bellwether, even though buried in bluebooks and freshman prose. The threat of dismissal hung over him daily and dismissal meant conscription. His wife left him. The tension took a terrible toll on him, leading to drink, drugs and psychiatry, the sad pattern of so many American poets. *Humboldt's Gift* and James Atlas' biography dramatize the tortures and the ostensible decline. The letters on the other hand testify to the sweeter uses of his adversities, the fertility of the poetry, plays and criticism, his sacrificial loyalty and his self-effacement. *The Last and Lost Poems of Delmore Schwartz* edited by Robert Phillips testifies to the unwavering flame of his genius. There is no sense in which the word failure applies to this poet.

This correspondence is not "literary" except in the early stages although its subject—if a lifetime of letters can be said to have a subject—is poetry. It is furiously engaged with modern poetry and the values that poetry bestows upon its era. Each serious problem is tackled head-on, the anti-intellectualism of Williams, Eliot's religiosity, the intransigent bigotry of Pound—in a letter to Pound Schwartz "resigns" from him—Auden's frivolousness, the machinations of Tate. There is no small talk but instead a relentless watchdogging of the progress and regression of the art. He is nothing if not judgmental and there is little or no temporizing.

Above all he concerns himself with the spiritual well-being of the poet in a world of war, nausea, nightmare, chaos and the debasement of all values. If he is quixotic about the power of art he is also heroic. If he is truculent he is also passionate. It is not by chance that these letters give us a summary panorama of the tragedy and the greatness of our age.

KARL SHAPIRO

New York City
August, 1984

INTRODUCTION

DELMORE SCHWARTZ was a man of letters in every sense—poet, fiction writer, playwright, translator, essayist, reviewer, and letter writer. During the years when his intellect was most active, the late 1930's and 1940's, he wrote as many as a half dozen letters a day. He would readily have agreed with William James: "As long as there are postmen, life will have zest." Schwartz's letters were not so much evasions of more serious work, I suspect, as they were five-finger exercises which prepared him for larger tasks. What he states in letters about, say, Eliot or Pound or James, would later be embellished in essays. Besides, Schwartz loved literary activity and controversy. He loved to champion a cause here, put down a rival there. He also loved to be at the center of things, scheming and debating with his literary contemporaries— who incuded John Berryman, Randall Jarrell, Saul Bellow, Dwight Macdonald, Philip Horton, Robert Lowell, William Barrett, and Jean Stafford.

Yet it is ironic how much of his own chaotic life the letters reveal. Many were written out of loneliness, after his first or second wife had left him. Others are a form of justification of his place in the world of literature, the calling to which he apprenticed himself at the age of seventeen. In this latter category are letters to his literary elders—of which there are a great number—correspondences with Ezra Pound, W. H. Auden, Wallace Stevens, Mark Van Doren, Conrad Aiken, Allen Tate, William Carlos Williams...

It is possible that Schwartz was, like Oscar Wilde, a man who put his talent into his work and his genius into his conversation. One of the pleasures of his letters is his voice: he was a great conversationalist, and next to hearing his conversation, his letters come closest to capturing the raconteur. In his letters he lets himself go in a way that makes even his most spontaneous poetry look studied. He seems aware of this. One entry from his journal carries this little poem:

> These pieces of the self are with my friends.
> They show me as I am, which never ends.

XV

The word betrays the heart and mind. And now?
Silence is empty violence, let me bow

Before the looking-glass and smile at last,
forgiving myself for the future and the past.
Most difficult of all is self-forgiveness,
Tied to the Siamese twins, self-witness and withness.

This collection begins in October 1931, with letters to Schwartz's New York friend, Julian Sawyer. Delmore was at the University of Wisconsin for one year, seventeen, and full of himself, correcting and hectoring his more reticent correspondent. These unusual letters, long and frequent, combine youthful pomposity with genuine brilliance and enthusiasm. (Letters to Delmore's immediate family written from this first year away from home do not appear to have survived, according to his brother.) His literary constituency soon grew to include Paul Goodman, whom Schwartz met as a student at New York University; James Laughlin, who founded his own publishing firm, New Directions, in the late 1930's and took on Schwartz's first book; Philip Horton, later author of a noted biography of Hart Crane; Arthur Berger, whom he met at Harvard and who later became a noted composer; and his lifelong friends, Nancy and Dwight Macdonald. The 1940's were his most fertile decade for correspondence. By then he *was* Delmore Schwartz, the golden boy, the young culture-hero of the liberal intellectuals. His first book, *In Dreams Begin Responsibilities* (1938), had received reviews writers dream of.

Afterwards one can trace in the correspondence a decline in spirit. His translation of Rimbaud and his *magnum opus*, *Genesis*, Book One, were not received well. His first wife left him. Other factors were the self-destructive and paranoid behavior which already had begun in the 1940's—exacerbated by insomnia, alcohol and nembutal. He began to quarrel with his closest friends, as some of these letters document. In another journal entry he writes of this period:

I must think of the house on Ellery St.: where I lived alone, drank until I was a problem drinker, fell in love foolishly and vainly and wasted the years when I should have been at the height of my powers: during most of the Second World War and after...

The letters from the 1950's are more perfunctory, or more concerned with the physical acts of publication and existence. The extant letters from the 1960's are briefer yet, and the penultimate letter, a diatribe against his landlady, foreshadows collapse. Many of these later letters in no way are examples of Schwartz's best prose or thinking. But they do push his story forward and help complete what I see as an autobiography in letters, the autobiography not only of a poet and writer and critic, but also of a professor, editor, failed husband, aging lover, baseball addict, cat lover, compulsive moviegoer, military historian, student of literature and music, and superb literary politician. The letters reveal all these aspects of Schwartz's personality, and more. He himself acknowledged his complexity. In a letter of May 18, 1951, to Laughlin he writes:

> It was pleasant to learn that you expect our correspondence to be read in the international salons and boudoirs of the future. Do you think they will be able to distinguish between the obfuscations, mystifications, efforts at humor and plain statements of fact? Will they recognize my primary feelings as a correspondent—the catacomb from which I write to you, seeking to secure some word from the real world, or at least news of the Far West—and sigh with compassion? Or will they just think I am nasty, an over-eager clown, gauche, awkward, and bookish? Will they understand that I am always direct, open, friendly, simple and candid to the point of naivete until the ways of the fiendish world infuriate me and I am forced to be devious, suspicious, calculating, not that it does me any good anyway?

This passage reveals rare self-knowledge. I hope most readers will see that Schwartz was all those things, certainly manipulative, but especially generous, and a friend.

I think of Pushkin's "That hour is blessed when we meet a poet. The poet is brother to the dervish. He has no country nor is he blessed with the things of this world; and while we poor creatures that we are, are worrying about fame, about power, about riches, he stands on a basis of equality with the powerful of the earth and people bow down before him." Delmore Schwartz did, as these letters reveal, fume about fame and power and even riches; but his primary concern was always poetry, and on that ground he stood with the powerful.

I have selected letters which refer to Schwartz's own work, to literature in general, and to other writers, for their interest to readers of literature. Letters that are of interest for style or humor are also included, and letters that contain biographical or other pertinent information about Schwartz. Sometimes the same anecdote or observation was repeated from letter to letter; in those cases I chose the most lively or fullest version and deleted the others. Certain short deletions have also been made for reasons of libel, invasion of privacy, obscurity, or general repetitiousness. These are indicated by an ellipsis within brackets, or a double slash (//) for deletions of a sentence or more. I have quietly corrected typographical, spelling, and some punctuation and grammatical errors. On occasions when the syntax is still unclear, I have employed the notation [sic]. Illegible words and phrases are indicated by the notation [?]. Dates and addresses that have been supplied through postmarks, return addresses on envelopes, or contextual evidence appear within brackets. Annotations have been as factual as possible. In some instances, identification of individuals or works has proven to be impossible. For these I apologize. I take responsibility for all errors.

ROBERT PHILLIPS

Katonah, New York
July 4, 1984

CHRONOLOGY

December 8, 1913	Born in Brooklyn.
September 1927- June 1931	High schools in Manhattan. Graduated from George Washington High School.
September 1931- June 1932	Freshman at University of Wisconsin.
1932	First published work, four poems, appeared in *The Poet's Pack*, issued by George Washington High School.
February 1933- June 1935	Attended New York University, Washington Square College.
1934	"Aubade" and "The Beautiful American Word, Sure" (the latter, Schwartz's first mature published poem) appeared in *Mosaic*.
1935	B.A. degree in philosophy, New York University.
September 1935- March 1937	Graduate studies, Harvard University.
1936	"Choosing Company," play in verse and prose, published in *The New Caravan*. Received Bowdoin Prize in the humanities at Harvard, for essay "Poetry As Imitation."
December 8, 1937	Moved to 73 Washington Place, Manhattan, with brother Kenneth.
December 1937	"In Dreams Begin Responsibilities," published in *Partisan Review*.
1938	Married Gertrude Buckman. Published first

	collection of poetry and prose, *In Dreams Begin Responsibilities*, with editor James Laughlin at New Directions.
Summer 1938	Residence in rented cottage in Bennington, Vermont.
September 1938-August 1939	In residence at 8 West 105th Street, Manhattan. Brother Kenneth with them for several months.
Fall 1939-Spring 1940	At Yaddo, Saratoga Springs.
1939	Translation of Rimbaud's *Saison en Enfer* published.
1940	Awarded a Guggenheim Fellowship. Second editon of Rimbaud translation.
September 1940-August 1947	Taught composition at Harvard.
December 1940	Delivered address, "The Isolation of Modern Poetry," at Modern Language Association meeting in New Orleans.
February 1941	Leased apartment at 41 Bowdoin Street, Cambridge.
1941	Verse play *Shenandoah* published.
August 1941	At Cummington School of Arts, Massachusetts.
1943	Became an editor of *Partisan Review. Genesis*, Book I, published.
1944	Appointed Briggs-Copeland Assistant Professor of English Composition at Harvard. Divorced Gertrude Buckman.
February 1945	Moved to 91 Bedford Street, New York, on 1-year sabbatical.
Mid-January 1946	Returned to Cambridge, 20 Ellery Street.
Spring 1947	Left Cambridge, failing to notify Harvard of his plans.
1948	*The World Is a Wedding* (stories).

1949	Moved to 75 Charles Street, Manhattan.
Spring 1949	Lectured at The New School, Manhattan.
June 10, 1949	Married Elizabeth Pollet.
Summer 1949	Summer in Woodstock, New York.
1949-1952	Residence in Greenwich Village.
1949-1950	Lecturer on T. S. Eliot, at Christian Gauss Seminars in Literary Criticism, Princeton University.
1950	The Guarantors Prize from *Poetry*. *Vaudeville for a Princess* (poems) published.
Summer 1950	Lecturer, Kenyon School of English, Kenyon College.
Summer 1951	Gave course on Eliot and Yeats at Indiana University.
1952-1953	Pro tem chairman of Program in Creative Arts, Princeton University. On advisory board of *Perspectives USA*.
1952-1957	Lived in Baptistown, New Jersey.
1953	Award from National Institute of Arts and Letters.
March-June 1954	Taught at University of Chicago.
1955-1957	Poetry editor and film critic, *The New Republic*.
1957	Elizabeth Pollet filed for divorce.
February 1958	Delivered lecture, "The Present State of Modern Poetry," at Library of Congress. Interviewed by Randall Jarrell.
1959	Received his second prize from *Poetry*. *Summer Knowledge: New and Selected Poems, 1938-1958* published by Doubleday.
January 21, 1960	President Kennedy's inauguration; Schwartz one of sixteen poets invited, and he and Lowell were the youngest. The peripatetic Schwartz received his invitation four months too late.

1960	Shelley Memorial Prize. Bollingen prize in Poetry for 1959, youngest recipient in history of prize. Reading at Yale
1961	*Successful Love and Other Stories.*
Summer 1961	Taught at University of California. Met Victoria Bay.
Winter 1961-62	Lived with Victoria on Gansevoort Street, New York.
August 1962- December 1965	Visiting Professor at Syracuse University.
October 22-24, 1962	Attended National Poetry Festival held in the Library of Congress. Read five poems.
November 6, 1963	Last poem published in his lifetime appeared in *The New York Times.*
1965	Foreword to *Syracuse Poems*, last prose published in his lifetime, issued by Department of English, Syracuse University.
January 1966	Left Syracuse unexpectedly and never returned.
January-July 1966	Lived in Hotel Dixie and Columbia Hotel, New York City.
July 11, 1966	Died at approximately 4:25 A.M. in ambulance en route to Roosevelt Hospital from the Columbia Hotel.
1970	*Selected Essays* published, edited by Dike and Zucker.
1979	*Last and Lost Poems* published, edited by Phillips.
1984	*Letters* published, edited by Phillips.

LETTERS OF DELMORE SCHWARTZ

BOOKS BY DELMORE SCHWARTZ

Letters of Delmore Schwartz (ed. Phillips), 1984.
Last and Lost Poems (ed. Phillips), 1979.
"I Am Cherry Alive," The Little Girl Sang, 1979.
In Dreams Begin Responsibilities: Eight Stories (ed. Atlas), 1978.
What Is To Be Given: Selected Poems (ed. Dunn), 1976.
Selected Essays of Delmore Schwartz (ed. Dike & Zucker), 1970.
Selected Poems (1938-1958): Summer Knowledge (reprint), 1967.
Syracuse Poems 1964 (Selected and with a Foreword by Delmore
   Schwartz), 1965.
Successful Love and Other Stories, 1961.
Summer Knowledge: New and Selected Poems, 1959.
Vaudeville for a Princess and Other Poems, 1950.
The World Is a Wedding (stories), 1948.
Genesis: Book I, 1943.
Shenandoah (verse play), 1941.
A Season in Hell (translation), 1939; revised second edition, 1940.
In Dreams Begin Responsibilities (poems and stories), 1938.

The 1930's

TO JULIAN SAWYER[1]

Adams Hall
[University of Wisconsin]
Oct. 1, 1931

Dear Julian,

First, to decide upon the business of this letter, and of the other which I shall write. I did not desire to write you disguised poetry. I do not wish you to write any unconscious or conscious attempts at literature. The purpose of our correspondence should be: to keep burning the "home fires" of the relationship (the bridge?) (the electrical current?) between us—not "apart from the night air and the traffic, and the jazz of the megapolitan world: taxis..." or "how beautifully stars shine in the forehead of each Wisconsin dusk"; O, no. We have decided, in other matters, that confusion is evil. True. If we gossip about ourselves, we will be writing letters.

I am very happy here. Does that interest you? Adams Hall, where I live, is an imitation of an Oxford College. It is divided into houses. Each house lives unto itself—in a particular section, has a special living room with a victrola, card tables, magazines (*The Nation* and *The New Republic*!), a special dining table in the refectory, and is, in a real sense, a distinct and conscious group. There is, to make lists:

A young man of Boston who was present when Gershwin composed the 2nd part of the Rhapsody.

A young man who can discuss Aristotle and Kant intelligently: (my dear friend).

A subscriber to the *Criterion*.

Three Russian Communists, very passionate, in America to study civil engineering.

A Gentleman and a Musician who can play Bach on the 'cello, has victrola records of Mozart, Brahms, Haydn.

A concert violinist (quite theatrical).

5

6

Three versifiers, entirely stupid. But no one who has read [William] Carlos Williams.

The library is a dream, has files of the *Criterion*, *Dial*, *Bookman*—fourteen volumes of Pascal, and Pound, Eliot, H. Crane, Kenneth Burke even.

As for [Louis] Zukofsky, I do not know if he has returned this fall, but he spent his time (poor authority for this) apparently figuring out reasons to fail 75% of his classes.

Madison is physically very beautiful: my room looks out on the lake, and many small birds, some red, some blue, waken me, as soon as light—the woods full of fresh-water brooks, springs and creeks, deer, too, and rabbits, squirrels. And the long quiet streets, tree-lined (tall trees!), New England white houses.

The imitation of German beer gardens (where everyone sings, and drinks).

The "quad": the internal lawn, park, of Adams Hall, where arguments are intense, sometimes reaching physical violence.

The whole provincial collegiate world.

But, best of all, most responsible for my emotion of happiness there is the sympathy, and friendliness of my reception, acceptance. For unconsciously, against my desire, an intellectual group is around me, looks toward me. Which is pleasing, and embarrassing, most of the boys being five and seven years older than I am, Protestant, Catholic— but I pose the questions, am the authority, and the kind of influence (through speech, I mean) that I do not want to be: everyone (the nine or ten) is reading Spinoza. I purpose a cleavage, that I may entirely devote myself to the clouds (such forms, I mean), Georgia O'Keeffe, the Picasso black storms, and the Wordsworthian lake, and walks. (Such is the pomposity of my soul.)

J.M. [John Middleton] Murry's second wife (Mary Arden) died last May: there's something about him, maybe: a compact handsome little epidemic by himself? //

Life is real, life is earnest, I am tired. Good evening Mr. Sawyer, my jewel, my plague, good night (I am always your friend),

Delmore

1. A friend of S, Julian Sawyer remained in New York City while S attended the University of Wisconsin for one year, 1931-32. Sawyer later became the bibliographer of Gertrude Stein. In the 1950's he committed suicide.

TO JULIAN SAWYER

Adams Hall
Oct. 6, 1931

Dear Julian,

I have your letter and it is the source of much pleasure. But I deserve to know exactly what my mother said. Your vagueness about this is annoying along with the apologetic undercurrent of "inconsistent and dull." Your letter, in spite of a misuse of words, is a reproduction of your conversation that gives me joy, lacks the burden of actual conversation, produces a vision of yourself, your mind. "Thou dost protest too much."

1. Supposing that your birthday was October 8th, I proposed to send a telegram: "April is the cruelest month. Delmore." But don't let this ruined project suggest emulation. I am not sorrowful, when the river of cheap cleverness is dammed. God's truth, the young gentles, my colleagues, lap it up like milk and honey, are uncharmed by Aristotle—joyful at verbal paraphrases of Joyce.

2. Gainst my desire, I am moved to a poem—translation of the beauty of the external world, the naked revelations of its playmate, the weather, and the utter (surely impermanent) harmony between myself and the temporal (i.e. scholastic, social) world. As for "veritable Nirvana," originally truly the word means freedom from the senses, illusions of life, desires, suffering and individuality. Contrarily, my impulse is to "think with the senses," desire, feel selfhood, very much. // As for Zukofsky, he has departed, the information relieving me for various (easily imagined) reasons. As for your reading I wish I had some of the books (C. Williams), I think you are only eating cake, no meat, no soup, no bread, no Shakespeare, Whitman, Dickinson, Racine, Webster, Stendhal. Two favors: I have asked Kenneth [S's younger brother] and C. (the lovely pig) to call you. Please help Kenneth with his English (!), entertain a lady apparently enamored by distance, a deliberately generated myth, a beautiful, new-born, not-existing shadow. And if possible send me C.O.D. *War and Peace* ($1.00 [*sic*]). As for your retreats, they prove, to me, rightness of sensibility. As for particular gossip, I have forbidden the mention of an infamous harlot of body, mind, personality, and voice. Enough for an answer to your letter.

Dear Julian,

There is little room for news of my world. I have been asked, theatrically implored, to write a series of essays on God for one of the school periodicals. I have not consented, cannot see a way of escape—but maybe. In preparation for this indulgence of vanity and inertia, social acquiescence, I have investigated the tradition, found Aquinas (*Sumum Bonum* only) in 22 volumes: "at which I was slightly abashed." In one subject, Botany, I have three teachers: a confession of impotence? I was taken from the freshman English class ("You don't belong here") and put to studying Shakespearean drama: education? I am a little weary of the Bard, have had enough. I feel insecure every time I open my mouth, considering the English department's sublimated passion for elevators. I liked the other class very much for irrelevant, primal, basic, constant, animalist, anti-moral reasons. But enough vaudeville— I promise you less hasty, less staccato "miraculously beautiful" subjectivities henceforth. Good morning, Julian.

Always yr. friend,
Delmore

TO JULIAN SAWYER

[Adams Hall]
Oct. 16, 1931

Program

For Messrs. Spira, Dan, Nelson,
Zellicoe, Brenner, Halpert, Love
—and Julian Sawyer

1. To read a page of the dictionary every day.
2. To read a chapter in *Logic* (Aristotle) every day.
3. To tell no lies.
4. To use words as translations of reality, not a cheap band music.
5. To read a poem by Blake, Dickinson, Dante, Milton, every day (choosing one).
6. To read Spinoza for a half hour every day, look at Cézanne, Daumier, Rembrandt (choosing one).
7. To spend an hour writing one sentence with the goal: approximate perfection of precision.
8. To see no moving pictures, read no cheap books, listen to no catgut music at all.
9. To listen to Bach every day.
10. To be pure of insincerity, laziness, anger, procrastination, discourtesy, inconsideration, affectation, misunderstanding, absent-mindedness, temporal desire, worry over time, vanity, sensitivity, dignity, loud

speech, insulting commentary, irony, arrogance, pomposity, luxurious-
ness, sublimation, misapprehension, uncleanliness, bizarre dress, consideration of money, jealousy, hero-worship,—and thusward.
11. To accept the actions as transitory motions, to be re-expressed
each day, to be known as indications, not consummations, not inflexible
determinations—only implying suggestions.

> Summon of Sermons
> Exhortations of D. Schwartz
> Sept. 21-Oct.16, 1931

TO JULIAN SAWYER

> Adams Hall
> Oct. 17, 1931

Dear Julian,
// I state for "the first and last time" that you represent a personal
entity, necessary (now) to my being. A violent adjustment of worlds,
perhaps impossible, would follow upon the loss of yourself. I speak
with immense conceit. Do I? I do not. I state facts, which there is no
reason to avoid. I pay the greatest respects I can conceive of paying
to anyone. Enough.

The future of American thought, poetry, and religion—the future
of the American world—is "intimately interwoven" with whiskey sours.
Two whiskey sours, and I could convert Ford to Communism, Gandhi
to war, and any young lady to _____. It is merely a matter of touching
the lights of my mind so that they burn with all their strength. Other
things, besides liquor, can do that. I cannot get drunk. It is my flaw;
my Achilles' heel. I get sick, fall asleep, but not drunk. Altogether the
bestial proud beauty has capitulated, much to my disgust. I caught
cold, stayed in bed, and she got sentimental. I have taken up with a
lady from Philadelphia, very stupid, very, very stupid, who calls
Stokowski "Sto," mouths musical platitudes, is very pure—which is
restful. ("Editorial Note": Sometimes for variety she calls "Sto,"
"Stoke.")

Reading your letter aloud at Perratoni's last night, I produced this
reaction: everyone wanted to come to N.Y. to kill you or kiss you—I'm
not sure which, not at all sure it wasn't both.

I shall try to write someone to call you. The length of the changing
season in N.Y. was the cause of much disagreement last night.

One more week, and I separate myself from the temporal world—

save for my classes. I shall read, see, think, write no more explanations of Zukofsky, Pound, Eliot, Kant, Hume, no more embraces—a farewell to arms. No more young men. I shall devote myself to clear vision alone. I shall, indeed, devote myself to clear vision alone.

Delmore

TO JULIAN SAWYER

[Adams Hall]
Oct. 22, 1931

Dear Julian,

Perratoni's is a speakeasy. But Julian, Julian is a fountain of evil delights. For it would be stupid to pretend your lyricism does not cause much pleasure, and foolish, too, to suppose there is any good in it. Formally, metrically, speaking, it is "pretty good." // But, dear sir, repeating myself: words are not used because they look nice, or sound good; they are used because they represent, with approximate exactitude, things that exist. Your very pleasing rhapsody derives its substance, its ways, its rhythms, from the desire to be emotional. I think that is true: I am not sure that you did not wish to indulge yourself in a mystical passage of your idea of good writing: instead of wanting to translate your feelings about me into words. I admit your sincerity. I admit that you must have feelings of some sort about me. But I am not a mechanism, nor a mold, nor a design, nor a carved effigy. My nostalgia is for Heaven, which you know nothing about. The world-pain I am aware of is a very common thing, among metaphysicians. I do not tremble, not even symbolically. Maybe I "stir" the soul, the imagination—but everyone does, to the true sensibility. I am sick of being called an "unusual personality." This is the effect your letter produced: it increased my affection for you, and confirmed my opinion of the confused state of your being.

You have feelings about me: keep on attempting to translate them into words. Send me the attempts. I will see whether your translation is good; I will be able to determine, in the end, if you have seen me truly. I could tell you in a sentence what I am. But it is infinitely better for you to find out for yourself.

And if I really mean as much to you, as your vague, excited music suggests, I desire to destroy that excessive meaning. I am a very important person, but quoting myself, I am not one of the "things that count." I am sinful in many ways—false, greedy, selfish—is it necessary to make some more lists? "All happiness or unhappiness solely depends upon the quality of the object to which we are attached by love." (Spinoza) Until "I die and go to Heaven," I will be a temporal and finite creature. The things that count are: as you say, the bridge, books, mornings, music—they have graduated to another state of being. I am a dealer in the things that count. Or, more accurately, I am the one dealer in the one thing that counts. But I always cause those who are near me more suffering than pleasure. I am an evil being. I have written these same things to another person: a young lady who is, she thinks, in love with me. Please listen to what I say as meaning, not as pleasant, vague profundity. The time is beautiful, Julian. Love God alone.

Delmore

P.S. Your handwriting has become very hard to read. And I'd like to have copies of [T. S. Eliot's] "Animula" and "S. for S." ["A Song for Simeon"]—on separate pieces of paper.

TO JULIAN SAWYER

[Adams Hall]
Oct. 26, 1931

Dear Julian,

Before I know what you have thought of my last letter, I write you another one. This is the reason: I remember so little of what I have written, that I cannot push away the feeling that I may have hurt you once more.

This is the kind of letter that I should write to you. At least to my judgement, this is the right way that I should write to you.

It is fifteen minutes after three o'clock, Central Standard Time. It is the last Monday morning of October. The trees near my window have become bare of leaves during the past week. The trees stand against the night of blueness, like tall flowers. As for flowers, (resuming two cadences) the small flowers of the night burn steadily and purely, like the clear eyes of my burning mind, when I am asleep. The sweet stars make me say my prayer, or my new thing which would have been a prayer in the time that is past: The Time is beautiful. I have looked at the stars again: the buds of morning? the infinite points of the compass of God? Whom I desire to love? God and the stars, too? Do not answer me, anyone! Being that such questions walk in the streets of my thought, like picketing Communists, of whose hope, of whose brutality and passion I am jealous. And why should I not nurse unanswered questions. To the cold stars, as payment, I will give heat with my belief in their fond interest in my life. I hitch the changes of time's world to the night's congregation. The connections I establish bridge the infinite spaces that terrify *me*, also. I inform you with sincerity the blood of my words, that I have seen bend earthward the black trunk of night, and towards some end (maybe that I write this letter) my forehead was touched by the shining thorns of the buds, buds?, of morning. Julian, I see these things because I fight the love of myself, and I try to love God, not myself.

For reasons less religious but the same, in all truth the same after all is meditated, the lake which is fifteen yards from my window, and the trees, and the slope of ground between my room and the lake are noble actors in the life of perhaps the most important being in the world of time. For, hurried by the winds, the lake drifts, runs, ever-unwrinkling, unravelling, comes southwestward toward me. This is during the day. And the lake drifts southwestward to me. But the trees and the ground stand still. Motion against perfect rest. The gray-blue influx parallel to the low brown and tall black and the thin grass, that is fixed. A pure movie—no intricacies of human beings wrenching its counterpoint, or let me say, rhyme with William Blake whom I read. The moving picture, and "Eternity is in love with the productions of *love.*" This was yesterday afternoon, or any afternoon.

It is important that you understand that I have visions. And I look up to the mirror above my desk, and I smile: for in the mirror, the light shining on my head, and face, and my face worried by the infinite possibilities of your miscomprehension of what I write—in the mirror I look like a snowy owl, comically serious, very childish. Am I becoming tender about myself? No more about this. I must write about what I see.

It is possible, of course, that Jean Arthur Rimbaud[1] did not come to see me last night, and that I suffered an enjoyed hallucination. I do not see the necessity for a judgement of the reality of the visit. Rimbaud was here. He spoke to me of the magic study of happiness— the practice I continue, as he hoped someone would. But he was the first, and will be the second and the last I think.

Naturally it is superfluous to say that I watched a young lady dive from a very high board into the sea, the young lady with sure, precise abandonment, the sea receiving her with pure acceptance, I could see very plainly, very simply, when, and how, in what way, sex can be beautiful.

I am very tired now. If I do not end this letter soon, if I read it, I will surely destroy it. And surely you must answer it as quickly as you can. Soon light will translate the world to morning, as I wrote almost a year ago. But it is still true, and that which I have seen will always be true. Good morning, Julian.

Delmore

1. S long identified with Rimbaud, and in 1939 published the first translation in America of Rimbaud's prose poem, *Une Saison en Enfer*. It was not a success.

TO JULIAN SAWYER

[Adams Hall
October 1931]

Dear Julian:

// Love is to feel about a thing, as if that thing were yourself; so that the seasons of its existence have the same meaning of hope, fear, desire, preservation, as the seasons of your own existence; so that your me is so united to that thing as to make it a part of yourself.

That which you see, you become a part of.

That which is near you, becomes a part of you.

The beauty of the natural world is the order of God.

That of which you have a conception, exists.

There is no good and evil (absolutely) but expansion and contraction of life. It is evil since it is a contraction to stop thinking, to murder, to read *The Saturday Evening Post*.

To eat when it is time to think is to live less: a contraction.

To think, to see, to make is to live more: an expansion.

The holiest act is to create, to bring more things into existence.

The justification of destroying is future recreation.

To see a thing is to possess it.

The artist gives his possessions new existences with words, colors, tones, shapes. But first he must see. In our time every writer, save one, is deficient in that he does not see to completely possess, or does not translate, give a new, greater existence to his possessions, so that nothing more need be done for them, so that their existence is fixed and eternal.

and do you want gossip?

E. E. Cummings is left-handed.

Lindbergh was discharged from Wisconsin.

H. G. Wells says Wisconsin has "a great Institution of Learning."

I. A. Richards was here last summer, and nearly drowned.
T. S. Eliot was a banker.
No more now, Julian.

Delmore

Postscript: you should read Stuart Chase's book about Mexico because
we are going there to live some day. And Chase said Madison was the
most beautiful city in America, when he was here.

TO JULIAN SAWYER

[Adams Hall]
November 1, 1931

Dear Julian,

1. As I address the envelope, a dear young gentleman enters. He
is wearing a trench coat and a beret, because outside there is a cold
and serious rain. It is his desire that I stop writing and discuss his
lady-bird, who coos for his vanity mightily. I refuse to stop. He calls
me a boor. I call him a lecherous sparrow. (I set down the conversation
as it occurs.) He calls me a gopher. I call him spleenful.—"There you
go confusing me with strange words, you pedant!" In reply I fondly
ask, "Don't you think people who wear berets should be betrayed, or,
at least, deplored?" He says nothing. I call him a poseur! He is sombre,
dignified, silent, and he thinks he is very funny. He informs me that
his seconds will consult me—and God bless my soul!—he departs, like
a winter wind, or three men running from [?], having enjoyed himself
with the expense of my time. Tarrant House repartee. And now for
my proper commerce with you. First examinations are done: I can
afford this indulgence.

Your last two letters were read after my reading of *The Waste Land*,
to the congregation of the amazed (my poor friends). Their wild acceptance of the letters was, maybe, caused by the pleasureful emotion of
understanding, a little, Eliot, minutes previously. But their unintelli-
gence is proven: they enjoyed them both—and only the second should
receive admiration. // Your writing improved immensely for this
reason: Your unconscious changed (I think). Not, except for lapses,
words that look nice, sound good, but the desire to employ words as
representations of things exactly as they exist.

I am very tired of knowing adolescents of the spirit. We have read,
in the way you remember, *The Bridge*, *Lycidas*, *Comus*, [Donne's] *Anatomy*

of the World, [E. Newgass'] *Everlasting Gospel*, St. Paul, Constant's *Adolphe* (this took a week) and Emily Dickinson. I am sick of managing these affairs because, done, I must go to sleep, and the fruits are, like as not, misunderstanding. Gradually I separate myself from everyone here. I must! Soon I will be alone, in the way I wish.

2. Now (the other start was false) for the business that should be between us. It is my duty, because of what I have done to you (or better, made grow in you), to give you, as you demand, I am very sure, a box seat to the evening and morning of that which I see. The performance (translation, composition) displeases me. Perfect clearness and exactitude, no. Major writing is to say that which has been seen, so that it need never be said again; so that which has been seen increases, changes in reality, in being. But I haven't surrendered myself "to the work to be done" in my letters. So that the qualitative equivalent of the poetry I write now—and sometimes slip in here—is not accomplished. But I am not writing poetry to you, of course. But I should write major prose letters, and I do not.

I dream at night. I dream of reading and writing. When I dreamed of reading I saw myself greeting and shaking hands with urchinous birds who entered my room on a tree, by my room, one of whose branches had extended into the room. Each bird dropped from his mouth numberless squirming twisting white fish which I delighted to touch. These images had followed my dream of reading Emily Dickinson. I saw the book of hers that I have, opened. Then, I saw what I have just written.

When I dreamed of writing, I saw clocks on the tree near my window—and snow on the branches. My arms stretched with pain from my window to the tree, which was far away, and my hands wanted to scrub, to possess, the scanty snow on the black branches. And beyond the tree was a great mountain of snow. I had to finish getting the snow from the tree before the clocks chimed six o'clock, so that I could go onward to the fields and the great mountain of snow. "Hurry up please, it's time." And the constant chiming of the clocks frightened me. This dream succeeded my dream of printing words, printing, not writing them, on huge white sheets of paper. My dreams are powerful symbols. Each object I had, before, used in poems. If you can't understand them, I will show you what I think they mean—if they have, truly, a meaning.

I've just spilled a bottle of ink over the desk, and part of the first page, because of the carelessness of my great tiredness (I didn't sleep last night). I'm too tired to recopy it; I fill in the inked words as best as I can—please excuse me for the difficulties you have in reading. Remember for whom your love must be.

Delmore

P.S. Thanks for "Animula"; I'm anxious to see "A Song for Simeon" and the new one. Do you save my letters?

TO JULIAN SAWYER

[Adams Hall]
Nov. 9, 1931

Dear Julian,

// Questions? My business is mostly answers. Here are some, anyway. Answer them, in just payment.

Do you use words because they represent something that you see, because they give a verbal existence to actual existences? (This is becoming a leitmotif!)

Do you love God or yourself, these being the only possible objects of the love in your self? (Every action of your life is for yourself or for God.)

Do you make illusions concerning Delmore Schwartz, who is at present a liar, pretender, cheat, lecher, sot, and a little tin Jesus to some unfortunate people who know him; who hopes, nevertheless, to become in time someone very grand, and is sure he is someone very important still unflowered?

Does it give you any satisfaction to have persons suppose that you are something you are not but only hope to become (which is, of course, one of the pre-eminent satisfactions of your dear friend Delmore)?

I end the letter with a little Meditation, because I desire to go outside and walk East, and see the light translate the world to morning.

(Did you think, in your sin, that Reality blushes with shame each time that you tell a lie? I have thought so, thinking about you. I have felt real terror—being afraid that Spring would give up the bursts of rain, and the sweet sickness it brings with its soft weather. I was afraid that Winter would no longer be passionate with such intense whiteness. I trembled for all treasures, because the blush being red might change to fire and consume our life, these riches, these riches: [Marie] Henri Beyle [Stendhal], whose taste is coolness, the stars which are the buds of morning and those that sing together; my dear thoughts which are delicate, these nerves, of tender meat, that extend through the whole body of the world. Shall we lose these things? Shall we lose them?) //

Delmore

TO JULIAN SAWYER

[Adams Hall]
Nov. 13, 1931

Dear Julian,

I've drunk all night at the springs—whose taste is of a coolness—of Henri Beyle, and the slippery things in the running currents were emotions: both fish and intellectual things! Black print to hastening water? See how I'm paid for my devotions! A sweet change, and cheaply bought: all night the fleeing of fish was caught merely by bending over the water. Love, hate, lust, ambition seen! Chill in my fingers, good to touch! Sense is disordered by the keen pleasure, apartness—for art is such, the hurting turn, is good to touch; is great, not mean. Then I read your letter.

You do not know what it is to fear that if the excitement in your mind, and mouth increases, you will become convulsive, very sick, and your body will die with an explosion. That is why I was reading.

Fabrice ne sortet de l'église qu' après avoir préparé la confession qu'il se proposait de faire dès le lendemain, il trouva Ludovic assis sur les marches du vaste Peristyle en pierre qui s'élève sur la grande place en avant de la façade de Saint-Pétrone. Comme aprés un grand orage l'air est plus pur, aussi l'âme de Fabrice était tranquille, heureuse et comme rafraîchie, and truly, as after a great sunset of vision, the air is purer, thus the soul of Fabrice was quiet, happy, and as if refreshed. But in between the great dawn and the peace, was the perfect measure of a great prose, bringing the quietness, happiness, refreshing rest. Then I read your letter.

// Julian has enormous sensibility, but absolutely no intelligence. I will write a book for you when I have the expense of time. Too sick myself to be doctor yet. The purpose of these letters has been to keep clear fires burning, to pile more wood on—a confession of sin, with summary half-fulfilled changes into seriousness—that was sinful, too, because it was not complete, but in little pieces. You have never heard my real voice—maybe your torn dream of it caused the confused eruptions. From now on, until I can speak with my own voice and you are able to hear me: conversation as,

There were four brothers Henry, William, two other Jameses.

There is a good story about D. H. Lawrence by K. Boyle in *B.A.S.S.* *[Best American Short Stories] of 1931.*

You are becoming a valuable myth in my postures before the intellectuals. A young lady of true generosity, when your letters, 3, were read to her, announced, "He's a homosexual!"—another thing to admire a nice person for her perception of a posture, her misunderstanding of a misunderstood and broken understanding.

My English teacher: "Do not come to classes unless you want to—cut whenever you feel like [it]. Why are you here anyway? Do you think there is anything to teach you?"

I have not read Rimbaud for a year.

Do not quote Waldo Frank.

I refuse to speak about yr. parody.

My first marks: English A, French A, History A, Botany D (passing).

William Ellery Leonard teaches here, Philo Buck too, Ellsworth Larson, Jean Toomer, Horace Gregory came here. Zukofsky beat it, the old wives tell, because he wouldn't leave his good-looking coeds alone.

I have read about 100 books since I came here.

Miss Wrinn[1] wrote to me—I laughed I thought I'd die at her letter— sent me five issues of *Poetry*, begged me to write to her (I did, signed myself always your pupil, and my mouth almost flew away with delicious laughter), begged me not to hand her address around, is in Massachusetts—"I am reveling in the outdoors"—and is going to Italy and France, at a sacrifice of salary.

I've read the *Dial* for five years.

// Do not be angry, if I speak this way, because I will see my body dying, if I do not control and order the periods of vision which any coveting excites. I hope you do not show my letters to anyone. Probably I'll be home for Christmas. Good night, good night, the bartender tells me it's time. I leave the saloon where I handed out the drinks—

Delmore

1. Mary J. J. Wrinn, who conducted the poetry club at George Washington High School, where S had been a student.

TO JULIAN SAWYER

[Adams Hall
January 1932?]

My best Friend—

Well, I was walking, in the gifted morning, with the young lady

[Fola, a Wisconsin coed] whose surrender is my greatest pride. She slipped and fell and hurt her dignity and broke her very loveliness in Anger, Pique, and Shame. And my smile broke over my chilled face overflowing control. How in that while war was resolved to bliss! That war of a smile meeting a sweet disorder, to say, with powerful allusion of meaning, that truly she then in that formal disgrace was lovelier! Sprawled on the snowbound path! O the profits of untruth!

In the round morning, our promenade was resumed. (On the white lake, in the little white city, the ice boats raced.) We walked then, on the water, like Jesus, toward the iceboats. I told that young lady of Lenin how strange it was that *The Phoenix Kind* by Peter Quennell should be so good and so much like *Laugh and Lie Down* by Robert Cantwell (so good). Both about 2 brothers, their jealousy for a lady. I thought that the theme was indeed rich, as was the reality, thinking of my dear Colonel Snowflake—who is about to fail all his classes.

Farther we walked across the lake, and skaters danced toward us skillfully, leanly and precariously. An airplane pulsed overhead, slowed, descended with dainty clumsiness. Fishermen were cutting a hole in the blue ice. When the lake is frozen, the fish have little food, and are quickly caught and many are caught. Last year there were trucks on the ice but one fell halfway through. If a round hole is cut in the ice it will not crack, no fear of drowning. Whatever color the sky is, the lake is.

The iceboats were sailing from us like birds and we started to run after them and slipped, both, and fell and caused a union of feeling (more really intercourse than various trillion coitus-es)—being one for minutes flowing with sweetness (sitting on the ice) because our beings in that moment temporarily were brother and sister of the one mother, laughter, clumsiness, pain.

In the recessive tide quietly we walked toward Adams Hall—for me to see if there was mail. My lady demanded the letters. The difficulty of informing her that my letter was from the Prime Dadaist [Julian], not from the author of *The Waves*. Do not do that again. Sooner or later such letters will become confused with ones of the real source. Naturally she only saw the envelope. Her seriousness is such that Dada, especially the impure edition of it (not pure since it also contains parody), is hateful to her.

I have a funny story to tell you about how my previously angered English teacher tried to give me a C, not an A, and was compelled to forego the excuse, and give me an A. (For our final examination we were questioned on S. V. Benét's overwhelming epic.[1] I wrote on my paper that I could not permit my mind to be profaned by such intellectual whorishness. Then I wrote an essay on Paul Valéry, making fifteen quotations in French (which he cannot read) and, in concluding, I denounced my dear teacher for being an accomplice of True Crime. So he gave me a C, for lack of self-discipline. So I went to another teacher, to tell him what happened. So everyone spent three hours discussing Paul Valéry, and then adjourned to the Registrar's Office where the mark was changed with much mock ceremony. Good afternoon, I'm going to Chicago until next Monday when next semester starts and I study,

Latin
Shakespearean Drama I
Milton
French Lyric Poetry III
French Literature 17th, 18th Century IV

One reason for taking Latin is: I'll be able to go to Harvard next fall, if I do. I read for my examinations everything of Shakespeare I and Milton II and Descartes II, Racine, Corneille, Sévigné, Voltaire, Bossiret, Molière, and Ronsard IV, Villon, Malherbe, Bellay, Vigny, Lisle, Baudelaire, Mallarmé and their company—but not, alas, Rimbaud.

Write me more Dada, but about yourself too. But Dada's based on destroying meaning, not making fun of it.

Nothing more beautiful than horses, Yes, horses, trees too, the opening of trees, and snow and your strongly young mind purely moving AGAINST the world.

Delmore

1. Stephen Vincent Benét's *John Brown's Body* had been awarded the Pulitzer Prize for poetry in 1929.

TO JULIAN SAWYER

[Adams Hall]
February 9, 1932

My dear Julian,

Your letter is very funny, but not Dadaist. Therefore, I am, one might say, sorrowful. Reading about your marks is an untroubled pleasure. In your generosity, let me think my word took you to the school again, in September, and caused your happy ending. I do not truly desire the truth to be so. My hope is that, with the force of a belief in my rightness, those matters which have meaning for me will be important to you, those attributes, which I regard with hope and desire, will become real in you—Real in You. My impulse now is to write your white-bearded Grandfather, but I have discovered that I try to be funny only when I am ashamed. Why should I be ashamed of the blue seriousness which I enjoy, which will pass, which deceives no one.

Thinking about books, I see that you have read *Towards a Better Life*. I would like to read it. Why did you think it was necessary to sign Kenneth Burke? Flatterer, Courtier! You won't like Robert Cantwell, but you will like Peter Quennell. Do you remember what I wrote in the last letter? Peter Quennell and Robert Cantwell write about the same theme, but there are sharper relations between the poems of Emerson, Emily Dickinson and Stephen Crane, between the general tones of Whitman and Melville, and between the styles of Henry James and Henry Adams, the purposes of Henry James and Robert Browning. I find *The Waves* very stupid: the personages and natures and interest sacrificed to a style which does not look especially good. If the consciousness of a different person is being given, the style should be different. In *Ulysses*, there is such a change; in Tolstoy the rhythms are too simple to interfere with the distinctions that meanings create. The world is too much of a seashore to your Mrs. Leonard Woolf. Suppose that the style is an attempt to represent The Waves of Life, not Bernard, Louis, Neville, Jinny, Rhoda and Susan. But the Waves have no significance until those human beings give them significance. But those people stay misty all the time; are never substantial. // No wonder Hart Crane is always drunk—having to write with [Gorham] Munson gazing on in rapture: "O, aren't we Bohemian, aren't we profound?" Everyone in Cleveland eats Hart Crane's father's candy. Crane's Inn, outside of Cleveland, is the place where my libidinous companion from that city took his father's stenographers.

Very soon I will have to stop hitting people. Already I have two knockouts to repent—once because when a young lady called me, she was told that I was up on the fourth floor, drunk. I was up on the fourth floor, drinking, not drunk. I am never drunk. Another time I became unexpectedly savage because I was writing, and my dear friends came to the door, and kept on knocking. After a while I awoke to their world—but I did not want to let them in. They knew I was in the room—from looking through the keyhole! Finally I opened the door and started to hit everyone. My unknown animal powers and its attitude produced by my fighting are altogether peculiar. Knocking a person out cold results in a delicious sensation of strength. And I've antagonized no one, but impressed everyone very much. Before, what I said made me look important—but in another country. My pugilism is concrete. I've become the Real Thing now. I do not know what to think or feel about this. Always, I fight with the people who live with me. Maybe I can sleep now. Write to me soon.

Delmore

TO JULIAN SAWYER

[Adams Hall]
February 16, 1932

My dear Sir,

You cause me to blush. My Latin book also does: "Sextus loves Marcus the sailor." "Galba loves his pretty daughter. Galba and his pretty daughter live in the little house." "Marcus and Sextus hasten to the fields." Incest and homosexuality wherever my mind looks. But to the pure— Nonetheless Marcus was quite a young man.

Poor Waldo Frank. Truly it gives me sorrow to read about his injury. The library always has five New York newspapers. I read about him this morning, and wondered if you would tell me, too. If he had been hit for some of his pompous generalizing, I should applaud, and delight you with that approval, didn't you expect me to cheer? It is true that his writing is sometimes profound—which you shouldn't be told. Why doesn't he understand that making speeches to miners is fruitless, that changing the social order will not destroy evil? Allen Tate stays at home. If the Christian religion were not sick in the minds of Americans, the greed and selfishness which creates hunger and unemployment would not be born. By changing the love of self to a love of God, such things will be destroyed, changing systems is changing clothes: a prostitute's still a harlot in the dress of a nun. I say this now, because Waldo Frank should know this, should not waste his time in Tennessee or before the Senate.

I should thank you for *The New Republic*. Last week's number "was like old times." I was becoming sure that my mind had changed—not *The New Republic*, that it had never been very good. [Malcolm] Cowley's review, and [John Crowe] Ransom and Tate, deserve gratitude. Orestes is still real; Aeschylus wrote about him in 440 B.C. Naturally you will buy Allen Tate's book of new poems. *The New Republic* poems of last week are inferior to the sonnets in *Poetry* and to "The Cross," "The Oath," and the poem in the current *Yale Review*, "The Traveller." Maybe Allen Tate is a great poet. In the Elegy can't you hear: it was a kind and northern face. //

Mr. Scheinmann, who lives above me, has just called out: "How do you spell "environment." "You don't spell it—you suffer from it" (answer). How has my wit wasted in this land! Of course, it may never have flourished.

My mark in French was A, but I do not know that examination mark. // A little theatrical group of undergraduates is producing five scenes of *him*;[1] I argued all this evening about the heroine's emotions in the second scene of Act One.

It has given me much understanding to read Milton with Blake's illustrations. I like Ovid, in Marlowe's translation, very much—how libidinous! lascivious! how pleasureful! I have discovered the existence of two great writers: Coleridge and Sir John Davies. I mean Coleridge's prose—*Aids to Reflection, Biographia Literaria, Lectures on Shakespeare*. After much thought one evening, I satisfied myself with this image: "Time is the fire in which we burn." Then I read quickly through Lewis' *The Childermass*—the more I read, the greater guilt I felt. Wyndham Lewis is an important writer—this is to say, he is important and not his writing. I mean that his attitude has value, benefit, for our age. His writing manifests that attitude sharply and fiercely but not with the realness of major books—even of that kind: *Gulliver's Travels* and the great Rabelais. Have you read about [Zukofsky's] *To Publishers* and *Contact?*[2] I would like to read [Williams'] *A Novelette*, and about Dr. Williams' new theory. //

I study seventeenth-century France, I study seventeenth-century England for Shakespeare and for Milton. I study "French Lyric Poetry" and Latin which makes me extremely conscious of the shapes of words. It is impossible to be imprecise in Latin. What I wish to show you is the unity of my classes: studying words, poetry of brother languages, the history of an age and its use in poetry. I also study grace in walking, table manners, and extreme neatness: that life may be a true poem, not for the sakes of conformity and social harmony.

The more I become conscious of individual things, the more I become conscious of God. Therefore, I study individual things.

But tonight, I am unreasonably sad. I do not know why. 'Tis bitter chill, and I am sick and hurt.

Delmore

Forgive me for the writing paper.

1. A play by E. E. Cummings, first performed at the Provincetown Playhouse in 1928.
2. A magazine founded in 1921 by William Carlos Williams and Robert McAlmon.

TO MERRILL MOORE

Mosaic[1]
298 Broadway
New York, N.Y.
December 4, 1934

Dear Dr. Moore:

We are advised by Mr. Dudley Fitts to get in touch with you, this advice being unnecessary, except that it is accompanied by your address, because we are acquainted with your first volume of poems [*The Noise That Time Makes*]. Unhappily our first issue, despite the presence of R. P. Blackmur and W. C. Williams, scarcely can be considered inviting to all good poets, and our inability to pay for contributions does not help matters. Nevertheless we are discriminating and for the most part intelligent about literature, and some poems from you would be received as a genuine favor. You will not be ashamed of your company in the magazine. May I hear from you soon?

Sincerely yours,
Delmore Schwartz

1. A little magazine which lasted only two issues, edited by Sigmund Koch and Alvin Schwartz. S was made an editor for the second issue. He was now attending New York University.

TO PAUL GOODMAN[1]

[Brooklyn?][2]
April 27 [1935?]

Dear Paul,

I've just finished what is little more than a paraphrase of the pages of your essay on Plato. I'm going to use it in the essay contest in school, and if I win divide the prize with you. You will have to forgive this announcement, which is made mainly for my own peace of conscience. If you remember, I did warn you that I wanted to do this, and you can still stop me.

I'll try to have the time to come to the library on Monday evening.

Yours,
Delmore

Excuse me for this improper envelope.

1. S met Goodman in 1934, and Paul contributed a story to *Mosaic*. S's story "The World Is a Wedding" is a fictionalized account of Goodman and his literary circle.
2. Probably written from his mother's house in Brooklyn.

TO PAUL GOODMAN

9 Story Street
Cambridge, Mass.[1]
Oct. 1, 1935

Dear Paul,

I've already tried to describe Cambridge, and I do not like to say the same thing often. Besides you've already been here. I am pleased with my courses and with my room, but with little else. An enforced solitude will probably be good, with all the work I must do, but it is not delightful—there is, so far, one boy worth speaking to, and his name is Gerson [Brodie], which is, perhaps you know, Hebrew for stranger. I am also upset daily by the effort of choice between my reading in philosophy and the writing of poetry: not that either comes easy. But I can make some unity of both is the well-known pious hope: an abstract project which has but little fact in my actual habits. Still I do find that the things I want to think and write about do deserve some kind of name in philosophy: revery over the essences might be an adequately dignified title for the activity of considering the tomato sauce on the veal cutlet, and the slice of tomato beside it as both a problem and a moment. Rereading what I have just written brings me inevitable self-consciousness. It shows that one exists mainly in feelings, not in air. If, by the way, you can tell me what feelings are, I would be grateful.

My courses are: Cosmologies with [Alfred North] Whitehead, Seminar in the Theory of Knowledge with [Ralph Barton] Perry, Advanced Ethics with [John] Wild and Comparative Medieval Philosophy with [Harry] Wolfson. Wolfson seems to be good; so far he has merely said the things about the Middle Ages that are no longer news. He has a terrific accent, which seems almost a parody at times. Wild is very poor and much too nervous to teach, and Perry seems quite uninterested, or perhaps tired. Whitehead, however, is certainly what is called a character. He is perfectly conscious of his role as a great man, and it delights him. Indeed he dresses for the part in a kind of prime-minister's collar and cravat, and toddles about looking for auditors, speaking of the autumn of 1880, "when I first went to college," and announcing that "I am really a muddle-headed man, you know, liable to speak the most utter nonsense, you know." As he has also said that "Plato was vewy (lisping) muddle-headed, you know," we now may feel that muddle-headedness is crowned. His contempt for scholarship and learning is constantly repeated, as in his books, and he speaks continuously about how inadequate language is, complaining that the French Academy has just published a dictionary, thus limiting the possibilities of meaning! No one will accuse him of being a scholar: "I skip the whole Middle Ages for two reasons: one, the theological bias, two, I know nothing of it"; "a...a... a...what *was* the name of that famous essay by Locke." In today's lecture, commenting on the *Timaeus*, this is what happened:

"Plato preferred the timeless, you know...
An utter mistake...absolute nonsense..."
And when the lecture was over, went up, asked Whitehead,
Shy and uneasy, "but I think that Plato
Thought that which is in time moves,
That which moves moves to an end
But that which moves to an end is imperfect.
Therefore the timeless is more perfect,
Therefore Plato preferred it..."
"But I can't think of a thing in time
But that it moves." "That's what I mean:
If in time, it moves: but then it is imperfect."
"But...a...But then he goes off here...
In the *Sophist*..." Turning the pages,
"...aaa...who are you?" And then my turn
To stammer: "aaa...Schwartz... ." "You've
Given me the proper answer, the proper
Answer: I'll take it up next time.
Remind me."
Will you write me soon, and will you give my regards to Alice?

Your friend,
Delmore

1. S began graduate studies in philosophy at Harvard in September, 1935.

TO MAURICE ZOLOTOW[1]

Brooklyn
January 9th, 1936

Dear Maurice,

Your letter calls forth so many memories that I am forced to think that I am very old or that nothing changes. My debt will have to stay unchanged also, because I keep on becoming poorer. I visited your home to tell you why I could not return your records until June—the way in which I came back to New York is the explanation.

I have many stories about Harvard, but most of them are best suited to conversation, gestures being necessary. Whitehead is the most charming, most delightful of all old men, but the most ignorant of philosophers. Wolfson, my own favorite, is so learned that he could drive Sidney Hook[2] into a convent, if each would join in dispute of the economic interpretation of philosophy; he says: Aquinas was a big man—you want to make something of it? This, I hope, suggests his incredible accent (Whitehead's is incredible, too, at the other pole, e.g., the jolly bark of the dog, I will bet heavily) and in Wolfson's class I often feel as if I ought to translate for the rest of the class. The big excitement in philosophy is a hysterical new German school called Existénce, and eveyone also remains preoccupied with systems of noting down logical relations, so that they will be entirely free of metaphysical consequences, and thus—but it does not matter—entirely free of meaning. The graduate students are haunted—each was a star back home and must work 15 hours a day to maintain his lovely idea of himself. Among the literary gents there is a lag or backwash which completely baffles me: Wilde and Swinburne ("would you believe it?") are on top.

Meanwhile I have been greeted with a widespread reaction which should certainly interest you. A good many of my short poems are being "accepted" in various places, and the *New (American) Caravan* is going to print the verse play which I mentioned to you last summer[3] and also, perhaps, a short story and several poems. I visited Rosenfeld last week, taking [Ben] Hellman [fellow student at N.Y.U.] along for bad luck and was startled by his announcement that the play was "genial"—I have had to say this myself to myself so often that it seems peculiar on another's lips. I was very pleased to think that this visit was in a way the completion of a circle. Because my infatuation with poetry began in 1927. Williams is having the libretto of an opera in this *Caravan* and no less a figure than Thomas Wolfe ("Sad like [?]," as Hemingway says) will be spouting like a whale—if it were not for

28

Wolfe, I would be sure that my short story would be printed. Rosenfeld says that he dislikes Wolfe but is forced to print his work.

You're wrong about Laforgue and Eliot. Laforgue writes good lines, as you say, but Eliot writes good poems. Laforgue lacks sustained meanings and rhythms, and Eliot does not. Also I dislike Laforgue's delight in "personality" and cleverness. *Ash Wednesday* is hardly more "original" than the other poems. The first line is directly from Cavalcanti: *"perch'io no spero tornar mai."* But Eliot's purposes are his own, and that is of course all that matters. *Murder in the Cathedral* seemed weakened and flat to me, except for that chorus on death. He's really tired now, and his wife, after years of mistreatment, has left him for an insane asylum.

I see that your joy in Hart Crane has not diminished. But if your moral sense is really sharpening, it should. Crane was musclebound, even paralyzed, on the love of apostrophe, apocalypse, and apotheosis—he was incapable of writing anything *that* he could not get immensely excited about. But his excitement is about inferior objects, and again and again there is no sign that he knows what he is doing. I don't deny that he is a great poet, but all these things ought to be noted: his method is entirely that of rhetorical allusion, and he seems so impressive mainly because he overpowers the reader with loudness and a grand manner. Measure the difference between Bach and Wagner, and you see how much is wrong in Crane as compared with, not Shakespeare, but Yeats, Eliot, Valéry, and Rilke. You won't be able to see that this judgement is just, unless you make many comparisons and forget your feelings.

Well! I see and you see that I am still capable of a papal air, for which you will have to forgive me. Remember me to Charlotte and write to me, when you feel like doing so, at my Cambridge address.

Delmore

1. Fellow student at the University of Wisconsin, who later became the biographer of Marilyn Monroe and John Wayne.
2. S took a seminar in contemporary philosophy with Hook during his second year at N.Y.U.
3. "Choosing Company," *New Caravan*, ed. Alfred Kreymborg, Lewis Mumford, and Paul Rosenfeld. New York, 1936.

TO PAUL GOODMAN

[New York City]
March 17, 1936

[No salutation.]

We might try to continue the argument so unpleasantly conducted at Gertrude's[1] house. You said that my analogy, art as knowing, was poor, because knowing always involves the universals. I used the word "knowing" as a contrast to "knowledge" to mark the analogy and signify the difference. My point is of course the likeness. Well, your objection falls down precisely because universals are involved in apprehending an object of art, just as they are involved in knowing a person or knowing a neighborhood. Knowing is not "scientific" in any of these instances—that is, it is not knowledge: but it is more like knowledge than "like" anything else, because in each instance we have a kind of conscious contact with the object. Now look how much support I have for this view: first, the "plain man" who says "I know that book—I know that person"; then, the fact that art is used to embody knowledge, as in Scripture, churches or merely a classroom example; and finally Aristotle, the remark about poetry being more philosophical than history being just as much in point as the other passage, that our pleasure in imitation is a pleasure in gathering the meaning of things.

I think my objection to [Alvin] Schwartz's article is worth mentioning also. Emotions, he says, tend to action, but music gives them musical action and thus teaches them. The trouble with this is its nearness to art as sublimation. If you push the point in any direction, you get absurdity: the musician in love who writes a composition in which his present emotions are involved thereby becomes less in love.

I have been spending some of my time in putting together a book of poems to enter in the contest called The Yale Series of Younger Poets. You ought to do so also. // There is also another magazine worth trying, *Transition*, which is now in America. //

Delmore

1. Gertrude Buckman, formerly a classmate of S's at George Washington High School. From there she went to N.Y.U. She and S were married in 1938.

TO ARTHUR BERGER[1]

700 W. 180th Street
New York City, N.Y.
March 24, 1937

Dear Arthur,

The notes are good, but there's no use in taking them, if you're going to be absent often. If you will, and you do not think you are doing too much, you can 1) get from Bernie my copy of Hook's first book on Marx, 2) and point out that if my reason were the one he supposes, there would be no point in concealing it (he can hardly think of the Bursar), 3) and mention to Prall,[2] not as your own opinion, but my message to him, that silence is money for me—[3]

I've looked through Paul's copy of Schwartz's thesis and should judge that its effect, such as it will be, can only be unfortunate. Not only its tone and method, but specific and repeated errors, are certain to have a disastrous effect on anyone who takes it seriously. The best thing would be for you not to read it at all: especially since it is sealed up in S's notion of an Aristotelian terminology (but he seems to know no Greek) and will thus be extremely difficult for you. If you must read it, you'd better not write about it. And if you must write about it, you'd better prepare yourself by listening to Wild. But I have little hope that any of this considered advice will be taken.

My own affairs prosper and will continue to do so, unless the Bursar is made suspicious by the Dept. of Philosophy. It's really pleasant to be among so many intelligent people for a change. You'll have to keep your silence in N.Y. also, for the time being.

Let me know when you get to N.Y. and give my regards to Gerson and Oscar [Handlin].

Delmore

1. Fellow student at Harvard, who later became a distinguished composer.
2. David W. Prall, Harvard faculty member whose book *Aesthetic Analysis* was posthumously published with a preface by Arthur Berger. S dedicated "Sonnet: The Ghosts of James and Peirce in Harvard Yard" to Prall.
3. S left Harvard without a degree, owing a large debt to the bursar. He intended to complete a book.

TO ARTHUR BERGER

[New York City]
July 31, 1937

Dear Arthur,

You will have to forgive me for not writing to you before this. I have little but my own ill fortune to set down. You will not be surprised to hear that Prall advised me as to the superiority of New York to a "barren academicism" for me with my purposes. This taken with what he said to Frieszel when F. complained about the lack of funds, is a fine example of balancing the budget, as I did not hesitate to tell Prall in a letter which will undoubtedly be our last communication in this life. But before this, the New York lawyer who now guards my father's estate decided that my father's will could not be abrogated, so that I must wait until December 1938 and my 25th birthday before receiving the remaining funds. (It seems that if I should marry and have a child within the next 18 months (until D. 1938) and die before D. 1938, then, when my child was 21, in the year 1959, he could sue these lawyers for the money which was paid to his father a little too soon. Naturally Gertrude and I cannot get married at present, although perhaps by next June; I can get somewhere by pointing out that a child requires nine months to arrive and thus could scarcely put in his appearance before my 25th birthday.) All of this reminds me of Kafka whose *The Trial* I am now reading with the greatest admiration. (When I add that my mother's illness has become much worse, I have completed the story. There is, as usual, nothing to do but work hard and think hard. You can see that the news of your happiness is a distinct pleasure which is increased by these dismal circumstances of my own.)

I have had to argue strenuously about the way in which music is "Expressive" of emotion, and the argument led me to several facts which will interest you. Most music, I said (hoping that I was right) has been set to a text. The relation between the meaning of the text and the quality of the music can be demonstrated. In the case of nontextual music, then, we must suppose a radical change in the character of the music (which is not apparent in its other aspects), and a radical change in the art of the musician—or we must admit that this music is "Expressive" in nature, "representative," "reflective" of emotion. However, my opponents were perfectly willing to admit the implication that nontextual music was new in this way. I think now that the whole thesis of Expressiveness has to be stated with much more care than Prall, you or I were aware several months ago and I hope you are continuing to think about it.

There is little news of Paul and company. I will bring your 2nd letter up there tonight and it will be read aloud with many comments; but I am sure that you do not mind. Philip Slaner [member of Goodman's circle], no less, was dispatched to France with a case of celery tonic as a token of the group's esteem. Meyer Schapiro[1] wrote him

32

an eight-page letter on seeing the sights, so that if you return to Paris in time, you ought to look him up for the sake of the letter. My dispute with Schapiro continues, by the way, through the mail and will probably result in another longer article in the *Marxist Quarterly.*

Gertrude would extend her regards if she knew that I was writing to you now. At any rate, our best regards to Esther and yourself, and I hope for another fine letter from you soon.

Your friend,
Delmore

1. Co-editor with James Burnham and Sidney Hook of the *Marxist Quarterly,* and one of S's teachers at N.Y.U. Later a well-known art historian.

TO PHILIP HORTON

700 W. 180th Street
New York, New York
Nov. 19, 1937

Dear Horton,

It was extremely gratifying to meet you and talk to you, and I hope we can talk again when you are once more in N.Y.C., and under less chaotic circumstances.

I am enclosing the unrevised version of my article about Crane [never published]. Almost all of my objections are made irrelevant to your book[1] itself by your reminder that you were writing a biography, and not a critical study, and in general I've done you less than justice by saying nothing of the vivid narrative power in the book. I intend to remedy this by adding a paragraph to the article. Perhaps you can suggest further revisions and tell me where I am wrong. I will be very grateful if you do.

I've also been thinking of your new project and wishing almost that I might be similarly engaged, so rich and interesting does the whole subject seem.[2]

Sincerely yours,
Delmore Schwartz

1. *Hart Crane: The Life of an American Poet* (1937).
2. Horton never published another book.

TO ARTHUR BERGER

700 W. 180th Street
New York, New York
Nov. 23, 1937

Dear Arthur,

I had decided that you were too busy to write, which was a pleasant thought after the celebrated Slaner reported your despondency upon his return. No doubt, a good deal else has happened to you since you wrote the letter of the 17th of Sept.; so many events—events—have occurred in my own life through the same course of time.

But first, to make myself a little clearer than I did, apparently, in my last letter. I meant to say that there was no radical difference between textual and purely instrumental music, no radical difference in the quality of the music. I should have said quality, not character, for that seems to have made you misunderstand me. But those who denied that emotion was inherent in music would either have to deny the obvious correspondences—such as you yourself have pointed out—between text and music in textual music; or, granting the reference to emotion in textual music, they might, as they sometimes do, maintain that the reference to emotion disappeared, was without meaning, when there was no text. But if they said this, they would be implying that there was some great difference between textual and non-textual music. And there is no great difference, at least none which an ignorant listener like myself can make out.

But the whole question is much more complicated than Prall seems ever to have been aware, or to have made us aware. There is a good attack, though poorly written, on Prall's view in the *J. of Philo.* for Nov. 11, I think, by Eliseo Vivas, who has previously shown few signs of being intelligent. I hope you look up the article. Vivas simply says that there is only this meaning for saying that an art "expresses" an emotion: it refers [to], that is, is a sign of an emotion. Thus the word "sorrow" is the symbol of sorrow the emotion, and in like manner, certain combinations of tones may be signs of sorrow. To say, however, that the music *is* the sorrow, or makes us feel sorrowful, is clearly false.

Of the friends we have in common, I can report that both Paul and Will [William Barrett] seem to thrive in Chicago, both of them being perfectly enchanted with a group led by a poet named Roditi, former expatriate who may be known to some of your friends in Paris. Gertrude is still her troubled self, but is doing very well with her sculpture and painting. // I had dinner with Oscar and his bride, who is a very bright girl, on the day after their marriage, spending my last five-dollar bill in doing so (but, after all, I hope that Oscar will only marry once, and in that case the expense is nothing), and almost committing suicide by eating oysters after drinking a number of rye highballs. My relations with Prall bloomed into an exchange of letters which was almost daily for a time, but I became tired of calling him names: in the end, it would have been possible to return to Harvard, but only without Gertrude, which made it impossible so far as I was concerned.

Most of the events I mentioned are entirely personal and I could scarcely get them down in a letter, but will gladly relate them when I see you again—perhaps next summer or fall in France. I ought to mention my various literary appearances, however, since I would like to have you get the magazines as they appear. My long piece on [Ivor] Winters for the *Southern Review* was extended by 10 pages, and this accounts for the fact it will appear in the January issue;[1] in addition, they have asked me to write an extended essay about Hemingway, who, as a source of so many fashionable attitudes, is a fruitful subject.[2] *New Directions* is a book like the *Caravan*, but better; and Henry Miller is also appearing in it, if you are interested. Dorothy Norman, friend of Rosenfeld, [Alfred] Stieglitz, et. al., has started a magazine [*Twice a Year*] and I am writing about Whitehead for her. But best of all is the *Partisan Review*, which changed from Stalinist to Trotskyite overnight. They wrote to Wallace Stevens and asked [him] not only for poems but to recommend a young poet and to my extreme pleasure he sent them my name. They published "In Dreams Begin Responsibilities" in their first issue, but although you have read this, the magazine is worth getting for a fine piece on *The New Yorker*, a review by Hook, and an article by [Edmund] Wilson—there are also some poor political cartoons by Picasso, and a story by [James T.] Farrell. All I ask, so far as literary fortune goes, is to appear always in the same issue with Farrell—the contrast is wonderful. I will have several more pieces in subsequent issues, and with this next issue begins the serialization of Gide's *Retouches*. You might also look about at the various English magazines in which some of my new poems will be appearing. By telling you this, I will be able to claim that I am increasing the circulation on the continent.

Apart from the fact that you did not return my books, did not pay the whole sum for the article, did not get the Hook from Frieszel, I have learned of an additional injury on your part, the fact that most of your records, including the Stravinsky octet, were left in Cambridge, either useless in storage, or with [Harvard classmate Louis] Harap, and thus equally useless. If it were not so difficult to be angry over an ocean, I would be extremely indignant. In any case, you've been bad as the worst capitalist about the records, since they're doing no one any good at the present. I've decided to say nothing at all, but the fourth item is too much. In view of all this, I send Esther my best regards; as for you, the enclosed essay,[3] which has since been extended and is going to be printed in the *Partisan Review*, is the best I can do.

Delmore

1. "Primitivism and Decadence," *Southern Review*, Winter 1938.
2. "Ernest Hemingway's Literary Situation," *Southern Review*, Spring 1938.
3. S's review of *The Man with the Blue Guitar and Other Poems* by Wallace Stevens (published in *Partisan Review*, 4 [Feb. 1938]).

TO PHILIP HORTON

700 West 180th Street
New York City, N.Y.
December 3, 1937

Dear Horton,

Many thanks for your letter and your marginal comments. I am certainly not offended, and I hope that you will not hesitate to say that I am foolish whenever you think so. My article won't, I assure you, be printed without expanding the quotations which you think misrepresent you, giving you the credit you certainly deserve for the many positive virtues of the book, and making other qualifications which I'll indicate in the course of this letter. I think that this is one way of making progress in literary criticism, and so long as neither of us think we are of an angelic intelligence, perfect at all times, there's a good deal to be learned by these disputes, although I'm sure the benefits are much more mine, than yours.

One marginal comment makes me think that the disagreement between us may be thoroughgoing. You write, "Does this kind of statement really mean anything?" next to my statement: "It is not that Crane was not a good poet, but that he might have been a very much better one." I may be misunderstanding you again, but it is just this that I meant by the non-inevitability of what the poet does. It seems to me that without the assumption that any act or work might have been better or worse than it was, all judgement, literary and moral, becomes impossible. To be specific about Crane, I think that he would have been a much better poet if, after writing *White Buildings*, he had worked the symbolist vein in himself, and—as you say—remained within lyric poetry—instead of attempting a Whitmanesque myth.

As for the rest of our disagreement: unless you do deny the objective basis of "might-have-been" judgements, I think that we would agree with one another if we discussed the matter sufficiently. I want to answer some of your objections, but only tentatively, until I can read your book again, as I intend to do in order to revise my article.

Point by point, then: "My book would encourage the idea that drunkenness is a source of great writing": I did not say nor think this, but I objected to the fact that you "preferred not to belabor the moral," at least in one general statement, and allowed "the story to speak for itself." Literary legends, I need hardly say to you, are generally vicious—I thought that your book did not guard against the fostering of one kind of literary legend. In fact, most of my objections came merely to this: that you did not guard against possible and likely implications. It seems to me that a literary critic really is responsible, to some extent, for the stupidity of those who may read his criticism. I've heard of homosexuality justified because Gide, etc., were homosexual, and I've known of one young poet who experimented with it because he had heard of Crane. As for the morality of the poet, in the title, I meant not morality in general, but morality in its effect upon the poet's writing. As for drunkenness and sensibility, here it is actually a question of fact easily verifiable. Liquor speeds up your reaction-time and makes many things seem pleasant and important, but you do not have perceptions when drunk which you would not have sober. Crane drunk saw things that no other drunkard would see. All of this is painfully obvious to you but would not be to the legions who accept the romantic idea of the poet. There have been elaborate investigations down at Johns Hopkins into the effect of liquor—R. Pearl is the man, the doctor, who has put them in books—and the net result is the one I've just mentioned, that liquor speeds up and colors perceptions which you would have sooner or later anyway, if you would have them at all. I ought to say, because I don't want to seem puritanical about this, that liquor seems to me to be a wonderful social thing, breaking down shyness and distance and making it possible for people to talk freely to each other; and the next time I see you the first thing I intend to do is buy you a drink.

Most of my other objections are, as I said, not so much against what you said as what you did not guard against in implication. When you say "the American spirit" many readers, a reader like Crane even, will see "THE AMERICAN SPIRIT," i.e., some kind of hypostatized entity, and you must have seen the reviews of your book—I can't remember which ones at the moment—in which your unqualified phrases about the plastic use of language and getting the poem thru its impact are taken to be evidence for [Max] Eastman's kind of attack on difficult poetry. The difficulty in Crane is, I think, even in "Possessions," a result of omission of connection; that is, the relation of one statement to the next one is not mediated by transitional phrases. I know that Crane thought otherwise, but perhaps we can look at the poems together some time and see if he was right.

As for Crane, things, and theology, it is Crane, not I, who mistook things for divine objects. You've said in your letter that this is completely false, that he took things for symbols of the divine—of what divinity, then, is the sea a symbol of? and the subway and the bridge? perhaps of Waldo Frank's sense of the whole, in which case they are not symbols but actually *parts* of the divine—c.f. the writing of Frank or [Jules] Romains, in the latter to be crowded in the subway is a religious experience. And in general, things have been taken as theological objects by primitive peoples—there's no contradiction here (cf. Frazer) although there is in the attributes conferred upon things, by the animistically devout.

You're right when you say that I take up too many matters in 9 pages, but what can one do, knowing that one will be given a chance to speak up only if one does not take up too much room? The day of the real Macaulay-like review is long past.

Your book *is* a highly dramatic and tragic biography and I should have said how good it is as a narrative. It seems to me a blessing that people like [Louis] Untermeyer, [Alfred] Kreymborg, et al., are being succeeded by a person like yourself. I've seen your poem in *Trial Balances* [anthology], by the way, but no poetry since then, and I hope—if you won't mind my presumption—that you're not permitting criticism and history to take you away from the writing of verse altogether.

Let me hear from you, when you have the time, on your reaction to my answer, and please let me know when you come to NYC again.

Sincerely yours,
Delmore Schwartz

TO PHILIP HORTON

73 Washington Place
New York City, N.Y.
December 14, 1937

Dear Horton,

At the risk of making a nuisance of myself, I am answering your letter immediately. Most of my correspondents find this rapid-fire reply very disconcerting, but I have the feeling that letter-writing aspires to conversation and needs a quick answer. I suggest, however, that you do not trouble yourself about answering this letter, unless you really feel compelled to do so—your time is probably much more "obligated" than mine.

I am grateful for both of your letters but sorry to say that they seem to confirm our initial and fundamental disagreement. Your most important point and the feeling behind much of what you say in your book of Crane's life is, I think, contained in the series of "ifs" about Crane. You say that his intimate friends told you "they often thought" that *if* Crane had not been a drunkard, homosexual, etc., he would not have been a poet or not been a good poet. You seem to believe this yourself, and you use the analogy of Goethe as an instance. Now it is precisely against this assumption, this pervasive sentiment, that my essay was directed. If you think thru this assumption carefully, you will find that it means this: that every item connected in any way with an event was necessary to the coming-to-be of that event. This is obviously an unverifiable proposition and against every canon of scientific method. (I should say, since someone—who could it have been?—says that I have adopted Thomism, an extremely inaccurate statement, that the only criteria involved in my essay and now are those of *verifiability* and *consistency,* that is, merely what the scientist uses.) The contradictory of your—or Crane's intimate friends'—assumption is fact which can be verified repeatedly, at any time. An event is the result of a limited number of factors—most of the concomitant circumstances of most events can be changed without affecting the event. This is by no means what you call "abstract speculation." A man writes poetry because he has acquired certain language and certain perceptions. The causal nexus between language and poetry, and perception and poetry is obvious. It is not in the least obvious that a causal nexus between homosexuality and poetry exists—the necessary connection is lacking as can be seen immediately in the fact that many homosexuals do not write poetry. I do not doubt that the circumstances of Crane's life affected his poetry a good deal—on the contrary, it is something which I must insist upon—but the primary gifts of language and sensibility are demonstrably based upon a responsive capacity of the sense-organs—and this, any psychologist will tell you, is prior to adolescence. It seems to me that your whole method—your belief that Crane's domestic background somehow made him a poet—flies in the face of scientific fact. It is superstition, nothing else, to think that, e.g. Dostoyevsky was a great novelist as a result of epilepsy, etc. The causal sequence has been reversed.

Your other remarks are less important. You speak as if a mistake can only be a mistake if it has not yet occurred. That is the only way in which I can understand your remark that to point out that Crane made mistakes which prevented him from being a better poet is at best abstract speculation and has no place in a *purely* literary criticism. Nothing, I think, could be further removed from what you call "pure speculation" than an evaluation of a man's actions in terms of the consequences which have already occurred. And in general I get the feeling, in your last letter, that your love of Crane makes you wish to prevent such judgements—you've used the word "great poetry" repeatedly merely as a bludgeon against my objections. To answer your point, the great poems in *The Bridge* are clearly those in which it is possible to use a symbolist method for the subject matter at hand—"Ave Maria" is of course a monologue, so is "The Harbor Dawn," "Cutty Sark," etc., all monologues, proceeding from the self-conscious meditation of the symbolist poet. One more answer: I must have made some mistake in typing: I said that I did not contradict myself when I said that Crane's sensibility was for things, and yet, on the other hand, that Crane's emotion was religious. No contradiction, because some people do have a religious emotion, merely about things, particularly primitive animists. No contradiction on my part. And yet, on the other hand, a contradiction on the part of the animists who attribute conscious attributes to wood and stone—or, as in Crane, to steel.

"O thou steeled cognizance whose leap commits," etc.

I maybe misquoted slightly, but the point is clear—a bridge cannot have cognizance or be cognizance—the engineer can; you seem to have answered that such attributions were merely symbols—of whose cognizance is the bridge a symbol?

But you must be very tired of my repetitious discourse by this time. I'd like by the way to use your letters—not in quotation, but merely as explicative of your book in revising my article. I won't do so—I won't refer to our private argument or make modifications because of it, if you object—but if I do not hear from you, I will assume that it is all right. Thanks again for all the trouble of writing.

Yours,
Delmore Schwartz

40

TO PHILIP HORTON

73 Washington Place
New York City, N.Y.
December 18, 1937

Dear Horton,

In view of your refusal, I have no alternative but to print the essay as it stands (although I intend to expand passages which do not refer to your book). I assure you that I will not quote from your letters, nor will I use our discussion. When the essay appears I will see that you get a copy.

There is obviously very little else to be said. You've contradicted yourself repeatedly in your letters, and despite your very fine intention, your book makes judgements which you think you have avoided. I intend to let you have the last word in this. These are your own words:

p. 124: "But eventually music and liquor became almost indispensable aids to his writing, regardless of circumstances..."

p. 166: "Aside from the part it played in Crane's life the relationship (of homosexuality) was the source of much of the strange mystical exaltation that inspired 'Voyages,' which must rank among his best work."

Note the words "indispensable" and "source." I've found fifteen other explicit statements of this kind, and there are one hundred places where the same idea is implied (although you like to think an implication which I see is merely a fancy). In your third letter, you say in capitals: "I do not believe that Crane's drunkenness, homosexuality, etc. were the causes of his being a poet... I do not believe they were even necessary conditions of his being a poet." You do not say this in the book, but it is full of precisely such statements as the above quotations, which directly contradict. You quote his friends in your second letter as saying exactly what I wish to deny, that had he led a better life he would have been a worse poet, so that you obviously recognize the existence of such a romantic and vicious view of the writing of poetry. It is because this view is so popular that I intend to print my article. I still think that apart from this aspect, you wrote a good biography.

Sincerely yours,
Delmore Schwartz

P.S. The above quotations and others were at hand when I first wrote my essay. If I should use them, please do not suppose that I have used our discussion.

TO W. W. NORTON

73 Washington Place
New York City, N.Y.
Jan. 21, 1938

W. W. Norton
70 Fifth Avenue
New York City.

Dear Mr. Norton:

Thank you very much for your letter and your friendly attitude. Under the circumstances, I would be glad to go ahead and write the first few chapters of my novel—indeed I would not approach a publisher until they were written—but I am faced with a personal problem which makes it necessary for me to accept Mr. Laughlin's offer.[1] The problem, if you will forgive me for dragging my private affairs into the mail, is that of persuading those who support me that I am justified in spending all my time in writing and can afford to turn down a job. A book is more persuasive than magazine appearances in showing that it is difficult to be a writer merely over the week-ends. I will have to give Mr. Laughlin an option on my novel in return for the publication of my book of verse, but he is an extremely generous fellow and I know that when my novel is completed, he will not stand in my way, if I have an offer from an established publisher. So that when the novel is completed, I shall certainly make it my business to show it to you.

Sincerely yours,
Delmore Schwartz

1. James Laughlin, founder of New Directions, who contracted for S's first book, *In Dreams Begin Responsibilities*.

TO JAMES LAUGHLIN

73 Washington Place
New York City
February 1, 1938

Dear Laughlin:

I am enclosing the signed contract with a few misgivings about being Quixotic, with much relief that I am finished with publishers for, I hope, the next twenty years, but really with the strong feeling that everything is going to come out well for both you and myself. I had better explain the misgivings, even if it means repeating myself: the offer I am turning down to go with you would free me from the parental grip once and for all and also get me a little more of the world, flesh, and devil than I have at present.

There are several things which are not quite right in the contract, but I am letting them go because I think that our interests are one, that though we scarcely know each other we have a friendly unity about the way things should be, or to put it pompously, that we both want to realize the same values. There is, however, one thing that I am going to insist upon—twenty free copies, which is the least an author is entitled to and which is as you know what he gets from everyone else. I need twenty copies because I want to keep my friends feeling that I am interested in their being interested in what I write— but seriously I have to have them and can't afford to buy them; and I'm taking the liberty of changing the number in the contract.

The book will be ready in July when you get back from Europe, unless I have another spell of sickness of the sort I had last year. After that's done, I'll revise the play you want to print in *N.D. 1938*.[1] Printing it there may sell a few more copies of the book of poems [*sic*]. The cover, print, and paper are hard for me to see, since I don't know what Bodoni is, nor cream-toned paper, but if it is going to be like the Faber & Faber poetry books, it will be fine. I'll have a device ready too before you send the book to the printer's.

I'd like very much to write ballet scenarios for [Lincoln] Kirstein, and have two ideas, one involving comic-strip motifs, the other a baseball game. From all that I hear it would be a chance to make some money, which I badly need, badly in the sense that a few luxuries are sometimes a necessity. I'd be grateful if you sent me Kirstein's address and told him that I was going to submit a short scenario to him—or perhaps it's enough to mention your name.

All these fine reviews[2] and all the rest of the things that I've been getting during the last few months are accumulating to the point where I am going to be terrified—because it can't last, I can't be being praised for the right reasons by so many people, it is much too soon, and it is taking my mind away from working. I hope that it does not make you expect me to progress in a straight line; but being a writer, I don't have to be afraid that you will have such expectations. The latest salutation, by the way, is from Wallace Stevens, who sent the *Partisan Review* a letter, which they're printing, saying that my review of *The Man With The Blue Guitar* was the "most invigorating review" that he had ever had. On the one hand, this, all of this, is going to help you get rid of my books, and on the other hand you don't have to be afraid that I will take this praise too seriously, forget how much one has to do to be a good writer, or rest on the laurels.

If I do not see you before you sail, goodbye, thanks for all your generosity, and I hope that old Pagany starts you writing again.

Yours,
Delmore Schwartz

1. No play of S appeared in *N.D. 1938.*
2. Of his poem and story "The Commencement Day Address" in *N.D. 1937.*

TO ALLEN TATE

73 Washington Place
New York City
March 8, 1938

Dear Mr. Tate:

You will know how pleasant it was to get your generous letter if I tell you that I have been reading your poems and your criticism with the greatest care and absorption since my fourteenth year. My first infatuation in literature, unfortunately, I think now, was *White Buildings*, and I strove for years with some of the sentences in your foreword which could not help being of a gnomic character for me at that time. And now, in fact, I think I must remember some of your early writing better than you do yourself—your reviews in *The Nation*, which I sedulously searched out, and your poems in [William Stanley] Braithwaite's anthologies. I hope that you will not be too uncomfortable at the thought of an unknown, all-examining pupil all these ten years; although twice, when I first began to study philosophy and when I considered myself a "non-Christian neo-Thomist," the very thought of your criticism infuriated me.

The subject of beliefs and poetry interests me very much, apart from the necessity of coming to some kind of provisional decision about it in order to write literary criticism. It seems to me that one must begin by taking as incontrovertible and inescapable and absolutely necessary Eliot's remark in the Dante essay that there is no such thing as literature or poetry, both disappear, if for one moment we permit ourselves to judge a poem in terms of the validity of its beliefs (qua beliefs). But this does not seem to me to mean that both poetry and literary criticism must restrict themselves to an analysis of craft and technique. I think that both you and Eliot have allowed yourself to be driven to this extreme. It seems to me that if you analyze what we mean by technique, craft, and style in the concrete, then we find that they are inseparable, in a certain way, from the beliefs and values of the poet. By the certain inseparability I mean that a whole set of alternative beliefs, for example, will all give rise to a lucid and intelligent kind of poetry. But I know that the only way in which to be perfectly clear about what one means in a difficult subject like this is to break up particular examples into their relevant parts, and I intend to do this, using as examples poems which will display the two extremes of accepting and rejecting the beliefs of the poem, while accepting the poems wholly from a literary standpoint. I hope that you will let me send you the article when it is finished and will in fact let me write to you from time to time for your help and judgement in other matters— you need not be afraid that I will take up too much of your time.

I am enclosing the piece I wrote on Horton's biography. There is a good deal in it which really needs more discussion and evidence, but I would like you to look at it. Horton himself was completely outraged and accused me of every critical sin in history, as well as of being a prig and Puritan. The last page, by the way, is a response to one point which you made in your own review of the book, as you will surely recognize.

Sincerely yours,
Delmore Schwartz

TO ALLEN TATE

73 Washington Place
New York City
March 14, 1938

Dear Tate:

You are quite right in reproving me for making critical remarks in passing and without arguing the point. I hope that you will reprove me whenever you see fit and with brutal frankness, and this goes for my poems and stories as well as my criticism, if you should see any of them. Naturally you have a great deal else to do besides correcting one apprentice among many, but I hope that I will be good enough to make my mistakes worth your comment.

If I recognize the remarks you object to, those about philosophy-mongering, there is at least this to be said for me, that I had in mind a good deal of evidence, especially with regard to Blackmur, who, despite all his virtues, scarcely ever utters a generalization but that some inane idea of Santayana is contained in it—I think I can show clearly that Blackmur misunderstands Santayana exactly when Santayana is himself engaged in misunderstanding something. I won't try to show this right now; but just regard this sentence from a review of Blackmur's as one example: "A good poem is a tautology on the plane of dramatic entelechy; which is another way of saying that it means what it *is*: meaning and being are identical." Both entelechy and the identity of meaning and being come straight from Santayana's misinterpretations of Aristotle. I know what Blackmur's trying to say and it is for that reason that so foolish and inaccurate [a] way of saying it annoys me so much. Besides, as stated the sentence is contradictory, for, of course, a tautology is just what cannot be an entelechy. This is what comes of getting terms from grammar and logic together with one term from ancient biology and making the brew even more inchoate by tossing in a few metaphysical ideas. But besides having in mind things like this, I felt it necessary while writing the review to right the balance by not attacking Winters without also mentioning the others guilty of the same offense. Blackmur, by the way, seems to me to be the chief offender, and that is why I thought it was so wrong for you to call him a master of ideas.

What interested me most in the review which you have just read was an attack on the romantic legend of the poet; otherwise I would not have engaged in a romantic discussion of possibilities, which, as you say, is out of the question except to define limitations. And yet I am not sure that you are right when you say that "a better understanding of his world would have meant quite possibly a better adjustment to it, and might have made him his father's pet candy salesman." I think that knowledge and discipline and a better understanding of his world would necessarily have meant quite the opposite. He would not have been taken in by his foolish friends, nor his grandiose ideas, it seems to me, if knowledge and discipline really mean what I think that we both agree that they mean.

In both of your letters you have been very generous in praising my criticism, but I am sure that when I do write good criticism I am merely extending something I have learned from Eliot or yourself, and in fact I find that the very words I use sometimes come from some passage in your own writing. There is no need to be falsely modest, and I am sure that I have been a good pupil; but I do not want you to think that I am unaware of debts, or incapable of gratitude.

Sincerely yours,
Delmore Schwartz

TO EZRA POUND

73 Washington Place
New York City
April 9, 1938

Dear Mr. Pound,

It was a very great pleasure to receive your letter. I am idolatrous or perhaps the word is "superstitious," and one of my superstitions is the great poet, especially the three or four who are not yet dead. Your corrections of my piece in *Poetry*[1] are thus very welcome, and I hope that you will be moved to correct me in the future. But you will not mind, I am sure, if I try to explain more exactly the notions to which you are objecting.

First, however, to answer your question about George Dillon and *Poetry*. Dillon is a very weak poet and not in the least intelligent. He was Harriet Monroe's pet child, he won the Pulitzer Prize once, and he translated with Edna St. Vincent Millay all of Baudelaire very poorly (using an alexandrine in English because Baudelaire used it in French). It is no exaggeration to say that he knows nothing. This obviously puts him in the same class as Harriet Monroe, and he seems to have like her one saving virtue, only one, the willingness to give all parties a chance to speak their pieces, and I should guess that he will be more or less as amenable to your desires as Harriet Monroe was. I for one have never been able to understand how you could tolerate so foolish a woman for so many years even with an ocean between the two of you. As for whether I was writing against the editor or with his consent, this question perplexes me. At any rate, I asked him to let me review your new book, expecting only two or three pages and he told me to write a long article, probably because he had read my long piece in the *Southern Review* in which I put Yvor Winters in his place. When the piece was finished, he said it was very good, and this probably means that I was writing with his consent. As for what I as contributor intend to do about the sabotage of your labors, let me know what you would like me to do and I will probably do it. But I actually cannot see why you should be concerned at all about *Poetry*. It has had its day and that day is long past, was over in 1920, so far as exercising a genuine influence goes, and the future for that sort of thing belongs or is going to belong to J. Laughlin IV. He has the interests, the energy, the ability and the intelligence which are needed where Harriet Monroe seems to me to have had nothing but a vague desire to be helpful, and it is obvious to me that you can go on with your useful labors with much more ease and satisfaction now than ever before.

Now for your objections. "suppose you Read some of these writers before telling grandpa he ain't been fotografted in his dress suit." This is only a shot in the dark and a pretty poor one at that. I have read with much care and attention Dante, Homer and Shakespeare, and also, though not as fully, Ovid. One reason, in fact, that I studied Greek was your own translation from the *Odyssey*—if Homer was like that, I wanted to read all of him. I found out that he was not really like that and as a matter of fact even better. All literary judgement seems to me to be comparative and on this basis it still seems clear to me that the best "frame" for a long poem is narrative. I may be very naive and literal about it, but when you say that "The *Divina Commedia* has practically no narration and no plot/it presents a scheme of values/ merely a walk upstairs to a balloon landing," I can only keep in mind the literal fact that the poem in question is about a man who was lost in a dark wood where he met various animals and then a great poet's ghost and learned that in order to escape from the wood and the animals, he would have to travel thru Hell, Purgatory, and Heaven. And thus the enormous exaltation of the cantos toward the end of Purgatorio derives from the character of the story, the narrative that Dante is going to meet the lady with whom he was very much in love for a long time and who has been dead for ten years. I do not expect you to take over broken-down values from fat Aquinas nor in fact do I suppose that the absence of narrative in your poem *as a whole* is a simple thing, a pure matter of choice. It seems to me that narrative began to go out of poetry when Coleridge had to write marginal summaries for *The Ancient Mariner* and by the time we get to *Sordello* it has become even harder to tell a story and again there are marginal summaries (at least in some editions) and all this is, I think, a part of a whole complex of both history and literature, partly the increasing quest of certain poetic effects which must of necessity eliminate or at least halt the story narrative—could Mallarmé, for example, conceivably have told a story using his style; and partly the development of the novel as a way of getting everything about a character into a medium; and partly the very breakdown of those values which focus interest upon the life and death of the individual soul—thus even the novel now tells almost no story and the leading beliefs on all sides are, as in Marxism, beliefs about classes, not individuals, about history as a whole.

I do not know how clear this is, and perhaps it is superfluous, but what I mean to say is that the very virtues of your writing *necessitate* the absence of narrative—at least some of those virtues, such as the wonderful excitement one gets as *The Cantos* move about the centuries. But given these virtues and with full awareness of your situation, I mean situation in a definite time, the contrast still exists as an objective fact, the contrast between what one gets in Dante and Shakespeare and Homer, and what one gets in *The Cantos*. It works both ways, of course, and there are, I need hardly tell you, effects in *The Cantos* which have never before been heard of. I said this in my piece. It also seemed worth saying that there is the correlative lack.

"NEXT/as to the seereeyus and solemp and perlite/'A tailor might scratch her where ere she did itch,' *'cul far tombetta.'*" It is right after this that you tell me to read some of these writers, so that it is only in fairness to the quotations that I point out that you seem to have misquoted both, if you are referring to *"ed egli avea cul fatto trombetta"* (Inf. XXI, 139) and that song from *The Tempest*. But really, you are mistaking me. By serious I do not mean solemn and polite. T. E. Hulme—there was a serious man, and that is what I mean by being serious, and I was trying to say that no matter what you, Ezra Pound, believe, the fact is that very estimable persons have all kinds of beliefs about life and death and uncontrollable mysteries which you as a poet sometimes (sometimes, I say, not always and who knows what the next 49 cantos will bring except yourself) sometimes neglect or pass over because you are more interested for the time being in some uproarious story (they are really uproarious). The marvellous comedy which takes place at the end of *Iliad* I, and the comedy in Shakespeare are proportionately less important in the structure of their writing than in yours. But notice this—perhaps I am repeating myself again—this kind of judgement and comparison is made only with the assumption that your poem is good enough to bear such a contrast.

At any rate, you can see that I have not been speaking without also thinking about what I was saying—not that that ever saves a stupid one from his own stupidity. There is a good deal more which I would like to say to you, but this letter is already too long.

Sincerely yours,
Delmore Schwartz

1. "Ezra Pound's Very Useful Labors," *Poetry*, March 1938, a favorable review of Pound's *Fifth Decade of Cantos*.

TO GEORGE DILLON

73 Washington Place
New York City, N.Y.
May 3, 1938

Dear Mr. Dillon:

In the letter from Ezra Pound which you forwarded to me, and in a subsequent letter which I received the other day, Pound expressed a great desire to hear from you. He apparently feels that it is your duty to write to him and voices bitter grievances against Mr. Zabel.[1] I know that none of this is my business, but it seemed to me that I ought to let you know about it. Pound's address, if you do not have it, is: Via Marsala 12-5, Rapallo, Italy, and one of the several remarks he makes about wishing to hear from you is this: "IF Dillon WANTS to remake the mag / and be useful / I am for having another heave at it / But it is the editor's place to indicate this desire / esp. / after the past 25 years of *Poetry* re / which he must know something / I have revived *Poetry* more than once when everyone else thought it was FINISHED (Harriet included I mean she was ready to quit)."

Sincerely yours,
Delmore Schwartz

1. Morton Zabel was Dillon's predecessor as editor of *Poetry*.

TO ALLEN TATE

73 Washington Place
New York City
May 18, 1938

Dear Mr. Tate,

I am writing a survey article, "American Poetry," 1912-1938 (as the editor calls it) for a little English magazine called *Twentieth Century Verse*, and I would be grateful for some advice from you to correct the arbitrariness which inevitably gets into one's judgement. My own taste is always too emphatic, for or against, and besides this, you may be able to suggest some aspect which I would forget or do not know about. I think this kind of piece must always make trouble—you can't back up your generalizations with sufficient examples and you always provoke resentment—but on the other hand, English pay little or no attention to American poetry, This is to be the "American number" of this magazine, and it is going to include a new poem by Eliot, which is exciting news indeed.

Suppose then that I mention a few of [the] things which perplex me. I would like to see your list of the poets who seem to you to have done something permanent and compare it with my own. I know the piece on [John Peale] Bishop in your book of essays, where you list four and make room for two or three more without naming them—which was, I thought, a beautiful piece of tact; but perhaps, you'll be willing to make a full one for me. Of the four whom you do mention, I would question the inclusion of Ransom as definitely minor, and certainly I would omit [Archibald] MacLeish, who seems to me to have been persistently third-rate, his whole subject being the nostalgic echo of an unclear memory of an imprecise feeling about Nature; and the dreadful things he has written since *Conquistador* show how little he actually has to say. And I wonder if you still think as well of Gregory as you did in reviewing *No Retreat*—I think he's especially interesting as carrying forward Eliot's method to a certain extent which is valuable, but the actual ground on which his poetry turns, once one digs beneath the fine surface, seems to be both sentimental and commonplace. Another problem for me is Harriet Monroe who seems to me to have been the editor with the worst taste in the history of poetry, but each time I have uttered this judgement everyone has claimed to be outraged. I know that *Poetry* was generous, but every poetaster in the Union knew the benefits of that generosity. I intend also to say something of the difficulty of getting a book published, the incredible corruption performed by the left-wing movement, and the stupidity of Wilson in speaking of the decay of verse, but I would like especially to hear from you how far you think Wilson is justified—it is true, of course, that good poetry for a long time has been merely lyric poetry, but the question of whether the medium of verse is less capable than in the past is a complicated one, and Bishop's sentence, which you quote, on making statements and yet retaining the post-Rimbaudian command of language seems to me to be the starting point. At any rate, I hope I can have the benefit of your advice.

Sincerely yours,
Delmore Schwartz

TO EZRA POUND

73 Washington Place
New York City
May 19, 1938

Dear Mr. Pound:
I have written to Dillon and he replies that he is going to write to

you. It still seems to me, however, that you are taking *Poetry* much too seriously. It is not subject to advertisers, but it is controlled by the taste of the subscribers, or so I am told. And besides this, it is not read at all, it is a dead thing which no one would think of attacking, like *The Atlantic Monthly.*

And your unawareness of this fact makes me wish to tell you that you seem—*seems,* my lord!—to have slowed up—if you will forgive me for presuming to tell you where you stand. What I mean is this: in the old days when you were busy digging up Joyce and Lewis and Eliot, and even ten years ago when you printed those wonderful poems by Yeats *next to* Zukofsky in *Exile,* you were in the middle of everything and knew what was going on with exactitude, and as a result everyone interested in literature was benefited. Now you seem to have your gaze trained on Jefferson and Social Credit and Harold Monro, and a phenomenon like Auden—to the author of *Lustra* and *Mauberley,* the satirist of the British ought to be an item of some interest—does not seem to exist for you—I mean, as a critic. Again, there is Zukofsky, whom one respects because he has tried as a poet to extend your method and because he has a certain feeling for historical fact, but who is, or was when he was getting printed, one of the worst critics in the history of literature, making mysteries out of maxims, taking over your mannerisms and omitting their punch, and substituting obliqueness and allusiveness wherever clarity and lucidity were a critical necessity. I mean: you could have corrected Zukofsky and perhaps even have kept him quiet. And again, it seems to me that you ought to answer some of the critics of *The Cantos*—especially Blackmur and Wyndham Lewis, who has, you know, been telling stories about you in his recent autobiography. You used to ride the "age"—if not for you, I would certainly have little notion of what it means to be caught up in a period of time, moved by it and attempting to move it. Perhaps Jefferson et al are more important concerns, but certainly, as I said, "we" profited more by your earlier interests. I ought to add, since you ask whether I have lived as near the starvation line as my elders, that I am poor and thus acutely sensitive to the economic in its concrete dollar-by-dollar difficulty. Well: what one wishes is that you continue to be our contemporary in the fullest sense of the term.

Sincerely yours,
Delmore Schwartz

TO ALLEN TATE

73 Washington Place
New York City
May 23, 1938

Dear Allen,

I am really delighted at the prospect of being permitted to write an essay about you, although, with my article on Dos Passos in the fall issue,[1] it is going to seem that they are running a serial. I hope too that Blackmur writes his essay soon. Last fall I did try to get your selection of poems [*Selected Poems*] for review, but both [Malcolm] Cowley and Margaret Marshall[2] looked at me as if I had just come down from high school. You have, I think, been unfortunate in your critics from the start, and I was angered not only by the intensely stupid [Ben] Belitt's review, and by the vicious passes of [Harry] Levin (whom I knew while at Harvard and who though learned identifies criticism with sneering), but also by Zabel's review. It is the sort of thing that one only says among friends, but writers like Zabel, [F. O.] Matthiessen, and Michael Roberts are actually very distressing and are not, in the end, of any use. They are on the right side, they mean well, they are nothing if not courteous, they always occupy the high places and are well paid, and it is just this "type" that is incapable of serious and exact perception and judgement. That dreadful abstract editorializing in Zabel's writing persuades no one, illuminates nothing, and is just not read.

Your remarks and your list are going to be very helpful to me in writing my piece. I intend to go through Ransom's poems again (I have read one of the poems you mention and like it very much), but I think there is still a sharp distinction between his verse and, say, Crane's or yours, or Stevens'. Naturally everyone is minor next to Shakespeare, but there is an obvious sense in which Auden with a few poems in his first volume (but nothing thereafter) extends the whole organism of English poetry (as Eliot would say), augments and modifies our fund of sensibility and feeling, while Louise Bogan, despite a few perfect lyrics, does not do so. It is of course (I need not say) not a question of being derivative, but of unique invention and response precisely by means of derivation. There is also the question, inseparable from [the] question of style in the end, of writers whose awareness grasps actualities of life and death (forgive me, for these terms), and those who like Léonie Adams and even Marianne Moore are special so that we sense the ignorance as well as absence of—forgive me again—an awareness of life and death. It is difficult to describe but I think you will know what I mean—it is as in reading a love story in

The Saturday Evening Post: not only is there no reference to sexual intercourse but the story is written as if there were no such activity. And it is in these terms that I would place Bogan, Adams, Moore too although with reservations, in a special place. As for Bishop, it seems to me that everything good in him is better in [Robert Penn] Warren and yourself. My one complete disagreement with you is [Marya] Zaturenska, and I would add Winters and [Howard] Baker and pay attention to Warren, as he deserves, although here, literary circles being what they are, it is certain that I will be granted only one motive in praising an editor [*Southern Review*] who has helped me. In fact, nothing has shocked me so much in this past year during which I moved from among the academic to among the literary than the ineluctable cynicism of the literary. I confess that I have like sentiments, but at least on an utterly different basis, a belief in the existence of God and the possibility of human nobility, rather than the sense that all acts spring from a competitive motive.

I hope that you decide to give *Twentieth Century Verse* a poem and that in the fall you will be willing to give me a poem, perhaps the same one, for an anthology which the *Partisan Review* has asked me to do. I am sure that I can get Pound and Stevens also. But I may decide not to do the anthology, especially if I can't get the writers whom I admire. Your reference to both [Mark] Van Doren and Gregory is interesting—I can see Van Doren as I see Bishop, everything good in him better in Hardy, in [Edwin Arlington] Robinson, and Dickinson. And there is a story about Gregory, yourself, and myself which I will have to tell you. He lectured at N.Y.U. four years ago while I was a student there and accused all American poets of being dishonest because they had their eyes turned toward the past and all that rot, and as an example he gave Eliot, about whom I had become pathologically sensitive, so that I arose, as if at a political meeting, and said that if it were a question of dishonesty, Mr. Gregory seemed to be dishonest in a much more literary sense, if the following examples were not too deceptive—the examples being a letter printed in *Poetry* in 1931 in which he said that you were "dead" as a poet, your review praising *No Retreat* a few months later, and his subsequent praise of you (although you had published no poems which he had not seen) in a letter to *New Verse*. Gregory's answer, to the shocked audience, was that the remark in *Poetry* had been a private letter to Harriet Monroe which he had never expected to be printed. This episode ended also in finishing me with the English Department at N.Y.U., the chairman and several professors being present; although until that unlucky day I had had a fair chance of getting a job teaching English there.

There is one more thing, about getting books of verse printed. I have been very lucky myself in getting Laughlin and for the time being at least he will listen to me, so that if you know anyone who really deserves to get a book printed, perhaps we can work together, and I think that in a practical thing like this one owes it to literature to be virtually Machiavellian for the sake of good writers. Your remark about the editorship of *Poetry* interests me very much because I had suspected some kind of palace revolution there. I intend to take advantage of your willingness to help me and write to you if some perplexity turns up in my essay.

Sincerely yours,
Delmore Schwartz

1. "John Dos Passos and the Whole Truth," *Southern Review*, IV, 2 (1938).
2. Cowley was literary editor of *The New Republic*, Marshall of *The Nation*.

TO ALLEN TATE

73 Washington Pl.
New York City
May 30, 1938

Dear Allen:

I would like to have a job very much, although my need of one is no longer as acute as it seemed to be during my six years of school. If you know of one, and can get it for me, I need not say how grateful I would be and in fact how grateful I am for the suggestion. I can get recommendations from [James] Burnham, Sidney Hook, Ralph Barton Perry and an ecstatic letter from Whitehead, if this sort of thing will do any good, and I could get my doctorate by returning to Harvard for six months, although I hope I do not have to do so and have no desire for an academic "career." I suppose it would have to be clear that the job was a secondary thing for me, although I would scarcely fail to do all the work required of me: I mention this because I was told at Harvard that I was hurting my chances in the Philosophy Department by publishing verse and criticism. But let's say no more about this unless something is actually in the offing; I don't want to create a burden for you, and I can take care of myself and my wife-to-be for at least two years, after which there is that great whore of Babylon and swank journalism, *Fortune*.

Laughlin wrote to me from Italy to ask what I thought of [George Marion] O'Donnell and about publishing a book of his poems. My own impression is—based upon ten poems—that he is good but that he might be improved by being made to work harder at single poems: the tragic manner of the poems I have seen seems both facile and somewhat premature. However, this is not a thing for either Laughlin or myself to tell O'Donnell, and I am going to tell L. to go right ahead.

I agree with you wholly about the rank of discoverers and developers and it seems obvious that the developers are really the great poets (I remember your own very interesting contrast of T. H. Chivers[1] and Poe several years ago). But I have in mind a more central criterion which cuts under the distinctions of technique and "content." The major poet sees the skull beneath the skin, he requires of himself the strength and courage to see himself *with* disgust, and this shows itself not only in his subjects, for of course anyone can take sublime themes, but in the quality of his images. Your own verse, if you will forgive [me] for using that example, is pretty bare of direct observation, but whenever it is there—the "smoky frieze of the sky," "the lunar interior of the night"—it seems to me to bear the heavy weight of sense organs which are penetrated by a mind aware that men must live and also must die. Everyone knows this, of course, but I don't think many poets have written with such an awareness involved in their writing. It is, I am sure, what Aristotle meant by high seriousness and also by pointing out that poetry was more philosophical than history. There are also further questions of individuality and "newness" (a newness made possible only by what has already been done), but I don't know why I tell you this, except to make it clear that it is in my own mind when I make judgements.

I suppose I have no business being harsh in judging Zabel, but I had in mind the wonderful work done in the field of art history by German academicians who occupy, or rather occupied, positions similar to Zabel's and Roberts'. The whole field of painting, sculpture, and architecture has been mapped out with the greatest exactitude, categories for every genre, all the facts at hand, and everything so ordered that all the analogies, resemblances, cross-references, and recurrences are waiting for the critic. The same thing is true to a certain extent of French literary history. Instead what do we have: anthologizers and the writers of editorials, [Babette] Deutsch, Untermeyer, [Eda Lou] Walton, and at best Zabel, and no one with the least conception of the solid journeyman work to be done, and which some of these people could do (not Walton, however, who sets an all-time record for stupidity).

My remarks about the cynicism of the literati were prompted partly by a cocktail party where James T. Farrell, a little tight at the time,

56

congratulated me on playing up to *S.R.* by referring to you in the Hemingway piece. The appalling thing was that he really approved of what he considered a deliberate strategy and it was no use trying to explain to him that I had been studying your criticism for ten years. A moment later he was engaged in telling Philip Rahv how he had just visited Clifford Odets and tried to get him to release the dramatic rights to a book by Silone by reminding Odets of the love letters O. had written to the woman with whom Farrell is now living. The remark about the first symptom of dishonesty being a belief that everyone is dishonest is the kind of observation that I write in the blank pages of my *Nicomachean Ethics*, with a half-hearted effort to put them in Greek, in the pious belief that Aristotle would have made the remark himself, if he had come around to it. The most recent entries are from Kafka: "Impatience is a form of laziness," and "There is a certain point onward from which there is no turning back: that is the point we must reach."

Sincerely yours,
Delmore Schwartz

1. Thomas Holley Chivers (1809-1858), American poet associated with Poe. In 1850 he was accused of plagiarism from Poe, and he retorted that it was Poe who had plagiarized from him.

TO F. W. DUPEE[1]

Overlea Cottage
N. Bennington, Vermont
July 6, 1938

Dear Fred:

The high point of our day is the mail and your letter was a very pleasant part of this morning's portion. Everything proceeds very well with us and the absence of distraction—I mean, of the possibility of distraction, the very minimum of which is the moving pictures—is just what I needed, so that I have some hope of finishing my new play[2] before my book goes to the printer. Every time hereafter that I want to get something done for sure I am coming to the country. Vermont—"Vermont"—is fine, although nothing near that Arcady of my youth (perhaps I should say: late childhood) Wisconsin.

I think your observations about Auden are very useful and original, and I hope he reads your piece. My own feeling about him is part of what you say, except that I think the elements which you consider rather recent to have been present in his first book. Two elements, I think: one that of a very sensitive mind which lifts up images of the greatest import and shows them in rugged, crabbed, hard language with the kind of "implicatory" power which always is a sign of poetic mastery; the other is the·schoolboy who is very clever, delights in his own cleverness, plays practical jokes and writes charades, and worst of all relishes the immediacy of effect which his cleverness brings him. The first one is all over the first book, especially in lines like

> Because I'm come it does not mean to hold
> An anniversary, think illness healed
> As to renew the lease, consider costs
> Of derelict ironworks on deserted coasts.
> Love was not love for you but episodes,
> Traffic in memoirs, views from different sides,

where every word, it seems to me, becomes rich with symbolic meaning, where such usually neutral words as "lease," "episode," "traffic" are brought into the vocabulary of poetic diction, and where such an image as "costs of derelict ironworks on deserted coasts" is the kind of image from the unconscious mind (the deserted factory towns of Wales, Auden's country, of course) which makes Auden so valuable a poet, a kind of Cumaean sibyl hearkening to the veritable Zeitgeist.

The other side is represented in the musical comedy style of "The Dance of Death," even in the later plays, and as you remark, when he tries to bring the two together (again because, I'm sure, of that immediacy of effect which is so intoxicating) he becomes, as in his last book, grandiloquent, Housmanesque. If he were a good satirist and funny, he might be justified, but as it is I think he has merely succeeded in partly suppressing the unconscious psychic in himself. Another thing is that he is not really intelligent, so that conscious concepts—Freud and Marx—merely get in his way, as in the ambiguous motivation—imperialism or Oedipus complex, or both—of the *Ascent of F6*.

Naturally success would tend to augment the musical-comedy man and make the genuine poet too facile—he is too facile, anyway—too uncritical, and ready to adore any idea that comes to him; to be his kind of poet one has to be not only absolutely sincere (as with the psychoanalyst) but also tough against most of the suggestions and seductions of the overt public world.

That's about all, and scarcely news to you, I suppose, although I think that in applying all to specific passages one could score heavily. I wish you would send me the copy in which your article appears, if it is not too much trouble, and let me know what goes on, if you have the time. Gertrude sends her regards and we both thank the *Partisan Review* for its very fine prize.

Yours,
Delmore

1. Dupee was an editor of *Partisan Review* at the time. He had arranged for S and his bride to rent a cottage for their honeymoon.
2. "Dr. Bergen's Belief," which S used to conclude his first book.

TO ALLEN TATE

Overlea Cottage
N. Bennington, Vermont
July 15, 1938

Dear Allen:

// The job [at Kenyon College] which you mention sounds fine and it is nothing if not pleasant to hear that there is going to be a good magazine [*Kenyon Review*] besides the *Southern Review*. But again, you know how grateful I am that you kept me in mind for that place. I think you're wrong, however, about jobs with *Fortune*. Besides the high-pressure work of getting things written by a given date, there is the rigorous imposition of what someone has just called a collective style and worst of all a crude indoctrination—ideology in the exact sense of the word. I am not afraid of being persuaded, but I don't care to spend myself resisting. [James] Agee and MacLeish have both quit and returned a number of times, I am told, for these reasons. In the end, however, I won't have much choice about taking such a job unless some college will permit me to teach.

I have a critical project in mind about which I should consider your advice decisive—although there's no need for me to know what you think of it immediately. The project is a book about Eliot. It would have to wait some time for publication, since Laughlin is printing a book of poems for me this fall, and I have another unfinished book for which I have the highest hopes—often despair—and which I want to get printed next, whenever it does get finished. But I think the kind of book I have in mind might be a good thing in several ways. I can see Eliot, or at least I think I can, in contexts which apparently have occurred to no one else. As almost the exact contemporary, in the widest sense, of Trotsky and Maritain, and also in his curious reading, for example of post-war German philosophy—"The natural wakeful life of our Ego," in "Triumphal March," is a direct quotation from Husserl's foundational work in phenomenology; and in general

I have taken the very interesting trouble of tracking down, so far as is possible, his roots in the books he has read. I should also have a chance to see how far I can get with the problem of belief and poetry. On the other hand, I undoubtedly have all sorts of limitations for a subject like this of which I am unaware, and which you see as annulling the whole business. Another thing: can one just go ahead and write a book about a man? I suppose one can and yet I should think some courtesy might be involved. Eliot has taken so many barbaric beatings that he has every right to wish that all would preserve silence, or at any rate forego a detailed treatise. If I do write the book, I would like to ask you to let me inscribe it to you.[1]

I think this takes care of all that you brought up in your last letter, except *Snow White and the Seven Dwarfs*—the aspects you mention are appalling enough, but the true abomination of that film has yet to be told.

Sincerely yours,
Delmore

1. An Eliot study is among S's unpublished manuscripts at Yale.

TO JOHN CROWE RANSOM

8 West 105 St.
New York City, N.Y.
Sept. 24, 1938

Dear Mr. Ransom:

Many thanks for your letter. I was delighted to hear from Allen Tate last spring that you were to edit a quarterly review [*Kenyon Review*], which means I am sure that the number of magazines with a genuine interest in literature has been increased by one, and the grand sum is now two. I will be only too glad to submit essays to you. I have several subjects in mind—the metrics of Yeats, an essay on Valéry's *La Jeune Parque*, an extended review of Joyce's new work (which is finished and will appear in January), and a review of Eliot's forthcoming play—and I will certainly be able to submit at least two pieces to you during the coming fall and winter, perhaps more, from among which you may be able to choose one that you will want. Perhaps you will like to suggest other subjects to me, or tell me which of the ones I mention seems most promising to you—without of course committing yourself to accepting any one of them beforehand. The suggestion of an article about the state of reviewing in America seems a very good one to me, but would unfortunately require too much room. In the course of pure abuse, I would want to quote extensively as a matter of fairness; and thus to show, for example, that all the reviews in *The New Republic* are written by Otis Ferguson, no matter who signs them, would mean an article of great length and much "journalism." There is one more thing: I would prefer not to appear in your first number, even if I should be able to send you something suitable by the 1st of November. The reason is that I have published a good deal during the past year, and my book of verse, an article on Dos Passos, one on Blackmur (which I hope you will see), and one on Tate will be coming out during the next three months, so that I will surely seem to be anxious, eager, voluble, and in a hurry to state my opinions.

There is one matter about which I am eager and that is the teaching job, the possibility of one, at Kenyon College. I was supposed, I think, to wait until the proper moment arrived and Allen Tate, who has in a very short time been kind to me in many ways, proposed my name to you. At any rate, although this may be premature, I would welcome an opportunity to teach very much, and I may have certain qualifications, academic ones, I mean, of which you do not know, and I would be grateful indeed if my name was kept in mind.

Sincerely yours,
Delmore Schwartz

TO ALLEN TATE

8 West 105 St.
New York City
Jan. 10, 1938 [1939]

Dear Allen:

Your letter pleases me much more than I can possibly say. And in writing to Laughlin, you are being extremely generous as usual.[1] What you say may take some of the edge off my article, but I think that my judgement is so obviously buttressed by a concrete analysis of your work, that it will make no difference to those who are genuinely interested, and as for the genuinely cynical, they would be cynical in any case about my writing such an article for the *Southern Review*.[2]

I hope that the next time you come North, it will be possible to arrange a meeting between Laughlin and you. He's a wonderful fellow, although as yet immature in taste and lacking in a sense of proportion. But his interest in literature is sincere and permanent, and he's humble enough to publish writing which is not especially to his taste. If he prints the worst of Pound, he also prints Winters. I mention this because L. apparently antagonized Van Doren when he came to see you last summer, and because it would be a good thing if he began to ask your advice, rather than Pound's or Dudley Fitts's. I can't do anything with him because he considers me an impractical child.

As ever.
Delmore

1. Tate had endorsed *In Dreams Begin Responsibilities.*
2. *"The Poetry of Allen Tate," Southern Review,* V, 3 (1940), 419-38.

TO ALLEN TATE

8 W. 105 St.
New York City
Jan. 19, 1939

Dear Allen:

When I wrote you last week I was upset by various matters and did not manage to speak my whole mind, to say, that is, that there is no one else in America or anywhere else, not even Eliot, from whom a kind word could mean so much to me. I hope that when you have the leisure you will make some detailed remarks. Added to this, you have gone out on a limb for me in public, knowing of course that first books are so often a flash in the pan, and at a time when silence would have been completely warrented.

I can't understand your doubts about *The Fathers,* which seems to me as good as your best poems and in a way a fulfillment or extension of them. The only question I would raise would be directed to the whole genre of novels in which everything depends upon the style. That is, Tolstoy and Stendhal seem to indicate prose which perishes as best for fiction—but when one remembers *Wuthering Heights* as the prime example of the other genre, one realizes that no real choice is involved. However, I am overrunning my article in which I would like to seem full of "news" to you.

I saw Van Doren the other day and found him, as at a previous meeting three years ago, one of the most attractive of persons. The reward of writing is best of all, I think, in knowing the kind of people who redeem the species, few as they are. But now I remember that the *Criterion* is through—have you heard about this—and that that is an omen of how foolish it is to be full of hope.

As ever,
Delmore

TO ALLEN TATE

[New York City]
Tuesday night
[January 1939]

Dear Allen:

Your letter has created considerable commotion, and I am not yet quite certain as to how things stand with regard to that job.[1] There are several pretty difficult barriers to overcome, judging from the prerequisites you mention.

First, as to the Ph.D. I can get it by writing my dissertation, plus paying Harvard all the money I owe them, which I don't have, plus learning German, and worst of all giving my mind up to philosophy for some time, which is what I want to avoid. The difficulties of the dissertation are increased by the fact that I am, it seems, [?] regarded by the department at Harvard, this having been the fourth or fifth time that they have spent a good deal of money on a graduate student, only to have him waste himself on so lowly a subject as literature. This attitude may make my Harvard recommendations less adequate than otherwise, especially since each professor has a number of Ph.D.'s on his hands, waiting about for jobs—it was this that made me quit.

Second, as to teaching experience, I have none. I've seen Sidney Hook and he is writing to Friedlander[2] this week and he wants to give me some of his classes, so that I can get some of the experience necessary, but I suppose that this does not do much good. Hook, by the way, is one of the most influential and important persons in philosophical circles, but again, since philosophers are not making the appointment, his letter may not be as potent as it should be. Perhaps it would be possible simply to say very little about the question of experience or announce that I was teaching for Hook this summer.

The question of society or sociability does not disturb me, nor would it make any trouble. Although both Gertrude and myself are by habit two recluses, we usually manage not to be regarded as monsters by strangers, nor would we fail to enter into the community spirit.

There is one more thing you mention in your letter. The fact that we are Jewish ought to be emphasized in advance. I'm sure that this makes no difference to you, but it certainly does to some, and at a time like the present any kind of ambiguity about the matter is likely to be misunderstood.

I am sure, apart from the above deficiencies, that I could give the college the kind of instructor they want. From friends of mine who teach philosophy out of town, I've gained a clear idea of what students usually expect from philosophy, or rather the normal curiosity which can be satisfied by that subject. Their interest ranges from a desire to discuss the universal significance of the cleverness of bees in taking care of honey, through questions as to the possibilities of reincarnation and a rocket to the moon, and it ends up, if the teacher does well enough, with a genuine awareness of their attitudes and beliefs and the reasons why they live by them. It would be a distinct pleasure to talk about these things and I would be able to learn a good deal in the process. The point is that I am sufficiently interested in the subject to make it probable that I would be a good teacher, and that, I suppose, is the main thing, or ought to be.

I've overlooked one thing; it would be foolish to raise my age, since it has been stated in print too many times already.

On the whole, though I really want the job, it would be a better thing if it were a less responsible one, or one in English. My interest in writing is primary and always has been, so that it is a matter by now not of will, but of habit. Perhaps if this project falls through, Ransom will find it possible to give me a job in English the year after (I will of course say nothing of your news in that regard; I suppose it means the *Kenyon Review* is a precarious thing and the job you mentioned last year very unlikely.)

Still one more problem: the interview, if it comes as far as an interview, may be hindered by the fact that I seem to look younger every year.

At any rate, here I am in debt to you again; I don't have to say how grateful I am for all the trouble you're taking.

I was very pleased to hear that you were satisfied by my essay on your poetry; I hope I will be able to write more later on, about your criticism by itself. Your corrections are helpful [...] //

We liked Marion O'Donnell very much and if people in the South are as charming as he seemed to be, we would certainly like them very much.

This seems like a hopeful note on which to close; will you let me know if my lack of teaching experience settles everything, so that I can avoid the futility of getting letters and, possibly, going up to Cambridge. Meanwhile I will be doing all I can.

Gratefully,
Delmore

P.S. You might point out that I am not interested either in rank or in a high salary. It may be that a low salary could reconcile the authorities to the risk of a year's trial.

1. Tate had recommended S for a job opening in the Philosophy Department at Women's College, Greensboro, N.C., where he was teaching.
2. Dean at Women's College.

TO JULIAN SYMONS

8 W. 105th St.
New York City, N.Y.
Jan. 26, 1938 [1939]

Dear Symons—

I am delighted to get your letter and wish only that it were longer. I suffer from the usual lust of authors to be praised, but I have also an overwhelming curiosity about the effect of what I write on another, especially a poet of my own generation. Your letter is full of things I'd like to discuss with you at length, particularly your amazing preference of Kipling to Yeats and Stevens. But about my own book: I agree completely with you about the play qua play. It is in the book in order to complete the leading theme expressed in the title; I would defend it only as a disguised poem in dialogue. As for CAHM ["Coriolanus and His Mother"], here I think the Atlantic, as you say, intervenes. If you could *hear* the poem spoken in American you would see how far from Shakespeare it is and why the elision is much different (much more minute in speaking) than the traditional one. Allen Tate, who occupies the position Eliot does in this country, wrote Laughlin: "Schwartz's poetic style is the only genuine innovation since Pound and Eliot. In his verse there is a wholly new feeling for language and in the regular versification a new metrical system of great subtlety and originality." This is extravagantly generous, and I am obviously not the one to decide if I am that good, but I do know this, that in the blank verse there is a new metrical system whose leading virtue is that it enables me to mention things usually kept out of recent verse and thus to write narrative poetry. However, this is matter hardly to be discussed in a letter—if we get to England next year before the whole place blows up, I hope to see you and speak of these things and also of your verse (I might, by the way, help you get some printed here, if you like. Perhaps JLIV [James Laughlin IV] can be persuaded to print your book. In passing, your poems seem to me to issue from the Id, not Ego, as so much post-Auden, but this is getting personal in the most devastating way.)

I can't write that piece for you [for *New Verse*], though I should like to, because I have my book of criticism, which LIV is publishing this fall, to finish. I am not, by the way, a Marxist, though Marx seems to me to have discovered all the connections—what is wrong is the *causal* direction, first productive relation, then value: one and the other are simultaneous and inseparable as a moment's introspection demonstrates; you can only *make* what you *want* to make. The remark about [Frederick] Prokosch, [Dylan] Thomas, and [George] Barker was unfortunate in that it seemed a condemnation and I meant only to establish a set of literary relationships. Will you tell him [Thomas?] so if you see him? I expect to write about his verse one of these days. //

I'd like to write to you again when life gets a little less crowded, and I hope you won't mind my volubility.

Yours indeed,
Delmore Schwartz

TO MARK VAN DOREN

8 W. 105 St.
New York City
Jan. 28, 1939

Dear Mark Van Doren,

Thanks very much for getting Holt to send me the copy of your poems. I am not writing to them, not for the reason you mention, but because my name obviously means nothing. There are many things I'd like to say about your poetry sooner or later and in particular I'd like to tell you the amusing story of my first encounter with them a long time ago when, being infatuated with the verse of Crane, I rushed downtown to get your anthology of world poetry (it had just appeared), and looked desperately for other writers as exalted as Crane, and found none except that translation by E. Powys Mather, and knowing that Crane could not really be the best of all poets, as he seemed to be, looked for one of your own books of verse, so that I could find out why your taste was so different from mine, which I was only too ready to suspect anyway, and ended up in a state of very involved perplexity and self-doubt.

By this time the whole business seems rather clear to me, Crane does not seem so very good, and I should think that my taste was much nearer to yours. And one of the things that impresses me most in going over your collection is how much I can learn about meter and about people in your poetry, and I need not say that there's hardly anything that seems more important to me. I'd like to speak with you some time about some of your variations of meter and hear how they sound when you speak it. Probably you remember an article Tate wrote for the *Bookman* just ten years ago this month (it served me as a guide to my reading); I am quoting it because I think it expresses my own sentiments: "Mark Van Doren is in some respects our most perfect craftsman. He found...a style...now equal to the demands of a highly complex vision. The surface simplicity is misleading: he is one of the most profound sensibilities in America." This reads like a prophecy of *A Winter Diary*, which I like best of all your books.

I am going to send you the essay on Tate as soon as I finish it.

Sincerely yours,
Delmore Schwartz

TO JOHN CROWE RANSOM

8 W. 105th Street
New York City, N.Y.
Feb. 21, 1939

Dear Mr. Ransom:

I was very pleased to get your letter, especially since you asked to see some of my verse. However, of the stack of poems which I've written since the pieces in my book, none sufficiently satisfies me as yet, although some of them, for all I know, may be good, and some others may turn out well with rewriting. I look forward to sending them to you when your examination seems justified.

How soon that will be, I don't know, and until then the following projects suggested themselves to me. An essay of considerable length reviewing the history of the *Criterion*, with special emphasis on its recent suspension. I went thru all the volumes several years ago (I would have to do it again) and I think there is a good deal to be said about the magazine in particular and all such magazines with regard to their influence, capacity, errors, etc. It is quite probable that you could get someone better fit to do this piece than myself, one, e.g., aware of the magazine since 1922. A second project would be one on Eliot as critic, more or less like my articles on Winters and Blackmur, if you have seen them. It is quite evident that Eliot is a great critic but still worthwhile, I think, to make clear all the contradictions and ambiguities in his essays.

If neither of these appeals to you, I can let you see the extended essay on poetry in general which I am now engaged in writing with a view to making it the backbone of a book of criticism. It was this essay which made me offer, rather pretentiously, I suppose, to submit several essays to you at once. As it now stands, it is too long to print, but parts of it could be recast for a magazine appearance. It would probably be some time before I could send the whole thing to you, but probably you could glance thru it and find something you wanted in different form (the essay is an effort at a sustained argument about poetry).

Sincerely yours,
Delmore Schwartz

TO MARK VAN DOREN

8 W. 105th St.
New York City
Feb. 27, 1939

Dear Van Doren,

I meant to say nothing about your review[1] partly because you've been concerned enough with me and my letters lately, and partly that I try to keep silent about praise and blame because my sensitivity to it is certainly a great weakness. But a review like yours is precisely the kind of thing that puts one in a state forgetful of such things and able to concern myself with, as you say in your review, what is not personal.

What especially pleased me was the remark about my knowing that Aristotle was the best and wisest tutor, although there are days when Shakespeare seems to put them all in the shade, and my only desire, as you indicate, is to be a late Shakespearean fool.

Yours,
Delmore Schwartz

1. Van Doren reviewed S's first book in *Kenyon Review*, calling it "as good as any poetry has been for a long while, say at least a literary generation."

68

TO EZRA POUND

8 West 105 St.
New York City
March 5, 1939

Dear Mr. Pound:

I have been reading your last book, *Culture*.[1] Here I find numerous remarks about the Semite or Jewish race, all of them damning, although in the course of the book, you say:

> Race prejudice is red herring. The tool of man defeated intellectually, and of the cheap politician.

which is a simple logical contradiction of your remarks about the Jewish people, and also a curious omen of a state of mind—one which can support both views, race prejudice and such a judgment of race prejudice, at the same time, or in the same book.

A race cannot commit a moral act. Only an individual can be moral or immoral. No generalization from a sum of particulars is possible, which will render a moral judgment. In a court of law, the criminal is always one individual, and when he is condemned, his whole family is not, qua family, condemned. This is not to deny, however, that there are such entities as races. Furthermore, this view of individual responsibility is implicit in the poetry for which you are justly famous.

But I do not doubt that this is a question which you have no desire to discuss with anyone who does not agree with you, and even less with one who will be suspected of an interested view. Without ceasing to distinguish between past activity and present irrationality, I should like you to consider this letter as a resignation: I want to resign as one of your most studious and faithful admirers.

Sincerely yours,
Delmore Schwartz

1. *Guide to Kulchur* (1938).

TO JOHN CROWE RANSOM

8 West 105 Street
New York City, N.Y.
April 25, 1939

Dear Mr. Ransom:

I have been ill for the past month, and though well at present, I do not have the freshness and energy of mind to do my best, such as it is, with my article on the *Criterion*. For that reason, I would like you to postpone it until the succeeding issue. Perhaps the postponement would remove some of the journalistic point, but the main concern of my article was otherwise, anyway—I was planning to show how the bound volumes in the library now constituted a permanent fund of awareness, so to speak, as well as a document, of the seventeen years (in which aspect it is, in fact, deficient). However, if you have been counting or rather depending upon my piece for the next issue and I have let you down completely, please let me know. I can force myself to work, of course, and all the forcing would be a matter of writing, for all the reading is done and I have a vast sum of notes. With apologies,

Sincerely yours,
Delmore Schwartz

P.S. I might add that I want very much to write the article, when my mind is really working, for the subject is an excellent one.

TO ALLEN TATE

8 W. 105 St.
New York City
May 16, 1939

Dear Allen:

I concluded weeks ago that the Women's College had decided to persevere without me, but expected some sort of notice from Friedlander, who had not even acknowledged my letter and the recommendations which were sent to him. I want to write to him and try to get my records back, but should like to know from you what, if anything, has happened.[1] I saw John Berryman the other day and he told me he had heard that you were going to be near New York next fall and since this was the most attractive feature of Greensboro, the news was very pleasant. We were supposed to spend the coming year at Norfolk and in Cambridge with Laughlin—my wife was going to be his editorial assistant—but Laughlin's aunt, who at present provides the cash for New Directions, "read" my book, decided that I was a sex-fiend and a Communist, and refused to permit Jay to give us the job. Thus both happy possibilities of a livelihood have vanished during the past two months and meanwhile I have been ill, unable to make the revisions on my essay on your poetry for which Warren asked, and otherwise stumped about this and about that.

Several other items have accumulated. One is that I asked Randall Jarrell for some poems for *Partisan Review* a long time ago and never heard from him. Then I met [Louis] MacNeice, but I will postpone until another time, when I feel more fluent, a record of our conversation: I doubt very much if any of those people will be writing poetry in ten years' time. And then, Winters with his inimitable gift for infuriating everyone has infuriated Laughlin and withdrawn his book of poems from New Directions. That man! He is as much an obscurantist as the writers he accuses of obscurantism, the pseudo-reference in his writing being to the kind of feeling which Winters likes to think is moral.

I look forward to your essay on Richards, and I've also looked forward to a letter from you on my book—having heard from Berryman, O'Donnell, and Van Doren how excellent, instructive, and patient you have been with them. But by this time, I've come to the stage where I want to forget about that book and save my claim to your attention for what I have been writing during the last year, whenever that is finished. I am sure the last one would have been much better—and shorter—if it had had the benefit of your scrutiny, but there is nothing I can do about that now, except wonder what Blackmur can conceivably mean when he speaks of my spontaneity and be perplexed by all the other varieties of praise and blame. //

Will you let me know what happened about the teaching job and will you ask Jarrell about my request when you next see him or write to him?

Yours as ever,
Delmore

1. No job was offered S, despite letters of recommendation from Mark Van Doren, Sidney Hook, and David W. Prall.

TO ALLEN TATE

8 W. 105 St.
New York City
May 24, 1939

Dear Allen:

Princeton is to be congratulated on getting the best poet and critic in America and practically everyone is to be congratulated on the poetry series you intend to edit.[1] My approval means nothing, obviously, but I might be able to help you in two ways: I might get a few subscribers for you and I can print your authors in *Partisan Review* as their books appear (I am the unofficial poetry editor) and I can also see that they get reviewed by intelligent critics.

I suggest that you speak to Friedlander before you leave Greensboro about getting my credentials back to me, so that I can get to work with them in another place. I will have to have some kind of job by next year and I don't want to waste any more time.

Winters and Laughlin parted, by the way, because Laughlin wanted to postpone his book of verse for one year—the reason was that Winters had published three books in two years and the reviews were just not being made any more. So you will probably have quite a time with him.

Yours as ever,
Delmore

1. Tate was to have edited a new poetry series at the University of North Carolina.

TO JOHN BERRYMAN

8 W. 105th Street
New York City, NY
May 29, 1939

Dear John,

The difficulty of getting away without spending too much money proved too much for us, particularly for myself in my present—continuing—state of dejection, and we will probably be here until August, when we may go to Yaddo, which will at least promise the possibility of seeing you sooner than I had expected. Your present place seems very attractive merely by virtue of its name; if there is a barnyard and a stable and country noises very early in the morning, then you are probably enjoying what is for both Gertrude and myself one of the most pleasant of life's false simplicities.

Thanks for getting "On the London Train" for me. It is a very beautiful poem and Warren can't have it because it now belongs to *Partisan Review*, and will soon be with the printer. I like the poem about the unfortunate Timothy, but suppose you send me "The Disciple" and "Ritual" and consider both of them accepted, unless you want to send me one of your new short-line poems. My extreme misgivings about the latter poem remain, but I think the vulgar shock may make some readers aware of your existence. This is a tactic and a relaxation of critical standards, but in printing it I am acting as editor, not critic, but really critic in the end, because I want to see your verse being read. (Casuistry justifies everything, but what can one do in the case when no one pays attention to a poet unless there is a scandal. Maritain observes that to refuse to use force, as of Gandhi, is to deny the fact that one has a body. The same kind of justification probably works for the editor, who prints insufficient work for the sake of all that is sufficient and is going to be so.)

I am convinced, after careful thought, of Blackmur's stupidity (and Tate agrees) in speaking of myself as spontaneous. Your gloss of "daring" for "spontaneous" is correct in itself, but hardly justifies Blackmur in using the wrong word. "Spontaneity" can't, obviously, be a critical term, for how can it apply to anything in the poet except what happens in the act of composition, which could scarcely be available to the critic. The artifice of spontaneity does exist in the book, especially in the long poem ["Coriolanus"], as a dramatic means; but the *artifice* of spontaneity is the opposite of spontaneity.

Tate mentioned his poetry series to me and also the fact that all six of the first year's series have apparently been chosen, which would free you from appearing with Jarrell and O'Donnell, but delay you one year. So I have taken the liberty of mentioning your book to Laughlin, and will continue to do so, unless you want me to stop.[1] It is hard to guess what will come of this or of anything else I recommend to him, but I think it is worth the trouble because of the effort he makes for the book which he does decide to issue. By the way, if you want to get in his next anthology, you had better send him your poems immediately or send them to me and I will do so.

But this is enough for an uninspired letter. With best regards from Gertrude and myself,

Yours,
Delmore

P.S. Will you send me the poems for *P.R.* immediately?

1. While Berryman wanted his own full-length collection, Laughlin was soliciting him to appear with Randall Jarrell, George Marion O'Donnell, W. R. Moses, and Mary Barnard in an omnibus *Five Young American Poets*.

TO R. P. BLACKMUR

8 W. 105 St.
New York City
June 1st, 1939

Dear Mr. Blackmur:
After considerable hesitation, I've decided to trouble you about your

review of my book. Your review seemed to me the only one which could be considered an act of genuine criticism (rather than a greeting to a new writer or an expression of personal feeling) and several of your remarks, particularly those concerning my play as not a play, my short poems as imitative, and my use of fable, seemed to me not only just but very helpful and illuminating. There are two points, however, which I do not understand in the simple sense of not knowing to what in my book they apply. One is the spontaneity you refer to, the other is the lack of subject matter. Both are applied to my long poem, in which I can see the artifice of spontaneity, but not spontaneity itself, and in which I am oppressed by a sense of too much subject matter (if I understand your use of the term). But I do not mean to argue with these points, but to ask you to mention the parts which you found corrupted by extended spontaneity, lacking in subject matter, and the separable parts which you say are not defective. It would be extremely kind of you to specify briefly the sections you had in mind. It is obvious that the best way of understanding such serious remarks as yours is in the text itself and since that is also one of the few ways of making any progress, I hope you will be charitable enough to help me, tiresome as it is for the reviewer to have the reviewed on his hands.

Sincerely yours,
Delmore Schwartz

TO MARK VAN DOREN

8 W. 105 St.
New York City
June 18, 1939

Dear Van Doren—

Thanks very much for writing Holt to send me your book on Shakespeare. I've gone through it during the past week and it is really amazing to see how well you've managed to be both comprehensive and detailed in every chapter—to present a focussing generalization and yet to hear the straw rustling by the measure or justice of your scrutiny. The book is full of observations which refresh one's capacity to pay attention to S. and look at that inexhaustible exhausting corpus of work some more. I was sorry that you said nothing of the wild men of modern Shakespearean criticism, who are always too comprehensive or too detailed and who apparently never read for pleasure, but anyway your book is an implicit correction of them. And I was glad to have you say how poor S. was often enough, something which Shakespeareans are so often forgetting or, when they admit it, attributing to another Elizabethan.

I looked for you several times at Columbia with John Berryman, and with your copy of Kafka's *Amerika*. I thought we would be passing your way in Connecticut this summer and so that I could return the book then—but Laughlin's aunt, who is the money behind the throne, read my book, decided I was a sex-fiend and Communist who would corrupt her nephew—and so we are going to Yaddo to see what happens when writers live together and where I am to be fed free but my wife must secure and cook her own food, which strikes me as a highly intellectual arrangement. With our regards to Mrs. Van Doren—

> Yours,
> Delmore Schwartz

TO ROBERT HIVNOR[1]

> Yaddo
> Saratoga Springs, N.Y.
> September 8, 1939

Dear Hivnor,

I am writing hurriedly and immediately because I want to get some projects in motion. First of all, send your manuscript to Laughlin, mentioning my name (I've already written him about your book). Then send me your verse. I think I told you I was poetry editor of *Partisan Review* and could print whatever I wanted; I'll print at least one poem in *P.R.* and insist, if it is necessary, that Laughlin print a part of your book in next year's New Directions anthology. So you can say that you are going to appear in those two places for certain, which may give you some kind of a lever in practical matters. You ought also to send some parts of your book to the *Southern Review*, mentioning my name there on the chance that it might heighten an editor's attention. And if you come East this fall, try to come by way of Saratoga: we are going to be here for some time, at least until the new year or America's entrance into the new war.

I'm very grateful for your remarks about my book. Many of your observations are extremely good; and it is helpful for me to hear them from you and from the outside, for when they occur to me, as some of them have, they seem moments of doubt and fear which come and go with the energy of writing or the aftermath of tiredness. I mention this especially because you may have to endure the same kind of self-suspicion without having as yet the good luck of external interest. I agree with most of the limitations you mention; that, for example, the imagery is too often that of the student, vacationer, paid admission. Is a limitation the same thing as a lack and a fault? I do not think so. Such a limitation as that of the imagery is the result, I would like to think, of an effort to be faithful to what I know, not to pretend to what I do not know. There is also a technical aspect to such limitations, my effort to develop a method which would make it possible for me to refer, with the least strain and the quickest transition, to anything from the purely personal to the international. I had the feeling that I had managed this in "Coriolanus," and at present I am enjoying what may be an illusion of having mastered the method to the point of such ease and familiarity as one enjoys when one has learned to drive a car. What almost no one seems to have noted in "Coriolanus" is that the hero of the whole thing is the I, the poet; and what he sees is what is important and constitutes the true action. Once you see this you are interested, as in that movie short, not in the sheep who wandered away but in the shepherd dog's inability to keep them all in hand. //

There is one thing, however, which I would shout at you: you have already said it to me; it is the necessity that you keep yourself going and living as a writer, no matter what demands the new war and the entelechy of revolution make upon you. By uneven analogy, the writer is like the doctor and like the shoemaker, and only by being doctor and shoemaker can he do any good; the revolution is a profession in itself, which it is the writer's part to support as a human being, but without ceasing to be a complete writer. The war's immense sensations may create all kinds of immediacies which tempt one to do something else; but one ought to remember that to live wholly in a crisis is like living wholly in the present moment, stupid and obscene. You have a good chance of being as good a writer as anyone of our generation, and good writing in the long run is as important as anything else to all human lives.

My wife sends her regards and I hope to hear from you again soon. Don't forget about the verse for *Partisan Review*.

Yours,
Delmore Schwartz

1. An unknown writer from the Midwest, Hivnor had submitted a story to *Partisan*

Review. S decided to try to help him publish. New Directions contracted to publish his novel but never did.

TO MARK VAN DOREN

Yaddo
Saratoga Springs, N.Y.
September 16, 1939

Dear Van Doren,

I've been reading your *Winter Diary* with so much pleasure and admiration lately that I thought it would be pleasant for me to write and tell you so. It is the kind of a poem which helps one especially in this new time of war. It makes me aware of how much will continue with its own species of eternity, whether there is a war or not. It's a great comfort to be able to think that there is a way of life in Nature or rather next to Nature which is gonig to last as long as men have to get food from the land, no matter what else is wiped out.

What made me take up the poem this time was that we had decided to stay here at Yaddo during the coming winter in the old farmhouse we were given when we arrived. This will be the first time that we have lived apart from the city, for a long span not a vacation, in our lives, and since both Gertrude and myself are both irreducibly the products of metropolitan childhoods, I expect a certain unrest at times, when the possibility of a dozen different activities which exists in the city is removed. But I have said so many times that I was a recluse by temperament, that it is about time I proved it. The prospect of America's entry into the war by next spring comes from the best Marxist source, Trotsky himself, and he's been right too often before this.

Our summer in Yaddo has been a mixture of many new impressions of the literary life. A generalization about writers drawn from the writers who have been here this summer is probably not a fair sample, since so many seem to have little more than a talent for journalism; but so far as that generalization goes, it makes me sick with the idea of how, as a class, writers are self-indulgent, full of self-pity, forever seeking reassurance, constantly occupied with what they consider the proper conditions of work, and the next thing to invalids in their demands upon life. One fine exception was a Kentucky poet and fiction writer named James Still, who had recently refused to allow *The Saturday Evening Post* to change the ending of a story for which they offered him $600 when changed, a refusal which seems to amaze some of the other people here. Mrs. [Elizabeth] Ames [the director] was also much better than I had any reason to expect, although the rubber pad worn by her female spaniel to circumvent the way of all flesh was the sort of thing indicated by all previous reports. And as if to remind everyone that life was not, after all, a vacation at a writer's colony, a German refugee writer dropped dead one night, partly I think as a result of the excitement of the news from Europe.

I hope that if we can get a car soon, I can take advantage of your invitation to visit you some day during the fall. I won't come without warning, however, and you'll have ample time to head us off if you are busy.

Yours,
Delmore

TO ALLEN TATE

Yaddo
Saratoga Springs
Oct. 1, 1939

Dear Allen,

I intended to write you long before this and in particular to thank you for sending me that fine poem; but practically everything has happened to me during the past weeks, among other events a request from my mother that I go to California and persuade my younger brother not to marry a widow woman with a five-year-old child, a complication of California resolved in the Polish Corridor when my mother decided that it was all for the best when one remembers draft exemptions during the war.

Now I'm rather ashamed to have to begin by asking you to write a letter to the Guggenheim committee for me when the time comes, and also, if you can and it will do any good, to put in a good word for me with Cowley, who evidently has much to do with the choices in poetry. I've also had the idea of submitting a second project, this one in criticism, though it is not what I would want. Does that sound sensible or efficacious to you? I'm troubled by the need of a detailed synopsis. I have a long outline of what I am trying to write, but I don't like to hand it out, since it is the kind of thing which may seem intolerably pretentious. Do you know if one can get away with a sentence or two?

I hope I will see you again, now that you are going to be near New York. We are probably going to stay at Yaddo for a long time; now that all the writers have left, it is very pleasant. But Christmas might

be a good time, and I can drive to New York before that, if you will
let me know when you are going to be there.

Yours as ever,
Delmore

TO ROBERT HIVNOR

Yaddo
Saratoga Springs
Oct. 25, 1939

Dear Robert,

I was going to write you and give you the advice gained from my
own experience as to how to deal with Laughlin, but since I had been
discussing you and your book with him and giving him asked-for
advice, I felt that I might be playing both ends for the sake of one.
By now I should guess that everything is sewed up and you need think
of nothing but the writing of your book, which is all that any writer
has a right to ask for at any time, even the present. When you get to
New York, it might be a good thing for you to talk to [Philip] Rahv
and Dupee about their impression of your writing. I think they're
wrong, but their particular view is one which, if you do not take account
of it now, you will certainly hear from the reviewers.

Your remark about my long poem still makes me think that you are
refusing to accept as a device what need be no more than a device, a
part of the form inhabiting the subject, and not the subject itself (if
it were the subject, then your objection would be valid; but the subject
is a certain man and various perspectives with regard to him or any
man). Think of the medieval dream poems or Dante's *Vita Nuova*,
where the dream system is used also not for what it is but in order to
see something else. However, I think your objection probably springs
from some other insufficiency either in the poem or in your reading,
and it is helpful to me to think about it and try to find out what it is.

Have you read Dostoyevsky's *The Possessed?* It is a wonderful book
in many ways, but I mention it right now because it seems to me the
best exhibition of all that is likely to be wrong with the revolutionary
movement, and how far any known theory of socialism is from being
an adequate philosophy of life. But that is the kind of statement that
one ought to discuss only among socialists.

Perhaps we will not be staying in Yaddo after December—the mon-
strous [Nathan] Asch [novelist] has made the place oppressive in some

ways—and we will come back to New York, in which case I hope we'll be seeing you, and meanwhile that you write to me. Gertrude sends you her regards.

Yours,
Delmore

TO F. W. DUPEE

Yaddo
Saratoga Springs, New York
Nov. 1, 1939

Dear Fred,

// I intended to write you before this, but so little occurs in our modest, studious, and quiet life here that I had nothing worth writing. By this time, no one of the five remaining guests (as they are called) is speaking to all the other four, with the exception of Gertrude, except that is when she is not speaking to me. There are all kinds of curious combinations of silence and anger; and it would remind me of explorers on Arctic expeditions but for the fact that the lack of harmony comes not from enforced isolation but from the contempt of one kind of writer for another kind. One fantastic creature named Anthony Wrynn maintains that only Marianne Moore knows what style and good writing are; the effect of this upon Nathan Asch can be easily conceived. However, the conditions for working all day long are better than I have ever had before, and besides, there is the saving of expenditures for rent. Unfortunately, this may not continue after the first week of December because the money to run Yaddo all year long has diminished so greatly as a result of the decline of dividends in some Mexican silver mines because of the Cardenas regime. This, for me, illustrates not only the far-flung character of modern life, but of my own life; we will probably be coming back to New York, unless something occurs to lift up Yaddo's income again. //

I enclose a poem sent to me by G. M. O'Donnell. I think one of you had better decide about it and write to him independently of me; otherwise Dwight [Macdonald] will certainly accuse me of accepting the poem because O'Donnell reviewed my book favorably, if Dwight remembers the fact. My best regards, nevertheless, and Gertrude's, too, to Dwight, Philip [Rahv], and William [Phillips].

Yours,
Delmore

TO FRANCES STELOFF[1]

Yaddo
Saratoga Springs, New York
Nov. 3, 1939

Dear Miss Steloff,

Thank you for your letter, which I would have answered before this, had I not been away from any place where mail could be forwarded to me. I am very glad to hear of the Gotham Book Mart's twentieth anniversary, and your catalogue sounds like a very useful and interesting thing. Enclosed is a paragraph on Hart Crane's poetry which I hope will serve your purposes.

Yours sincerely,
Delmore Schwartz

HART CRANE

The virtues and the faults of Hart Crane's poetry are inextricably combined. Crane's gifts made possible a certain rhetorical elevation of language, and an intense apprehension of the *things* of modern life, the subway, the bridge, the harbor, the metropolis as a whole. But he lacked the understanding of ideas and of human character which would have made him sufficiently critical of his age and of his own mind to write the kind of poetry his ambition proposed to him, poetry in which a comprehensive vision of life is realized. Nevertheless his wish to write that kind of poetry is responsible for the unique quality of language, the exaltation of emotion in his blank verse, which gives a good many of his poems their permanent interest and value.

Delmore Schwartz

1. Proprietress of The Gotham Book Mart in Manhattan, whose catalogues were entitled *We Moderns.*

TO ROBERT HIVNOR

[Saratoga Springs]
Nov. 27, 1939

Dear Bob,

Six per cent is all that I get—what it amounts to generally is fifteen cents for every book sold—but I hope you can get more. The day should come when the steelmaster scion [Laughlin] is faced with a perfect strike from two of his most politically conscious authors. But for the time being, the main thing for you, I should guess, would be to have the assurance that your book will get printed.

We are going to New Orleans, all right, though I much doubt that anything I say will have any effect on anything whatever. I intend to speak about what will be called "the isolation of modern poetry,"[1] but what will really be an effort, to explain the kind of problem you mention in your letter, the difficulty of uniting straight narrative with poetic sensibility. My hypothesis is that there is no room for sensibility in modern life as lived by most people. Hence the obscurity of the modern poet, his isolation from an audience, and other sad effects. The point is not so much that people are not cultured, no matter what class they belong to; but that culture and sensibility do not fit in, have no usefulness, no working relationship with the rest of modern life: so the poet often takes this as his theme—W. Stevens, e.g.—and often his subject is art and culture itself, for this is the only place where sensibility can function well. However that may be, the only solution for the novelist that I can see is to give his plot such a development and his characters so much intelligence and sensitivity that the passages of poetic apercus are necessary growths. I should guess that this already has been done by you. In any case, the problem, in different ways, is old as the Greek dramatist's need for a chorus which could spout philosophical comment, and I should think that the question has to be answered over again in every age; any given moment of life seen from the outside is obviously too bare, narrow, and incomplete a thing to be a sufficient subject for good writing: and that seems to me to be why naturalism always collapses. One always has to find some standpoint which makes any moment more significant than it can be in itself, seen from outside. I don't know how lucid I've just been, but you'll recognize that the same problem has been troubling me.

I hope you try to write poetry as well as work on your book—I think that once you had a little more formal usages at hand you would write well and you would have a more natural container for your kind of seeing than the novel.

Yours
Delmore

1. S gave the talk, with that title, at a meeting of the Modern Language Association in New Orleans. It was later published in *Kenyon Review*, 3 (Winter 1941).

The 1940's

TO ARTHUR MIZENER[1]

Dear Arthur,

We managed to get back here on Sunday afternoon, much to our surprise. The heater would not work and the starter never did start, but the only consequence was that we were too cold to pay attention to the mileage, so that the trip seemed very short. //

Many thanks for helping me with the committee man. So far as I can make out word of mouth is always the most effective means of getting something done in the vicious Guggenheim circle, and I would not be surprised if your oral help had done more good than most of the letters. But I doubt that much more can be done. I'll send your letter to Jay and he will send a book, if any are left, but neither Wilson nor Tate could do much good. Wilson has said pleasant things about me, but he does not think there are going to be poets any longer, as you know, and an idea like that would just about annihilate my project. Tate, working with Van Doren, another of my sponsors, denounced the Guggenheim committee when they asked him for an opinion. Matthiessen would be a good man, but I have been troubling him for months about that job at Harvard, and I can't bring myself to write to him again. If you happen to write to Ransom, or if you have any occasion to write to Matthiessen, you might mention the matter.

My impression is that all external goods are unexpected and not the result of effort. Virtue, on the other hand . . . I mean to say, I feel rather apathetic about making any more of an effort than I have already. But again, thanks very much.

It was with sadness that we attempted to go to a movie in Saratoga, for two seemed to be lacking; and in fact neither Gertrude nor I can bring ourselves to conceive of the time when we did not know you and Rosemary. With best regards to both of you from Gertrude, who

85

has just decided to speak for herself and thus made unnecessary the first half of this sentence.

Yours,
Delmore

[A postscript by Gertrude follows.]

1. Future biographer of F. Scott Fitzgerald and Ford Madox Ford. The Schwartzes had met the Mizeners in New Orleans.

TO DWIGHT MACDONALD

[Saratoga Springs
January 1940?]

Dear MM [Master Mind]—

Thanks for the financial assistance and please let me know the veritable deadline for the next issue; don't tell me Feb. 5 because I know it is not.

I will now make a few remarks on the present issue; not that you will listen to me, but just for the pure sake of the spleen. When a rat makes his departure from a sinking ship in the most rat-like manner, is it necessary that he turn up in the *Partisan Review*? I refer to that rat, Gregory; why do you let him perform his political manoeuvres over Lorca's dead body? It is disgusting and obscene. Second, the review of Hook's book was of a painful, of an almost arthritically painful stupidity. Otherwise, it seemed like a fairly good issue, and [Lionel] Trilling's article seemed very good except that I wish he would not make the most obvious remarks in the tone of one who has just discovered the cure for cancer, or a new continent. I also wish it were possible to print poems on a single page; it is your contempt for poetry coming out again, old master. Smaller print would be better than your present arrangement.

To continue our discussions, I would point out one logical fallacy in your masterly argument. You say that I should strike out for myself, not look to authority. But then why in God's name do you commend your authority and your views to me? You did not say: follow your bent, do what you want to do. You said, listen to me (and I am not alone); my authority is superior to that of Eliot's, because he is old hat. Well: I would be willing to admit that in addition to being a master mind, you are already a minor historical figure *if* the SWP [Socialist Workers' Party] negotiates the revolution; but I need hardly say that this does not make you any more authoritative on literary criticism, though I suspect that you really feel that your connection with the revolution really does, you history-snob!

I enclose the letter from Blackmur just to complicate the issue further. As you know, he is not disposed to be lenient to me, yet he pays me an immense compliment in suggesting that I go on to translate Baudelaire. Somebody must be crazy! maybe you, maybe Blackmur, but certainly not me. When I made that translation [Rimbaud's *Une Saison en Enfer*] I had nothing in mind but an adequate pony to instruct me in my own writing; it did; and it should serve a similar purpose for other poets who are interested. There are several minor mistakes— the kind of thing which is as inevitable as proof errors—but I think it is an adequate pony and that is why Blackmur suggests that I undo the evil committed by Arthur Symons and [Edna St. Vincent] Millay. I can't see that any other notion of translation is permissible; the idea is to bring the object closer, not to create a new thing, which is an activity for unsuccessful poets to kid themselves with. //

None of the poems were worth a damn. I wish that when you get somebody like [Theodore] Roethke with a poor poem, you would write to him yourself; obviously one can't just send him back a pink slip and I get worn out being polite.

In affection, admiration, and profound disagreement,
The Journalist (Delmore)

P.S. Gregory is a fine poet and if you could get some good poetry from him that would be something else again.

TO MARK VAN DOREN

Yaddo
Saratoga Springs, N.Y.
Jan. 19, 1940

Dear Mark,

Thanks for your letter which comes just as I was beginning to feel that remorse which seems inseparable from publishing anything, at least for me. The demon of the absolute has me in thrall. When I made the translation, I wanted an adequate pony, nothing else, for my own edification, and now I look for something new in English— which I had enough sense not to try for when I was actually at work.

I was glad to hear that your new poem is extending the ideas in "America's Mythology"—or so I thought you implied. If ever I get my own poem *[Genesis]* finished (it is not the one of the Guggenheim synopsis), I will have to say in an introduction how reading that sequence in the *Southern Review* gave me a fresh start when I needed it most.

I was also glad to hear of your justified indignation with the Guggenheim people. Anger has a fatal attraction for me and you had every reason to be angry.

Our Southern trip was a weird and wonderful thing. Most of it was spent in N.Y.C. waiting for Laughlin to arrive, while everyone else came to pay us a visit, from Auden to John Berryman, who fainted in front of the pity and terror of one of Picasso's blues at the Museum of Modern Art. The actual trip began and ended at Princeton, N.J., under Allen's [Tate] supervision (from the point of view of our sentiments and what to eat and drink in New Orleans, before we went, and cynical remarks about the whole thing on our stopping there when we came back). Our first glimpse of the sunny South was Louisville covered with snow, and the most impressive thing was Katherine Anne Porter trying to stay up all night with her husband[1] and your sleepless correspondent and talking all the time—this was New Year's Eve—of being 20 years older than either of us. But I will never get to the end if I try to tell you all that happened.

Will you give our best regards to your wife and boys—

Yours always,
Delmore

1. Albert Erskine, then an instructor of English at Louisiana State University.

TO JOHN BERRYMAN

Yaddo
Saratoga Springs, N.Y.
Jan. 26, 1940

Dear John,

I've been troubled at not hearing from you, hoping that it was because you were working hard, but afraid that your health might be keeping you from writing me.

Your poem in *The Nation* seemed very beautiful to me on this second reading after several months; although the last line seems incontestably bad to me. It is about time that you were giving me a poem for *Partisan Review* again.

Our Southern trip was too exciting and too much in a hurry and too much a flood of impressions to be sensibly narrated in a letter. But the pleasures which I remember most were the meetings with Ransom, Katherine Anne Porter, and Cleanth Brooks with whom we spent several days in Baton Rouge. My paper appears to have been a success, at least with Ransom who asked for it for the *Kenyon Review* and with Kay[1] who decided immediately to print it in a special edition and give free copies to all members of the Modern Language Association. I had the sickening experience while reading the paper of having people get up and go all the time, which convinced me that I was speaking poorly. On our way north, we stopped at Princeton for a second visit with Tate and found that you had been there about a week before; this visit made me want to know very much what he had said to you while you were there; my curiosity in the matter of his opinion is now unbounded and the contrast between what he said to you and what he said to me would help satisfy perplexities that have been troubling me since then.

I came back here to find that my job at Harvard is secure. I had heard in New York that my Guggenheim chances were very good and in New Orleans that Ransom had told Brooks of the fair likelihood that he would soon ask me to come to Kenyon to teach and to be an editor of the magazine. This has excited me immensely but also presented the possibility of an embarrassing rich choice some time soon. Of course I am lucky and happy to have any choice at all. Will you keep these possibilities a secret, however.

I hope you're going to send me a long letter and poems very soon. I ought soon to be able to tell you of a new project of Laughlin's which will I hope involve you.

Yours always,
Delmore

1. Wife of Theodore Morrison, who directed the Freshman English program at Harvard.

TO ROBERT HIVNOR

41 Bowdoin St.
Cambridge, Mass.
Feb. 25, 1940

Dear Bob:

If you want to go to Yaddo, get Dwight and Jay to write letters to

Mrs. Ames for you; this is the way it is done, editors must recommend you. However, the season starts in June and only people who have been there before can, sometimes, get asked for the off-season.

Here we are in Cambridge. Gertrude is helping Jay run N.D. [as business manager] and I have a job, beginning in September, at Harvard.

I did not see Auden—we were in too much of a hurry to get back to Yaddo in order to get here.

I am glad to hear that your book is moving on and look forward to reading it in a complete organization.

I'd like to know what you think of my story in the forthcoming *Partisan Review*.[1] I never understand what I write until I hear what others have to say.

Have you read at all in Henry James? I've been going through him again lately to be convinced once more that he is the greatest of American writers—the geat theme of freedom and necessity is taken care of once and for all in *The Portrait of a Lady*.

Yours,
Delmore

1. "America, America!", *Partisan Review*, VII (March-April, 1940).

TO JOHN BERRYMAN

41 Bowdoin St.
Cambridge, Mass.
Feb. 25, 1940

Dear John,

I decided last week that it was impossible, for a number of reasons, to go on reading poetry for *Partisan Review*, and so I am returning your poems to you in the hope that you will send them on to Dwight. The poems gave me a great deal of pleasure, as yours always do.

Above is our new address, and I wish you would write me more often. At the moment, I am troubled by a sense of the inadequacies—not to speak of the inexcusable errors—of my translation. Fortunately, the edition has sold out very quickly and I am preparing what will be virtually a new translation, to be published very soon. What happened was that I took so much time with my criticism, editing, and other wastes of time, and was so excited by my own writing, that I did not go over the translation, though it had been done five years before.

This is one of the reasons for giving up reading for *P.R.*; another is my inability to write letters explaining why I do not accept the poems submitted.

I wish there were better news of your health. There is every reason to think that it would be possible for you to get the job—teaching Freshman English—that I am going to get in the fall and perhaps if that could be done, you would enjoy better health.

Your friend always,
Delmore

TO JOHN BERRYMAN

41 Bowdoin Street
Cambridge, Mass.
March 7, 1940

Dear John—

I've made a few general inquiries and my impression is that it would be difficult to get you started on a job here right now. By next year this time, when *Five Young American Poets* have made their bow, you should have the record needed. The kind of job I am getting is given on the basis of literary work, nothing else except an A.B. degree. However, there would be no harm in your applying this year.

I did think "The Dangerous Year" improved, though I did not remember the old version very well.

The translation is being gone over carefully by two people who have lived in France for years, so thus there is no sense in your taking any trouble with it. Actually there are about 10 inaccuracies... //

I am still completely in the middle of my long poem, and whatever verses I write in addition are too hurried and relaxed to be worth showing you. Every time I read or see the long poem as a whole, my hair stands on end at my own daring or shamelessness or whatever quality of character moves me to do what I am doing! Perhaps I will be able to finish it by the fall, perhaps not.

I am going to have a long story in the new issue of *Partisan Review* and the essay I read at New Orleans in the *Kenyon Review* and I'd like to know what you think of both of them—

Yours always,
Delmore

TO ALLEN TATE

41 Bowdoin St.
Cambridge, Mass.
March 9, 1940

Dear Allen:

I've intended to write to you ever since hearing from Mark Van Doren that your operation had been all right, but I've been too ashamed of my translation of Rimbaud to want to do anything but keep quiet. I was excited by my own writing when I looked it over— after five years of not glancing at it—and everything looks beautiful to me when I am in that state of mind. However, Laughlin is going to print a 2nd corrected edition and perhaps that will constitute a partial penitence and atonement.

// I hope we'll be able to persuade you and Caroline [Gordon, Tate's wife] to come here for a week-end when we get enough functional to have guests.

I've been seeing a good deal of Blackmur, who is an extraordinary charcter, I think—of Baker, Horton, and Matthiessen; and thus for the first time in my life I am near people to whom I can talk about poetry. I confess that the situation leaves me with mixed emotions.

Some time when you're looking among your papers I wish you would find the 1st version of my essay on your poetry. If I decide to publish a book of essays in the fall, I may try to write the whole thing a third time and the 1st version would or might help me.

With best regards to Caroline,

Yours always,
Delmore

TO ARTHUR MIZENER

41 Bowdoin St.
Cambridge, Mass.
April 2, 1940

Dear Arthur,

In putting away my letters of the last month, I noticed a phrase in your letter which I should not have missed: "...out with it at once," whether we don't want to pay a visit right now or await a definite date. This means that I should have answered your letter immediately and I am upset that I did not. You can guess my frame of mind during the last two months from this omission.

The fact is that neither alternative had anything to do with our vagueness about coming. It was a question of Gertrude's getting started on her job and getting ahead with the work sufficiently to permit a weekend's vacation. Orders come in every day and the last incumbent of the job (and one of the worst living poets) had messed up the books. In addition the car stopped running for the duration of the cold weather. It is being fixed at present.

Now new problems face us. I've been given a Guggenheim (thanks, I'm sure, at least in part to your help) and I have to make out whether I can take it and then take the job at Harvard, or get a promise of the job for the year after next, or take it for six months until the fall term begins. And I am also engaged in trying to undo all the disgraceful harm I did with my Rimbaud translation, for the edition sold out and Jay is going to publish a new one as soon as I can write it, in the effort to redeem what respect I may have had before I went and foisted my college pony on the poor people who wanted to read Rimbaud.[1]

Life is very difficult, I find, and I am very lucky, more so than I can ever deserve. In two weeks' time, I ought to have enough straightened out to write you and let you know what is what.

How is your tennis game? I've waited so many years for an opponent who could make me play well, that probably I can't play well anymore for lack of practice. But I am glad you're going to be in Cambridge for many reasons other than that.

With best regards to Rosemary and you from Gertrude and myself,

Yours,
Delmore

1. S's translation had received exceedingly unfavorable reviews in *Kenyon Review*, *Poetry*, *Saturday Review*, and elsewhere.

TO R. P. BLACKMUR

41 Bowdoin St.
May 2, 1940

Dear Richard,

I've been reading your novel,[1] but hardly with the right kind of attention. The attempt will have to be made again when I'm not suffering from varieties of tiredness. Despite not being a good reader, I've liked it a good deal, and this is enough for our particular practical purpose. I'll give the book to Jay and tell him in as many ways as I can think of that he ought to publish it.

The main barrier, if I can imagine ahead, is Jay's old idea that he ought to publish only innovations and the certainty that he won't find your novel innovational, if that is a word. But this barrier may not get in the way this time. As you probably know, Jay has a fine natural intelligence which works itself free of that kind of preconception often enough. //

I have no news to report, otherwise, and no energy to communicate sentiment or observation, except to say that I seem to have come to the pretty pass where my unhappiness and happiness depend mostly on my being able or unable to satisfy myself in writing. With our best regards to Helen and you,

Delmore

1. *King Pandar*, Blackmur's unpublished first novel, submitted to seventeen publishers.

TO ARTHUR MIZENER

41 Bowdoin St.
Cambridge, Mass.
May 7, 1940

Dear Arthur,

It looks as if we are due to be continually disappointed in wishing to get away for a week-end to see you. Gertrude just manages to get her work done by doing on Sunday what she had no time to do all week, and the return of President Laughlin is going to bring new complications. Jay now conceives of me as rich. Share the wealth, he writes, and the result will probably be that by fall New Directions will move on. I would not care at all, except that Gertrude seems to get some profound satisfaction of the psyche out of doing something and earning her keep—you know, in New York, we used to call her The Independent Subway; but perhaps that is too local an allusion.

However, we're looking forward to the arrival of the Mizeners in Cambridge. How soon do you expect to come and how long will you be here? My tennis is not what it used to be before I stopped playing for two years and unless those old conditioned reflexes come back soon, you're going to take me for an idle braggart; but maybe if you are here long enough toward the fall you will let me use you to see what my new book does to someone besides myself. It raises my hair on end and makes my knees shake, sometimes; and sometimes it just looks peculiar and full of private obsessions. I've had a longing to go to Mexico and I would, for a month, if I did not want to try to finish by next fall and thus get the book printed before M-day. But probably I won't finish that soon.

The idea of going to Mexico is one of those dreams of self-indulgence for which the Guggenheim Memorial Foundation is responsible. Do you and Rosemary ever think of going there? Perhaps if you did, it would be possible for me to persuade Gertrude to come, too, after Jay decides to get a new helper. Thanks to Guggenheim, also, I've purchased a secondhand *Encyclopedia Brittanica*, and it now seems unlikely that I will ever read anything else. On the other hand, I might have lived my life out without ever knowing that tadpoles are not affected by light, and the kind of objectified free-association one gets from turning the pages of a volume gives me a fine vicarious pleasure.

With our best to both of you,

Yours always,
Delmore

TO JOHN BERRYMAN

41 Bowdoin Street
Cambridge, Mass.
May 8, 1940

Dear John,

First, for practical matters. The man to write to about a job here is Theodore Morrison, Warren House, Harvard University, mentioning all the periodicals in which you've published verse and all the people who would write good letters for you. There have been an extraordinary number of applications this year for jobs in English A (which is just what you do now, I think, freshman composition) and as I said, it is probably too late to make headway this year. But it would be well to apply, anyway, to start things moving. This is about two months before I started to work on getting the job last year for last fall, and I think the process might very well work a second time. What are your plans otherwise? Gertrude and I are staying here and I am going to take just one class because of the Guggenheim. I've looked for a job too long to let a mere sum of money make me give one up, and besides the Guggenheim term will be more than half over when school begins again.

I know just how you feel about Jay's anthology[1] and it's obvious that you have every right to feel as you do. Tate said, when I saw him in January, that Scribner's were going to do Jarrell's book in the spring of 1941, which is rather a headstart for him, a point which might be used in explaining your feelings to Jay. But then you're not yet sure of any other publisher, and the proverb about the bird in hand still seems good mathematics. A complicated and unscrupulous scheme occurs to me right now, which, if it worked, would probably be best of all for you, but I'd better save it for when I see you. Can you come here for a night on your way back from Detroit? I hope so very much.

I think "At Chinese Checkers" is easily one of your best poems; that is, if I am not too much flattered to say.[2] Not only the mastery of diction, but the easy movement from one frame of reference to another, from the game to the landscape and the age and the past, make me feel that this poem marks a great deal of progress in opening up for you the most complex subjects. If you come here, we ought to spend some time discussing some of the poem's minute particulars.

As for my own poem, I have the illusion or the actuality—which I can't tell yet—that I have answered my leading problem and that the only thing I need now is continuous hard work. I may be finished by the fall, but the only consideration which would make me publish the poem immediately would be the likelihood of M-day. I've learned one other thing, how much more I can do if I avoid criticism and fiction and lyrics and stick at every difficulty without interruption of any kind whatever. Now, with all my recent luck, I'll have no excuse for yielding to anything else. With Gertrude's best regards, and the hope that you'll write sooner this time and let us know if you are coming (please be sure to let us know, because we may be in Maine with the Blackmurs during the week when school is out).

Yours always,
Delmore

P.S. Jay and I argued about the question of introductions and I agreed that it would hardly look well for me to write an introduction for you while the four others wrote their own. Some other similiar occasion should come up sometime, and when it does, I'll take full advantage of it.

1. *Five Young American Poets* (1940). Berryman objected to the use of photos, facsimiles, and self-introductions by the poets.
2. The eleventh stanza of the poem is devoted to S and his "marvelous faculties."

TO MARK VAN DOREN
> 41 Bowdoin St.
> Cambridge, Mass.
> May 8, 1940

Dear Mark:

It was delightful to hear that something substantial has been done about restoring the prestige of the Pulitzer Prize poetry awards.[1] It is obviously the first just choice in years, and when I heard of it I thought I was going through the same process of error as last year—when I thought you had won it seeing the name Van Doren on the list first of all and not seeing that it was your brother.[2]

Gertrude and I have been here since February—and will be here for a long time, I think [...] Gertrude's office is one of our apartment's bedrooms and it's a curious thing to have the apotheosis of all the little magazines in one's house. But the volume of mail every morning is one of the great satisfactions of my life, even if most of it is not addressed to me. Never the empty mailbox which makes the rest of the day seem rather dreary.

With best regards to your wife and you from Gertrude,

> Yours always,
> Delmore

1. Van Doren had just won for his *Collected Poems*.
2. Carl Van Doren's biography of Benjamin Franklin had won the Pulitzer Prize in biography for 1938.

TO NANCY AND DWIGHT MACDONALD
> 41 Bowdoin St.
> Cambridge, Mass.
> May 28, 1940

Dear Nancy and Dwight,

I wish you had written us a week or two ago. We decided to go to Maine for a few weeks in June because that is probably the only time that Gertrude will be able to get away from all the work she has to do for New Directions. It's just possible that some need of Pres. Laughlin's will keep us from going, in which case we will let you know.

The war is all the rage here and the college boys have been going about inviting the Departments of History and Government to declare war on the German government. Three weeks ago one boy killed himself because he was an "interventionist" and felt "isolated" among so many students who were against the war; and some of the older professors, when hissed by their classes for urging immediate entrance into the war, have called their students physical cowards, and been perplexed by the students' cheerful acquiescence.

The last *Partisan Review* seemed one of the best of all time, even if "East Coca Cola" [T. S. Eliot's "East Coker"] is a disgraceful piece of writing; especially Hook's piece and the piece on Newark. And "Labor Action" looks very good also. Enclosed is my dollar.

We're delighted to hear that Mike is talking; no doubt he will soon be as talkative as his father.

Affectionately,
Delmore

TO DWIGHT MACDONALD

Cambridge
August 12, 1940

Dear Dwight,

I thought your editorial in *P.R.* and also your recent piece on the same subject in *L.A.* were eloquent, persuasive and illuminating. I hope to God you know what you're talking about. The rest of the issue seemed to range from disappointing to disgusting, when you begin to point bad critics at bad poetry—I mean Babette Deutsch's review— the time has come to retire.

If the next issue is the last, I would like to appear in it, partly as a matter of sentimentality. Will you let me know the actual not the specious deadline? Also I'd like to write a one-page plug for F. Fergusson's Bennington play,[1] a version of an episode in *Huckleberry Finn* in which music, dance, stage-design, and drama are all worked together. I saw a dress-rehearsal. How about it? Just one page.

It will take me some time to get through Hivnor's novel, which remains unfinished. It looks full of good passages but also full of disorder and without a unifying structure. I will send it to you in a few weeks. I've only had it a few days. //

It seems to me that the time has come for the old master mind to produce a book. Enough of this guerilla warfare.

As for what I have been doing this summer, my life is consumed by my art.

Best to Nancy, and Fred, William and Philip.

Yours,
Delmore

1. Francis Fergusson was a drama professor at Bennington College at the time. S dedicated his verse play *Shenandoah* to him.

TO JOHN CROWE RANSOM

41 Bowdoin St.
Cambridge, Mass.
Aug. 18, 1940

Dear Mr. Ransom,
I'd like very much to have Van Wyck Brooks' new book for review. *New England: Indian Summer* seems so wrong to me in its whole method and the reviews which have already appeared seem so fatuous to me that I'm particularly eager to say something about it. After seeing Henry James and Henry Adams abused and misunderstood and misrepresented by Brooks' impressionism, which pretends to be above literary criticism, I more or less boiled over by the time I reached the passages on Eliot and Wallace Stevens:

Wallace Stevens of Hartford published the polychromatic poems that suggested Henry Adams' old French windows. For, reading these poems, one felt as if a window of Chartres had been shattered, and the lovely bits of colour lay on the grass, and one forgot the picture, which one could scarcely reconstruct, in the pleasure of letting these fragments fall through one's fingers.

I hope at least one dissenting voice can be raised to this kind of systematic superficiality.

Yours sincerely,
Delmore Schwartz

TO ALLEN TATE

41 Bowdoin St.
Cambridge, Mass.
Sept. 22, 1940

Dear Allen:
I must correct Arthur Mizener's story about [Theodore] Spencer. I've been guilty of tale-bearing too often myself to adopt a righteous attitude about such matters, but in this case you seem to have been given a story which is inaccurate as well as unnecessary.
We were all dining with Spencer and Richards, both of whom had been encouraging themselves with gin all afternoon, and I was arguing

with Richards about Eliot's new poem, "East Coca Cola," and getting more and more annoyed because Richards would not admit that "undisciplined squads of emotion" was an inept metaphor. After citing Confucius several times to add to the general daze, Richards informed me that I ought not to take lines in isolation, thus rendering me speechless, and Spencer followed through by saying that that was the trouble with the whole *Southern Review* school of criticism, they tended to take lines in isolation, and Blackmur was especially guilty in this regard, not that he did not do that sort of thing very well. There was no question of 1st, 2nd, or any other rate, and so far as I can see of any malice in Spencer's passing remark. I don't like Spencer, I do like Arthur who is a man of good will—sometimes of too much good will—but it seems a shame to have you angry about something like that; especially when by *Southern Review* school of criticism Spencer obviously had in mind mainly such old Confederates as Blackmur and myself.

My book of criticism is scheduled for February, but if it doesn't look more adequate to me soon, I'm going to postpone matters a few months and try some more revision. The twenty-sixth year, I find, is the most difficult.

Yours always,
Delmore

TO ROBERT HIVNOR

Cambridge, Mass.
Oct. 3, 1940

Dear Bob,

I was about to write Jay for your address when your letter came. I've been reading a book called *The Craft of Fiction* by Percy Lubbock and find that, with qualifications, it expressed my feelings about what formal necessities the novelist has to accept and work with. I wish you would read Chapter 3, especially; it has to do with the deficiencies of *War and Peace*, which is, I'm sure, the greatest of all novels, but only when its deficiencies of structure are not in view. When you read it, I think my main misgivings about the structure of your book will be more intelligible than I seem able to make them. Lubbock's book is as good as any on the subject I know of, though he's too much the literal Jamesian (and the James of the Prefaces at that) to suit me. I can understand your wish to get your book done and into print and to get the claim of dignity one needs to face family and friends; but it seems to me that your book will be so good if you get the form to work for you and it will be so much a matter of just brilliant passages of writing if you don't that more work and more patience seem to me your only choice. I can hardly say that I can take my own advice, so I ought perhaps to be ashamed to give it, but I've had two sad experiences of what happens when one does not work hard enough and patiently enough.

The day after your visit, I started to move up again on the manic-depressive roller coaster, and within a week I suppose that my poem will again present the illusion of being very good. It's very interesting to me to see how every time I get started, what starts me is a new *formal* dodge. My main problem right along has been to get the kind of structure which would make reasonable and articulate and symmetrical the kind of international consciousness which keeps growing bigger all the time in the world—in such strange plants as the radio and the newspaper—and which is the only point of view from which I can see my subject. If you remember my poem about the children of the Czar and myself, you'll see the beginning of what I'm trying to do. But the point worth communicating is that when I make progress or get the illusion of progress, it's always by means of some invention in the form.

This brings me back to the form-subject relationship or union. I'd been using the word "relationship," but decided it was probably too general—a union is one kind of relationship and I have some other names, though how it will be finally named in my book, I don't know. I dislike the word "content" because it keeps you in literature, but if you want to use that word, let's say that experience is always form-content in some way—everything save prime matter, says Aristotle, is a union of form and matter, save the Deity—but with respect to the forms of any art, the subjects an artist chooses are relatively un-formed. By submitting them to the particular forms of his medium, he makes a new experience of them, a new form-subject relationship; and this is what makes it something available only in his work itself in place of the old one; nowhere else. I don't know how clear this is, but it's the only way I can understand all my feelings about specific successes and failures in the writing I know.

I hope that by this time you're more adjusted to New Haven; the only one I know there is Norman [Holmes] Pearson, whose address would be in the catalogue; but he would know everyone worth talking to, I think, though he's not very much more than one kind of literary parasite himself.

With best regards from Gertrude,
Delmore

TO ROBERT HIVNOR

Cambridge, Mass.
Oct. 13, 1940

Dear Bob,

I've hit the top again and now expect to begin going down soon, but feel like yelling Eureka! The Indias! America! The glory, the power, the illumination of form! But I've felt this way before this many times, the excitement of writing for the excitement which should have come *from* the writing, objective on the page.

The trouble, for me, in this up and down is that, knowing it won't last, I rush to get as much done as I can while I can, and the rush and the excitement destroy my powers of discrimination, such as they are where my own writing is concerned. Somewhere someone reports that Joyce has always hated and tried to avoid these periods and tried to keep himself at work at a daily routine drudging level. It is the classical man in him and the Jesuit discipline, I think; anyone can see that it pays. But we were brought up not only a hundred thousand miles away from anything of the kind, but in the American public school system, where one is supposed to "elect" one's courses before any good habits of work have been formed. I suppose I will have to spend the rest of my life trying to get free of the habits I contracted in school.

I would send you what I've done if I could bear having an unfinished work looked at; but I can't; it is the neurosis of form again; or perhaps something less high-sounding makes me hate the unfinished so much.

Your project with Katherine Anne Porter's story sounds very good. I should think all her stories might bear dramatization quite well. What do you mean by "cantos of prose rugs work"? It sounds pretty persian, while I find that what I've been doing seems to be based upon the telephone, as "IDBR" on the movie.

Great works may be making, but I think it would be best if one tried not to think of greatness; it becomes less likely then, for obviously the mind is diverted somewhat by its sense of glory. A Pax Americana, Trotsky's North American militarism, would certainly provide some of the conditions, but probably for the boys who are now beginning high school. Don't forget a period of war will be necessary before America's imperial grandeur can really begin; and anyway, we may be thinking in too literally Marxist terms about this coitus between national power and great art. Imperial Rome produced nothing very good once it became imperial, though I suppose Virgil can be said to be the product of the conflict between the old republican Rome and the new day. It's the city-state, I think, the Athens and Florence, which generates great art with great social power; and probably that's because the national state tends to spread out its energy, while the city-state contracts and unifies it. Someone pointed out that Dublin was the last city-state, and Joyce and Yeats and the Abbey theatre, the last such products. There is a moral problem somewhere at the center of this relationship between culture and the community. I mean, the national citizen can't love and unite a life based on spread-out imperialism; the city-state citizen can do so, since such injustice as he sees can be understood, placed, and condemned. You can see this in Aristophanes.

I don't see why you think I would disturb one like Richards with my making the form-subject relationship the center of literary criticism; "so much mystery has been raised about the identity of Form and Content, or about the extirpation of the matter in the form, that we are in danger of forgetting how natural and inevitable their cooperation must be"; *Practical Criticism*, p. 233; the whole discussion and I intend to quote for my argument.

I'm glad to hear you're beginning to like New Haven; I've found myself, that the college community was the best place to live in general, because of the optional mixture of solitude and society. If you're stealthily making friends with two drama girls, the virtues and defects of plurality must be plain to you; there's safety in numbers but no distinction, but on the other hand safety is the last irreducible value remaining to us in modern life, and on the other hand it can be purchased in the drugstore, if one is not too bashful.

Probably I ought not to write letters when in this state of mind. Let me know what you think of Lubbock. Gertrude sends her best regards.

Delmore

Probably I mean uniqueness, every soul is something special, like the color blue; I was trying to show this in "Coriolanus and His Mother." Give my regards to Pearson and tell him I've not forgotten what I owe him, but still can't find them (viz. the magazines).

TO ROBERT HIVNOR

[Cambridge]
Sunday, Nov. 3, 1940

Dear Bob,

A great deal of work has kept me from answering your last letter before now.

I wish I could try out my essay on you, now that the first draft is finished. I should never have spouted about it as I did the evening you were here.

I lectured and read my verse on Weds. and quoted your remark about my images being those of the vacationist, student, and paid admission. It made a great hit. I also read some relatively self-contained passages in my new poem and unless everyone is lying politely and gently, it exceeds my greatest hope.

Muriel Rukeyser I dislike intensely, both as a poet and as a person; she's one of the people for whom energy takes the place of intelligence, she played the Stalinist game for years because it was useful, she is stupid and she knows nothing about poetry. Forgive me for being so violent and emphatic, but I'm convinced it is so.

I read the new Hemingway novel *[For Whom the Bell Tolls]* and was almost persuaded; when the messenger goes back to the loyalist lines the brotherhood of man becomes the bureaucracy of man and the book's morality is shown as inadequate. But if you have not read the book, there's no point in saying this; I'm adding a postscript on it to my essay on Hemingway in my book.

Sorry to hear about Warren's sending back your excerpt;[1] why don't you try Dwight; a passage there would do the most good, anyway. The *Kenyon Review* might be persuaded also.

I'd like to see you sometime when I was feeling high, not abysmal as has always been the case since June 1939. Have you read the Lubbock book or don't you care?

Delmore

1. Robert Penn Warren co-edited *Southern Review.*

TO ROBERT HIVNOR

[Cambridge]
Nov. 16, 1940

Dear Bob,

I think maybe Eliot in *The Waste Land* and "Sweeney Agonistes" might be helpful on poetic speech.

Cleanth Brooks wrote the other day trying to get me to send him something for his winter issue [of *Southern Review*], and I wrote back suggesting that he ask you for something and making as if I did not know they had just sent something of yours back. It may work, since they seem to be in desperate need of fiction and verse.

I'm sorry to hear New Haven is not nourishing you. But do you remember Auden's remark about Eliot's unhappy marriage? He was looking for his life, and prepared to generate his misery.

Have you read Dostoyevsky's *The Possessed*? Besides being the best political novel I've ever read, it raises a question that you have to face, Is morality of any kind possible without a belief in the existence of God? I don't think so.

How did you make out in the draft lottery? It was a pretty revelation for all to see: in order to be *just* it was necessary to commit the whole thing to the complete *irrationality* of chance. Enough to make Plato vomit in Heaven.

I hope you come here any time you feel like it. Maybe we will have room for a spare bed soon, since the whole of N.D. is moving here, but to another office.

Delmore

TO R. P. BLACKMUR

41 Bowdoin St.
Cambridge, Mass.
Jan. 5, 1941

Dear Richard,

// Is it not clear that a reviewer's psyche, like an iceberg, is seven-eighths beneath the surface?

But that farm like a poem (though I would prefer a poem like a farm) how much does it cost and would you throw in borrowing privileges on all your books? Located there it would be too expensive to make phone calls to me, concerning reviews. How much would it cost to fix so that I might live there next summer, during the coming wars? How different from the city life is it? Will you let me know? Probably you won't, but I will ask Philip [Rahv]. Merely the idea of being so far from Cambridge and New York would console me, in Cambridge and New York. //

I wish you and Allen would see Jay in his special context, benumbed by wealth, but learning fast, and really with a good will. The only good thing in the world is good will.

Your haunted lover Zabel was here through Christmas, still speaking of you like the fallacy of pseudo-reference.

I do not think I managed to get to tell you the immortal story of English A. This boy, G. F. Post, Jr., came in with a paper two hundred words in length when he was supposed to write twelve hundred. One is supposed to be stern about such things:

BRIGGS-COPELAND CREATURE:[1] This is a little thick, two hundred words, two-thirds of a page, when you were supposed to write six times that many.

POST: The Sermon on the Mount was less than two hundred words, *Sir*!

B-C C: Well, then: if you will come down to the Charles and walk on the water for me I will give you an A for this paper...

POST: I will wait until it freezes over, *Sir*!

B-C C: Some say that some winters it does not freeze over. I cannot wait that long...

> Signori, *you* go and enforce it!
> With our best regards to Helen,
> Yours always,
> [Unsigned]

1. S was the Briggs-Copeland lecturer at Harvard, which allowed him to teach part-time.

TO ALLEN TATE

> 41 Bowdoin St.
> Cambridge, Mass.
> Jan. 27, 1941

Dear Allen:

Many thanks for sending back the copy of my essay. It is the second version, and it was the first I wanted. But I've postponed my book of criticism until next year, anyway, and won't be trying to rewrite the essay for some time, so that I don't need it right now. I would be grateful if you did get it back to me when you get to your papers again. I'm very dissatisfied with all but a few pages of what the *SR* printed and want to try the third time, bringing in again some of the things in my first and not my second version. I hope three times will end the business, as in drowning and batting a baseball.

I've been girding my loins (and my spleen and my temper and my anger) to reply to Winters on Eliot. Ransom said not to abuse him, and I can understand his editorial caritas. But really that man's become a kind of small-time Lucifer. His reading of Eliot, when it is not pretty close to dishonesty through distorted quotation, reminds me of myself translating French. Did you stop at the part where he quotes Eliot as saying poetry is autotelic, and then goes on to say that this shows Eliot thinks poetry is *about* itself?

The only thing that makes me want to hold back somewhat is my feeling, which can't be mine alone, that Eliot ought to be examined very carefully right now; but of course not with Winters' stupidity. I was reading something the Old Possum had written about Empson's poetry (if that's what it is) and came upon the enchanting phrase, "(Empson's poetry is) brilliantly obscure." In English A, Section 17, any Freshman who tried that would be failed. The best I could do with the thing was to think that Eliot must have been thinking of a torchlight procession through a cave.

With best regards to Caroline,
Yours always,
Delmore

TO DWIGHT MACDONALD

41 Bowdoin Street
Cambridge, Mass.
Feb. 16, 1941

Dear Dwight:

The enclosed attempted *jeu d'esprit* [*Shenandoah*] (ah, my French), written last summer but just typed, is sent to you on the off-chance that you might want to print a scene or two, though it will not change the world, as Malcolm Cowley would say, and though some of the verse needs to be pared and firmed, it seems good to me, though I have been wrong many times before. The great Levin thinks it is good, which proves something, although I don't know what. Though obviously personal in a painful way, I feel that the dramatic idea is sufficiently generalized. I am also sending a copy to Warren.

In line with my recent policy of keeping you *au courant* with what cannot interest you too much, I might say that my long poem is now so long that I feel like a driver going sixty miles an hour who finds his brakes have gone dead. I do not know how to stop anymore; it is a veritable hemorrhage. Have now used every meter but the knocking the radiator makes when the steam comes up. Do you know where I could purchase a time capsule cheap in case the war...Seriously, I'd like to know where you will be this summer and if you would reserve a weekend for the reading of my poem: with your *imprimatur* and [?], I would fear no other reader—

It occurred to me reading the last issue of *P.R.* that perhaps you were not a member of the advance guard, but rather an archaism, born too late: a great muck-raker, a greater [Lincoln] Steffens? This explains your joy in critics like Jarrell who substitute wisecracks for perceptions.

The last issue of *P.R.* seemed very good to me, especially your piece, Greenberg's, and [Robert] Fitzgerald's. To me Zabel was, needless to say, too wordy with a sure-fire project. The verse as usual stank. I have now given up the reading of magazines, however, on the grounds that it keeps me from my work and I do not think I will read even *P.R.*

Tell Phillips that if he's interested in Jay as a publisher for his book on the hero, which Gertrude reported to me, it could probably be arranged with ease and he might be better off than with anyone else.

Is it true that *The New Republic* is going under? Ah, happy day! //

Yours with a vengeance,
Delmore

TO DWIGHT MACDONALD

[Cambridge
March 7, 1941]

Dear Dwight:

I'm very pleased that you like my *jeu d'esprit*. How much do you mean when you say, "could you shorten it a bit"? Would it not be possible to run it all in book-review type and save more space by not giving stage directions etc. separate paragraphs? If not, keep your copy, but let me know how much to cut and, if you will, the reason why it seems superfluous to you. After sending you the ms. I had an idea which made me add several pages, but I will let this go, except for three lines about Trotsky which seem to fit.

Shen[andoah] was supposed to come out in June in the ND pamphlet series. I can put JL off a month, but hardly more than that, so you'll have to use it in your next issue, also say that it is an abridged version (minus the recent addition).

I don't really think you are an anachronism, but it does sometimes seem that you have made a profession of against-ness. Thus I note that all critics who do not write like Jarrell or Macdonald, you generally label and damn as urbane, if not genteel. Furthermore, Jarrell makes dreadful mistakes just because he's engaged in wisecracks. I hate to agree with Cowley and [Conrad] Aiken is a second-rater, but it's impossible for me to understand how Jarrell could have read that sonnet sequence and missed the spine of narrative in it. He's much worse on Pound, whom he says has no meter. But in general, what happens to the muck-raker? He disappears with the muck. Consider the sad shades of [H. L.] Mencken and of [George Jean] Nathan: have you looked at them lately? I mean their writing as of 1927: it reads like a discarded collapsed condom looks. And one reason is that they were too busy being funny men to *describe* their targets.

As for me, I have founded what may be a new school of writing, the peripatetic-dart-throwing school. I write for fifteen minutes, then walk about and throw darts at my dart-board to free the caged sedentary animal... Next month I may go further *and write standing up*!

Hivnor writes that he's sending you some more and on that subject I want to say one more word, if you don't print anything of it you'll be sorry, you'll be sorry; prophecy as of the 7th day of March 1941: members of the editorial soviet will engage in mutual recriminations as to who rejected it for what reason. Philip is right when he says Hivnor is provincial, but that is not as damning as it might be, seeing as how Hivnor comes from the provinces and makes something out of it.

Henry Miller wants to call his new book *The Enormous Womb*. Jay is going to print all of Kafka's short stories, also Pasternak, who, even through the veil of translation, seems to be easily the best of living poets, that is, if he's still living. Could you not get someone to translate him for you? Let me know soon about cutting, because I'm very busy, must get back to my Leviathan/Frankenstein/Iliad.

> Regards to one and all, and to Nancy,
> Delmore

TO DWIGHT MACDONALD

[Cambridge, 1941]

Dear Dwight,

With a speed I have only for this purpose, I hurry to defend myself from your sentence: "I take it the $100 means more to you than the regional motivation you spoke of."—Not at all; the money was not in question; the main factor was your unwillingness to let me print the play in *P.R.* and then as a pamphlet. Since Jay had already had illustrations made, he was justified in not letting me substitute another play in verse. In addition, you wanted to cut it and were lukewarm, anyway. I will send you my brand-new play after you print Mary's [McCarthy] story and I will send you a poem for the next issue; not that I really believe you want my writing so much. //

The new issue came yesterday and I read it with much interest, especially interested in your article and Burnham's. The contrast of the two touched the critic of style in me once more, and I can only say again (I am not kidding) that I think you have developed a wonderful expository style with more energy and clarity and what Eliot once called ordinance (that is, arrangement and structure proportionate to the subject matter) than anyone I can think of since Bertrand Russell was an honest man. I think you ought to get along with shorter quotations and use verbs of less hackneyed-metaphorical quality ("threatens," for example), but otherwise the contrast with Burnham's slow laborious chewed-over writing was very marked.

The analyses interested me intensely, too, but I need hardly say I make only tentative fearful ignorant judgements about such matters. However, to my unequipped mind, the following problem in Burnham's view was nothing if not striking (perhaps he takes care of it in his book, but even if he does, he has little evidence to go on): how does the managerial class perpetuate itself? Presumably property rights won't work at all, as under capitalism, and thus the father-son relationship, that profoundly human fact, will have no social-economic expression (Nijinsky[1] Macdonald will not inherit an editorship on *P.R.*). Will the managers choose the graduating class's stars every June, and if so, will they be full of desire in that regard? Does this not open the way, *in an economy of plenty*, to a managerial class which, for the sheer historical prestige of it all, will try to give the populace a good society? In addition, as must have occurred to you, what social use will managerial exploitation perform? *How* do you exploit *what* in an economy of plenty? Yes, this must have occurred to you, and I wish you would let me know what the answers are. I try to use this problem for dramatic-narrative purposes in my long poem, though in a very clumsy way. Seriously, let me know.

I thought Bellows [*sic*] was very interesting and I wish you would either send me their addresses or tell them—that is, the whole group you mention—that N.D. would pay much attention to their manuscripts. Probably that Kafkaesque novel.[2] //

The uncensored reports from France were very moving and had the toad-chill and moist-warm-hand feeling of actuality, as did Jarrell's and [David] Schubert's poems. But the conjunction of Greenberg's and Goodman's chronicles brings me to further remarks about taste. The sense, the explicit feeling for the man as a product of a milieu, and the careful and numerous *observations* in Greenberg's piece should show anyone a little less receptive than you how senseless Goodman is. Let me mention just two stupidities which stand out among the many; first, the assumption that it is wrong to abstract technical innovations from a work of art (thus it would be wrong to abstract the blank verse Surrey invented to translate Virgil, which made possible Elizabethan tragedy); and second, technical slickness equals a professional style (thus technique and style are identified). For vacuous cleverness and ingenuity unrelated to fact, this is the counterpart of that poem in which Trotsky is the chief of excitement and the Russian Revolution becomes by obvious implication an amusement park. To pay attention to the Breen-Irish[3] Catholic morality which is, in fact, the ethics which Hollywood falls back on (note the unconscionable number of priests whenever anyone dies and the transformation of urban-garage-truck-driver-taxi-driver types such as [James] Cagney, Spencer Tracy, and Pat O'Brien into priests during the last four years)—to pay attention to anything like that would be to relinquish the transcendental-homosexual-infantilism which gives Goodman that ease, grace, and false air of deep thought. When you give up close attention to facts and to actuality, you can say anything with ease.

Finally, let me say that I have now removed you from the muckraker rubric since seeing Nancy work so hard for the refugees. I see you now as part of that great non-conformism which began when Roger Williams moved to Rhode Island. Yet, suppose that you have the long life I wish you, what will you do in the good society, if it ever comes? A new neurosis! nothing to which the non-conformist can direct the resistance in his soul!

Sincerely,
Delmore

P.S. // By the way, did you see Cagney's *Strawberry Blonde?* Though a bit disingenuous, it was full of a new self-consciousness about cinematic usages.

1. S's affectionate nickname for the Macdonalds' son Nicholas.
2. S may be referring to Saul Bellow and his novel *Dangling Man* (1944), though S's biographer, James Atlas, indicates their friendship did not flourish until 1945 in New York.
3. The Breen Office was responsible for censoring movies in the forties.

TO ALLEN TATE

41 Bowdoin St.
Cambridge, Mass.
May 2, 1941

Dear Allen:

I've hesitated for several weeks in acknowledging your new book [*Reason in Madness*] because I did not know exactly how to say the only things I can honestly say about it. But having refused to review the book because to say such things in print might seem peculiar for several reasons, it seems to me that I ought to avail myself of the privilege of the devoted reader privately.

Many passages throughout the book, but in particular "Literature As Knowledge" and wherever you make use of philosophical terms, are shocking in their inaccuracy and misunderstanding of the matters you are talking about. This sort of thing existed in *Reactionary Essays* but one had only to break through the surface of verbal contradiction and misused terminology to get to your fine insights on Crane, Mac-Leish, Emily Dickinson, the South: the actual subject of your discourse was always something you knew very well.

In this book the opposite is true, and you seem most of the time to be using literature for the purpose of stating a general point of view and attacking a series of other positions which you lump together as positivism. As a matter of surface, the essay "Literature As Knowledge" contains on an average of two errors per page in the references to Aristotle, Hegel, Lessing, and above all the nature of logical positivism. I don't want to list them because it was precisely that kind of superficiality I was going to attack in Hook (who deliberately ignores, it's obvious, the fact that you were attacking the tradition of historical studies in this country for reasons he would agree with). The important point is the misrepresentation of your opponent's position as a whole and the self-contradiction which the statement of your position contains. To say that "the world of positivism is a world without minds to know the world"—and you say this again and again—is not only complete misunderstanding, but it is the equivalent of Max Eastman's discussion of the modern poet as simply engaged in talking to himself: that is, it springs from prejudice which is uninformed. Moreover, you identify positivism with instrumentalism and pragmatism in a way which again suggests the Eastman analogy: it is just like identifying Gertrude Stein, Joyce, Pound, and Eliot on the grounds that they are all "modernists." And when, on p. 28, you state that the meaning of a sentence is, "from the pragmatical point of view," and say that lighting a cigarette, looking the other way or swearing are all included in the effects of the sentence, "This country has an annual waterfall of fifty-one inches," one is ready to abandon all hope.

Worst of all is the way you state your own position. I know, or I think I know, what you mean by knowledge and literature as knowledge because I've studied your previous criticism with care and can piece together isolated observations and statements. For many readers, however, the statements on p. 60 and p. 61 must seem either very vague or contradictory: "the completeness of *Hamlet* is not of the experimental order, but of the experienced order; it is, in short, of the mythical order." Just what you mean by an experimental order is not clear, but is one to suppose that experiments or the experimental order are outside of experience? Is one to suppose—"in short"—that that which is of the experienced order (a philosophically barbarous phrase) is mythical in its entirety? What it is you mean by myths which will keep them from being Richards' pseudo-statements you do not say. They are "hard realities in projection" in Richards: the only way I can understand this identification is to refer to the passage in *The Fathers* which I quoted in my essay on you, but which is not made available in your essay, so that to the reader who has not followed *all* your writing with care, your conclusion can only seem a form of obscurantism: you have simply not given your position objective expression.

It would not be worth saying this and risking the further presumption of advice, if there were not so many passages in the book which came to the same incoherence and misrepresentation. But the suggestion that came to me again and again in the course of reading the book was that the proper convention, the one which would be adequate to your insights (and which is sometimes discernible here and there), would be some concrete "existential" form of discourse. I think it was [F.] Cudworth Flint who said that you ought to write your autobiography; that's not what I mean, but it suggests the convention I mean, an expression of your judgements in terms of the experiences which brought you to them (as Coleridge began to explain himself in *Biographia Literaria*, but unfortunately did not continue). Your objections to naturalism seem to me to be profound, but as expressed in discursive terms in this book—from the initial error of identifying naturalism with positivism to the end—the only result one can see is further multiplication of prejudice and misunderstanding on each side: this is clear, as I said, in Hook's letter and Hook commits the same sin you do out of a like but reverse ignorance.

Yours always,
Delmore

TO ALLEN TATE

41 Bowdoin St.
Cambridge, Mass.
May 23, 1941

Dear Allen:

I am sorry to have disturbed you by not answering your last letter. You said that "there are no particular points left to discuss." It seemed to me that there might have been and that you might have said something of your view of your book. But I did not want to force a discussion on you. What else was there to say?

Now I don't know what to make of your present letter. Personality, temperament, and repudiation of friendship have suddenly made an appearance, to my immense surprise. Our correspondence has broken off repeatedly, to my regret, during the three years I have known you, so that it is hard for me to understand why this breaking-off should appear unusual. Of course during the four years of my bare-faced pretension to authorship, I have had most of my speech and silence interpreted. But I do not seem to be able to get used to it. If you think there is a nigger in the woodpile, I wish you would bring him out.

It occurs to me that the only possible reply until he makes his appearance is this: to list some of the passages which upset me. I don't expect you to share my view of your book, but I would like to be sure that the ground for my objections was perfectly plain. Then perhaps what I had to say will seem—though not wholly convincing, as you say of my last letter—wholly convinced as an impression of the book. I think I had better make the list on another piece of paper. But before I do that, I should say that this whole unpleasant discussion is of course wholly a private matter so far as I am concerned and I was very pleased to see that you felt as I did.

Yours always,
Delmore

TO JAMES LAUGHLIN

[Cambridge]
July 15, 1941

Dear Jay:

Your idea about poems and comments strikes me as brilliant, but you ought to put in the proviso that it be some other poet's poem, preferably of the past, thus no charge, and keep out the half-wits and three-quarter wits.

Hivnor says he is getting near the end. Keep your fingers crossed. //

My masterpiece proceeds triumphantly—it is indeed a masterpiece—and I hope you are keeping in mind my desire, indeed my
demand, that you reserve two days in late August or early September
for the reading of it, early in the day when your mind is fresh and
strong, so that you will know what a treasure you are getting.

I like your poem indeed, but merely did not think it as good as your
last one. Have never exchanged a word with H. M. [Howard Mumford]
Jones. //

My masterpiece will present the problem of censorship. Your aunt
seems to be the secret queen of American writing.

I was very glad to get the case of the sex change: it is enough to
make a fellow nervous. As I said while reading it to myself: what is
the plural of penis? Answer: testicles. //

// Did not get my July retainer.

I have put off revision of my play until the third week in August,
so that nothing will defer the triumphant progress of my masterpiece.
But quiet yourself, you will get it in time, the revision will take no
more than a week at the most.

Rumor says that the *Southern Review* and Bennington College are
both in plain danger of ceasing to exist.

How is your titanic novel? I wish you would send all communiques
to Bowdoin St. They are so busy at the office that they sometimes
forget the dispatch to me.

Gide and Brecht books came back as if they had been moving about
with Panzer divisions through the Steppes where once my fathers
yearned with Dostoyevsky, Pushkin, Tolstoy. Try to send back the
Kafka book a little less bruised, and don't send it to the printer, which
is what you did with the last book by Kafka borrowed from me.

I see that I am a paying proposition. I added up my earnings for
four years the other day: $1610, exclusive of Guggenheim and Har-
vard. I see that *Shenandoah* is still a problem play.

Delmore

TO ARTHUR MIZENER

908 Memorial Drive
Cambridge, Mass.
Sept. 18, 1941

Dear Arthur,

I was very glad to get your letter, and hope that henceforth you will tell me what you think, even when much less pleased; sternly correct, reprove, and yet encourage.

At the moment I am as low in spirit as I have ever been and hardly able to know or say how much I agree with your kindly said reservations. I hope you are exactly right about the versification, and I had hoped it was really a play on the stage. It occurs to me that if you can have a ghost from the supernatural, perhaps you can also have a ghost from the future; but maybe not; or maybe not in this case. Anyway, I can only write poetry that pleases me in this way, by trying to get the actuality and the transcendence into the structure and the texture at the same time.

We are delighted to hear about the new child, and I would like—if you will forgive my presumption—to express the hope that this one will be a boy, although if this one is going to be as pretty as the first, perhaps it had better be a girl. During the last few years seven of my friends, including my brother, have had children, all girls, including Harry Levin our next-door neighbor ... If the educated classes produce such a disproportionate number of female children, I foresee dangerous and immoral social tendencies in the years 1960-1975. With our best to Rosemary and you,

Yours always,
Delmore

P.S. I can't find your address, and in fact can't find anything in this house[1] except a reflection of the moral chaos in my soul.

1. S and Gertrude had moved from 41 Bowdoin St.

TO R. P. BLACKMUR

[Cambridge]
September 22, 1941

Dear Richard,

Phillip quotes you as expressing the hope that I would not turn on you as I had turned on Allen, the consequences of June Cannan's[1] report of what I had said at Cummington. So I am in a great hurry to vow and avow eternal friendship, if you will but accept it, and to propose to write you a letter once a month, however unanswered, unless you stop me. But since / Nothing is ever wiped out, no matter what / Jacky Christ says, / I had better say too that I have not turned on Allen, only on his last book, of which your opinion, I would bet, was even less favorable than mine, and what I said at Cummington was that the boys and girls must expect me to say some things contrary to what they had heard from Mr. Tate, Mr. Blackmur, and Mr. Cowley because literary criticism, like many other things, was like a see-saw and I was of the next ten years. I should have known that something was not said properly when June, that wonderful unsteady girl, came and said to me that she did not care what I thought of Mr. Tate and Mr. Cowley, but she did not see why I was hard on Mr. Blackmur. I mentioned the see-saw again, but it does not seem to have been a very lucid example. //

At the moment I am so low in spirit that everything seems to need to be guarded against misunderstanding, so I must continue with [. . .] who went about saying dark things about my being afraid of her, as I was told as soon as I came by Klonsky,[2] that pure type of the *vieux pays*, for me. Since what she said seems to have received an erotic interpretation, a horrifying thought to me when I think of her appearance, I had better say too that she rang my doorbell in New York in 1937 and asked to show me a story and I read the story and tried to tell her that it was not very good, but could not because she could not hear me, so that when from time to time she wrote me demanding with shy aggressiveness further interviews, I did not answer and she waited where I lived and I snubbed her in an awkward unkind way; which is what she meant by my being afraid of her.

Then, there are the afterthoughts I have written for my essay, "The Isolation of Modern Poetry," in which I tried to mention and answer the comments made to me. You are anonymously but perhaps recognizably among the questioners I tried to answer: "A distinguished poet and critic said to me, after reading this essay, that he did not *feel isolated*. This author, although recognized as valuable and important, had been unable to earn a living by writing through fifteen years of effort. His prose was subjected to abuse because in it his use of words was special and self-conscious and sometimes obscure, another moment in the modern author's extreme cultivation of his own sensibility and his own medium. And, O intimate oblivion! his wife says that she does not understand many of his poems . . . Here I think my questioner was laboring with a complex notion of the way in which good poetry at any time must achieve objectivity. This is granted; but it is necessary to distinguish the objectivity the poet, however isolated, can achieve in language from the objectivity of the common mind of the community. The community has often not known *the very words*—not to say, symbols and techniques—the poet used and had to use *in order to gain objectivity*. Thus perhaps an engineer among primitive peoples might seem to be a maniac when he attempted with the most objective means to build a bridge." Am I taking unfair advantage of a conversation twice unfinished? Essay and appendix are being reprinted, but I would like to omit this passage, if you do not like to have your casual remarks used as an example. I would also like to know what you think of the answer as an answer.

Yours always,
Delmore

1. A young woman with whom S had a brief affair at Cummington School of the Arts that summer.
2. Milton Klonsky, young poet whom S met at Cummington.

TO MARK VAN DOREN

908 Memorial Drive
Cambridge, Mass.
Oct. 16th, 1941

Dear Mark,

Many thanks for your book [*The Mayfield Deer*]—not so much for the printed copy as for the writing itself. When it came the other day, I was taken aback by your supposing that I could think it too long, since it is just such copiousness, fullness, and richness that I with many others, I think, look for and long for and do not get in modern poetry. I've been reading in the poem since it came with the kind of continuous and cold pleasure which was, I should guess, just what you aimed at, and when your letter came I had just finished the passage where David ends by choking the old hunter to death—the passage began by reminding me of Hamlet looking on as his uncle prayed and ended by being as enthralling and exacting as the action in a movie, but what was most moving was the defeated expectations, which kept coming back, that forgiveness would win out—as if Christianity was one of the new gods surrounding the reader's head.

As far as I've come in the poem, two things seem to me to be wholly successful and to be marvelled at. The versification, which has a fluency, sweetness, and singing quality which I am in a good condition to appreciate after hacking away at my own blank verse, and the *wholeness* of the writing, which I suppose is made possible partly by the mastered ease of versification—I mean the wholeness of the story, the speech, the perceptions, the theology, and the fundamental imagery of sound and silence, and light and darkness which goes through the whole poem. These elements do not look like elements at all, but pure substance, poetry, which makes me sure that you've done what no one else has done for a long time, written a genuine narrative poem. The only doubt that suggests itself to me, and perhaps it will go by the time I have read the poem well, is whether or not the plot is in itself worthy of the sensibility and imagination it is given. The fact that the poem is in a way a revenge poem suggests revenge plays and subplots and further complications which would be more adequate to the richness and darkness of mind which makes the poetry, and which seems to demand the larger-than-human, epic, fabulous action.

But the incidental felicities and the continuous unfurling, triumphant felicity of the versification keep doubts of any kind in the background. I've tried in reading to make out the particular metrical devices which make the blank verse what it is. At first I thought the use of unaccented syllables at the end of lines always was kept fresh by not being done without the firmness of a line ending with an accent coming after two or three or four such unaccented line endings. But after a time I became aware of the fact that there was often a sort of pulse unaccented syllable which moved about in the line, sometimes as overflow, sometimes as a caesura, which kept the lyrical fluency and the tone going and yet let genuine speech come into the poem. //

Yours always,
Delmore

TO R. P. BLACKMUR

908 Memorial Drive
October 23, 1941

Dear Richard,

My monthly communication would have been written before this, but nervous depression, or something which suggests that word to me, has kept me from having any thoughts or observations to communicate. Strengthened by the emotion of two cups of tea, which will not last very long, the news that I can think of is that Tessa's[1] return caused general joy which was profound, perhaps, because Tessa is or seems a beautiful instance of vitality; the freshmen at Harvard this year are shocking both in thought and in expression; most of the few that I know in Cambridge seem, at least to me, to be in a state of becoming reconciled to their particular kind of stabilized defeat; and I myself wish I were a bird, for then I would go south for the winter.

Also, my last idea, ten days ago, was that if one were to start a magazine, perhaps one might entitle it *Byzantium*?

A week ago I broke through numbness to pain again by shocking myself as often before by reading about primitive man and the age of the planet which always brings a certain putativity into the idea of the maker of heaven and earth: what a nineteenth-century activity!

If I continue to write about my state of being in this way, this letter will be like coming into a bathroom full of steaming air from another's bath, so let fresh air come in by way of the freshman who wrote on his first theme that one of his chief abstractions was swimming. When corrected, he looked at the explanation of what an abstraction is in the English A handbook and found that Germany was given as an example of an abstraction and said then that he didn't think that Germany was an abstraction, which made a difficult moment for me before the whole class, for I think too, and don't you? that some abstractions are rather concrete, not to say, motorized and armored.

By next month, the manic-depressive roller coaster should be carrying me up, so that I will be able to write a better letter. Gertrude sends her best regards and was delighted to be called crisp.

Yours always,
Delmore

P.S. I will give your message to Philip [Horton] when I see him tomorrow, and am sending a copy of my play with an inscription which represents ten years' thought. I hope you will send me another letter soon, although I do not really expect to break the habits of a lifetime, and intend to write you once a month, in any case, like a subscription.

1. Tessa Gilbert Horton, Philip Horton's wife, Blackmur's first love, a painter and beauty.

TO R. P. BLACKMUR

[Cambridge]
January 22, 1942

Dear Richard:

I still feel ragged and unfinished about the war argument, and compelled to send you the following example (although I have never won an argument and [never] expect to win one), suggested by something I read or heard about in T. E. Lawrence:

M (a moral being) is captured by soldiers, and told that he must commit sodomy with P or with P1, if he wishes to keep his life. P is well-dressed, clean, kindly, cultivated, even charming; P1 is a filthy cruel Arab. What does M do? Does he not say with the Cumaean Sibyll, I wish to die? or the very least, I choose neither, I reject both?

I admit that this is a vast over-simplification, but nevertheless it is a question which seems to me to commit one to denying the kind of argument based on the lesser evil, or on the argument that there are only two alternatives. Is it not true that for the moral being a moral choice is always possible, and necessary, however unsuccessful it may be?

Anyway, I wished to add this to what is no doubt an endless disagreement.

Philip tells me that you asked him for serious literary criticism of your Yeats essay. Though unasked, I would say it was very good, almost as good as the first one on Yeats. I note that Allen has now reached the point where he mistakes irritability for originality, but don't say I said so, since there is enough ill will in the world right now. But anyway, what an amazing thought, that Yeats was not a romantic!

The ms. of my book was lost in the express on the way to Utah, and I have no copy of about sixty pages plus many pencilled-in corrections. This was the first time in years that I did not keep a carbon of something I wrote (ever since hearing that only Bohemians did not keep carbon copies), and the reason was that I was writing with an emotion of goodness that I knew would not last.

Any expression of sympathy would be gracefully received, but I suppose my run of luck has to be corrected by something like this. I feel like one who, having thrown up and known delicious convalescence, has just been advised by his nervous system that he is going to have to throw up again soon—the best sixty pages.

I have decided not to read any more reviews of my play, since my own weakness of mind is shown when I resent and argue for days, to myself, when fools call me sophomoric, adolescent, pompous, pretentious and dull...“until he thinks that face must be his face.”

Best to Helen,

Yours always,
Delmore

TO MARK VAN DOREN

908 Memorial Drive
Cambridge, Mass.
March 22, 1942

Dear Mark:

I spoke to John [Berryman] and by the indirection of speaking of seeing a doctor myself found that he has no Boston doctor, but one in New York named Ben Segal, who is in the phone book and would know whatever there is to be known. The Detroit doctor, who, I think, started the whole business, sent John to him, and John has gone to New York several times to meet him when he has come to New York, so that it might be worthwhile writing him.

My own impression, whatever it is worth, is that the only thing wrong with John is some kind of hysteria. The fainting fits he has occur when he is spoken to sternly or contradicted; I don't think they're sheer frauds, but if they spring from his secret disease, the disease is an open secret, and beside the fainting, there is no sign of anything wrong with him.

However, if [Beatrice's][1] inquiry means that she is thinking of coming to America, and if you are going to advise her about John's general circumstances, I think that her coming to America and marrying him would do him an immense amount of good, for what he needs in the most obvious way is some kind of situation to cope with besides his own feelings. Living alone as he does, in Boston not Cambridge, and seeing no one at all for days at a time, he is really not well off; and being improvident, he sometimes spends all his money and then tries to feed himself on chocolate bars, until the 1st of the month. Gertrude and I do what we can when we know what is going on, but usually we don't.

My manuscript is pretty definitely gone—at any rate, the Railway Express is willing to admit that it is, and I have made almost no progress in getting back the pages which I have no up-to-date copy of. But the whole business is beginning to seem a blessing in disguise, anyway, because I have found defects in the whole I might not have seen for years. And then, despite the lack of progress, I have begun to get the habit of trying to write all day and walking up and down the room between lines; instead of rushing along as I always have, before the intuitions wore off. It makes me feel like a professional for the first time and no longer at the mercy of periods of inspiration and drought. It reminds me of how pleased I was when I read, years ago, Cocteau's exclamation, "I want to live. I want to travel. *I do not want to become a fountain pen.*" And now these words hardly impress me, perhaps because I have become a fountain pen, and it is a pleasant enough thing to be.

With best regards from Gertrude to you and Dorothy,

> Yours always,
> Delmore

1. Berryman's first fiancée. The name "Beatrice" is "used by agreement" in John Haffenden's biography of Berryman, and I extend the same courtesy.

TO MARK VAN DOREN

> 908 Memorial Drive
> Cambridge, Mass.
> April 27, 1942

Dear Mark,

I'd like to take advantage of your offer to read my book for me, and come down to New York this week or next with the ms. The ms. was finally found (under the floor boards of Jay's station wagon!), and I had gone off on a new tack in rewriting and am now in a state of profound bewilderment, in which your advice would be of course very helpful.

But if you are busy with your own work, or reading end of the term papers, and so on, please don't hesitate to head me off. I would send you the ms. if I did not now suffer from a superstitious unwillingness physically to part with it.

I am bewildered about poetry but not so much that I can't see how good your new poems are, not only in themselves, but as the beginning of a new period for you and a new subject-matter.

> Yours always,
> Delmore

TO MARK VAN DOREN

> 908 Memorial Drive
> Cambridge, Mass.
> April 30, 1942

Dear Mark:

Many thanks for being so kind about the reading of the manuscript.

At Gertrude's insistence, I am having copies made and will send you one (by Railway Express!) as soon as it is ready. I thought of this before, of course, but was immorally impatient and unwilling to wait the perhaps two weeks or more the typing would take now, when all the typing bureaux are busy with theses, etc. However, I've decided not to publish it until the fall, if then, and there is plenty of time.

You're right, I'm sure, about the dead staying dead and the lost, lost; but of course, they never do.

Jay, who is on his way into the army, wants to start a quarterly and put me in charge. I have in mind a review which would *not* be like the *Southern Review* and which would try to bridge the gap between the elite (forgive the presumption of the word) and popular culture. But I don't want to say anything more until I am sure it is worth starting the whole shebang at this moment of time.

Yours always,
Delmore

TO R. P. BLACKMUR

.   [Cambridge
May 20, 1942]

Dear Richard:

Do you have the time now or soon to look quickly at *Genesis*, Book One and let me know whether or not I am publishing a blunder 261 pages long?

As you predicted, the ms. was found under the floorboard of L's station wagon just after I had finished the reconstruction and just as I was to get $150 insurance: thus were four months of my life destroyed.

Let me know, etc., and would you keep the request a matter of confidence, especially from Major Tate, the sometime distinguished author.

And in any case, don't forget to come to dinner on your way to Maine.

Yours always,
Delmore

P.S. It seems to me that I ought to get a free copy of *The Second World*[1] since I can't read well while standing up in the Grolier Book Shop.

1. Second book of poems by Blackmur.

TO MARK VAN DOREN

908 Memorial Dr.
Cambridge, Mass.
May 21, 1942

Dear Mark:

I've just had a note from Jay, saying that he was going to ask you to get *Genesis* I for review in order to thwart my *enemies*, as Jay calls them. I know you know that I had nothing of the sort in mind when I asked you for your advice and judgement. But Jay is always running amok in this way. I hope you tell him that you can't do anything of the kind just as a matter of helping me to keep Jay from such tactics; otherwise, I suppose it will all end with my being unable to ask anyone whose judgement I trust to give me advice.

Many thanks again for the reading. I slept the sleep of the innocent, just and happy on Saturday night as a result of your favorable impressions. With best regards to Dorothy and the boys,

Yours always,
Delmore

TO CONRAD AIKEN

908 Memorial Drive
Cambridge, Mass.
May 26, 1942

Dear Aiken:

I'm sending a copy of my ms. to you today. All kinds of chores connected with school and New Directions will keep me from accepting your really kind invitation to visit you during the next few weeks; but in place of the detailed criticism you might be able to give me then, two or three sentences of a quick general impression—such as, you had better not print this—would be very helpful. This is the best copy I have, but please go ahead and cross out anything you think too poor, etc., and when finished send it back to the above address express collect.

I can't really say how grateful I am for this aid.

Yours sincerely,
Delmore Schwartz

TO R. P. BLACKMUR

[Cambridge]
August 16, 1942

Dear Richard,

Gertrude was very pleased to get your letter, and we both feel that it contains several of your most beautiful sentences.

I do not think that I owe you a letter, except that you want to know why I left Cummington too soon. The truth is that sleep was diminishing at both ends to the point where I had no energy during the day to be fluent or sensitive enough to teach anyone. I told the dying lady[1] of this upon arrival and she was agreeable enough about my departure. As to the reason for my sleeplessness being so extreme at Cummington, if I know the reason why, it will be difficult for you to guess.

You were a great hit and popular success and some cried out, when I came, "All instinct skun [sic] away!" And it was, truly enough, when I lay down to wait for two hours' tense sleep. //

But while I was still in the place of the Playhouse, I learned that you seemed to be full of unhappiness. Klonsky brought me all the news quickly and received a summons from his draft board in Brooklyn, at which he went and blew his nose in the Stars and Stripes, Rimbaldian [sic]. He then wrote right back that he was an artist, he could not be disturbed on such short notice, he was in the middle of a poem. The school waited to see what would happen and when the mail came two days after with the Draft Board's name on it, he came with his mail to me, enjoying the attention he had awakened. He opened his letter from his girl first and began to knock his head, saying, "I am a cuckold!" He gave me the letter to read, and it developed that he had advised his girl to sleep with someone else in order to ascertain if he were the cause of her frigidity. This project had often been discussed, but Klonsky was inconsolable, saying, "How could I know that I would feel this way?" The Draft Board gave him six weeks.

// I was drunken every night of my stay, and feel that few things can equal drinking in the open air in summer.

It would be senseless to start a magazine now, for Jay tells me that sales have been cut in half since December. I do not want to throw away such a chance by beginning under the worst possible conditions. I think this is probably why your book has not been reviewed yet, the editors know that no one cares very much for poetry right now.

When I came back to Cambridge, Edmund Wilson was here, there was a party for him, he explained to me how the critical essay I wrote about him, which you did not like very much, was wrong,[2] and as he explained to me, I saw how wrong I was, but not for the reasons he gave me. Then the other day Ransom was here, and Theodore Spencer strove to arrange for me not to see him, but Ransom wanted to see me, and Theodore Spencer was once more frustrated. Ransom said how much he liked your essay on *The Sacred Fount*, which seemed to have suggested to him a James number in 1943.

And then, I saw an old copy of John Walcott's[3] novel the other day, and I did not read much of it, but it seemed to me, if I am not wrong about that prose, that to be a friend of yours is to deprive oneself of the full benefits of your criticism. It is of myself that I am thinking; I would soon accustom myself to the idea that I am not a really good poet; what is hardly bearable is the endless shift between the illusion that I am, and the disillusion and disappointment when again and again the whole poem looks blank or foolish, until the illusion returns.

Do not, as I am sure you will not, let John or Nela ever know of this impression of his book.

Give my love to Tessa, my favorite woman, and to Helen, who, since her moving narrative about seeming peculiar, belongs to the same club that I do; in fact, we are two of a kind, except that she is much better-looking. And now you owe me a letter.

Yours always,
Delmore

1. Katherine Frazier, director of Cummington. She was quite ill at the time.
2. "The Writing of Edmund Wilson" appeared in *Accent*, 2 (Spring 1942).
3. Husband of the painter and heiress Cornelia (Nela) Walcott. The Schwartzes and the Walcotts were neighbors. S spent a good deal of time with Nela in the early 1940's when her husband was overseas with the armed forces. His novel was never published.

TO JAMES LAUGHLIN

[Cambridge]
August 31, 1942

Dear Jay:

A boy named David Newton at Cummington asked me if I thought you might have almost any kind of job for him at ND. If so or not, would you please write him a postcard there and let him know. He is really a fine boy, he was running everything at Cummington because Miss Frazier was very sick, he is very intelligent, the army won't have him, he has been helping with the printing there, he worked for some time as advertising manager of a newspaper and he seems to me more efficient by far than anyone I ever saw work for you. If you have nothing at all now in Norfolk or New York, he would be worth keeping in mind for the future. //

I have altered the framework of the poem, without at all changing the substance, by giving the choruses definite names (this cuts out the big moment of unmasking, at the end, but one can't have everything), and making the narrator not the young hero, but one of the dead. Much of this change was suggested by your own doubt, which I had to hear not from you but from Van Doren. Are the voices necessary? The new framework should make them seem natural and necessary. The story itself, by being removed from the mind of a sixteen-year-old boy, becomes more plausible in point of view. However, all of this takes time, and I have been careful not to make the lines in which named characters are given credit for comments seem either interpolations or mechanical. Hence you had better not count on any definite date. I get free of this summer school, which is nothing less than the Black Hole of Calcutta, on the 16th of September and there are twelve full days before I must again mark freshmen themes: perhaps I will be able to get through during that period, if the process of moving to 20 Ellery St., the old Horton homestead (where the rent is twenty-seven dollars less a month) does not upset everything. But you will understand my desire not to deliver myself to my enemies before I have done all I can. The poem is too important, and I think too good not to be given evey benefit. Consequently don't tie it to any definite date of publication.

Yours,
Delmore

P.S. Berryman is enraged about his pamphlet [*Poems*], not without cause I think, and you had better blame everything, including the words on the jacket, on somebody in the New York office.

TO JAMES LAUGHLIN

20 Ellery St.
Cambridge, Mass.
Sept. 20, 1942

Dear Jay:

Genesis is all dressed up in Sunday clothes, ready for the printer, posterity, and my hated enemies.

Let me know immediately whether to send it to you or straight to

Beilenson, and don't forget the format you promised me, that of Thomas' *PXYD*, but with a blue cover.[1]

It might be rushed and made ready before Christmas, I don't care whether it is or not, but you may—but I am in a hurry to get sheets to show [Henry Allen] Moe of the Guggenheim Board, for I seem to have a good chance of another Guggenheim, on the basis of *Genesis* as a half-finished work in print. Let me know how soon this can be done.

This is no doubt the worst time of all to publish such a work, the war being what it is. But I must get free of it and move on to the novel which my head is heavy with. I hope you are ready to do what must be done to give the book any chance of success, and at the very least preserve the prestige of a valuable property. I can see how you may well be skiing when the time comes. When copies are ready, I will send you a long list of suggestions, such as, visit Irita Van Doren,[2] and tell her what Mark Van Doren said of the book, write to Ransom and move him to tears as you moved me by telling him of the cabal, visit J. Donald Adams[3] and persuade him to read the poem, and explain to him that a cabal of enemies is ready, visit Margaret Marshall[4] and point out that every one of my works has been attacked in *The Nation*. The main principle is to get these editors *to read the book*. The experience of sending it to many hearts and minds this summer makes it overwhelmingly patent that it awakens the intensest interest and at any other time there would be a chance at popular success.

I want a three hundred dollar advance on the novel [*A Child's Universal History?*], and this is not meant as the beginning of bargaining. I can get three times as much anywhere else, you gave Hivnor and Nabokov that much, the ever-rising cost of living, the end of Gertrude's job, the necessity of not writing critical essays while I teach and try to concentrate on the novel—make me need that sum very much. Moreover, such an advance was part of your promise last Christmas. If you feel like gambling, I will go to the trouble of getting definite offers from other publishers, and then you can give me *half* of what they are willing to give me, which will be more than I am now asking you for.

Yours,
Delmore

1. The cover was tan and green.
2. Editor of *The New York Herald Tribune Books*.
3. Editor of *The New York Times Book Review*.
4. Literary editor of *The Nation*.

130

20 Ellery Street
September 28, 1942

Dear Richard,

This is pretty quick as a rebound, but I wish to deliver myself of a difficult, unpleasant request, that our next meeting may be as dedicated as the last one to the same things, and this time sans any slowness on my part, for I do not understand why I should let anyone become more drunken than myself in my presence, especially when the results seem so happy.

First I ought to say, if you have heard from none, that George[1] was not wanted by the army, because one ear was not suitable.

The request is that you review my poem if you think it is really worth reading, as you should, for if it had not been for a sentence of yours on your visit, I would not have sent it away to the printer on last Thursday. I enclose a sweet note, which please return, from the young tycoon [Laughlin], as one witness among many of late as to what is in store for me. The book was announced for last spring and as a result everyone who dislikes me for some reason or other has tried to get it for review. This is the first and I hope last time I make such a request of anyone, and I am pressed this time by the knowledge that those who are really interested in poetry in this country will read a book which you say is worth reading, no matter what is said elsewhere. It is not that I want to be applauded as an eighth or ninth wonder, but actually and sincerely that I want this work to be read, a deep-dyed craving, which would surely be satisfied then, and surely Ransom would give you the book.

Enough of this, it is outside the circle of friendship, it will certainly not intrude again, no blur or shadow will remain.

The day after your flying and brimming visit, so just a coronation of the house, I protested the loudness of the next-door radio, and the old lady next door shouted out, "You go to Harvard!" and then spoke of our midnight music. And then there were a whole new set of early morning sounds to get used to sleeping through, especially a man with a motorcycle at seven going over the top with gunshots, and the children going and coming to school three times a day. But now I am used to the waterfall or Elevated; but not used to the many ghosts here, dead and living, for here we saw for the last time in this difficult and beautiful life Harry Zimmerman[2] and Jack Wheelwright,[3] here the stairway, as I think I told you, must be entitled Nella Falls, here many a time Tessa ate with inimitable zest and drank so that she might soon throw up like Roman, Elizabethan, or Peeperkorn,[4] here Haskett[5] wooed Libby fast as light, here Winfield [Townley] Scott was much drunker than anyone I have ever seen. What profound subliminal intuition drew us here, not to speak of the economic determinism of twenty-five dollars less rent? For this has been the only place to be comfortable and have social joy in all Cambridge, and it makes me think of what your witness Adams[6] had to say about polar bears in Cambridge. At any rate, I think it was a happy omen, and evoking a serene smile, to see you coming from one side as the moving van came from the other and the task of living here commenced.

Nela was here the other night on route to Washington, and we met her at the North Station to encounter her inimitable disorder, for there was the whole business of getting her sleeping tickets and getting her bags on the train, and before the evening was done, the only thing on the train was herself and that only by means of a hundred-yard dash, and a telegram had to be sent to wake her up at three o'clock in the morning, so that she might get her bags which she had arranged to put on the train without knowing or remembering that she had done so. Yet, she has a wonderful openness of nature and grasping desire for joy and the intellect, which makes me like her much more than you do.

George and Wallace[7] were here on Saturday morning and George had, through the passage of a week, lost the dignity which the imminence of the army had aura'd him with, and the quiet joy which getting out had brought about in him. After a brief period, Wallace became much beBacchused on merely some native sherry, and wished to visit his sister's house to dance in the ballroom, but when we arrived, exerted himself for hours in accusing his mother of riding herd on him for thirty-nine years, to which she replied with much dignity by reminding him of the strange costumes, such as Russian blouses, which he had worn through childhood. And now and then, seeing that I listened because I could hardly get out of earshot, he would accuse me of filing all these things in my filing memory, as I do I suppose because I suffer from total recall.

This is all the news I can think of right now, except perhaps that a telegram from one of your *Chimera* boys which asked me to review Jarrell's book [*Blood from a Stranger*], possessed the obscure phrase, believe we have tentative approval, which suggested your hand?

Yours always,
Delmore

1. George Anthony Palmer, Blackmur's Cambridge cousin, who published poetry under the name "George Anthony."

132

2. Harold Zimmerman, painter and teacher of Hyman Bloom and Jack Levine. Both Helen Blackmur and Tessa Horton studied painting with him. He died of brain disease at the beginning of the 1940's.

3. John Wheelwright, Boston dandy, bachelor, and poet, who was killed by a drunken driver.

4. Character in Thomas Mann's *The Magic Mountain*, who represented the sensual.

5. Haskett Derby, who married Harold Zimmerman's widow, Libby.

6. Blackmur was writing a critical biography of Henry Adams, which was published posthumously in 1980.

7. Wallace Dickson and his wife Rose were friends of S.

TO DWIGHT MACDONALD

20 Ellery Street
Cambridge, Mass.
Oct. 5, 1942

Dear Dwight:

The enclosed billet doux from the young tycoon, which please return, is one sign among not a few of the fate which appears to be in store for my poem. Will you then, whether it pleases Sir Clement Greenberg or not, give the book to Blackmur to review and all by itself, not with others. It will then probably be the only serious review which appears. Your impression of the poem was unique, almost all other readers being at the other extreme; but I would be grateful if you kept that impression and this request to yourself a while longer.

I was disappointed that you did not come by here on your way back from Nantucket, and especially since I wished very much to explain orally why I did not write about the war. I delay the explanation again, until we come to New York, perhaps at the end of the month. But in brief, the stand I wished to expose was as follows, and I do not know what you would think of it, having been dumbfounded by the belief that I agreed with Goodman's meaningless verbalisms. The initial assumption is that no political position is possible for intellectuals at present. Second, the intellectuals must, as a necessary myth, conceive of themselves as a class, or rather a club, or at any rate, a group which, by the very nature of their profession, have a vested interest in truth, an interest which must be defended more than ever in wartime. Needless to say, it is a myth that the intellectuals are such a fine class, but it is one of those myths which come true to an extent, if believed and acted on: just like the Elks and the Free Masons. From the point of view of this vested interest in culture and truth, it is possible to proceed to a detailed and constant criticism of the war. This is as a matter of fact what you have already done in attacking [Van Wyck] Brooks, and from just such a point of view. But the point of view is just as important as the particular targets, and ought to be stated in abstraction. That it is an abstraction is undeniable, but no more so than the professional standards of doctors. Since surgeons are not asked to throw overboard their activities in wartime, those who are doctors of the spirit ought to continue their professional engagements also.

This does not strike me as particularly original or enthralling as a stand; but it is workable, as is made evident by the fact that some fall back on it naturally and of necessity. It is also a position from which one can advance to a political stand whenever such a one is made possible by the movements of the well-known masses: O grandeur and misery of socialism! I thought Orwell was bringing in the old and obvious stupidity by attacking the pacifists with, All who are not pro-War are working for defeat.

Be that as it may, the times make me sick at heart. Soldiers and sailors drill in the Yard, the students speak of nothing but various makes of planes, and the college courses have been made into a cunning scheme to keep some men's sons from any chance of an early grave. If you feel moved to see a great institution in wartime, why don't you and Nancy come on the long-delayed weekend. We have a whole floor for you, and will give a party.

Yours,
Delmore

TO JAMES LAUGHLIN

[Cambridge]
Saturday [October 1942?]

Dear Jay,

Sorry about the state of the ms. Some of the inconsistencies of punctuation are deliberate; others are the result of my attentive scrutiny of the words as carriers of meaning. Like a great engineer or savant, I relaxed so much after sending off the ms. that I contracted a cold.

I will attend to the markings necessary with complete promptness. //

The novel contract should be half on England and Hollywood (the former I think not unlikely), ten per cent, twelve and a half, and fifteen, on one thousand, fifteen hundred, and two thousand copies respectively, ascending after that in the way that every other good contract does. I think that, plus the advance, takes care of all possible points of dispute.

I think perhaps wrongly that I can have it finished by a year from now, so much progress have I made and so clear is it in my head. If not, then I have another book just like *IDBR* for next fall's list; that is, story, lyrics, play, and poem of eighty pages. By the spring, I will know for certain if the novel is going to be finished in time. I take it that you would want the other one, too. I certainly hope I can get the novel finished by then and have enough money for some necessities of the spirit.

Will y' please use the beautiful ND centaur on the title page and cover. It is much more beautiful than any of the new ones, and has happy associations.[1]

I have gazed at some of Goodman's novel and will send it back with the next express parcel. What a waste of cleverness and ingenuity on private unimportant feelings! There is just one word for it, self-abuse, for if Goodman could only realize that fiction must have its roots in experience, no matter how attractive a fantasy may be, his eloquent style might be put to some use. I used to try to tell him this in the old days, and his answer would always be some false analogies with music or the plastic arts. He does not understand that even the sculptor has to accept the actual nature of his material; and that the material of the author is human experience, not puppets who spout homosexual bons mots and move about wherever the prose style wants to go. It is probably too late, but perhaps it is worth expressing such sentiments to him, for if enough people tell him this, he might as an experiment try to write a novel based upon what experience is. Needless to say, the other extreme of Miller or Farrell of just typing out case histories is just as worthless. I hope you are careful not to involve me in any letter of rejection you may write. //

A new book on Shaw has just appeared, as you may have seen in the *Times*; hence you had better move Theodore [Morrison] the Dispenser to another subject. It was a poor subject for him, in any case, for it would not be possible to find anyone less able to understand the social context in which Shaw was involved.

Ever,
Delmore

1. It did not appear in the book when published.

TO R. P. BLACKMUR

Dear Richard,

There is no coffee here, too, and if God and Pharaoh do not wish to have mercy on my living soul, they have chosen the proper means, for the whole morning passes in a half-awakened state, during which I read letters in *The Times* in denunciation of the bogus shortage, full of high-toned political and economic arguments, but obviously inspired by nothing but the sensibility depraved and deprived of coffee. I read a book by a German once in which the whole lucid glory of the eighteenth century was attributed to the arrival of coffee in Europe.

The lack puts me in the right frame of mind to answer your optimism about our society, which seems plastic and buoyant to me, too, but with whatever buoyancy a deathly sickness brings about. But first, to say that I did not mean to suppose or suggest that you spoke from the same box as Philip [Horton], who does not mean what he thinks he means, I hope, and who suffers now, I think, from a lack of vocation plus a naive notion of what being sensible is.

The disagreement, so far as there is one between your senatorship and my belief in critichood, in such a period as the present, seems to me to be a question of how radical it is necessary to be in order to place the struggle of human life on a reasonable basis. Consider once more the complex fact (I do not pretend that it is not complex) that in the Thirties the New Deal's expenditure's for playgrounds, swimming pools, schools, and many other things, not least the support of the arts in which Helen participated, brought about immense protests until finally the whole procedure was given up; so far as one can tell, it certainly has not established itself as an integral part of our society. The war, however, costs many times the cost of the positive things of the New Deal, and draws overwhelming support, not merely vocal support, but the support of heavy industry and organized labor, both thriving wonderfully on the needs of the war. Complex as this contrast may be, it seems to say that one must be radical and cut at the roots of private property, especially the private ownership of heavy industry, so that our society can thrive on the creation of positive goods and not the instruments of warfare. Anything less than this by any senator is trivial amelioration, for crisis, depression, and unemployment must return as soon as the goods of war are not active needs.

Returning to such a one as Philip, it seems to me that intelligence must either corrupt itself or be rejected. Is this not one of the lessons of Adams? They did not want him as senator because of his intelligence. And does not the proper place of intelligence in our time show itself in the fact that the *Education* [*of Henry Adams*] was a best-seller for eighteen months? This is what I mean by critichood. Intellectuals even in wartime and especially in wartime ought to act on the necessary myth that they ara a class with a vested interest in the truth and in the active telling of the truth, instead of being bandwagon chasers and whores [. . .] What would happen if you were appointed Ambassador to Cuba or Chile, after the war and during the Pax Americana? Would you not be compelled to give up either intelligence and honesty or your job as soon as the first serious ambassadorial issue arose?

Be that as it may, I do not see why you take with any seriousness such a minor vocalist as [Alfred] Kazin, whose piece I just glanced at, but who is just trying to keep up with the rest of the chorus. Horace Gregory put you in an icebox in 1934 and [Granville] Hicks and some others sans any perceptible effect on you or your readers, who will not give out because you have your roots in immortal literature, while the Kazins merely have their hands on the handrail of the bandwagon, so that when the war is finished they will be crying out for belles-lettres once more, and then with the next depression, for social consciousness. I wonder how many times we have to go around this particular merry-go-round. I was born with a postwar soul (a thought inspired by Wallace's remark that he was born with a hangover), but as [J.L.] Sweeney [Harvard friend] remarks, once is enough!

We thought of writing to Helen before you said so, and have, and this makes me think of the possibility of a possibility of a grand and monster party at Christmas with perhaps even Commissioner Morton [Zabel] persuaded to return to old haunts.

Last week Gertrude and I walked down Irving Street from the lower to the upper middle class, wondering which was your house, which Cummings', and which [Irving] Babbitt's, and then we walked further and in the semi-slum street which industry brings to Cambridge, we saw four children standing in a very small yard and chanting, "Five cents to come in!" and then, an hour after, walking on Coolidge Hill, we saw a six-year-old boy who said to two girls from his fine lawn, "I will kill you, if you come on my property," waving a mock rifle at them, and they came on the lawn, and he hit them until they ran away. This was not serious, but neither was it charming.

Yours always,
Delmore

TO JAMES LAUGHLIN

[Cambridge
October 1942]

Dear Jay:

I will learn something about preparing a book for the press before my next book appears.

Howard Baker gave me his new work to read, a play about Negro swing musicians doing the Orpheus story, like *Green Pastures* but much better, with the two lines of the Negros and the classic story kept going all through beautifully. He is going to send it to you and asked me to express my opinion. I think it would go very well in book form, or in the yearbook, which apparently would satisfy Howard. His agent thinks a B'way production possible, and I think it might even be a popular success on the stage. As verse, it is unimportant, but this does not matter because the rest is so moving.

I think Kazin would do very well with [Thomas] Mann. He wrote a fine review of the Joseph [*Joseph and His Brothers*] books once.

You did not reply about sending books about to the right people before sending out review copies. This might be a great help. Please answer.

My preface is not really negative; but quite pretentious; and yet it may relieve the feelings of those who said, I am told, when they heard of this long poem: "Who does he think he is, Dante?"

Sometimes I find it hard to follow your views in politics. I too detest Roosevelt, but for far different reasons. One would think, to hear you on the artist destroying himself by descrying the conditions on which art can flourish, that, one, the artists elected Roosevelt, made the printers' union strong, and determine at all the conditions under which they live; two, that when Hoover, his cheeks mounting to his eyes, and Quiet Calvin [Coolidge] ruled, all the great poets thrived by writing verse, Joyce in a Berlitz school, Eliot in a bank, Pound in a garret, Stevens in an insurance co., and the much greater number of gifted ones, whom we will never know about, because they did not manage to come through the way the few do, but gave up, as many always do. And in general, what do you think brought about the present war, the artists? the bankers? Surely it was Capitalismus, which corrupts you who are rich as it corrupts me who am not, too much and too little always being forms of disease.

I must admit that the present war has very pleasant aspects. The death of generals, the stupidity of the British, Hess dropping down in Scotland, but above all, Darlan, greatest of politicians, for who before him ever changed sides three times in one war? His career will be studied in days to come as Caesar's has been. Did you, however, see Churchill's sentence, I did not take office in order to preside over the liquidation of the British Empire. What cynicism! to say this before the war is won.

Did you hear about [Walter] Winchell's prophecy and guarantee, the war will be over in forty days, and if it is not, I will pay one thousand dollars a day for every extra day to a recognized charity. This is insanity, but maybe four hundred days will be enough.

I saw some of the new poems of June Cannan, the poetess of the year before last at Cummington, and they were very good, better than Jean Garrigue's. Would you think of two girls in the next FYAP, why not? Anyway, would you write a polite note to her, invitingly, at Student Mail, Barnard College, NYC?

Yours,
Delmore

TO R. P. BLACKMUR

[Cambridge]
October 30, 1942

Dear Richard,

I was flattered and pleased to get your long letter, and especially because it relieves me of some of my misunderstanding of some of your remarks.

The health of your distrust of ideas as formulae and of the intellecutal / as one who with a system blocks off the actual / I know about now as only one can who has suffered from not knowing it for a long time at the right time, just as in infancy I had to learn about fire in the frying pan. At the height of your most eloquent intoxication here in September, full of prose and verse, you declared, "Anybody can have ideas," in ignorance of which truth, and in the most stupid pride of intellect, I spent years in love with philosophy, contemptuous of all who were not high-toned intellectuals, disdainful of fine arts with their actual glories, and, to be more concrete, convinced that it was most noble to be a teacher of philosophy, but ignoble to teach English, ignoble to write stories and poems about actual things, noble to tap out thin allegories of high-sounding ideas, in love with the platitude of statement and ignorant of what Warren justly called its poverty. What stupidity!

Thus I assent to all that you say and the attitude you elaborate seems to me the only right one for the citizen of a reasonable society. I say reasonable society, because I do not, of course, suffer from Utopian delusions, nor expect that any order will eliminate inadequacies on every *purely human* level of experience, nor the necessity for heartbreaking toil and effort. But the question is whether or not this our society is not diseased, rather than inadequate, with inadequacies which may by long effort and reform be corrected. There is a time for healing and there is a time for surgery. It is not, I think, that private property is irresponsible, but that it must be irresponsible; the manufacturer must exploit his workers by holding down their wages in order to make a profit, or he will cease to be a manufacturer. He must shut down his plant when it is not making a profit. The wheat must be plowed under and the cotton must be destroyed, to keep up prices: it is in this sense that the New Deal's failure was inevitable. And then the whole thing must lead to depression and to war. In bringing in these worn instances and in using mustness so many times, I do not deny at all your willed purpose. But willed purpose is always limited and always surrounded by necessity, so that one can will a walk in the country, but one cannot fly to the moon. The frames and the institutions of capitalism create this limitation, this mustness, and this necessity that the economy must move for a profit, the profit must impoverish the purchasing power of the market, new markets must be found, nationalist and imperialist wars must come again and again. I trot out these old paradigms precisely because they are old and are confirmed by the present war, which no one wanted. Roosevelt tried everything else from post offices to swimming pools; nothing worked, nothing reduced the number of unemployed until the war arrived, the one policy which succeeded in making all the wheels turn. In the same way, given a highly industrialized country, Hitler had to go forward in one direction, there was necessity and not choice in front and in back of him.

All this is intended as evidence that the institutions and frames which you grant to be bad, but expect to correct, cannot be corrected. It is a case for surgery; any economy which cannot support and give work to all who can and need work must be cut out, so that willed purpose can exist. The Senate can be corrected; private property in an industrial society cannot.

I say all this at the same time that I suffer from the deadly fear that capitalism is immortal, for it survives the most exhausting crises and wars with matchless stamina, a stamina which, so far as I can make out, draws itself from the fact that the populace for the most part wants to be rich, every girl in the 5 & 10 believes in the long shot hope that, although she is not Barbara Hutton, she may marry a Rockefeller, as the silver screen reveals repeatedly. In this sense, I suppose that the root of the matter is a moral failure on the part of the whole populace.

To turn to matters of less enormity, Gertrude heard from the fearful Mrs. Gilbert[1] that Philip had received a raise and was riding high, but that they were still unable to find a place to live and Tessa was so much distracted by this that she asked old friends to forgive her for not writing.[2] I think too that the various strains and stresses on the old friendship during the last few months are the product of Philip's break, effort to find himself a place, departure, and the effect of that departure on Tessa, who seemed to me to do pretty well in a situation where most women would have indulged in yells and appeals. I hope you are not serious about the nineteenth year of your friendship with Tessa. How, by the way, did you figure eighteen years as the normal length of friendship?

There was a letter from Nela saying that [Maxwell] Perkins had sent back John's [Walcott] book and with the customary stupidity of editor's tact praised him very much as a man of ideas, but not properly a novelist. Nela said, too, and I hope I am not repeating something that John did not mean to be repeated to begin with, that John now felt so ashamed that he did not want to see any of his friends. It would be pleasant to be able to do something for someone in such a state, especially when one has been through it oneself. But I suppose such ventures are vain. //

This is all I can think of right now, except that we were disappointed to miss Helen, to whom Gertrude, the Ellery St. Blue, sends her best as she does to you too.

Yours,
Delmore

1. Helen Gilbert, Tessa Horton's mother, a Cambridge eccentric.
2. The Hortons had gone to Washington, D.C., where Philip worked in the Foreign Nationalities Branch of the O.S.S.

TO WILLIAM ARROWSMITH

20 Ellery St.
Cambridge, Mass.
November 2, 1942

Dear Mr. Arrowsmith,

I would like to review the Stevens' *Notes Toward a Supreme Fiction* very much, and if you like, it might be well to get the other new book, *Parts of a World*, into the review also. You had better let me know how long you want the review.

I thought the first number of *Chimera* was a good piece of editing, but was somewhat perplexed to find Booth Tarkington cited in one of your brochures.

There are a number of good young poets worth asking for verse, particularly June Cannan, care of Student Mail, Barnard College— Blackmur may have spoken to you of how good she is—, Jean Garrigue, 120 West 10th St., New York City, Howard Moss, care of University of Wisconsin, John Malcolm Brinnin, care of Vassar College. Sorry not to have better addresses. And why don't you ask John Berryman for something? His address is 49 Grove St., Boston.

Yours sincerely,
Delmore Schwartz

TO R. P. BLACKMUR

[Cambridge]
November 30, 1942

Dear Richard,

Your letter comes just at the right time, for this has been the kind of a day when one meets one's face unexpectedly in a sudden mirror and does not for a moment recognize it. One of my students at Radcliffe was in the Coconut Grove fire, and between the weeping of the class today and my own feelings about all accidents to anyone I know, your letter was the only thing that took my mind away from what happened. This girl was very pretty in a doll-like way—if she had been less pretty I suppose she would not have been as likely to have been taken to a night club—and very shy, eager, and charming. As it happened, I had a conference with her last Wednesday, and by those ironies that so fascinated the great and unconsolable Hardy, I corrected her last two themes, one on Keats' "When I have fears that I may cease to be," and the other on a childhood friend of hers who had just been shot down in the South Pacific. This led to some talk of sudden death, and her obvious grief made me give her a higher mark than her paper actually deserved. I tried to say something to the tearful girls, and then said that there was nothing that could be said, and went on with the class work, and then, preoccupied with what I was saying, asked a question and pinned the dead girl's name to the question, because I suppose it had been in the back of my mind all the while. This led to a fresh flood of tears. Patriot of the actual, though you be, this kind of pointless death must make you feel how senseless actuality is, after all; not that I suppose you to be unaware of this unengaging aspect. I need not remind *you* that we do not live much in the actual world; and hence, Gentlemen, the sensation of irreducible distress—always death.

All this seems rather an excess of feeling, on re-reading, and hence I should turn to other matters. I wondered no little if Nela would keep going when she arrived in Princeton, for the night before, she talked to Gertrude all through my first sleep which begins at 12:30, if the sherry will do, and ends between two and three, after which I arise and slug myself to sleep all over again with more sherry, except when Nela is here, for when she is, as she was this evening, she seized on me, and let Gertrude go, her project and issue this time being the annihilation of all the youth of Germany after the war is won. I don't want to go over the varieties of barbarism—and the reversed kind of anti-Semitism which was actually at the bottom of her argument—suffice it to say that Nela has a good chance, if the liquor holds out, of using more words than any other human being of our time, and probably with as little sense as anyone else. Nevertheless, and despite all this, I still think Nela is better than most human beings because her being is opened up to everything. And this reminds me of June Cannan, who was here last week, and really looks as if she might turn into something fine, if she does not destroy herself in the course of doing so.

It turns out that we will almost certainly have to be in New York through Christmas because of the illness of Gertrude's mother, so that the chances of some pleasant evenings are increased, rather than diminished. But if it happens that you are going to come to Cambridge, after all, let me know, for then we may be able to put off our departure for New York a day or two. I see my Christmas party glimmering away, though at least one other is eager enough, Nela, who would certainly be willing to fall downstairs again.

I too have been reading Dostoyevsky and with the feeling as I get into the middle of the story that here is more insight than anyone else ever had; partly, of course, because he had Christianity to draw on; acceptance of guilt and punishment, acceptance of one's own self without further illusion or evasion—what else is worth learning to do? Next to this view, Tolstoy's good life seems fat and easy, and in addition requires an inherited estate. Not that Tolstoy did not end Dostoyevskian.

I think maybe I am going to try to write an essay on Dostoyevsky's criticism, transposing his recognition of the evil of the separation of the intelligentsia and the populace to post-war America.

I am piqued to have you suspect that I have not read *The American Scene* and also piqued because I appear not to be asked to write about James, although I suppose that I can't expect to be in on everything. The part in *T.A.S.* about New York Jews (how James shudders) I was tempted to use as a quotation for *Shenandoah*, especially since my mother and father both lived at just that time in the part of New York James was looking at. And then there are the sentences about the football game and the roar of the crowd, which you ought to quote in your book, for the sake of your audience. How too too refined James sometimes permitted himself to be.

Nothing would give me more pleasure than to reconcile Jay and you, but after *Genesis* appears I am not likely to see or hear much of Jay, such is his infatuation with success and the roar of the crowd. I don't see why you don't finish the James book first, however, since so much is already written, and since it is going to be done, anyway. I think there would be an additional pretty penny in it for you, for Eliot is taking all the books of the series apparently, and in any case, as you know, expressed the wish to get you started in England. //

With my best to Helen, with whom, when next we meet, I must work out some secret sign and signal for our particular kind of exile,

Delmore

TO R. P. BLACKMUR

[Cambridge]
December 19, 1942

Dear Richard,

Our plans are uncertain again because our trip to New York has to be synchronized with some stage of Gertrude's mother's illness, so that we won't have to make two trips. Also my mind—and my emotions— are an unholy mess at the moment. I can't go from the living room to the study without losing my temper. I have insulted about ten people in the last week, and in short I am afraid to circulate among dear friends. But maybe I will feel more amiable soon, and if not, then we will come to New York in January. As I get older, I seem to have less and not more control over my feelings.

Nevertheless it was pleasant to open *Time* this morning and see you described as a remote and excellent poet[1] by some mind that has enough sense to admire Stevens and to see that Harry Levin is blind to the grandest and plainest virtues of Joyce.[2] I don't suppose I have any ground to stand on when I think you ought not to get upset, since I get much more upset. But Greenberg is a clever and dishonest fool, as I know at first hand, and as can be seen in such a howler as the remark that you divide your lines with monotonous and mechanical regularity. I am not sure what he means, but either he is condemning all blank verse, or blind as Harry Levin, for I open at random and find ten instances of overflow on p. 22 of your book. If you want another test, objective and free of personal reference, read "Darkness and Light," one of the poems described as showing that [Stephen] Spender is a great poet.

(I would have said this in my last letter, but I thought maybe I ought not to, because you were going to review my book. On further thought, however, it seems mean and selfish not to say it just for that reason, since I thought it and since you might give my opinion as much weight as you give to people like Kazin who don't read poetry from year to year.)

One reason for these attacks is the war (in the dirty Thirties it did not seem infamous to protect one's own pigeon-hole by shouting that everyone else is narrow and limited. This is what Kazin is doing. But I don't have to tell you these things, nor that the reason for some expression of perplexity is that when you write that you are trimming your own snaky locks in your own glass, most people just don't know that you are bringing in the Medusa as a conclusion which lights up the whole poem. This is what I meant when I wrote you last summer that you depended too much on diction; after all, an allusion like that would have been better, not that it is not good, if it had stuck out more. Do you agree? Also, the fact that you make yourself out to be at once Perseus and the Medusa is not put strongly enough.) (This reminds me, be careful as with fire what you say to Nela about poetry; you told her last winter that poetry ought to have an immediate effect, or it was no good, and she then argued for ten hours that Stevens was no good because *she* felt no surface excitement, turning the pages.)

Anyway, what can be expected of light and intelligence if a genius like Van Wyck Brooks turns into an hysterical and abnormal advocate of normality and declares in *Oliver Allston* that "there is no trace of religious feeling in all of T. S. Eliot's writing." Next time they take him to the asylum, they ought to keep him there, for only an insane man could read "Ash Wednesday" and make a remark like that. Do you agree?

I intended to say before this that William Phillips wrote me and asked me who I wanted to review my book, and I wrote back not to him but to Rahv, whom I had to write to about other things, that you and Matthiessen would at least be honest and sympathetic. Rahv wrote back that this was a good idea and also that he had been planning to ask you to do some reviews, anyway. Should I not have done this? When I get scared, I get devious, and Laughlin just won't stop telling me what other people say of me. Some people go through life without knowing what is said behind their backs, and some, like myself, are told *all*; not really all, but it sounds like all.

Harry Levin, speaking of Matthiessen, seems to have fixed me with M., by repeating something I said to M., who then called me up to ask about it. This was in June and I made a special point of asking Harry not to repeat it. M. smiles sweetly when he sees me, but we have since not been asked to his house, not even to the Christmas punch when all are asked. I've never liked M. very much and can forego the visits, but it makes me feel a fool not to be able to keep from alienating someone who befriended me again and again. No doubt, I should have kept my mouth shut, but I can't help expressing my opinions some of the time. We heard the other day that Levin had told Wilson to his face, in L's own house, that he did not know what he was talking about and was "a mere impressionist critic." Wilson did not like this and, strange to say, was angry.

Do you really think I am a nut? This, you said twice, in Harrington[3] and at the Athens. But like your wife, my fraternity sister, I feel quite normal, although the notion that I do not seem so is an agent in making me morbidly self-conscious and thus "peculiar."

Your [Princeton] boys' poems about the Grove fire must be good, will have to be very good, to console one for the fire. What do you mean, "a hymn in new whim"? Is this chance flowering to choice again? Let me ad lib forever.

Has John [Walcott] left the country? If you see Sage Walcott [son of John and Nela], look long at him, I think he is going to be President. Give my love to Nela, although just between us I feel rather ambivalently about her right now, and to Helen.

Yours always,
Delmore

1. Blackmur's *The Second World* had just been published.
2. Joyce himself had praised Harry Levin's commentary on *Finnegan's Wake* in a letter to Laughlin.
3. The Blackmurs had a summer home in Harrington, Maine.

146

TO DWIGHT MACDONALD

20 Ellery St.
Cambridge, Mass.
Dec. 19, 1942

Dear Dwight—

Although I get nothing but memoranda from you, I will now write you a long letter because I feel rather lonely and want someone to talk to who will regard what I say as *funny* (at Xmas 1939 you flattered me greatly by maintaining—as [no] one else ever has—that I had a sense of humor).

First, many thanks for the invitation and offer of the house. I don't think it would be wise to take it up because I am now in the middle of a story (which Sir Clement Greenberg (O.M., Ph.D., D.Litt. (*Horizon*), W.C. (Oxon.), *PMLA*, DT. [*sic*]) will first maintain ought not to be accepted and then will decide ought to be revised in the light of his critical standards as communicated to the author, thus enacting a superiority ritual), and I want to finish the story before my energy wears out, and while school does not get in the way. I've finished the first writing of the essay on Eliot,[1] also, and I want to keep at that, too, so that travelling and visiting in New York would be a waste of a good period. But I will certainly come to New York in January or February, and before that, it occurs to me that perhaps you could be persuaded to come back from Ohio by way of Boston, staying here with us. Philip [Rahv] has promised to come in January, and it would be pleasant to have two lions in the same month to show off. I get blamed for much that appears in *P.R.*, so that I might as well get some credit from the putative connection. I will explain this remark lower down, but seriously, is it not about time that these discussions of your visit ceased and you actually came, with Nancy and with young Nijinsky? If you don't want to come on your way back, then please regard any week-end from now on as one in which we would be really overjoyed to have hot arguments with you and have you laugh at my weak jokes. I also want to show you the data that... No, I will withhold this news as an associate feature.

Anyway, it is kind and characteristic of you to repeat the invitation, and it reminds me of how I always defend you among the academic and the genteel (two of your curse words, by the way) by saying, Yes, antagonism for its own sake is his appetite and neurosis, and none of his political predictions seem to come true, but he is a master of expository prose and more than that, he opens himself up to all kinds of being and beings, Open House Macdonald ought to be his name. I am eager, by the way, to see your fish.

That reminds me, you say, "I am anxious to lay before you a journalistic project." Being a teacher of rhetoric, like St. Augustine, I must, such is the occupational disease, point out to you that "anxious" is incorrect, "eager" is correct usage. What is this project, or are you trying one of my devices, or is it the new political monthly Jay wrote me about? If so, I have a poem for the first issue which begins,

A Wise Question

Some Rockefeller said to me one day
(He saw me hide a poem inside my coat)
"If you're so smart, why ain't you rich?"
What could I say to the son of a bitch?
"If you're so rich, why ain't you smart?"
(Had I but irony like Thomas Mann's
I'd turn it on myself! If I were he
Before I'd be the President of Germany,
I'd turn it on myself, if I were he!)

I hope this poem is of simple enough versification to hold your attention, for will I ever forget what a triumph of insulation you have achieved, managing to maintain an immunity to an interest in poetry through five years of editing a literary magazine and gloating over the receipt of poems by Eliot which insist that the only meaningful event in History is the Incarnation of Christ. Perhaps I exaggerate; you *have* been busy.

As you know, I've written William and Philip about getting an honest review of my book in *P.R.* It was not very good of you not even to answer me when I suggested Blackmur. In the early days, no, I mean, in the last years of the dirty Thirties I was helpful as an author to *P.R.*, and what has been my reward? apart from Farrell's praise of my ability as a third baseman? You send kind and hospitable invitations, you laugh at my jokes, you seal me up in Martinis, and then you tell me what a big fool I have made of myself by writing plays in verse or criticism. Nevertheless, I love you, being irrational.

How long can my esssay on Eliot be? Remember, I am not going to cut it, once it is written in final draft.

There is no use in continuing this argument, but I must say again, Why has antagonism *an sich* a fatal attraction for you? Sometimes it seems that the less it is backed up by observation and analysis, the more you like it, as in the cases of [Lionel] Abel's review and [Weldon] Kees's also (I admit this is not true of things you are really interested

148

in, such as politics and the films). Muriel's [Rukeyser] bad poem and her bandwagon riding from the proletariat to the Marines should have been exposed, and Levin's confusions and bad prose also. Instead of that, you print a jealous wisecrack from Kees and four *mots* from Abel, excited by Stewart's Cafeteria coffee and some bedraggled girl's outcry that he is a genius! Please answer.

I hope you feel like coming back from Ohio by way of Cambridge, and if not, we will see you in Jan.

Ambivalently, with affection predominant,
Delmore

1. Possibly a draft of "T. S. Eliot As the International Hero," not published until 1945 in *Partisan Review*.

TO DWIGHT MACDONALD

[Cambridge, 1942?]

Dear Dwight,

Last night *you* were my insomnia, but I love you anyway, and also Nancy and Mike, and I am sorry I took the keys, grateful for the pea soup, against the war, and full of hope with nine lives.

Delmore

P.S. Please preserve your silence until other hearts and minds have pronounced judgement.

TO DWIGHT MACDONALD

[Cambridge, 1942?]

Dear Dwight,

Is it true that *PR* is quitting and would you consider coming to live in Boston (change is creative)?

Jay is starting a quarterly, though on too modest a scale, and putting me in charge.

How much does each issue of *PR* cost?

Hurriedly,
Delmore

P.S. Do you think we are sufficiently compatible? And yet, on the other hand, conflict is creative, as Hegel observed.

In Boston or Cambridge you might write your great book, *Western Culture Seen by a Yale Man*, or *The Education of Drite Macdonald*, or *A Thousand Arguments with Philip Rahv and Other City Jews*.

TO MEYER SCHAPIRO

20 Ellery St.
Cambridge, Mass.
January 20, 1943

Dear Meyer:

Many thanks for your article on Cain's jawbone. Reading it, I was strongly reminded of an incident last year when I lived next door to a learned coxcomb [Harry Levin] to whom, in passing, I made the remark that you were the most learned man I had ever known or expected to know. The foolishness of making this passing remark became clear to me during the next six weeks, for I began to receive from my neighbor an intensive course in cultural history of the nineteenth century, then the eighteenth century, then the seventeenth century, concluding, I think, with an exposition of the usual curriculum of Italian universities in the fifteenth or sixteenth centuries, I can't remember which. In any case, by this time I had caught on: I made the same remark again and thus ended my neighbor's efforts to impress me.

I think I remember someone saying that you were in Vermont this year; if so, perhaps you may be coming to Boston, and if you do, I wish you would let me know.

Yours,
Delmore

TO R. P. BLACKMUR

[Cambridge]
January 22, 1943

Dear Richard,

I did not answer your last letter (with the Idea of a Literary Education in it), nor come to Princeton for reasons so complicated, intimate, and silly that if I put them in a letter, I would spend the next few days full of new anxiety feelings, these from shame at having said too much to my friends.

In my youth I thought that Life was Shakespearean, but it becomes more and more obvious to me that it is Dostoyevskian.

Doubtless you have seen a big German police dog or some strong dog trembling on a streetcar, terrified by every clang, hiss and skid; so it has been with me; and through this suffering I come to new knowledge, as Aeschylus says. A non-literary source! of one of Eliot's lines which is at the same time not one of his wife's hysterical remarks— becomes clear: "trembling at dusk" is obviously the trembling which begins at dusk before the first drink.

Many new lines have been added to my Xmas poem, "The Doggerel Beneath the Skun," [*sic*] and this is the second of the innovatory evasions of my twenty-ninth year, first to make endless notes; second to write couplets. I quote some lines which Helen may applaud, since they were applauded by Gertrude and Eileen, John Berryman's bride:[1]

> All poet's wives have rotten lives,
> Their husbands look at them like knives
>   (Poor Gertrude! poor Eileen!)
> Exactitude their livelihood
> And rhyme their only gratitude,
> Knife-throwers all, in vaudeville,
> They use their wives to prove their will—

I can't remember the rest of this passage now, but it was received with many recognitions and sighs.

I went into a bookstore and discovered going from book to book that I have a sensibility that can be violated by *any* idea; which puts me at the North Pole from H. James.

At present I am wasting some of my time in a profound brawl with Jay, as who is not?, and if it were not for my deep desire for a magazine as soon as the war ends, I would cut the cord that binds me to that spoiled child. But magazines, to be trite, do not grow on trees. However, if you see Harcourt, Brace, and you want to get a scout's commission, you might say to them that I would *try* to write a novel for them (they have asked me several times in the past), if they were willing to take a chance on a big advance. Never mind, if you don't feel like saying anything. //

What would you think of, for the fun of it, writing a play with me next summer, a short play, of an evening in Cambridge in the Eighties in which the brothers James try to elicit through innumerable dodges and subterfuges the reason why Henry Adams' wife killed herself? asking Adams many devious questions in their beautiful styles, while

Adams deliberately leads them on, somewhat to punish himself, and to tease them, with, at a key point, a veritable Jamesian moment when the ghost of Marion Adams actually puts in an appearance? and the whole thing ends in immense ambiguity which Edmund Wilson will proceed to destroy, explaining that it is all sex? Answer me that.

Yours always,
Delmore

1. Later Eileen Simpson who published her reminiscences about S, Blackmur, Berryman and others in *Poets in Their Youth* (1982).

TO R. P. BLACKMUR

[Cambridge]
January 28, 1943

Dear Richard,

I did call Princeton 1903 three times (something like 1903) and took the silence as Balaam's ass, for if I had come I would have talked too much, not that I would have said anything not already guessed, since you are one of the best guessers I ever saw, and my face is an open secret anyway. Philip's [Rahv] idea of my being in fine fettle is characteristic: when I start talking a mile a minute, he thinks I am in fine fettle.

Anyway, I will probably be coming to New York once every two months henceforward, and will come straight to Princeton next time, and when I start talking too much, let your eyes blaze at me as I have seen them do, and I will shut up.

I like your emblems very much, at the first reading and at the tenth, and everyone for whom poetry is daily bread and wine will like them too. But the common critic who wants everything on a silver platter will say of them what has been said of your verse before. I don't think it matters (like most, I have great courage for the book reviews of others), but when you use *valiancy* instead of some more familiar word for *courage*, you are mistaken if you think most book reviewers will look the word up in the dictionary; the same thing is true of *severalty*. However, it does not really matter, if you are willing to let your poems grow as you rightly said Stevens' did in the mind [...]

But wholly apart from these poems, which justify themselves, what I would like to know is why you don't draw more often not only on the knowledge and love of people I have seen and heard many times; not only on that, but on the unseen drama in their very scabs, which gives them tension and depth, and not a living action, [T. S. Eliot's] Sweeney shaving while his poor bedpal shakes the bed unsatisfied? or for that matter, Tessa's first husband stepping into the dish of ice cream hidden under the bed and thus summing up all possible marriages to Tessa?

I think maybe it is that helpless strength of yours, that overwhelming consciousness of the possibilities of meaning of single words, which if it continues will make you end up like Samson dragging the temple of the whole English language down on your head, in order to prove to yourself that you don't care what the Philistines and the Levins say.

Who am I, however, to tell you? especially since my sense of language is increased every time I read anything you write. And besides, I may be wrong, a thought strongly suggested to me when I read the courtier Arthur Mizener's *Kenyon* review a few days after I last wrote you about the diction as your fatal Cleopatra; for what Arthur says can't possibly be the truth, his life is dedicated to pleasing Major Tate, which must have been one reason why he made such a point of kicking John Berryman in the face.

I hear, by the way (since I am one of those who always hear everything) that you think I am paranoiac about Tate? This is at fourth hand, so that maybe it was Tate and not you who said it, but in any case, let me cite one example. He wrote me that *Shenandoah* was wonderful while he told everyone else he did not like it, as I learned the first year at Cummington (*after* I protested against the stupidity of his book of criticism). //

To turn to pleasant things, to turn back to the dish of Tessa's husband's, I was so haunted by your story that I wrote to Tessa suggesting that if we live a second time, I would like to be one of the first to step into her dish of ice cream, to which she replied, What flavor? to which I made the obvious reply, tutti-frutti! and intend to continue this discussion when next we meet.

I yearn to hear Helen's stories of the industrial life. Her story of her sister's entrance into a sorority was like a looking glass to me, I saw my own face there, for in my youth when I went to four different universities, God only knows why, I did not ever perceive that nobody liked Jews because not only was I not asked to join the Aryan fraternities, I was not asked to join the non-Aryan ones, mad as the mist and the snow.

Since this is a hundred years since, I thought maybe we ought to have a masquerade party in memory of James. Perhaps we could get Philip Horton to play Merton Densher, Gertrude would be here as *What Maisie Knew*, John Berryman could come as Roderick Hudson,

Harry Levin as Gilbert Osmond, Helen as the actress in *The Tragic Muse*, Edmund Wilson as Henrietta Stackpole, Eileen Berryman as Milly Theale simply because she has beautiful red hair, Tessa could be *The Spoils of Poynton*, I would be present as Edith Wharton, and you could come as R. P. Blackmur.

Yours always,
Delmore

P.S. One of the best poems is "Second Drawer" but I don't get *chartered ease* unless it is the desk they gave you for the Creative Arts Project at Princeton, which is obviously too private. Also the last line of "Wisp o' the Will" or rather the word *humiliation* sounds wrong to me as rhythm, unless there is elision.

TO JOHN CROWE RANSOM

20 Ellery St.
Cambridge, Mass.
February 11, 1943

Dear John:

I received your telegram this morning. I meant to write you before this to say that the combination of a succession of colds, many freshman themes and bluebooks to read, and my inevitable mid-winter staleness had kept me from writing the Kazin review, so that I would like to have it put off until your summer issue. I've accumulated ten cards of notes and want to do a thorough job because, as I think I said when I last wrote you, the very fact that Kazin is so good, in some ways, makes it important that in admitting his critical gifts, his whole point of view be attacked as sharply as possible. The burden of his attack on you, Winters, Burke, etc., appears to be that it is *infamous* to analyze the structure of a poem. Yet there is no sign in his chapter on criticism between the poles [in *On Native Grounds*] that he has read the poetry of which the new criticism is an elucidation. But more than that, it seems to me that the success of the book is a sign that it is part of the New Philistinism, which of course always grows up in times of crisis, but which seems especially dangerous when it has the authority of someone like Van Wyck Brooks behind it. It occurs to me then that perhaps you might find it possible to let me write an extra-long review—of the size of an article, but in your review type—in which I could show in detail how empty and how full of contradictions Kazin's point of view is. I don't have to have the extra space, but I think I would be more persuasive if I engaged in a detailed analysis. Yvor Winters' new book, *The Anatomy of Nonsense*, might be added to the review of Kazin, in order to round out the whole business.

In any case, I am sorry not to be prompt about getting the review to you, and I will certainly be on time for the issue after this next one, when I have fought my way through all the chores which teaching has thrust upon us this year.

Yours always,
Delmore

TO R. P. BLACKMUR

[Cambridge]
March 16, 1943

Dear Richard,

I do not really have to tell you, for you must know that your essay on Dostoyevsky is very good, not only good on the subject, but better still on guilt and love: "to love is to impose the most difficult of burdens": this and some of the other sentences have the force and lightning of great proverbs. But the news of your academic assurances makes me wish to say again that I hope you will not permit yourself to be defeated by your handsome minor successes.[1] Anyone who can see so much in such a book as *Crime and Punishment* might well write such another book.[2] //

Upon coming back to Cambridge, I found myself in the midst of an academic-comedy scandal which may well issue in my not having my job much longer. It is a beautiful story of the nature of an institution, but I will not try to tell it until I see how it comes out in the end. I am all innocence for once, as everyone admits, but that may not do much good.

And I found myself in one more slump of energy and feeling, and went to a much-commended doctor to discover that for years I have suffered from a profound endocrine imbalance, so that I must be with injections punctured like a dartboard six times a week, and take nine pills from day to night, from waking to the moment when I start to climb the peak from which I jump to sleep. The doctor declares that he will make a new man of me, a promise I think of with mixed feelings. To think that my exaltation and my boredom have both been supported, if not engendered as the doctor says, by my dark body! Will you tell Nela, who listened with much sympathy last summer to my many descriptions of emptiness and numbness.

Your "Language as Gesture" might not be the best thing to send right now to *P.R.*, for the other editors as you must know are not interested in essays of that kind of generality. If you like, I will start everything moving by writing to Philip Rahv and telling him to write you. But it might be better to await a later date, for I do not have a vote (everything is decided by ballot) until I permit my name to appear on the masthead, and in addition, with all your lectures, you will soon have several other essays about which there would be no question at all. There is also soon to be a Joyce issue, so that you might tie this prospect to one of your lectures. But let me know if you want [me] to write Philip.

As to your queries about Harcourt, Brace and my poem, the one has come to nothing but amiable sparring. [Frank] Morley was very pleasant, but seems to wish to be sure that I would write a masterpiece; and the poem has been delayed because Laughlin wished to ski for two months in Utah, but it should be out by the end of the month. I have a paperbound copy which Gertrude read, to announce when she finished, as I nearly fell down with pleasure, that she waited impatiently to see what the chorus had to say about the narrative. Since Gertrude maintains a studious silence about almost everything I write, this gave me the courage to look at it myself and to find, wherever I looked, looking with fear, that I was at least honest, honest in that everywhere I found an effort to state a perception. And it seemed to me too that poetic form, far from being a barrier, had actually lifted the perceptions from my mind into the open air. But I suppose I will go to the grave without knowing the truth about this book, since I do not know the truth about less complicated efforts, although years have passed.

I was sorry indeed not to see more of Helen, and I hope that next time she will not be so middle-class about going to sleep, although I know she had to get to work the next day.

I will seek to have "Survival Was His Hobby" inscribed on your tombstone, if you die before I do; if, as is more likely, you promise to see to it that "Metaphor Was His Salvation" is inscribed upon mine, should I put off the body of this darkness before you.

Yours always,
Delmore

P.S. Would you explain to the *Chimera* boys that I may have to delay my review of Stevens some more because of illness. All the little energy I have goes to teaching, and my mind won't work, especially after the injections.

156

1. According to Russell Frazer, Blackmur at this time had "a fair chance of being kept on at Princeton" (*A mingled Yarn*, p. 183).

2. Blackmur professed for years to be writing a full-length study of Dostoyevsky. However, all that surfaced were a handful of essays and some inspired seminars given at Princeton in the late 1940's and early 1950's.

TO R. P. BLACKMUR

[Cambridge]
April 6, 1943

Dear Richard,

I did not answer your last letter because I wanted to have a conclusion to the academic farce. But the conclusion may be delayed. Hence I had better tell you while the stupidity remains fresh in my mind. All of this is for the esteem you expressed for Harvard two letters back.

When I returned to Cambridge, Morrison told me that the Dean had appointed a committee to pass on my five-year appointment. This was curious because I had been told that the Dean as well as Morrison had written letters of recommendation already. The committee decided then to visit my classes. I objected strenuously in principle, because all other promotions in the English Department during my three years here had gone through without any visiting; and I also objected because I was in a frozen slump and bored my classes to tears.

Morrison persuaded me, however, and the committee began to visit. [James Buell] Munn, [Samuel Hazard] Cross, [Delmar] Leighton, [Robert S.] Hillyer and Howard Mumford Jones were the five judges. Munn came first and departed in pleasure and admiration. Then Cross sent his secretary, instead of coming himself. This was at Radcliffe, and I thought she must be some Radcliffe functionary. It was just luck that I found out who she was. I went to Morrison with much indignation, and then he, Hillyer as chairman of the committee, and the Dean began to apologize to me. Hillyer remarked that this kind of thing would drive him to drink, Morrison declared that there was only one man at Harvard who would behave in that way, and the Dean stated that he wished to apologize for Harvard, adding that he would ask Cross to apologize to me. Cross refused. I said I wanted an apology then, and the result was that Cross was fired from the committee.

Then Munn discovered that the essays, stories and poems I had written, which he had brought from his library, had disappeared, and he became very angry, asking me from time to time whether his collection was complete as different items were returned, one by one, by

Cross's secretary, who kept saying that she did not know where they were. Here, at this juncture, I was tempted to withdraw myself from the whole business, for the news arrived that everyone would have to teach full time. I told Morrison that I did not want the appointment, the terms of which permitted part-time teaching, after he declared to the whole composition staff that those who were not willing to teach full time ought to be prepared to be taken by the army. The visiting was resumed then, and my classes went off well, because the boys and girls knew something was going on, and then Morrison assured me that I might choose to teach as much or little as I wanted.

The committee then questioned me for an hour. They had all presumably read all my published work, but Jones asked me if I had ever written any short stories. Leighton declared that he knew nothing at all about literature, and it was obvious that one impression was that I was a Dadaist. It was decided to recommend me without reservation, but to suggest that these appointments ought not to be given to the kind of an author that I was. As matters stand now, I should get the contract, unless the Dean or one of the overseers should see a copy of my new book.

Is this not a pretty story of a great institution? But I wish you would not speak of it in Princeton. When it is all over, and if all goes well, I want to write a letter to the Dean, describing the whole process from the point of view of the profession of Letters.

Meanwhile they appear to have decided to let go Berryman, although they know he is an excellent teacher. If you hear of any place for him at Princeton—I know it is not likely right now—you might let me know. He is much improved by marriage, and he is really a good teacher.

Little else has occurred, except my becoming very thin as a result of many injections; and the interesting experience of feeling full of energy, but without any thoughts or language in my mind; more evidence of what I am unable to doubt, the unidentity despite much mixing of the body and the soul. //

It must be Karenin who is Harry Levin's prototype in *Anna Karenina*; or did you have another character [in mind]? It must be Karenin. I was sad to hear of Helen's sleeplessness, but not in the least surprised, for it belongs to our kind. With best regards to her and to Nela,

Yours always,
Delmore

158

TO MARK VAN DOREN

20 Ellery St.
Cambridge, Mass.
April 8, 1943

Dear Mark,

Your letter came the day after I had read your extremely fine poems in the *Kenyon Review*, and two weeks after Jay's fourth gratuitous declaration (the first one came on the eve of publication, when it was too late to do anything) that my book was no good at all. Hence you must know how welcome your expressions of interest and pleasure are. If I can please you, I will gladly waive Jay's good opinion.

Academic matters are in a state of profound disorder here. My own job hangs in the balance right now, after my classes have been visited, my writings read, and my teaching praised in the most superlative terms by the committee of five appointed to inspect me. I feel an indifference I do not understand about the outcome—hard to understand because I like teaching very much ever since I discovered the wonderful professional secret that the teacher learns much more than the students. He learns not only the conditions of absolute intelligibility and clarity, but also how much he knows. But this must be an old story to you.

John's stay here, however, is probably at an end, I am afraid, and this is especially a shame because he is such a good teacher. I know that because I know some of his boys, and the higher powers know it too, but it seems to make no difference to them. John throws his whole being into teaching in a way that no one else does, so far as I know, and his classes get an intense interest in composition, which is unusual because freshman composition is considered a penalty course, which the best students are permitted to forego. I am sure that if you are able to get him another job somewhere, you would certainly not only not be sorry, but very pleased by the results. But I know too how difficult it is now to get anyone a place anywhere.

Someone quoted the Talmud to me several weeks ago, under the impression apparently that I knew it well, so that in order not to be caught napping again, I took a volume of selections from the library, and amid much trash, protocol, and mere intellectual ingenuity, found this sentence all by itself without context or commentary: "The world is a wedding."[1] I have tried without success to figure what this means. At any rate, it suggests delightful variations, such as The world is a misalliance, a marriage of convenience, a royal mating, a shot-gun affair, and all the other kinds of marriages.

With best regards to Dorothy and to Charley and Johnny,

Yours always,
Delmore

1. S squirreled the phrase away and used it five years later for the title of his 1948 story collection, as well as for the story which lent its title to the book.

TO DWIGHT MACDONALD

[Cambridge]
April 8, 1943

Dear Dwight—
Everything is very difficult right now for me. My job hangs in the balance, my mind is empty, and I yearn to return to New York. While the higher powers are making up their minds about me, it would probably be best to keep my name from the masthead for one more issue—that is, until the July-August number. But I want very much to be an Editor and no matter how matters turn out here, I will play a more active part soon; for example, go after young authors I know through New Directions.

My essay on *The Waste Land* is giving me an enormous amount of difficulty, partly because of the theme, and partly because of "the profound endocrine imbalance" to correct which I visit a formidable doctor every day. //

I am very pleased that Rahv and Dupee like my book, but unhappy,— even a year after!—that it made so little impression with you. Perhaps Parts II & III will please you more, and if Nancy, that mysterious character, expresses interest and pleasure, my joy will overflow.

How is your book coming? Forgive me if I say that you ought not to permit minor successes and objectives to get in the way.

Yours always,
Delmore

TO GERTRUDE BUCKMAN[1]

[Cambridge]
May 1st, 1943

Dear Gertrude,
I had better restrict myself to a plain and flat recital and say nothing

of my feelings, so that I will continue to get your letters so full of cheer and light.

After you left, I went to buy myself a pair of shoes, to distract myself, and to the doctor, and back to meet Roslyn Brogue, fat and vain as a sultan, voluble with her many successes, which she bracketed in affirmations of abstract humility. She inquired frankly if she were to be asked ever again to come for a visit, and if she had done anything wrong. No, I replied.

I did not go to Wallace's fortieth birthday, but corrected more of the last papers of the year.

On Wednesday morning, as I foretold you, a telegram from Fairfield, Connecticut gave me to know that my mother was on her way and I was to meet her at the station. This act of grossness and gall destroyed all but one feeling in me. I did not go to meet her, but when she came, I said quickly that you were with your mother and I was going to the Cape the next day for the week-end. The evening passed in the most degrading recriminations. I learned that my suit was three sizes too big for me; that Kenneth regarded me as a crackpot and remarked how in last September's photograph I still wore one of his ties of 73 Washington Place; that I was miserly, the house unpleasing, and cold, for the fire had gone out, and the dining-room table disgraceful.

To my surprise, I hardened my heart against many descriptions of unhappiness and pain, which were mixed with the critical remarks, and in the morning managed to persuade her to go back to New York by resuming the twenty dollars a month. Her purpose in coming, she said, was to explain to me what "they" had done to her there, and what that girl had done to Kenneth—"he gets two cents for gum," "he is afraid of her," "everything is bought on the installment plan." Something has happened to you in the last nine months, she said to me, when I showed myself unmoved at all, except by the infant Harry's skin disease, with which he seems to have left the womb. //

But she left with a check for twenty dollars, given on the condition that she say no more of these things.

How appropriate, however, that she should come the day after your departure; how often Life has a literary design.

During the morning as I waited for the time to pass, and corrected more papers, Harry Thornton Moore [biographer of D. H. Lawrence] called, just back from England, Scotland, and Iceland; and in the evening after the catharsis of my mother's departure, I went with him to dinner at the Athens Olympia, and called George and Rusty [Eileen Berryman] too. He had many stories of the girls in England and the girls in Iceland, of Frieda Lawrence and Paulette Goddard; and his

Middle-Western Smithness, untouched by the war at all, was pleasant after my mother's discourse and my own anger.

Yesterday there was a cold rain all day and I drank gin neat with Sweeney late in the afternoon, saw the first review of *Genesis* in the *Advocate*, and sat with some of the sentences in a bar through the evening, for to the undergraduate I was pathetic, inadequate, too intellectual, and like Whitman. //

This house is full of your style and idiom, in the curtains drawn back each morning and in the arrangement of the dishes. Today is cold and sunny; the wind is blowing hard between the houses, and this is the first of May in New England.

I will match you letter for letter; how articulate you have become, with all your observations. What a pure job it is, to use the mind to look and to see, and for nothing else.

Very much,
Delmore

1. The Schwartzes had separated.

TO GERTRUDE BUCKMAN

[Cambridge
Spring 1943?]

Dear Gertrude,

// I miss you very much but grow a little more manual every day. It is probably good for my images. //

It is very cold. The sunshine hard, pale and clear.

Have they caught your mother at an early stage? Some say cancer comes from anger, in which case I should have it shortly. //

I wish you would look in on my mother for a half hour. What a scandal I will have if she hears of your presence and absence!

O Lord we are not worthy
but speak the word only.

You may recognize my early morning trains of association.

Letter from Ransom, asking me to write of but not abuse Winters, best regards to Gertrude. Conversation with H. Levin who asked about The Dark Lady of the Schwartzes! Ransom says I have been nominated to Breadloaf, will I accept?

// With helpless inept devotion,

Delmore

TO GERTRUDE BUCKMAN

[Cambridge
Spring 1943?]

Dear Gertrude,

You have not heard from me because I went to New York on Monday night and to Princeton on Tuesday, trying to get away from the boredom and emptiness here. I should have thought of your letters to your mother, but I did not, and after much thought I did not try to get you in New York because it seemed unlikely that you would want to see me so soon, as I see by your letter where you tell me not to call you. I came back last night, although I was going to stay longer, because I had to run away from New York and Princeton, everyone was too unhappy or dead to bear, and be with.

I suppose you must tell your father, but if you do, be sure that he promises to tell no one else. Philip lives on 10th St. and William on 9th, Fred is nearby, the Zolotows go back and forth, and on 8th Street you will certainly meet some of the boys all of the time. The only thing to say when you meet them is that you have just come to New York in order to visit your mother in New Jersey several times a week. I told them you were at Morristown when they asked for you, and Nancy took the address because she wanted to write to you. It might be best for you to pay a state or official visit to the Macdonalds and Phillipses, to maintain the deception. Besides, you will be lonely and it is better to see them than to be at the mercy of the abysses of loneliness, as you know.

// Dwight liked your review very much, and Richard liked it very much, but felt that there was not enough of the lenience in you and you were a woman with a woman with Kay Boyle. But it reads very well, it reads as if you had written literary criticism for ten years. I will send the copies today.

I was told by Dwight no sooner had I crossed the doorstep that Paul Goodman was going to attack *Genesis*, and from William I heard that Frank Jones, which might as well be Clement Greenberg, would review it for *The Nation*,[1] and that there had been a row at *Time* about reviewing it at all. Matthiessen had not written his review, although Philip asked for it several times, and Richard had not written his, and spoke of putting it off, and when I looked dismayed, consoled me by a description of how Allen Tate had praised the book. Meanwhile Jay has written all over to say that he does not like the book, but thinks it deserves a serious review.

My last classes ended with surprising delightful prolonged applause, especially from the girls, and made me think I had perhaps not been as poor a teacher this year as I supposed. I boarded the train with Gogol's *Dead Souls*, determined hereafter to read a masterpiece on each trip, and when an RAF officer sat next to me after Providence, and seemed to want to hold a conversation, I was divided in half by Gogol delightful [*sic*] and the feeling that I ought as a matter of conscience to hear what this instance of a great historical reality had to say. But Gogol was too profoundly farcical and I let the great historical reality go.

Dwight was speechless with a sore throat and nothing if not annoying, which made me go to Princeton where Richard and Nela were in their own ways annoying, Richard with his class which I went to and with his detailed activities, Nela with her stories of Richard, Helen, and Nela. But I stayed for two days and came back with Nela who had to come to see Christine, and then went to the Wilsons, asked there because I had been answering Dwight's phone during his speechlessness, to find Lionel Abel, Dawn Powell, and Rolfe Humphries there, but also [Roberto] Matta [Echaurren] the painter, an effervescent soul who had brought Lionel, and Lionel's girl friend, and his own wife pregnant and from Ohio. Matta wanted all to take off their clothes. This would be truth and consequences, he declared. No one spoke to Lionel, because he had not been asked to come, and finally I spoke with him and heard him prove that Sidney Hook believed in God. Consequently the next day Lionel went about to tell everyone what a fine fellow I was. Wilson was very attentive to me for several hours and called me Mr. Schwartz when I came in, Schwartz after the second highball, Delmore after the fifth, and Mr. Schwartz once more when we arrived at the eighth refreshing. Now I will never know what would have happened at the tenth and twelfth, although I was tempted to stay just to find out. //

The next night there was a foolish party at William's, and Diana Trilling asked me if I thought I looked like her? to which I said after a stunned silence, it is very kind of you to ask me. Later William and I tried to decide what it could possibly have meant, and we went to see Meyer Schapiro and asked him, and he had several interpretations, but he was not sure. He looked worn out and old, and he said foolish things, and he told Philip Rahv that he did not know what he was harping about as they discussed the war. He had just written a piece for the magazine entitled "The Nerve of Sidney Hook," making Hook look like a fool and maintaining that if Hitler won the war, there would nevertheless be the possibility of a revolution in Europe.

But I see that this must sound as if it were a happy trip, but it was not. I felt immense depression to see everyone paralyzed, unable to go forward with their work, not different or better than in 1938, and having nothing to say or foolish things to say, most of all Schapiro who lost his temper with Philip as if he were Dwight, and reported himself unable to read *The Ambassadors* from beginning to end, and remarked that Joyce hated the English language, part of a typical theory that only an Irishman could have written *Finnegans Wake.*

Your little pictures make me remember how you were beautiful then as you are now.

Except for your letters, there was no mail that was interesting when I came back last night. //

I dreamed about your room last night, and I did not like the way it looked. But in your letter it sounds like a fine room, and the fireplace must please you.

I will write you more and more, but I went to get this off right now to end this silence and waiting, which I should have thought of, except that I did not think of your difficulty with your father. If my mother hears anything, she will come here again and refuse to go, and maintain that she wants to take care of me, and then there will really be a scene.

Very much,
Delmore

1. It was an enthusiastic review; Jones echoed Eliot's description of Pound's *Mauberley* by praising *Genesis* as "a positive document of sensibility."

TO GERTRUDE BUCKMAN

[Cambridge]
May 11, 1943

Dear Gertrude,

I feel guilty about making you wonder about my silence. It must have spoiled your pleasure in your job, which sounds like a very good job, although I can't make out just what it is you are to do, and I hope you do not permit it to keep you from trying to get reviews to write and trying to write short stories.[1]

Morrison wrote me a note to say that all was favorable and by Commencement I would know for certain, and there was no reason to doubt the outcome. He wanted me to know that the appointment was a personal tribute, extraordinary in wartime, important by "local conventions," however it might seem to me measured by "the standards of the universe and society." I went to thank him for the note yesterday and brought up the question of deferment obliquely. [...] but since the University will only ask for my deferment if I am teaching the army or navy, I think I will be cautious and teach one of them, although it means teaching six times a week through the Cambridge summer.

Sunday and yesterday passed like a patient train ride. I have not seen anyone since I came back, although I spoke with Mark and John on the phone. No, that is not right, I saw Linscott[2] and it seemed from what he did not say that my chances are really not very good, for he said that he liked my poem in a way that meant that he did not like it very much. But I do not think that this is very important right now, for the idea of writing a novel does not quicken my mind at all. .

Yesterday I bought a dozen oranges for forty-five cents and brought back a suit from the tailor's. Both activities gave me a feeling of efficiency. Today I will go to get my shoes from the shoemaker's and perhaps buy a box of cereal.

Of my more important feelings, I must not say anything now.

In Princeton, Richard and I made much of Nela's job, driving a truck with flowers each Saturday, and going from door to door. She was enraged by our view of this as pure farce, but somewhat appeased when I pointed out the link with Mother's Day, and thus not to be taken seriously. Sage has diminished somehow, he is lacking in verve and even in hauteur, but Susie's eyes are miraculous;[3] they look as if she were hiding something—it is hard to find the expression—they look like innocence and evil at the same time.

But now I must try to make something of today, although to write to you is easier and pleasanter by far; if I wait my energy will fade as it does, as you know.

Very much
Delmore

1. After leaving Cambridge, Gertrude held various jobs in New York; they included acting as secretary to Kurt Wolff at Pantheon publishers, working for the Bollingen Foundation, and serving as fiction editor of *Collier's* magazine.
2. Robert Linscott, editor at Random House.
3. Sage and Susie Walcott, children of John and Nela.

TO GERTRUDE BUCKMAN

[Cambridge]
May 12, 1943

[No salutation.]

Your letter lifted me more than the coffee this morning. I do not think you know how well you have begun to write and how you are getting your own unique sensibility into language more and more.

Can it be that you are a nurse? How can this be? Where is your certificate? I like your doctors very much as characters in a work of fiction; perhaps you have found yourself a real subject, especially with your pathological interest in illness.

It has been raining without conviction since Monday night in Cambridge, and I broke the wooden stem of the umbrella I gained at the Signet;[1] broken as I tried to open it going through the hall. Roslyn Brogue wanted to come to say goodbye before she left Cambridge, and I put her off with one of the most obvious lies of an old liar.

To repeat once more Ivan Karamozov's profound remark, "I am a scoundrel," the more because I know and love goodness.

You are wrong in your own essential way about Jean Garrigue's postcard. You remember we lived at the house by the Charles when I last saw her, and she does not know who Gertrude Buckman is. Only God, dear sister...She must have chosen to write you because of an interest in your stories.

Last night I had the most literary of dreams, first in the first sleep I dined with Horace Gregory and Kenneth Fearing, and marvelled at Fearing's beautiful tweed suit, which I discussed with Gregory, and woke pleased to note that at least in dreams I have a perception of physical detail which I cannot even think of when I think of the writing of fiction. And then in the second sleep, I was in Harry's [Levin] house and tore off the vulgar wallpaper in his hallway for a reason I cannot remember, but there was a good reason, as Harry said when I volunteered to put it back again. He had brought me in to show me his paperbound copy of T. S. Eliot's *Complete Collected Poems* (I looked twice at the *Complete*), he wanted me to see that Eliot had written a sentence to him, and I read it to see that it was merely a note on the derivation of one of the lines, and turning the pages wondered that the book was very thick and full of prose and stopped at a chapter heading which said in large type "R. P. Blackmur in an Airplane," and then asked Harry how much it cost to send a book to England, thinking that perhaps Eliot would send me a copy too.

The night before, I dreamed of finding dimes and quarters going downhill in a dump heap with my mother. We were both very pleased. It was a most obscene dream, if Freud is right.

John is sick and there is no job for him anywhere, unless Richard can get him one. He promised to try at Princeton.

The Civil War on *Partisan Review* continues in this morning's mail, and I am the crucial vote, but something is going to happen if this

continues. I don't think I told you that I quarrelled seriously and trivially with Dwight before I left. The true cause was Dwight's resentment of my long afternoons with Phillip and William, and my pleasure that Tunis and Bizerte had been taken, which Dwight interpreted as support of the war.
[Rest of the letter lost.]

1. An undergraduate club at Harvard for aspiring poets; the Secretary gave minutes of the previous meeting in rhyme.

TO GERTRUDE BUCKMAN

[Cambridge]
May 16, 1943

Dear Gertrude,

Solitude has been my bread and wine for the past seven days, so that there is not much to tell you, except that each new stair or step down brings me new kinds of feelings.

However, in the intermissions Howard Blake, Sonny [composer Harold Shapero], John, and Rusty, Wallace and George and Margery [Palmer] have appeared, all more and more unwrapping the endless folds of their natures, for Howard Blake has applied to be an announcer for WEEI, obviously his station in eternity, Sonny has declared his belief in God, it is impossible that there is no God he feels, Rusty justly entitles John "Laughing Boy," Margery tries very hard to be the meek one who is permitted to stay, George finds new moments in preciosity, and Wallace is pleased to hear that nothing can be well for him until Rose is well.

From Sonny I gained a description of my grossness, his word and not the word he should have had, but nevertheless with the look of simple and obstreperous truth, like a big boulder or a cow on a railroad track, not to be passed by without stopping. It is as if I wore blinders, he says, and to be kind, names it Beethovenish, and when I asked him as if idly if it was with you that he had seen this, his two instances were an exact description of a boor of the feelings. How much you have to forgive me—how much I cannot forgive in myself, nor feel able to alter.

If you had married some bon vivant of the heart, your charm and beauty might have been like a new school of lyric poetry. And the more I think of it, the more I see my wrongness, for no one may *ask* from anyone, what I wanted, and asked for.

But it is also wrong to speak of these things and in this way and now.

One of the benefits of solitude is that it brings back the powers of memory.

I have been trying all week to write a review of Eliot's new poems. Linscott wrote me to say that the contest has been postponed until November and reduced to one prize, which is the end of that for me. And I had a letter from Maurice [Zolotow] to announce his purchase and joyous reading of Book One, but chiefly the narrative. This Sunday is the ninth one since the book appeared, so that my faint hope that this poem would actually get attention is more faint than ever. But I think that I mind less than if this were four years ago.

// I wish very much that I did not know that Kenneth had said that I was a crackpot, not that I am, but clearly that is what I am to him.

For you always,
Delmore

TO GERTRUDE BUCKMAN

[Cambridge]
May 19, 1943

Dear Gertrude,

Much of one more wasted morning has passed, and again the one thing I find myself able to do is to write to you. //

Your Sunday was unlike mine in that I had no desire to see anyone, and I have had none since you left. To be alone, even to do nothing, satisfies me that I am not running away from my feelings or the possibility of effort.

You are right, we must forgive each other, and remember the fact established by ten years that we made no life for each other, nor any happiness. //

Practical matters go well enough for me. I make my own breakfasts and lunches, and get a mild satisfaction from completing an activity.

Again, you are wrong about Jean Garrigue; if you knew her, you would know that she would not try to please me in that way, or whatever it is you think she had in mind. //

The extraordinary beauty of your voice is a plain fact. Why don't you ask for an audition somewhere?

After some thought, I decided to stop going to the doctor, at least for a time. Eighty dollars a month, which is what it must come to when the druggist's bill is counted, makes this seem merely an expensive experiment, and that is what he is known for, experiment for its own sake.

The chapter in *The Brothers Karamozov* is important to help define Ivan's character as an intellectual and his moral failure, which shows itself most of all when he makes his departure at the height of the conflict between Dmitri and the father.

School does not begin until July, but I won't come to New York before then. I can be empty and benumbed here as well as there, and if I am not, I don't want to waste a lucid period.

Your doctor was only lucky in his guess about your age. You do not look twenty-two, or rather one does not think at all of your age. The sadness of seeing the withdrawing attractiveness in Eleanor Clark and Mary McCarthy, mostly in a flattening out of their features, makes me think that the absence of sexual desire is at least part of your appearance of being fixed as a young girl.

Dan Aaron [Harvard professor] was here yesterday afternoon to ask me if I might like a job at Smith the year after next. I tried without success to shift the chance to John. Apparently, if I wished to, I might become a veritable professor. But this is but one more elaborate way of evading myself.

And this letter is another, and I must stop.

To you, too much,
Delmore

TO GERTRUDE BUCKMAN

[Cambridge]
May 24, 1943

Dear Gertrude,

// But to continue with the *longeurs* and the blankness of my solitude, it is a kind of deafness, pianos are struck, trumpets are puffed, violins are crossed and recrossed, and I hear nothing, knowing there is something to hear, seeing it. Meanwhile I still feel in myself some not-to-be-named destiny, and this illusion will not go no more than my gross need for affection which makes me cut off one by one those who come near me and violate it, the whole train having the same kind of form each time, as when I gave Lincoln [Kirstein] thirty-five dollars and thus made him avoid me.

// It is not astonishing that your father was not thunderstruck, we have always been a perplexity to him, but what did he say, what did he ask and what did you answer?

For four full weeks I have not been to the pictures, not since the last night with you, and now I have no desire to go, and this has not been like other times full of something else, so that the abstinence is something new, not abstinence but indifference.

For the cruel and the just, what will equal the ascent of the two shares my mother gave me, now 14? She must turn to the financial page each day to see the growth of her error. So too when I crossed Quincy Street, the stock Italian played his barrel organ as the officers-to-be marched in formation and shouted emphasis with one-two-three-fours's, yet were unable to keep from their step the music's influence, which made me give the musician a nickel as one profoundly against war.

Last night I dreamed that my grandmother quarreled in a store because she wanted to be paid more for a holla bread; and after that I dug two graves for something concealed and valuable, while she directed me, making me pleased with the detail and the invention, but unable to conceive what fears and memories seek to sign to me. This, and the hair growing on my face and the brown stains increasing on my neck make me see how much more I am than my conscious mind, what unknown sources well up. But whatever the moreness and the mystery, I am to you always, and to you only, with my heavy-lemon face, and my cannonball eyes.

Too much,
Delmore

TO R. P. BLACKMUR

[Cambridge]
May 25, 1943

Dear Richard,

// Yesterday I read through the second volume of *The Golden Bowl*, depending on my memory of the first volume. This may explain my growing sense as I went forward of the cruelty of Adam and Maggie, the cruelty of the screw in Maggie's forcing the end, the metaphors of the cage in which Charlotte and then the Prince are seen, and "the silken halter" in which Charlotte is taken back to America, and Maggie's view of the Prince and Charlotte as the last of the art objects bought by Adam in Europe made me suppose that the evil of the father and the daughter was perhaps intended. And yet if it is, is not the irony of Maggie's triumph of possession too faint? First she possesses him because she is as he says "deep" and has forced him to see her clever-ness. Perhaps I am too much a character from the *Old Testament*, but

I find the final justice absent. If it is ambiguity, it is not the right ambiguity at the end of *The Wings of the Dove.*

Yours,
Delmore

TO GERTRUDE BUCKMAN

[Cambridge]
June 3, 1943

[No salutation.]

// My contract has not come through yet, although it was due last week, and the Draft Board has started with me, sending me for the first brief inspection to a local doctor who placed me in tentative 1A, but said, when I showed him Sieve's[1] description of my condition, that at the induction center I might or I might not be rejected. I had no intention of letting it get that far, if I can, and I spoke to Morrison right after that, getting [him] just before he left for Vermont and he said that the University would ask for my deferment but only if I took two military classes. I consented although it means three classes to teach, but I might be looked on differently if it were known that I did not have to support you, and I would probably not get a class at Radcliffe, which is so much less work. None of these things are very likely to get in my way, but I think it would be best, if it is not too much trouble to you, to be prudent. When the contract comes through, as it should unless something very unlikely has occurred, and then the Draft Board sends me an official deferment, then there will be no reason for silence on your part. I prefer to say nothing myself until it is unavoidable.

// Paul's review was in *The New Leader* some time ago, and Philip has just written to say that perhaps he ought not to reply, for Paul speaks of making a rejoinder with even more calumny.[2] I told Philip to go ahead. Meanwhile he is coming here for a visit and to see Houghton Mifflin and I suppose I will have to hear more about the review.

Thanks very much for the tablets. All of them have come and they will be a saving because the price of the sleeping tablets has gone up much like my shares, now 18.

After two false starts, I broke through my idleness with an enormous flow to find myself before I really knew with an endless subject which responded to every movement of my mind. I was upset and today I am again because I can't make this a short novel in which I might hold myself back and see how far concentration would get me, concentration and the sense of being on top of the whole thing. But it is no use, I am carried forward by a headlong rush which I don't foresee and which means, I think, that the subject in me writes, running like a wild horse, and not my will, and which is always a good sign, for it is the knowledge we do not know we have which is most worth bringing into the light. The title, for the purposes of composition at least, is *A History of the Boys and Girls*, and the sadness is that I had this in me for at least five years, but was stopped by the imagined difficulty that I had to write about myself in order to write about the boys and the girls. This is for you to think about too, for so many of the blocks are imagined.

Meanwhile I have been reading a great deal of the time in the way I did once, now that I see no one, and do not do anything about the coarse necessity, and do not go to the pictures, and *Finnegans Wake* is for the first time lucid and interesting, but much more than that, Bergson, whom I should have known years ago, if not foolishly fashionable in my ideas about authors. What he found out about memory is what excites me most. He showed that memory could not be localized in the brain because some with aphasia had no brain injury, some with brain injuries had no aphasia, and some who had had lesions of the brain recovered full memory with the growth of new tissue. This seems to mean that memory is not physical at all, but merely acts through the body, and it is thus an experimental proof or help to proof of the immortal soul. My own devotion to memory you know, and yet I had never before made this explicit connection with the immortal soul, and this all becomes more important to me because of Bergson's linking of memory and freedom of the will, but I have not yet gone far enough to see what this comes to. Meanwhile I cultivate my memory which rises up as never before. //

Too much,
Delmore

---

1. Dr. Benjamin Sieve, Commonwealth Avenue physician, who treated S for his "glandular" malady. Dr. Sieve later committed suicide.

2. Paul Goodman's review of *Genesis* referred to the book as a "combination of ineptitude and earnestness," written with a "calamitous lack of language, inaccurate learning," and other weaknesses.

TO ALLEN TATE

[Cambridge]
June 11, 1943

Dear Allen:

The announcement of your new appointment[1] was a very pleasant thing to see, and it made me think that perhaps I might have the liberty of asking you if you might not know of some job for John Berryman. He has been let out here by the higher powers (although they know and have affirmed his excellence as a teacher), because the war makes fewer men necessary, and for the same reason he has found it impossible to get a place elsewhere, even with Mark's help at Columbia. Since his marriage last autumn, he is much improved in the ways in which he used to be difficult, and I think you would be glad to have him about, as well as competent and responsible in whatever he did. I hope this won't seem a pressing forward on you just as you took on your new job.

With best regards to Caroline,
Yours sincerely,
Delmore

1. To the Chair of Poetry in the Library of Congress.

TO GERTRUDE BUCKMAN

[Cambridge]
June 12, 1943

Dear Gertrude,

This has been a difficult week, but all seems to have come out fairly, except that I have not been able to [...] tie your boxes. I was classified in 1A and this led to much commotion, for there was a story that the Draft Board would refuse the University's requests for deferments. But then I went after the powers and authorities and today I am in 2B and my five-year appointment has come, and it looks as if my job will be more comfortable than it seemed. No one can understand the details, but if I understand them, then all members of the faculty are to get one term's vacation in every four. There are only three terms in each year, but this only makes the arrangement complicated, and the vacation of four months' duration. My deferment lasts only until December, so that I may not be able to stop until next summer, to keep the deferment, but that is better than any other prospect if I were elsewhere. Not only that, a full schedule is now defined as teaching seven classes in the three terms for which the salary is thirty-seven hundred dollars a year, plus an increase to pay the income [tax], plus the amount the university pays for an insurance [policy], which comes to a pretty penny in five years. This will give me more money to spend than ever before, not that I have any longer any need of more money. //

The external things have taken too much time and I have not gone forward with my novel as I should, but the difficulty is the kind which is best of all, the difficulty of having too much in the subject and being dumbfounded by the richness and unable to respond with a careful and pleasing form, and having the beginning of new poems come to me when I was in the midst of prose fiction.

I saw [Donald] Davidson's review and thought it good enough, although John and George, who are now cronies, were indignant, and George wrote a precious, protestant letter. Then there was Louise Bogan's new meanness[1] and profound [Richard] Eberhart in this week's *New Republic*, oracular but good enough too.

At the Weismillers,[2] Francis [Fergusson] wanted to know when you were coming back, and [was] emphatic when signifying surprise, and then [Andrews] Wanning [Harvard colleague] who came late from just having had a son wanted to know where you were and Ruth called to ask us to dinner and then asked how long you have been gone? The truth appears to be coming through like the slow morning light, but until school begins, I won't make it official. Hillyer and his wife are now no longer one, which will ease whatever shock occurs.

George the other night wanted me to help him decide between Phoebe and Marjorie,[3] but I replied that I admired both and felt that one ought not to marry unless one felt that one had to marry, and George said he ought not to ask me for I had just lost the most charming creature he had ever known.

John is going to New York next week to try to get a job and that probably means that he won't come back, except to move his books, for Eileen will go too when her vacation begins, so that I keep coming back to [*sic*], they are all gone into the world of the unfit, of the night, and I alone sit lingering here, where many a party rose with the wine and the laughter.

Wallace and Rose were very interesting one night when we returned from a dinner party of George's, most Georgian, and in the subway Wallace held Rose's hand and she looked as if the held hand had turned to stone.

I wish very much that you were able to write me of some kind of pleasure or satisfaction.

[Unsigned.]

1. Bogan never liked S's poetry. Her review of his first collection, in *The Nation*, ridiculed what she thought of as his "modernist" pose, and she thought he borrowed too heavily from current literary myths.

2. Harvard colleague Edward Weismiller and his wife.

3. Eventually he married Phoebe, but not until after marrying Marcia and Marjorie first.

TO JAMES LAUGHLIN

[Cambridge]
June 12, 1943

Dear Jay,

Here is a suitable quotation from profound Eberhart to add to the ones I sent you last Sunday:

Genesis represents a triumph and control over time and events, in their inexhaustible meanings, the triumph of an elaborate plan. There is such a freshness of perception, such understanding of childhood, such a cohesion and order in the writing, and indeed such splendid areas of poetic feeling that one acknowledges the satisfaction of a harmonious work of art.

One good ad in the *Times* on Sunday, where I will be writing reviews soon, will repay the expense.

I want you to send me a contract for my next book. My novel is finished, but it is a big thing, it will take time to get ready to print by whoever I give it to, and I want to let it cool off, anyway. The book I want a contract for will have five stories, one hundred pages in all, and an equal number of pages of verse. You have already seen three of the stories, "America! America!", "The Commencement Day Address" (but in a new version), and "The Statues"; one of the others is going to be printed by *Partisan Review* and another one will be in *Best American Short Stories 1942*. The poems are a selection from the hundreds written during the past five years, many about America, so that I think a good title would be, *America, America!* Will you write a contract right off, binding yourself to publish the volume by April 1944?[1] I don't want to have the Matthiessen business occur again, and if you don't want it, I intend to get another publisher for it right now, but in that case I will give you my novel and whether you want it or not, the terms of my contract will have been fulfilled. I don't intend to print the second and third books of *Genesis* until the war and the war books subside. Send me the contract immediately, or a waiver, for I am free of school now for the last time in the next six months, and this is the only time I can go to New York with the manuscript.

Yours,
Delmore

1. The book was not published, though the stories later became part of *The World Is a Wedding*.

TO GERTRUDE BUCKMAN

[Cambridge]
June 22, 1943

Dear Gertrude,

Your news and reports were pleasant especially together with John's report that you were very witty and very gay. I told John of your departure because he wanted to get you in New York and that was a way of forestalling him. You can break the news as you like now, although I intend to say nothing to most for a time. //

I like Rose more and more, she is really one of the goodest pesons, except to her husband, and as for joyous Jeremy,[1] he becomes more of an infatuation to me, and I am afraid that the unborn Shenandoah, if he ever arrives to this difficult world so beautiful and interesting, will find that his father has given his heart away. Rose was much pleased by your letter and she speaks of how disappointed she is not to have you here, and she really feels that.

If you see the *Partisan Review* boys soon, it might be a help to tell them the news, for Philip speaks of coming here next week and I want him to know how little comfort he will have. The house becomes more a pen every day, for I can't get a servant, not by any effort. Mrs. Roberts has gone to an all-day job.

At the Athens-Olympia [Boston restaurant] I am not recognized, I am known as Mr. Palmer's friend. At George's I heard beautiful catches by Purcell,

> I gave her cakes and I gave her ale,
> I gave her sack and sherry,
> I kissed her once and I kissed her twice,
> And we were wondrous merry,

and also a lyric which began, "I love and I must."

I have a summer cold in the very dead of summer to add to my new disorder of the skin.

Sonny on the telephone remarked, to say that my voice seemed to show good health, "You seem equivocal"!

I was much tempted to a kitten left at Rose's by Marcia whom John Bovey[2] is actually marrying, much to George's pleasure, for he seems like a father whose daughter is marrying well. The kitten was like one *persona* of your infinite variety and was helpless to keep Jeremy from stepping on her back. But I decided to be sensible, thinking of how difficult it would be and how many nuisances, when I wanted to go to New York.

In honor and recognition of accident, I have composed a brief will so that all that I have will be yours if some Massachusetts car succeeds at last. This is my true wish and will.

It may be that we will be lucky, the army may not come until September.

The other day, I took your picture to place it in the small study,

> I took her picture down,
> The *Jacob* plant died,
> *Dear heart, how like you this?*
> My double cried.
> *Let Nature take no part!*
> Shouted my trembling heart.

One thing I mean to get, as soon as I can, and that is that we should live in the same city, so that each week I will see you, and then all of your goodness, which really existed, will not be stopped, and perhaps this will be the year after this year, for I mean to return to Brooklyn where my dark body began and to stay on the tree-shaded street with the brownstone house, backyard, English breakfast room, and period quality.

Kann nicht anders,
Delmore

P.S. Your trunk and suitcase were taken by Railway Express today. If you come upon the Zevros book, please buy it for me, and also Joyce's record of *Anna Livia Plurabelle*. I will send you a check when I know how much they cost. The gramophone shop must have the Joyce record.

The editor of *Poetry* [Peter DeVries] has written a poem about reading *Genesis* and it is in the June issue.

1. Young son of Rose and Wallace Dickson, in whom S took special delight. He quoted Jeremy to his classes at Harvard.

2. John Bovey, a writer, married Marsha Palmer, George's first wife.

TO GERTRUDE BUCKMAN

[Cambridge]
June 27, 1943

Dear Gertrude,

// Rose, who has virtually adopted me, has arranged to have her girl come here every week, and that makes the house orderly enough. I've been to the Dicksons twice for dinner this week, partly because you asked her to drag me out of my cell. Last night Elizabeth [Dicksons' daughter] inquired, "Why doesn't Gertrude come?" and I said I did not know and she said then to tell you she wanted to see you. Meanwhile Jeremy bounced up and down in his bed like the infant Dionysus, pleased to show his private parts. // George announced as if from a great distance that he supposed that he was going to marry Marjorie this summer. Neither Rose nor I said anything for the moment, although we were expected to, and then I said that Wallace ought to give the bridegroom away—Wallace had gone to sleep by then—and George replied that Wallace was not to come to the wedding, for he did not approve of this marriage, Rose quickly denied this and said, "George Palmer, you will certainly be a doting parent," and when George expressed horror, she wished him twins. //

I dreamed one night that I sat in a big kitchen and waited, my hands on the linoleum of the kitchen table, for you to get through having a child. The kitchen was full of other new fathers, but I was more than any of them afraid. When I went into the bedroom to see you, there was the child who looked just like you, a big girl of five, whom I did not like because she was so big.

In the *Book of Common Prayer*, I found the old version of the wondrous marriage solemnization, and in the old version "to love and to cherish" is "to buxom and honour at bed and at bort," though the Victorian commentator explains that "buxom" means "obey" and "honour," "be gentle," as in "debonair."

Jay has sent me a check for three hundred dollars, for what should be my next book, *America, America!*, five stories and my new poems, which I think you will like, all under the title of *The World Is a Wedding*. Jay is now seven hundred dollars gone with me. When this reaches a thousand I will be tempted to depart, for apparently others will print the second and third books of *Genesis* willingly.

Tessa wrote a most Tessaesque letter, directed to me to tell me that I was a great poet, and with love to you, and sadness because Philip soon goes to England for the rest of the war.

It was helpful to get news about some of the boys and girls and I wish you would tell me more and especially what you remember about Ruth and Adrienne.[1] The narrative and the method is such, as you will see, that it won't keep you from telling the story yourself. I think you will be delighted with yourself as Wilhelmina or Billy. It is an enchantment to look for the right names, [Julian] Breene [N.Y.U. friend] as Otto Taylor, Red [Robert Penn Warren] as Bertram Mims, Paul as Rudyard Beil, Eugene as Ferdinand, Arnold Canel [member of Goodman's circle] as Francis Felt, Sarson as Basil, and myself this time as Richmond Rose, and my mother as Aunt Leah, not to speak of Professors Long, McKenna, and Suss.

I wish more and more that this might be a short book, but the subject does not exist like that for me, it is the slow change, degradation, and defeat which is more important and which can't come as straightforward drama, although I think I've overcome my fear of the scene with dialogue, and really enjoy it very much.

With John [Berryman], whom as you see, has his really good qualities, and with Philip [Rahv], I should think you would not have too much difficulty in finding yourself in the midst of much variety of a social life, as much or as little as you like; but especially with Philip you ought to be able to see the kind of persons you are most likely to be interested in and with Dwight and Nancy.

Too much,
Delmore

1. Adrienne Koch, sister of S's N.Y.U. friend Sigmund Koch.

TO JOHN BERRYMAN

[Cambridge]
Tuesday, June 29, 1943

Dear John,

This is just hurriedly to say that the State Dept. called me to ask about you and asked me among other things if you were a good loyal American, and I said, O yes, he is a descendant of Ethan Allen and shifted with great quickness to your fluency in French and at acquiring languages, which is one of the things I know they are interested in and which this Mr. Norris was interested in very much, as well as in your health and why you had not been conscripted, to which I replied (the idea is to see how long this sentence can continue) that you seem to suffer from the colds of New England, making Norris comment with chuckling, "Don't we all?" but the main point is this, you had better keep your pamphlet [*Poems*] out of sight, for it does not seem to show you as a good loyal American.[1]

The fact that they are making inquiries must be a good sign. With the best of luck, and my best to Eileen,

Yours always,
Delmore

1. Berryman had applied for a job with the State Department that summer, after Harvard did not reappoint him.

TO GERTRUDE BUCKMAN

[Cambridge]
July 2, 1943

[No salutation.]

That I am equable is perhaps maybe and I hope an improvement, long-delayed in my character, for it was just the other day that I denied myself an opportunity to punish Louise Bogan and Horace Gregory, whose review of my book is the worst I have ever had; not that the temptation will not recur. //

I was unable to be specific about the effect of the Army's delay because I did not then know. Now I know. The Navy is here and I must teach two Navy classes and two Radcliffe classes, to justify the deferment the University gave me. This means teaching on every day but Sunday and Monday for the next sixteen weeks, beginning in the middle of next week. And the likelihood that I would be rejected by the Army makes me wish there were a way to get definite word, but this is not possible before classes begin.

The one note of promise is that Morrison told me that the grand-daughter of Sigmund Freud is to be one of the students. She is probably neurotic. I have gone all over to make this remark which does not seem comical to anyone but me. However, this completes for me, that gratification of the snob and historical sense which has been provided, the brother of T. S. Eliot, the granddaughter of Melville, the grandson of John Singer Sargent, the descendant of Aaron Burr, the nephew of Christy Mathewson, the granddaughter of Grandgent, the descen-

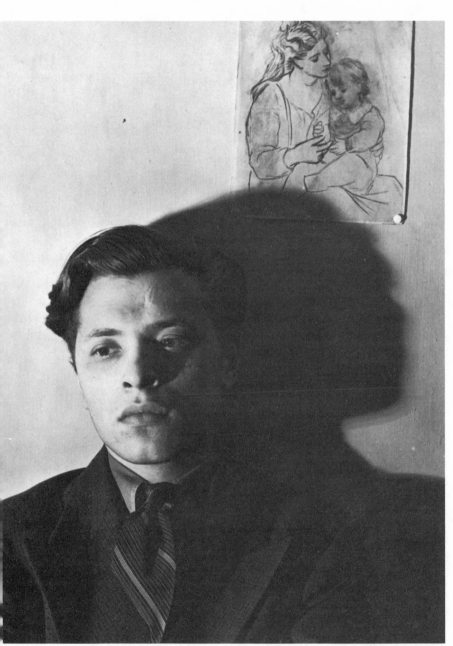

Portrait study made in 1938, shortly after publication of first book.

On Ellery Street, Cambridge, in the 1940's.

Circa 1949.

Photo by Wallace Dickson/Courtesy of Rose Dickson

With Gertrude Buckman, 1943.

Elizabeth Pollet at the farmhouse in Baptistown, New Jersey, in the 1950's.

Photo by Rollie McKenna
R. P. Blackmur in his Princeton office, circa 1951.

With Randall Jarrell at the Library of Congress, 1958.

Courtesy of the Library of Congress

Tuesday

Dear Richard —

I am at the hotel Marlton on 8th St between 5th + 6th Aves. When you + the Bouyways get to town on Thursday, call me here or better still write me, saying where we are to meet for drinks. As Van Dorens are coming too, + perhaps Philip Rahv.

I am haggard-feeling so much that, unless I feel better by Thursday, I may want to go right back to Cambridge. Then you would read the old + beautiful poem "Altre Verru", on Thursday night.

Yours,
Delmore.

P.S. The lobby of this hotel might be as good as any place for us to meet —

Letter to R. P. Blackmur, circa 1946.

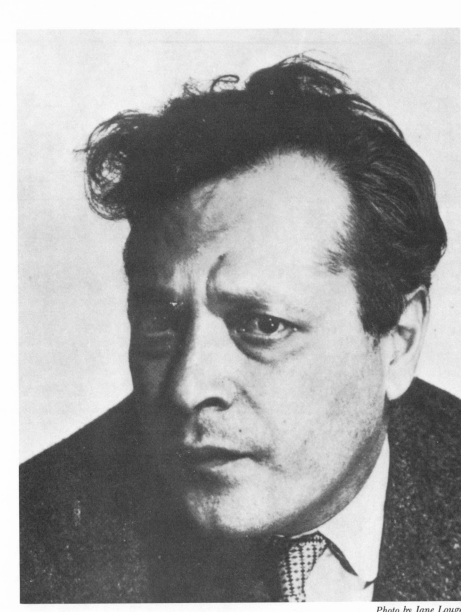

Circa 1958. "Nobody should look that unhappy."—W. H. Auden

Circa 1961.

Photo by Hi-Lite Studios, Syracuse/Beinecke Library, Yale Universit

Portrait made by a Syracuse studio, October 18, 1965.
Perhaps the last photo taken of the poet.

dant of Edgar Allan Poe with haunted rolling beautiful blue eyes, and other fine relatives. //

I won't publish any of my new poems before I hear what you think of them, if you will tell me. They are different than anything I have written, or they seemed to me to be. In the month of June I wrote more than in the past two years and more than in any other month before, and with more pleasure and certainty, although it is a first version, big blocks. //

Can it be that you do not know who concludes triumphant in *The History of the Boys and the Girls*? Not that this triumph is shown as a victory of virtue and goodness.

Are you writing at all? Have you tried to get reviews?

I am pleased that my mother has moved, for now I can visit my grandmother. I sent my mother the shares as her monthly allowance, unable any longer to bear the tension of this rising stock.

I heard from Arthur one of the most pathetic of all stories, the story of Scott Fitzgerald and his wife, an explanation among other things of the obscurity of *Tender Is the Night*. Apparently, Zelda Fitzgerald has been in an insane asylum for years now. But I will keep this story for another time.

Cambridge is pleasant, now that the great heat is gone. It is impossible without living here to understand the question, What is so rare as a day in June? The answer is that it is virtually unique. //

Beaucoup,
Delmore

TO R. P. BLACKMUR

[Cambridge]
July 8, 1943

Dear Richard—

This is to invite you and Helen to come here for a week-end at least, if you can, and it is to ask you to write to me, which you can.

Gertrude and I are now separated—all amicably and with the exchange of two letters a week—and this is very sad but I think for the poor best. Thus it is lonely, everyone is gone into the world of the night and I alone sit lingering here—with memories of Ellery Street parties—everyone meaning you, Helen, John, Nela, Tessa, Philip, Gertrude.

Faced by a choice between two fine suits, I—or rather you—bought both, a Blackmurian choice. I should never have gone with you to Rogers Peet.

I have to teach four classes—and only Sunday is free, and the tread-mill continues until November.

From my Navy classes, a note anonymous from one of the Navy boys, "Fuck the Jews!"

—forth from the dying republic.

Because of you too I have written most of the first version of a novel, and this you will have to read, since it could not have been written if you had not said that I could write a novel.

I think your best essay is the one on Herman Melville, which I did not recognize as best until I was inside a novel.

How about writing some poems for me and *Partisan Review*, which is being renovated? If there is any book that you want to write about, will you tell me? //

When Nela passed through—all circus ménage and disorder—I saw with joy that no matter what the local pastor is to say—so long as Nela draws breath, speculative metaphysics shall live.

> Best to Helen, and to you,
> Delmore

P.S. Wait until you see what Winters says about Henry Adams, that so great man.

TO GERTRUDE BUCKMAN

> [Cambridge]
> July 15, 1943

Dear Gertrude,

Almost everything has been difficult since I last wrote: the heat and teaching have been grueling, I have had an upset stomach which made me vomit for hours, succeeded by a cold which seems to me not cricket when the heat is at ninety. //

Some of the news, some of which may not be true, is that [...] I have broken the truth today to Mark [Schorer] who will see that all Cambridge knows by nightfall, and there are other items which don't leap to mind right now.

There is now no reason for not being explicit with anyone but my mother.

I liked your poem except for your reference to yourself as a vulture which is untrue and banal also.

Today Philip Slaner was here, seeking a scholarship, just released by the Army, fat and about to become a father; a becoming he announced at four-minute intervals at lunch.

John wrote briefly to say how good you had been to them, and that you hardly knew this. One reason for his difficulty is that he began to look too late, another is that there are not any jobs, right now, in universities. //

I have four classes to teach, two Navy classes and two at Radcliffe, and the schedule is such that I must teach every day but Sunday, and the Navy classes are ten and eleven on Tuesday, Thursday and Saturday, which stops the habit of writing in the morning. It went well until yesterday, when I went blank at Radcliffe and today too I was slow and awkward with my Navy class, and with Morrison on a visit. But this can hardly matter very much.

Auden was here, and Spencer asked me to lunch, and Auden seemed ageing, unhappy, and disquieted. //

I have a new and good friend in a bartender who has every virtue possessed by Nathan Asch, my uncle Irving, [Eddie] Cantor, [Al] Jolson, and Sonny, who is like all of them, and of the same origin, and it must be a strong tradition, for the sense of humor and of expression is the same. He told me of a friend of his, "He is his own worst enemy, his tongue is too big for his body!" His name is Robert and in my glass the liquor is always long enough for a party.

I wish I were able to write more, but the heat now, and the thought of the papers I must correct, drive every other thought from my head.

Yours always,
Delmore

TO GERTRUDE BUCKMAN

[Cambridge]
Tuesday, July 20, 1943

Dear Gertrude,

I decided not to come to your mother's funeral because the only one to be pleased was your father, and the possibility of pleasing him any longer is too limited. I could have come only for the day, such is the treadmill I now run, and the consequent exhaustion would not have been any help.

What an ordeal the last few days and today must be! but you must feel now that a [?] has been set to what exacerbated you so much.

The heat here has been Turkish, and I feel very worn, and although

I go forward with my new book, it is "the thin excited conversation at the end of a party, after midnight."

The one indeed pleasant thing was a letter from Meyer Schapiro to say how much he liked *Genesis* and, more than that, how he found there his own life experienced. This is the best possible praise, now that the Eliot of 1928 no longer is likely to be available.[1]

Rose asked me to tell you to come at any time you were able to, and I hope you do, and if you do, you stop by to see your old friend.

In going back to the old days of the boys and girls, I had one of the strongest impressions—perhaps an immense illusion—what a good boy, with all my shortcomings, I was *then*, how full of the desire to be good, generous, friendly. It is very sad to think about.

Yours always,
Delmore

1. T. S. Eliot wrote most of his best criticism in the 1920's.

TO MEYER SCHAPIRO

20 Ellery St.
Cambridge, Mass.
July 25, 1943

Dear Meyer,

It was really very kind and good of you to write me about my book. I can't think of anyone—except perhaps the Eliot of 1925, obviously no longer available—whose pleasure would mean so much to me. And in the last few weeks I've had a series of reviews which look like madness itself, ranging from Horace Gregory's comparison of the book to "Potash and Perlmutter,"[1] and the statement, with a notation showing how foolish it is, that I say that Jack Green is just like Henry James—from this to a remark in the *New Republic* that "sex is without subtlety in Schwartz, as was to be expected"—whatever that means—and other reviews in which an effort to praise the work reminded me once more how unsatisfactory good will is without intelligence, and how unpleasant it is to be praised for the wrong reasons.

Will you give my best to Dwight and Nancy,

Yours sincerely,
Delmore

1. An old comedy based upon two Jewish businessmen who bumble and stumble in their efforts to keep their firm alive.

TO DWIGHT MACDONALD

[Cambridge]
July 25, 1943

Dear Dwight,

Come any time with Nancy. There is plenty of room, four beds and the fourth can be doubled. I will not throw you out of the house no matter what happens unless you mention *Genesis*, the big frog.

It is time to tell you that I live among the *longeurs* and blankness of solitude, for Gertrude and I have been separated for the past three months, which is very sad, but I am afraid for the best, the famous lesser best.

If you have any coffee, bring it with you, because I have none. I drink tea since I mislaid the ration stamps.

Let me know two days in advance and then maybe we can have a big party.

If I had known that you were going to depart from *PR*, I would have tried to dissuade you. I wish you had not resigned, and I think I should have been told about it.

It is useless to discuss my book any more with you, but I should make some general remarks since they come to mind (however, if you spoil the happiness of our meeting by resuming the senseless argument, I swear to God and History that I will seek to effect your departure while I try to persuade Nancy to remain and become an adultress). Unless because you confess that you have not read it at all, and all that you say is either Goodman's unreal guff or has its own lack of relevance to anything whatever.

Thus, you bring up again the unreal imputation that I am just trying to be a second Eliot, as you did last year, saying, "You are trying to be an Eliot," just like I tried to be a Trotsky. Eliot never wrote a long narrative poem, nor tried to use prose and verse with each other, nor made the effort at directness and clarity which I make, nor was motivated by the alienation which only a Jew can suffer, and use, as a cripple uses his weakness, in order to beg.

As for the choruses as unnecessary (this is what was said of the choruses of *Agamemnon*, and what is always said of choruses), your own experience of modern life should have reminded you how essential a part of it is the occurrence of an event and then the discussion, comment, and interpretation of it, from many and conflicting points of view. Wait and see how this kind of thing is done more and more, as the self-consciousness of the modern intelligence increases; I don't doubt that it will be done with much more skill, and ease.

And so too with the verse as such; when you say it is pompous and verbose, I can only suppose that you did not see how much irony, how much of the colloquial, and the ear and the conversation there is in it. The verse is meant to lift up the narrative to a generality in which all its implications are exhausted. I don't doubt that this is done with awkwardness, or a blindness to some implications some of the time, but when you say that the narrative carries its own implications sufficiently, how sadly you show that you did not see how the chorus has several points of view which are utterly different from that of the narrator.

And for pure fantasy, it would be hard to surpass your metaphor of a congress of Freud and Marx and such fellows. The connotations you mean to enforce in the word "congress" are immediately drained by the mention of such congressmen. Did you ever hear of such a congress?

To argue in this way obviously places an author in a false light. I know that the book has shortcomings and imperfections and that I do not yet know them all. But now, a year after finishing it (and having done much new work and heard the impressions of many others), I feel sure that it is genuine and solid throughout, everything is there, for the sake of representing some perception or emotion, which I actually knew or felt.

But this is vain, and if I have a naive improbable hope that your severe judgement will vanish in three years, like your declaration that I was unable to write literary criticism, my sense of probability makes me turn to the next generation, to Michael, undistorted by Yale, *Fortune*, and arguments with such a jackass as *Sidney Hook*, who also is full of contempt for the sacred art of poetry.

Since you threw me out of the house, I have finished a new book of stories and poems, and almost finished the first version of a novel, and both seem better at the moment than the poem in dispute, but they could not have been written, if I had not first written the poem, that is, the whole thing, the second and third books also. Some of the stories will be a true trial of your disinterestedness in urging me to prose fiction, and also of your power to distinguish between the use of real life as a *donnée* and a fictive elaboration, not to say exaggeration.

It is not my fault if you are of a marvellous suggestiveness to one prone to the picaresque and caricature. When I read about Grant Landis,[1] I laughed myself sick and then burst into tears, it is like nothing so much as Quixote, also skinny and tall. It remains to be seen if you too will know the same helpless laughter and tears.

I have much more to tell you, particularly if you are still interested in going forward with popular culture as a subject. But it can wait until you come, except for two ageing incidents, first that I went with zest to my new Radcliffe class, having been told that Sophie Freud, granddaughter of the Viennese, was to be one of my students. She is probably neurotic, I said to myself, but on the contrary, she turned out to be a veritable butterball, full of assurance, and when the class read *The Turn of the Screw* and I asked *Sophie* what she thought of it, she said, "A clear case of paranoia!" Second, the textbook especially designed for the Navy classes contains Thoreau's *Civil Disobediance* and it is assigned in the syllabus made by the Navy, which perplexes me [...]

> To you and to Nancy,
> An Arch-Shakespearean Radical.

1. Character based on Macdonald in S's story "New Year's Eve."

TO WILLIAM CARLOS WILLIAMS

> 20 Ellery St.
> Cambridge, Mass.
> August 10, 1943

Dear Dr. Williams:

Sorry about the delay in writing you about your "A Fault of Learning."[1] What we would like to do is this, print it, and print a reply to it, sending you the reply beforehand so that you could withdraw, or answer back. (All this will take a little time.)

(For myself, as one with intense admiration for your work for a long time, I'd like to say that I have been unable for ten years to understand your hatred of intellectuals. I understand and agree with the whole business when it is aimed as Lawrence aimed it, at the way abstractions get in the way of real love and real living. But surely to say that intellectuals prepare the way for totalitarianism is strange in view of what Hitler as a practical man did about intellectuals. It reminds me of the point of view which attributes the rise of Hitlerism to Wagner and Nietzsche. No doubt, you remember James J. Waller's just remark,

"I never heard of a girl who was ruined by a book." It is a question of *which* intellectuals and what their particular ideas are, it seems to me, and not the intellectual in general.)

In any case, will you let me know if you consent to the above arrangement, and needless to say, we would like to see any of your new prose or verse.

Yours sincerely,
Delmore Schwartz

1. The essay had been submitted to *Partisan Review*. Dr. Williams castigates intellectuals for attacking Stalinism at a time when Russia was our military ally. He goes on to attack the "intellectual establishment" generally, saying its beliefs are contrary to the mainstream of U.S. history.

TO WILLIAM CARLOS WILLIAMS

20 Ellery St.
Cambridge, Mass.
August 20, 1943

Dear Williams:

I like your little poem, "These Purists," very much, and we will use it soon, with Miller's "It's Not What You See, But How You See It." I'd like to take several more of Miller's pieces, but we're full of too many unused accepted verse right now. At some later date, I hope you will send us not just one poem, but a group, for I've noticed that readers tune in on what you write when they look at several poems, one after another.

I don't have your last letter here because I sent it to N.Y. to show the boys that there ought to be no more delays, about answering anyone (but they've been preoccupied with the business end of the review for the last two months). So, without your letter, I risk being told again that I did not read what you said. I risk it, anyway, letter or not.

However, the gist of the reply to your essay will be as follows, so far as I am in on it: Dr. Williams is an important poet and author of fiction. This essay is significant for that reason. In it, he maintains that the best kind of statesmen have been boobs, or at least none too bright. Intellectuals are too smart. They are smart to such an extent that they ought to be used very carefully, like any dangerous thing. They are by nature only "superficially colored by democracy." Jump. Maybe then they are fascists. They don't like to see a whitewashing of the totalitarianism of Soviet Russia (where two million peasants were deliberately starved in 1932) because such a whitewash has no military value whatever. Jump. Hence intellectuals, or at least [John] Dewey and Eastman, are aligning themselves with those who bombed Guernica. *Mission to Moscow* not only distorts the truth about Russia, but it also distorts the book on which it is based. Jump. This shows that intellectuals are too smart, and Russia may have its faults, but the fifth columnists (and, as you may know, the best living Russian poet, Pasternak) are behind barbed wire, unable to do any harm.

You can certainly reply to this in print if you like, after the other editors have added their remarks.

As I remember, you ended your letter by remarking that you and I were not intent on the same thing. So far as intent and intention go, this is not true; so far as performance goes, if I am half as good as you at fifty, I will be a lot more pleased with myself than I am now. But the intent is a common one: the exact description of what is loved and what is hated. If I may be even more personal about this, I might say that I guess my teaching at Harvard puts me under the general stigma of being academic. You have as much notion of what the academy is like now as I have of the care of infants. I teach the freshman how to use English, and when one boy writes that a neighborhood is slightly ugly or a person has an outstanding nose, I try to explain that they have misunderstood some words and might do better with other words. Or when a girl writes that "a liberal arts education makes a girl broader," I try to explain that words have idiomatic and metaphorical qualities which require careful handling. When the high school gets done with them and when the newspapers, films and radio get through with their minds, they arrive here to be repaired. Thus, obviously, I am a kind of dentist, as you are a doctor, and it is an honorable calling. The textbook the freshmen use, as you may know, contains not one, but two pieces by you, "The Use of Force" and "The Destruction of Tenochtitlan." The only other author with two pieces is your old chum, T. S. Eliot. It is in this way that you are treated by the academy. Meanwhile there are also the Navy boys to be taught, and it grows on me that the war will be over long before some of them learn how to spell, which I mention to explain the perhaps harassed tone of this letter.

The boys and the girls, by the way, seem to see no serious difficulty and inconsistency in reading both you and Eliot, nor do I, and your notion that Eliot keeps any good poetry from print is just as much fantasy as your idea that Macdonald likes Eliot. He resigned, saying among other things that he never wanted to run a review which printed such authors as Eliot. Another fantasy is that Lincoln was not an intellectual; how do you think he learned to practise law and to make the best speeches any politician is ever likely to make?

Well I've never won any argument with anyone and being in the middle of my twenty-ninth eternity, I don't have the energy of old to nourish often-defeated hopes, but I cannot resist adding that your view of the role of Eastman and Dewey is identical with the view expressed by Alfred Noyes that Proust was responsible for the Fall of France. By your jumping logic, this makes you the same kind of poet as Noyes, if Dewey is aligned with the Fascists who bombed Guernica.

Perhaps I ought not to argue with one of the few of my elders I admire very much, but it occurs to me that the difference in age between us is not likely to diminish, so that this is as good a time as any.

Yours sincerely,
Delmore Schwartz

TO R. P. BLACKMUR

[Cambridge
August 25, 1943]

Dear Richard—

257 papers a week [. . .] keep me from answering your last letter as I should.

But this is to ask you if you could be persuaded to participate in a new *Partisan Review* symposium: The Future of the Left. Silone and Niebuhr are some of the other probable symposiasts and though it won't be printed until winter and spring, the contributors have to be settled soon.

This might be the launching of your campaign for Senator. You can count on my vote.

Also, the delightful Miss Caroline Greene unnerves me by telling me she will tell her father[1] to tell you what I say in class. In defense, I have asked her to write a character sketch of you, and hinted loudly that I would tell you what she is like in class: E.g., one of her papers read:

"A liberal arts education makes a girl broader."

When I objected to this, she said, "If you have that kind of a mind . . . !"

I've decided never to marry because I would like to be wedded at the same time to Tessa and Helen, and these ladies seem preoccupied.

Please let me know about the Symposium. You don't have to write the piece until about Xmas. Best to you and to Helen,

Delmore
An Arch-Shakespearean
Theocratic radical

1. T. M. Greene, then in the Philosophy Department at Princeton.

TO DWIGHT MACDONALD

[Cambridge
September 1943?]

[No salutation.]

This is part of a much longer letter, which I've decided, in the early morning light, not to send, but because I don't think that such a letter will do anything but make you angry, and such things are best said in conversation.

It concerns *Partisan Review*, from which you should *not* have resigned, you, and the effect of such on one as myself to be a friend of yours.

We will have it out when I come to New York in someone else's house perhaps, so that you won't be able to throw me out of the house.

Sadly,
Delmore

TO GERTRUDE BUCKMAN

[Cambridge
September 1943?]

Dear Gertrude,

Today ended the 2nd week of classes, & they went off well enough, without the stage fright I suffered when I stopped teaching in February.

Before school began I went to Truro for a week-énd, to see Fred, Dwight and Nancy. It was very pleasant except for the long trip by train and bus, which will keep me from going more often. Dwight cried a loud invitation to a dinner of roast capon from the tennis court and I yelled back that he was still clipping capons, but he did not hear me, & later we had a long argument about whether I had made the remark or not.

// It is distressing to hear of my anger in your dreams, since denunciation has been in most of my dreams; but not of you. I dreamt one night that you had fallen from a window and been killed, & then I was very unhappy. Thirty years of denunciation have I known—it interests me to see, now that I know the pathological connection, how much I can avoid denunciation.

I was given $100 for going to lunch at the Ritz with an editor of the Atlantic Monthly Press, to tell him what I know about anthologies. I think I must know more about private life in Cambridge than anyone in this line: "Nobody fools anybody much," to quote H. [Humphrey] Bogart. I saw *The Uninvited*, which I liked somewhat because the ghosts were real, and two girls were Lesbians. I don't know if it was good or I enjoyed my ability not to depart before the end.

The State Department asked me about W. [William] C. Barrett, whom I compared to Aristotle and Kant. Why don't you write a film chronicle for *PR*? Shall I suggest it to Philip? The idea of another gun girl at Mary's side will please him.

As always,
Delmore

TO R. P. BLACKMUR

[Cambridge]
September 15, 1943

Dear Richard,

If I do not hear from you soon, I will think that you are not interested any more in the senatorship, the Left, or friends of your Cambridge period.

Probably I ought to resume the practice of monthly newsletters, to keep you *au courant*, if I may quote Harry Levin. But then when I get no answer, I become uneasy, and think, I have said something wrong again.

The little Greene girl continues to delight and unnerve me. She told me that as I came into class the first day she just knew that I was one of those persons who admire T. S. Eliot, whom she detested until the other day when I showed her how she admired Picasso for doing the same kind of thing in painting as Eliot did in verse. Then she promised to regard the poet as an open question. Then she read my character by looking at my handwriting on her themes and said quickly, "You get very despondent, but then you keep trying, anyway, and you are warmhearted"—and I had to break in with, "Stop, you know too much already," or some such fearful embarrassed remark. Her quotations from her father are also rivets of attention: "Daddy says he does not like women because they interrupt," "Daddy says he wishes I would emerge" (I feared the womb was meant—my impure, Freud-bent mind—but it turned out to be adolescence), and then her own comment on a liberal arts education, already hailed as making a girl broader: "I wish some man would marry me and put me out of my misery!"

If all students were like that! There was a robbery in her dormitory and she was the first one to be robbed, at five in the morning, when first she thought it a joke, and then with a gun in her ribs, said to one of the poor crooks, "Don't be a silly and take away my lipstick and locker key." They left her a dollar too and received twenty years that week, while she was scolded by the house mistress for not screaming.

Speaking of Harry Levin, I am about to begin to show what a learned jackass he is, and the only sublunar being who can stop me is you, but only with good reasons and not a noble gesture, for I've been reading *Finnegans Wake* with care, and it is shocking to see how he invents with inexhaustible ingenuity and foolishness when he doesn't understand what Joyce is doing, and much of the time, the ingenuity is for exhibition, nothing else. That, and *Ulysses*, and his [Maurice C.] Bowra [*The Heritage of Symbolism*] review where he takes the symbol of the rose in the Symbolists and lists, among other recurrences, the fact that Rilke died of a rose-prick? How he left out rose fever, Rosie O'Grady, and Abie's Irish Rose troubles my midnight reflections.

I meant to say before this that I was much moved by your sentences about Gertrude and myself; but it is a great sadness to say that here you permit the poverty of statement to bar you from actuality; our Lady Actuality with whom I have lived so long, in the dark, in the early morning light.

The effort to get the news of Gertrude's absence told without separate awkward difficult statement to each one produced a phenomenal farce, too long to tell. In the good society, gold engraved cards will be proper protocol probably, just as for the marriage.

I have figured out the meaning of "The World is a Wedding." It is that picture of Breughel's now on my wall, and it is motto for my tombstone, under "Metaphor Was His Exhilaration."

If you do not write me soon, I am going to write to Helen.

Is it not true that teaching is a great seduction, too easy and too pleasant?

If you saw Gregory's, Bogan's, [Dudley] Fitts', and some of the other reviews of my book, perhaps you saw what Jay meant and that your own review was an enormous help. // Bogan said I was too serious, Fitts too coy. Goodman's review which you did not see was some kind of new record. It appeared in the *New Leader* and marked copies were sent to members of the English Department. I mention all this as a postscript to having asked you to write your own review, which was very good, no matter what you say. To you and to Helen,

Delmore
a wedding usher

TO DWIGHT MACDONALD

[Cambridge]
Sept. 21, 1943

Dear Dwight:

Your silence strongly suggests that you like to write angry or dununciatory letters, but you do not like to receive them. This is interesting and not astonishing, but again my hopes for the future make me postpone comment and the temptation to send you the rest of my letter, which is all about you. In much detail. What I want to know is if you are going ahead with your review and if you would be interested in a column by myself about all current criticism, entitled "A Review of Reviews" or something like that. I found enough howlers in just this week's literary supplements to make not one but three columns; and this attracts me also as a way of proving to you the courage and honesty you have from time to time found lacking in me. But as a condition of writing such a column, I would want absolute freedom to say whatever I think, whether you liked it or not, and to speak also of the criticism in your journal.

Also, your silence suggests that the sending of marked copies of Goodman's review of my book to people here did not impinge upon your much-vaunted moral sense?

Why don't you and Nancy and Michael come up for any weekend and we will get drunk in this which is now the Cambridge Ghetto, for renting agents here, since there is a housing shortage, ask unAryans if they are Jewish and tell them they can't find anything for them then. If you stay here long enough, you will be taken for a Jew and Nancy will be arrested for miscegenation.

Yours strainedly,
Delmore

TO GERTRUDE BUCKMAN

20 Ellery St.

10, 1, 43

Dear Gertrude,

I wish that you did not think it pointless to say a thousand things.

The term ended with the house in a state of pure disorder, and now I can't find that list of things you want. Would you mind making a second list? Do you want the piano? I would like to have the space for book shelves.

I now have a month's vacation from school, for it was decided that since I had been teaching more students than anyone else and since I looked as nervous as a bride all the day and every day, perhaps I should have a rest.

The aftermath of Paul Goodman's review was the sending of marked copies to members of the manly English department. I am afraid I am not good enough to be able to feel forgiveness about that. I heard too that Paul and his wife had been separated, and of how, at a party, Paul sat [...] on his lap and put his hand in the [young man's] fly that all might see. //

// George and Marjorie were married the [*sic*] Saturday and Wallace as well as I were forbidden to come to the wedding. //

Jeremy, taken to Sunday School for the first time, declared, when asked what did God do, God makes water. When I ask him his name, he says it is Delmore. When I ask him my name, he says, "Jeremy Dickson." You must admit that this is breath-taking genius? //

Yours always,

Delmore

TO DWIGHT MACDONALD

[Cambridge]

Oct. 3, 1943

Dear Dwight,

If I must choose between friendship and saying what I think (rightly or not), I choose friendship. (I hope this does not seem immoral.) My letter was not meant to hurt you, but to defend myself from the accusation of being Stalinist about Goodman, and seeing your review spoiled by space given to Goodman's ideas, which never achieved anything for him or anyone else.

Your insults to me date from the Yaddo days, when you told me I was a brilliant undergraduate as a critic, to your letter, on the heels of Schapiro's very pleasant praise, denouncing *Genesis*. I was upset very much, but I did not consider you a foe. It is the dishonesty, attack, and the "who asked you to come here?" alienation tactic (which occurred just after Gertrude and I separated) that make me angry.

My behavior for years and my letters (in your file) should prove my friendship and admiration for you, despite recurrent provocation. I do think that you are not using your gifts (which make you ten times better than Lincoln Steffens and Orwell put together), as you should. But if I discuss this, you will get angry again, and I want to be a friend if possible.

Yours possibly,

Delmore

P.S. If I wanted to hurt you, why did I withold most of my letter?

TO GERTRUDE BUCKMAN

[Cambridge]

Oct. 18, 1943

// But also, the old Adam in me is dying because I know now that I am good, somewhat of a goodness, because I have always wanted to be good and became evil because I expected too much of other human beings and tried to force them to behave as I thought they should. But now I expect nothing, because the desire to be good is enough, it is a great pleasure to be one who tries to be good, and I hope this does not sound complacent. So far as I can make out, it is enough to believe in goodness to have the strength to try hard to be good.

// Please don't be angry because I say these things, since you don't seem to take pleasure in my not writing to you and I must say what I think or lie or write something which will distress you. You are my only sister,

As always,

Delmore

TO R. P. BLACKMUR

[Cambridge]

Oct. 18, 1943

Dear Richard:

I can't write you a real letter now because, despite your impression, school here has turned into the perfect industrial system, and since July I have been teaching 87 students, more than anyone else in the manly English Department. At the moment, three batches of papers from each class stare me in the face and I just stare back, unable to concentrate because new epithets occur to me continually, such as Glasshouse Hershey.[1]

Also I can't speak of the new publishing venture because I know now that the only way to keep a secret is to shut up. By now, Consultant Tate has probably telegraphed all the authors in America about the project, thus making it necessary for me to change the project somewhat.

As for good work and enormous, it is enormous enough but how can I know if it is good until you tell me? Not only that, but I have written from 6:30 until 10 each day and then run off to class, and not dared to look back at the previous day's work because I know what happened to Lot's wife and I don't wish to be discouraged.

When you finish the book about Adams, then we will talk Turkey [*sic*] with all the stuffing. However, as your admirer and disciple since the dead year 1929, I know you too well to give you a lead dime before you write anything. I hope this does not sound disagreeable, and if I am wrong I am willing to take Helen's word for it, since she is my sorority sister.

Tessa affirmed that she was pleased by my poem, but objected with obvious pain to the line, "She gets as wet as soup each time she cries." "You have never seen me crying," she exclaimed, and now I have to change the simile to dew. The *amour-propre*, if I may once more quote Harry Levin, is not to be satisfied. I thought I had never written more favorably of any character.

Gertrude's address is 225 E. 19th St., and I wish you would look her up without saying that I gave you the address because she suffers from the imagination that no one likes her, not even I.

John loses his temper in arguments and behaves like a maniac and it is not his fault, but not everyone knows that. I mention this to you because there is no one at all he won't blow up with, but the saving grace is that he does not mean to be personal and all is serene and amiable the next day. Eileen is a saintly character, and of a cleverness which is somewhat concealed by the most nasal of all New York accents.

I am afraid of Nela because her mind has a curve like a distorted looking-glass and also because she suffers from [...] panvanity. Nevertheless I like her very much, but for other reasons.

Right now, eighty-seven students are writing eighty-seven bluebooks which I will have to read eighty-seven times. I know just how a treadmill feels, and I suspect that I have written the same poem several times during the past three months.

I spoke to Tessa about my desire to marry her and Helen, and she said she was willing. Will you ask Helen for me? It is all academic, of course, but then I am an academician, as Paul Goodman observed in his review [. . .] At this academic wedding, I want you to be the better man and give me away.

More and more,
Delmore

1. Hershey Green, who is the protagonist of *Genesis*.

TO W. H. AUDEN

20 Ellery Street
Cambridge, Mass.
November 16, 1943

Dear Wystan,

May I have back the volume of Kafka which was part of our rather strange exchanges in summer? I do not like to ask for the return of books since I do not like to return them; but nowhere in Cambridge can I find a copy of "The Great Wall of China," and I have to have it for a piece I am trying to write (about an effort last week to find a friend of mine in New York), which begins, "This Kafka was just a journalist," and concludes, "This Kafka was just a city-desk man."

The first term of Navy English ended for me in a not-to-be-believed denouement, for one of the examination questions was to correct a misspelled passage, and to single out the misspelled words, writing "misspelled" next to them. Consequently, "misspelled" was misspelled in fourteen different ways among my fifty-seven bluebooks, and sometimes misspelled in several different ways in the same bluebook, "mispelling," "misspelling," "misspilling," "mis-spelling." Thus it will be possible for me to reply with dignity when asked by my grandchild the classic question, "What did you do in the war to make the world safe for the lesser evil?" "Grandchild," I will be able to say, "I was in the Navy, defending the English language."

Yours,
Delmore

TO GERTRUDE BUCKMAN

Dear Gertrude,

It is *Partisan Review*, my own writing of the whole summer, all the small things in the house, and Jay, which keep me from writing to you. I came back to Cambridge quiet and empty, all the passion of the summer and the fall exhausted, and now I have been trying to get things in order, so that I can get to work once more. On Monday next, I must begin to teach again, perhaps without an intermission until the war ends, for Morrison said to me, as a member of the faculty, you are entitled to one term in four as a vacation, but this will probably prove merely theoretical. //

It is unpleasant to hear that Nela has been unable to keep quiet. Did I tell you that John found out about Nela's feeling for me, as you entitle it, by finding a letter to me in one of her books? This made me feel sick to my stomach. What has Nela said exactly, do you know? And can you think of some way for me to make her silent? I am not likely to see her very much, but I intend to tell her how much harm she does herself and John. She wrote me a note about seeing you, and she spoke with warmth of her delight in you. *Quel enfant!* I hope you will believe me when I say that I do not make love to her, nor to anyone else (I would not, even if I could), and I will not again become drunken with the wife of another man, even if I am not guarded by a sad immunity.

If you make a new list, I will get Mrs. Massey to look for your things and to send them to you. I've looked everywhere for your list without success, indeed with much frustration. The best thing would be a flying visit here some week-end, and you might stay here or with the Van Keurens[1] who have a big house.

Apparently it would be unwise for me to be divorced from you because of adultery. Murdock was asked to resign as Master of Leverett House because of that, and I think next year I may want to stay at one of the houses, where there would be no rent or board bill at all, and where I would have no chores day and night. //

I am really pleased to have you tell me that you do not like my sonnet because perhaps it means I can depend on you to tell me what you think of my new books, when I send you copies before sending them to the printer. I still like the poem myself, but probably this is because of my private feelings, and it is consistent that you should not like such feelings, for if you did, ten years might have been different.

Your own poems are not finished, and I think you do not hear how they sound. They are the first version of very good poems.

How strange my life has become will be obvious to you when I say that I've been to the pictures only twice since April, and for the first time since 1922 I did not know each day what the results of the World's Series games were.

The new conclusion to my poem (or did I tell you?) is, Jack Green as one of the ghosts says to his son, as part of a mounting chorus, "Don't be like me, Hershey, it is to be damned," while as Hershey Green awakens, his mother, very much in this life, says repeatedly, "You are just like your father!" and the chorus, all unmasked, presents him with a choice, if he forgives his parents and accepts his own guilt, then he can live. If he refuses the responsibility for what he is, then he must die, because this is a denial of the freedom of the will and the possibility of human goodness. Meanwhile the snow which is the snow of freedom and forgiveness is falling down as if a new world were beginning, and Roger says, "I don't like you, I wish I had another kind of brother, I wish you were not what you are." Right now I intend to conclude on the ambiguity of two choices present to Hershey, without resolution, for this is the way dear Henry James, I think, would prefer. What do you think? It was partly by reflecting upon the guilt I accused you of that this conclusion occurred to me. I think I will publish the whole poem as one thing, entitled *The Singers*, as soon as the war ends.[2]

In the 30th year of my rage/When all my guilts I have booed—

Yours always,
Delmore

Postscript: One of my guilts and foolishnesses was this
To ask and try to force a human being to love one
As in deadly sin: this is like trying to make a child
American because of a love of America.

1. Mr. and Mrs. William Van Keuren. Van Keuren actually owned the stuffed duck said to be S's in Robert Lowell's poem "To Delmore Schwartz."
2. He never did.

TO JOHN BERRYMAN

[No salutation.]
This had better be sent soon, if it is not to be dismissed as too late. Perhaps some of the words ought to be altered so that they will seem less of my own usage.

Sir:

Mr. Richard Eberhart's review of Delmore Schwartz's *Genesis* in your June 4th issue [*New Republic*] arrives at such a peak of inexactitude that something should be said in reply. It is urgent that your readers know that this important work has been misrepresented.

Mr. Eberhart says nothing of the actual character of the work, its form, imagery, diction, use of narrative and ideas, variety of tone, emotion, attitude and subject matter. Instead he treads repeatedly on the verge of the meaningless, so that one is unable to understand the cause of his favorable judgement.

Consider the consecutive sentences in which the poet is said to be photographing the middle class and hitting a nail on the head, only to be compared soon after to a long-range bomber. To be a photographer, carpenter, and airplane at once is a Protean feat; but not only one to make your readers aware of anything but the rapidity with which metaphors may be mixed. Consider the contradiction in saying that the emotions are declared, not evoked, and then asserting that the verse is written "with strong emotional flow," and "with the emotions masterfully pointing at the story." Or, as one last instance representative of virtually every sentence of the review, I would like to be able to understand Mr. Eberhart's strange remark that "sex is without subtlety in Schwartz, for that was expected." What can this mean? What is sexual subtlety? Is Schwartz's lack of sexual subtlety a thing of public expectation and knowledge? Can anyone know what sex *with* subtlety is? Do the cognoscenti want sexual subtlety?

Mr. Eberhart is chiefly impressed that the work was written at all. His impression is unjustifiable, for the book does not exist for him, and your readers have been seriously misinformed and subjected to an attack on the English language, especially in the use of words like "probation," "emotion," and "evocation"; they are used with such subtlety that they are deprived of meaning.

Yours, etc.

TO R. P. BLACKMUR

Dear Richard,

No one believes the stories I tell, but in New York I wrote a telegram to you on a slip of paper, asking if you were able to come to town that night or the next night. I gave the telegram, written on a memorandum slip, to a friend to write out at the nearest Western Union office, for I then was so much involved that I might not have turned my head if assured that Jesus Christ was playing the harp in back of me. Then this friend went to the subway, the train approached, the slip of paper was blown off into the artificial depths, and I heard about it all two days after, as I prepared to return to Cambridge. If this seems peculiar to you, accuse Life and not myself of fantasy, invention, and strangeness.

Partisan Review is poorly off because, with the departure of Nancy Macdonald, there is no one for the business work, and William and Philip are harassed by the necessity of earning a living, and no one will help, very much because of some groundless fear of the review's political views. Philip can always get enough money to pay the printer's bill, and he will, since he has put too many years into keeping it going. But obviously more than the printer's bill is necessary, so that one step has been to become a quarterly, until the end of the war. I did not know they had written you, and where my stamped signature came from perplexes me. But since you have been thus accosted, and if you know ladies and gentlemen of means who can make deductions for gifts from their income tax, it would be a great help. The kind of pressure against politics in the magazine has made the boys dubious about The Future of the Left. Another kind of pressure is illustrated by Leonore Marshall who gave the Review several hundred dollars on both previous campaigns, but has not replied to this letter, but has expressed great resentment of my review of her book [*No Boundary*]. "The only unfavorable review I received!" she told Dwight, and Dwight said to me joyously, "You have a new enemy!" Perhaps there is no connection between her silence and my review, but anyway it is not pleasant to have to think of such things. But all of this ought not to be common knowledge. //

A voluble visitor has just arrived, which means that if I don't finish this letter now, I won't finish it for two days, for tomorrow I return to the academic treadmill. Are you and Helen coming to Cambridge for Xmas? Please answer, for if you are not, I am going to sell some of the six beds which now are with no little irony unoccupied. Ora poor las Animas, as Anna Livia sighs, we're umbas all,

Much enumba'd,
Delmore

TO JOHN BERRYMAN

Cambridge
Dec. 8, 1943
Dear John,
and Rusty, wife of John, the black days are back, prolonged stage fright before the class, and everything else that you have seen for yourself, and that is why I did not finish the letter I began to write to you, full of strange stories; at least I tell the truth, and then I am told, "How strange!" "Are you sure?" until now, like James's governess, I do not know what the truth is, perhaps it is all my interpretation; so they say; so Gertrude often told me.

Today is my thirtieth birthday, and I had thought of a Gold Rush birthday for myself in the dining room, plates with melting ice cream, all flavors, even tutti-frutti, for friends absent, dead, misunderstood, offended (this list will take too long)—but then I corrected myself, enough of this self-pity, I said to myself, you have no kick coming, and don't forget, there are too many unwashed dishes as it is.

Instead, I am going to hear the London String Quartet play some more of all of Beethoven's Quartets, as they have been playing them all week long, and then I will hear the phrase that began its reiteration with the news of John Walcott's death,[1]

Why him, not me? Answer me that, if you can!
Him and not *me!* Answer me that, if you can!

Fluency is all gone, as in the classroom difficulty, so that I had better hold myself to news: [...] perhaps I will see you Xmas week, perhaps I will not. I must now think ahead just one hour. Here I go down on the roller coaster,

As always,
Delmore

1. A vehicular accident while serving overseas.

TO JOHN BERRYMAN

20 Ellery Street
Cambridge, Mass.
Feb. 8, 1944

Dear John:

There is nothing to tell except that publishing matters are entirely in abeyance—and I suffer from silence, blankness, apathy and all amid good health, which makes a new enigma. My distress is so obvious that I've been given next term off, so that I will certainly spend a weekend in Princeton, and perhaps bring Aileen[1] with me. But truly, Aileen apart, there is no mystery, and no news. I've turned the other cheek, but consented to nothing else.

Will you give my best regards to your dear wife, to Nela, Richard, Helen, Sage, and Susie.

Yours always,
Delmore

1. S was dating Aileen Ward, then a graduate student in English. She was in love with Professor Perry Miller, who was off to war.

TO GERTRUDE BUCKMAN

Cambridge
February 16, 1944

Dear Gertrude,

This has been a time indescribable: stage fright, torpor, boredom, anger, and a simple paralysis of the will before papers that had to be corrected. But now there are no more classes, only seventy-eight blue books, and then I will be free until the 6th of July.

The reading is on the 2nd of March, but I will come to New York before that, if I manage to get some things into order. The number of unanswered letters, unread manuscripts, unpaid bills—it is useless to make a list. I have the feeling we used to have before examinations, when we fell into arrears all term, and had so much to learn the night before, and were unable to study because the idea of how much had to be studied kept appearing. If you have seen a lawyer, perhaps you can find out if I ought to commit specious adultery and how I ought to commit it during my next trip to New York. I would like to have that done with as soon as possible, and especially for convenience, during the period when I am not teaching a class.

The day before, William Barrett (so he announced himself on the phone) was here, and yesterday too, and we spoke much of what has been and what has not been. He has been teaching mathematics in a small school in Albany, to keep out of the army, and he is crushed and helpless and hopeless in the way that he began to be in 1941.

What is it that troubles you? Is it that you did not get the job you wanted?

I heard a curious thing, that Michael Macdonald's case history is full of references to Delmore.

Paul and Maxine Sweezy have just been divorced. We appear to have been part of a trend. Matthiessen spoke of their being congenial with the same astonishment which has greeted my own references to you. But, as I begin to make out now, one is supposed to regard the end of a marriage as a personal failure and not to speak of it as one does not speak of any other kind of failure. //

In squeezing orange juice some of these mornings I've known the consolations of philosophy: a success, however modest, which was not to recur for the rest of the day.

One will surely say, "You are all a four-F generation"; for did you know that the extent of neuroticism in the Army and Navy, and the necessary discharges because of it, has been so great that in Washington they ask each other, "What has been happening in America for the last twenty years?"

I can no more; I have no thoughts and no sentences, except the phrases of unwritten poems,

"Now half of life is past: well! what of that?"

With love,
Delmore

TO GERTRUDE BUCKMAN

[Cambridge]
March 8, 1944

Dear Gertrude,

I suffered waiting-room or railroad-station disappointment, interpreted five unlikely distant girls as you, and then thought that I had better get back to Cambridge before disappointment and haggardness arrived at the next frustration, no sleeping berth on the midnight train. I thought of looking for you or waiting at your apartment, but then decided that you must have gone out and stayed out during the afternoon, otherwise you would surely have received my telegram, which I did not send at an earlier hour because I did not know what train I would take.

Princeton was pleasant enough, but full of disorder for me because I do not have travelling habits. Richard has become a kind of marriage broker or general intermediary or promoter, and he has the idea that he can get me a job like his with the Institute for Advanced Study. Not a job like his now, for he is now entitled an economist, but some sinecure as literary critic; it is all very vague, but apparently one would function like Einstein, lecture twice a year, and hold conversations with other advanced students. Then, when the war is over, Richard speaks of my becoming his assistant, and helping him to edit the review which the Princeton University Press may give him. None of this awakened much interest in me, because it is all mere possibility; and only the dinner Richard and I were given by the head of the Rockefeller Foundation made me suppose it was anything but Richard's daydream.

I was impressed by Helen's paintings for the first time. I don't know how to describe what moved me very much in them, except to say they were full of darkness and intensity which made me think of my own emotions of the past three months. John was John and Nela was Nela and did not look well, and apart from the friendship and peace between Helen and Richard, each one seemed to be moving about in the same half-chosen half-given cage. But perhaps the cageness is in the gaze of the beholder. For I am still with an empty mind and it has taken me almost an hour to get this far in a letter I owe you because I enjoyed your letter so much.

The only pleasant thing about my trip was our own accord or concord, and I've been haunted, as by the idea of falling from a brink, by the idea of how it-all-might-begin-again. The mind has its reasons which the heart can never understand, to invert Pascal, and I try to remember exactly what you said on Tuesday night: "How awful it must be to be in love." Was that what you said? Whatever the exact words, it was what I did not remember and should have remembered: your own distance from love for ten years, for only love can make everything acceptable and accepted.

It is noon, the furnace has gone out again, small things weigh me down, and I am afraid that if I read what I have written, I will not send the letter. I will write you as soon as possible, and answer you about the business of the divorce; the only reason for being prompt is the possibility of a newspaper item, which I would like to avoid while teaching a class. But it will be four months before I teach again.

If you feel lonely some evening, why don't you call me up and reverse the charges.

Your only brother,
Delmore

TO PHILIP RAHV

[Cambridge]
March 11, 1944

Dear Philip,

I've tried all week to write the Winters review, or rather to rewrite the version I did for the *Times*, and I've been unable to get through a page. I am sorry to let you down in this way, but I can no more write at present than I can fly to the moon. According to my doctor, my present state is the consequence of six months of overwork, and this seems plausible, since I was teaching four classes and forcing myself to write fiction, verse, and criticism more than I had ever done before. I promise you that as soon as I get started again, I will concentrate upon something substantial for *P.R.* before I try to do anything else; and if it is at all possible, I will try to get Laughlin to let me give my novel to the Dial Press. However, I feel much more certainty about my being able to get free from L. than I do about the novel being anything the Dial Press will want. //

I wish I could be more helpful and I certainly ought to be, but my mind is just not functioning.

Yours,
Delmore

TO JOHN BERRYMAN

Cambridge, Mass.
March 29, 1944

Dear John—

Your news makes me think of the argument after midnight about Helen, Helen's job, and the war (in the midst of which with no little temptation to resist, I refused to permit myself to ask you and Richard why you did not get to a war-production plant as soon as possible).

This long sentence, just written, gives me much pleasure, since it is the most extended piece of composition of my 30th year.

At any rate, stupid, foolish and unjust as in nothingness of the

Guggenheim Committee [*sic*], I hope you do not permit yourself to forget that it has nothing to do with the worth of your poems.[1]

I wish you would let me have some new verse to improve the pages of *Partisan Review*.

There is little to say of myself that I have not said before. I sit recumbent or supine, in emotionless vacancy, or murmur sentences such as,

> As for *this* world, it's
>   hardly worth a sneer—

> Now 30 years are passed: Well! What of that?
> (the caesara is marked by a French shrug).

But then I do not intend to take my emotions seriously any longer: the peaks and the depths are both illusions. Yet, to repeat,

> You never thought to pass your ageing youth
> On this cold shore: Never knew
>   how shabby was the truth
> Did you, Delmore? so...

Will you give my love to Eileen, Richard, Helen, Nela, and also Pomfret [the Blackmur's cat] the fat white beauty.

Yours always,
Delmore

1. Berryman had been rejected for a Guggenheim Fellowship.

TO R. P. BLACKMUR

[Cambridge]
April 11, 1944

Dear Richard—

I like your poem very much on first and second reading. Unless the next issue of *P. R.* is crowded with already-accepted verse, it will appear in the July issue. Meanwhile Rahv must have written you about commenting on Eliot's new essay. I hope you don't hold back on that.

More than once I've tried to write you a decent letter, only to be stopped by whatever it is stops me. But I will write the letter I ought to write as soon as I can.

Until then there is one urgent thing. Tate told Rahv that the *Kenyon Review* had been given $8000 a year for the next three years by the Rockefeller Foundation. What chance has *P.R.* to get support like that, which it sorely needs, and which would lift it from the amateurish business on which it has been run? Will you let me know what we can do about asking for the support? The question of a budget is an involved one because much of the detailed secretarial work for *P.R.* has been done by this or that editor's wife for nothing. Something ought to be done soon, since the magazine simply can't continue to have a financial crisis every other issue. Please let me know what steps can be taken.

Yours always,
Delmore

TO GERTRUDE BUCKMAN

[Cambridge]
April 17, 1944

Dear Gertrude,

The facts are—that the house is full of the smell of dead oranges and dead cigars; two months have passed since last I taught; I went on Tuesday and Thursday night to see and hear *The Marriage of Figaro* and *The Magic Flute*, with Aileen; and I've consulted with Aileen and Phoebe Raus [Radcliffe undergraduate] as to your description of my shortcomings. These ladies profess bewilderment; but they do not know me very well, certainly they had not your advantages. And then how near to the facts can we come? I don't mean this with unamiable intent, but only to puzzle at your puzzling that I did not fail to send you the books; which I interpret as an interpretation of my failure to send you the piano.

Richard has written a fine poem about John Walcott. //

It is cold and of a penetrating chill both outside and inside; inside because I've not tried to start the fire again, having decided to coast to August in the dry air of the kitchen. //

Wednesday.

I stopped because my mind stopped the other day and by late afternoon I felt that a thought might be seen to be crossing my face like a caravan on the Sahara.

The other evening Sonny rang and once more I heard that I was to be married. Did you speak about this to him? It is truly astonishing to hear this so often when there is so little reason for it now, no matter what may occur in the future. And truly, all other obstacles apart, I feel the element of the flattering—of the marriage which will look well from the outside—as an accusation against thinking of the possibility. Marriages not made in heaven ought to be made in the id, and not in the ego, ought they not? I think it is ego at the other end of the gulf also.

If some of these sentences give the impression of an active social life, they are not true.

I think I learned very much from my visit to New York, especially the horror of Saturday night and what William said to me as well as what you said. That it is some deep anxiety that drains off my energy illuminates the ending of every period of energy; for each time, as I look back, I see the growth of anxiety, the outbreaks of anger and accusation, and then the helplessness of mind, as if that were the way I succeeded in hiding from myself what made me anxious.

Please write me news of getting a job and of your white knight. I hope you do not expect of him too much of whiteness, nor much resemblance to

Your black knight,
Delmore

TO ROBERT HIVNOR

[Cambridge
Spring 1944?]

Dear Bob,

I wrote Mrs. Ames as persuasively as possible. Yet, I hope you won't go there [Yaddo] unless you have nowhere else to go. It's not, I think, a good place to finish a book: too many impressions and persons striking against one's mind.

You're rather kind about Cooper Union.[1] Not contempt, perhaps shyness, but most of all lack of physical knowledge keep me from speaking well to a big audience. Immense muscular strain and unease from the idea that many strangers are looking at one. I try hard, however, practice, and have improved very much in the somewhat different arena of the classroom.

I was struck, as many times before, by your facile cynicism when I asked you to wait for me at the side. Not that I wanted to keep you from hearing whatever nothing I might say, but that I wanted to recognize a friend, not handle him as any stranger come up to the platform.

How is your book now? I looked at it the other day, trying to find something to send Warren. While looking, the following possibility occurred to me: perhaps you start too often with an idea and then look for a story to embody it (a story, incident, characters). If you were able to reverse the process, everything might flow life-size on the page. Just as the poet begins and binds himself in the tapping of the meter, refusing all that does not fit the meter, so too—perhaps—if you would insist on the story to begin with... I've been wrong many times and renounce whatever presumption of knowledge this suggestion may contain.

I found nothing, so far, which seemed complete in itself for a magazine. Your play, "M.G.'s P"[2] ought to go to Ransom, however. He has just taken an old play in verse of mine[3] and I'm sure he would be much interested. Tell him I said so.

I spoke with Burnham about his book [*The Managerial Revolution*] while in New York. One important question which he seemed unable to answer was: How will the managerial class perpetuate itself? Property rights and thus inheritance being eliminated, they would have to choose the stars of each June's graduating class, but I fail to see the human or the social motivation which would keep this going, especially in the economy of plenty, which a country like ours would surely provide? I also fail to see what they would "exploit" in an economy of plenty. But I must read his book and find out in detail what motivation is attributed to this managerial class. Perhaps they are said to like power as a bird likes to fly, but, in my experience, human beings want power not in itself but in special contexts which, presumably, would not exist in an economy of plenty.

Yours,
Delmore

1. S had given a poetry reading there, with Allen Tate and others.
2. "Martha Goodwin's Possession," a one-act play. It was inspired by Katherine Anne Porter's piece on Cotton Mather, published in *Partisan Review*, but based directly on Mather's diaries. Never published, the play was given numerous performances in colleges by a travelling troup from Bard College.
3. No verse play of S's was published in *Kenyon Review* after *Shenandoah* appeared there in 1941.

TO JOHN CROWE RANSOM

[Cambridge]
April 20, 1944

Dear John:

Thanks for suggested revisions:

"Tinkled and tapped out on the xylophone" is an improvement. Will you use it, and use as the title:

The Starlight's Intuitions Pierced the Twelve[1]

—which is, I think, the subject of the poem, once starlight is seen as the symbol I try to make it as the poem continues.

Yours always,
Delmore

1. When he included the poem in his 1950 collection, S changed the title to "Starlight like Intuition Pierced the Twelve."

TO GERTRUDE BUCKMAN

[Cambridge]
May 3, 1944

Dear Gertrude,

I have almost no news.

I have been better than for months, since I can read and practice a lot of note-taking on some days—but nothing else, and it is now almost six months since I've actually written anything. Today I feel rather hopeful, however, despite a poor night which might not have been poor had not Nela rung me at 11:30 to incite [sic] me to a Princeton party—just as I was half- and three-quarters asleep—hopeful I mean of taking hold of my mind again.

I received a kind of state visit from the Kazins, the critic and his extremely nervous sister—it was very literary.

// How the truth makes us free—so that, to know that an unknown anxiety reduces me to utter dullness is at least not to blame myself.

In recent dreams I was with you—in one at a theatre. You were reproaching me for some inappropriate behaviour, and the ladies ahead of us turned to say I would be taken off the list—some list which seemed very important. //

As always,
Delmore

TO GERTRUDE BUCKMAN

[Cambridge]
June 14, 1944

[No salutation.]

This time six years ago! and six years hence? We all go into the dark / but sentiment is so easy.

The news reached my mother at last and she wrote me what I must take to be a letter of condolence. She feels that I may feel that she may feel this to be a reflection on my character and she wishes to reassure me.

The days slip into each other as they have for almost seven months now, one alert and wakeful day and then a poor one. School begins again on the 5th of July, and as a consequence of my going back to civilian sections, I was shifted back to 1A by the draft board. However, last month it was announced that no men of 30 years or more would be taken for the rest of the year probably; or at any rate until the 1st of October. I received a request for my doctor's address, among other things, but for the time being my thirty years will keep me in this civil life-and-death.

Tonight Fred Dupee is coming here, on his way to two weeks on the Cape; and next Wednesday I go to Vassar to read my poems, which is a junket I would not undertake now, if it were not that I do not wish to disregard the seventy dollars entitled "honorarium."

In order to give a minor semblance of accomplishment to each day, I force myself to read, and in the last two weeks I've read a play by Euripedes, and a book by Kierkegaard, both without enjoyment or understanding; *Cousin Bette*, without admiration, a short biography of Pope, and a long poem by Stevens with admiration but without understanding. Then I've forced myself to the pictures too—really compelled myself, astonishing as it would have seemed years back—*Gaslight*, *The Bridge of San Luis Rey*, *Lifeboat*, and *The Man from Down Under*—all a waste of eyesight except for Akim Tamiroff's gusto. //

You must remember to describe Maurice as a witness against me; it is too neat, for it was he who spurred me on when I saw you again in the distance, at a table.[1] //

One tract of possibility which I tried last week and the week before to get into was *A Child's Book of Knowledge*, for a little boy named Jeremiah and his tutor Noah—full of things a little boy should know, the true, the good, the beautiful, the just, Flaubert's cigar, how to choose the pairs for the Ark, how to tell if they are in love—a book not only children but also adults would be forbidden to read. But so far, after a few deluded days, the idea has been fruitless.

// The reason I don't see anyone is vacancy; the vacancy is in me, no doubt, but when I think of the possibilities (the other day I wrote them down) the vacancy appears to be out there. "O Lady, we receive but what we give." So, with the same projection, I think of returning to New York, and no matter how often I tell myself it is an illusion, nonetheless there would be a difference in being back in New York again, although I suppose also there would be now-unsuspected difficulties too. But if all goes reasonably well, I will surely be back for a year and a half next March. I wonder if you would be pleased at how often I think of you. Doav you are [*sic*], and Will's phrase should have been, "Charm infinite," charm untouched by the years.

This is the longest letter I have written this year; and now, if you will but answer me, I will try to write to you once a week, although as you see I have little enough to say.

As always,
Delmore

1. S is referring to the time he pointed out Gertrude to Zolotow in the N.Y.U. cafeteria, the first time he had seen her since high school.

TO MARK VAN DOREN

20 Ellery St.
Cambridge, Mass.
July 4th, 1944

Dear Mark—
I've been like the seven sleepers for more than seven months now, and that is why I kept putting off the letter I wanted to write about your new book [*The Seven Sleepers*]. And now, after all this time, I still have no hope of any early return to being articulate, but the way in which phrases and perceptions in your book keep coming to mind makes me want to tell you not only how much wisdom the poems contain but how the wisdom is stated and defined in some of the poems. One phrase which comes back especially is "Eternity is Now," or rather the "is Now" with which the poem ends; once the poems are read with that truth in mind, the particular statements and observations are transformed, for they have become descriptions and predicates of what Eternity is. I kept thinking of how much better—simpler, more direct, and more illuminating—your line is than those of Rimbaud I used to admire very much—his cry that he had found

Eternity and that it was the sea fused with the sky. And how much better it is, too, to see the presence and the present of eternity than to speak of having seen Eternity the other night.

So too you tell the reader how to read your poems when you wrote "Consult the showy. Believe in the unshowy" and the underlying unity of imagery and statement among the poems comes through when one sees how a line like "when scent is servent to understanding" and the connection between red and "the dark unheard idea" are consistent and bound up with consulting the seen and believing in the unseen.

I think there are about ten poems in the book which are slight and unimportant especially when set against the important ones, but even these grow more and more interesting as one takes in the context of the whole book and the rest of your poetry.

I don't know how well this communicates the impression which deepened each time I opened up the book again; but I was prompted to write you when this morning, for the nth time, as I emptied out used coffee grains and crushed oranges, "Eternity is now" came spontaneously to mind.

Yours always,
Delmore

TO MARK VAN DOREN

20 Ellery St.
Cambridge, Mass.
July 10, 1944

Dear Mark—

.I meant to list the poems that seemed slight to me, but in looking at them again as I wrote to you I became less and less sure. They are—for whatever the list is worth—"New York Unbombed," "Armistice," "Observation Poet," "Song," ("To be at all, your birdlings"), "Gift of Kindling," "Berkshire Express," "Latter Day," and "The Second Leaving"—and I see now that I was wrong about the other two. I can't make out any characteristic they have in common, unless the subject seems to be not plumbed and dug into as much as in the other poems.

Your saying that you were not entirely aware of the connections I mentioned makes me think of one of my favorite remarks about poetry—Goethe's saying that one defect in Wordsworth's poems was that he always knew why each was there. (I think Arnold quotes this with approval.) Which I take to be another way of asking that the poem be not wholly the conscious Ego, but derived as well from the

Id—from both, really, from the whole being, and not merely from the skill of the man of art.

I'm very pleased you like my *New Testament* poem ["Starlight like Intuition Pierced the Twelve"], which, though not very new, was the last piece I managed to finish. The trouble, for me, with being unable to write is that it goes with an inadequacy in most other directions—and the contrary is true, too, so that I find myself teaching well when I am writing new things. I think that involved in this is part of the professional secret: the teacher learns more than any of the students and the poet enjoys himself more in writing poetry than in any of the subsequent benefits, such as they are, and the self-enjoyment of the mind and the whole being which comes from writing make the attendant pleasures—the ones like publicity, etc. which are taken as essential motives—look pale or unreal. I angered Frost once by saying that one could be spoiled by inspiration. What I meant was that inspiration made an unholy touchstone for the necessary periods of insensitivity, and that is one more way in which it is really salutary and wholesome to be reminded that Eternity is now.

Yours, always,
Delmore

TO JOHN BERRYMAN

Partisan Review
45 Astor Place
New York 3, N.Y.
August 26, 1944

Dear John—

I should have written you long ago but kept waiting for the proper mood, as if a poem and not a letter were in question. In fact, I am not yet used to your not being in Cambridge, so withdrawn from the actual world have I been.

I am much revived and full of new hopes and illusions. The doctor, at any rate, thinks the past eight months of utter distress a turning point.

I wish I were able to try out new poems on you. Perhaps I will have copies to send you and a long red pencil.

How about some verse for *P.R*, and since you are writing stories, how about a story—the only sustenance, as it turns out, of *P.R.*?

Are you coming to Cambridge this fall? I expect to be in New York in October and if all goes well, to take a year off next winter.

Goethe thinks that as we grow older, the ordeals become greater: he is right. To you and to Rusty always,

Delmore

P.S. I am now the proud owner of all of the recording of *Don Giovanni.*

TO GERTRUDE BUCKMAN

[Cambridge]
September 12, 1944
Dear Gertrude,

I was disappointed to get only a note from you, but know very well at the moment the difficulties of letter-writing. Though I have seen some people during the past month, much of my time has gone to keeping up with my classes and to writing or rewriting the poems and stories of a new book. It is nothing if not strange to write a story again five years after.

After visiting [John Malcolm] Brinnin at Rockport, I went back again and saw both Williams and the Dry Salvages, which seem over-rated. Will's marriage is an interesting one, for his wife is as devoted as a serf and appears to like it that way. Will spoke of you as being a genius, an unexpected product of Washington Heights, and when I remarked that this did not seem to make you any the less unhappy, he said platitudinously that that was the price one had to pay for genius. So too John Brinnin spoke of your bringing inspiration to Poughkeepsie.

Agee and Mia Fritsch [Agee's third wife] stayed here overnight on their way back from Maine, and then Richard and Helen came the week after. We had an extraordinary party at George's, a party whose scenario must have been written by Dostoyevsky as you can see when I say that Wallace took a poke at Richard, Helen burst into tears and became angry with Richard, Wallace became drunk to the point of not recognizing anyone, and I tried hard to start a fight with someone, but found only a stranger who insisted on using the word "nigger," but submitted to my correction. When we came back, I responded to Helen's criticism by accusing Richard of anti-Semitism, but he did not seem to mind. On the whole, the most unpleasant thing was that everyone enjoyed their behavior throughout. On the other hand, I would not like to have this version of the party recounted to anyone.

Now you must write to me and tell me how you are and give me the impetus to write a longer letter.

As always,
Delmore

TO JOHN BERRYMAN

[Cambridge]
January 23, 1945

Dear John,

I like your poem[1] so much less than most of your other poems (although it is much better than most of the poems in *PR* with the printing of which I had nothing to do), that I had better send it back to you, hoping against experience that I can get some of the songs you showed me two years ago. Anaesthesia has come again, no poems please me very much, I've just decided that I must write all my new poems again, which is to say that my impression may be an old and incontestable stupidity (the one you saw when I was unable to understand *Henry IV*, Part I), but for what it is worth my impression is that the complication of images often takes the mind away on digressions, rather than giving one an increased and increasing knowledge of the subject. What a piece of jargon this last sentence became! But anyway: from trash to rascal to glacier and April's revelry is an example of what I mean and the ninth stanza is an example of what I think the whole poem ought to be, and the eighth stanza, and the one about Mozart. The image of marriage as a music and as a trial is difficult for me, too, even if one imports the notion of a laboring violinist. The versification is as it always [is] with you of wonderful skill, but here I suspect or guess it may be responsible for the forced quality of some of the images and phrases. I hope I am wrong and you have Richard at hand to correct me.

Now if only you might be persuaded to send me more poems or to write a story for *PR* or to write a short Variety; but how shall I persuade another when I cannot force myself?

Will you say to Richard that *PR* has heard of no money, and neither William nor Philip ever hear of any money, except the money which is given to other reviews?

I will be back in New York in the middle of next month.[2] Can you wait for your books until then? With my love to Eileen and to you,

Yours always,
Delmore

1. A draft of "Canto Amor," in which Mozart appears in the eighteenth stanza.
2. S had been granted a sabbatical leave from Harvard.

TO JOHN CROWE RANSOM

91 Bedford St.
New York, N.Y.
April 30, 1945

Dear John:

I'd like to take the liberty of recommending to your attention one of the stories submitted in your new contest, "The Unconscious" by Elizabeth Pollet.[1] She's as gifted as any writer I know through my own reading of manuscripts, and my own habit and fault of missing the qualities of new writers prompts me to write to you about her.

Yours,
Delmore Schwartz

1. S met Elizabeth, the daughter of painter Joseph Pollet, in the spring of 1944. She became his second wife on June 10, 1949.

TO KARL SHAPIRO

91 Bedford Street
New York, New York
May 27, 1945

Dear Karl,

I was very pleased to get your card. Your idea of a polyamericana sounds like good politics as well as good poetry.

Let me know if you come to New York, or just ring my bell. You'll probably find me illustrating to myself the inexhaustible maxim I mean to use for future contributors' notes: "DILIGENCE IS NOT ENOUGH."

Yours,
Delmore

TO R. P. BLACKMUR

91 Bedford Street
New York, New York
July 19, 1945

Dear Richard:

If you'd care to renew the invitations of previous years, I would immediately take advantage of your hospitality. But if you are hard at work, please don't be embarrassed to say so: I have three invitations elsewhere and will not be at a loss. And if I were in the country hard at work, I would not very much desire such a visitor as myself: the most I can say of myself at present is that I am full of long silences.

Also, could you be persuaded to review Marguerite Young's *Angel In the Forest?*

I have a new sentence for my tombstone: "Diligence is not enough."

Yours,
Delmore

TO JOHN CROWE RANSOM

91 Bedford Street
New York City, N.Y.
Oct. 28, 1945

Dear John:

Would it be possible for me to be paid for my story in advance?[1] I'd like to see proofs, too.

I meant to write you before this to say how pleased I was that you liked it, especially since it is the only thing I've brought to a successful conclusion in almost a year of trying. With best wishes,

Yours sincerely,
Delmore

1. "A Bitter Farce," published in *Kenyon Review*, VIII (Spring 1946).

TO R. P. BLACKMUR

91 Bedford Street
New York, New York
[November 3, 1945]

Dear Richard,

Joyously I would travel far farther than Princeton to see you or to see your poem, but that the effect of any travel is to derange such concentration and purpose as I possess. The fact is that I expect to have all the time in eternity to discuss fit subjects of conversation with you in Purgatory, where no doubt sinus and insomnia will be replaced by suitable equivalents.

I wish very much that you would send me your poem. I can't see how a place would be open for it very soon, since the spring issue is to be devoted to French authors wholly, an enormous backlog of accepted poems by inferior poets has accumulated, I have just concluded an ordeal made necessary by John's sending in of eight poems, some poets such as George have waited more than a year now to appear, and the summer issue may well be the last one, unless matters change very much in the interim.

I've raised the issue of Pound more than once and more than a year back I wrote an editorial on the subject.[1] The majority view, which seems reasonable to me, is that Pound is not being tried as an author. If he is attacked as a poet, then we will certainly defend him strongly and at length. But meanwhile it is observed that no one's actions can be defended on the ground that he is a great poet, as he is.

If you can't make John your assistant, you might do worse than importing one of the children of Israel from Cambridge, Massachusetts, an importation you once mentioned frequently and then ceased to mention. As my pony Horace says, "I will do the office of a whetstone, which serves to make the steel sharp, itself incapable of cutting; I will teach the duty and the office, myself writing nothing; whence subject-matter may be secured (in the obscene abysses of the heart); whither virtue, (promiscuity, ambition, anger and hope) may lead. Sound judgement (and conquered neurosis and overcome evil) are the ground and the fountain of writing well. The Socratic papers (and *Finnegans Wake*) can show you an (inexhaustible) subject; and spontaneous words will follow (the submission to overt form)."

Yours,
Delmore

1. Pound, who had been arrested by the U.S. Army in Italy the previous year, was about to stand trial for wartime treason.

TO R. P. BLACKMUR

91 Bedford Street
New York, New York
November 12, 1945

Dear Richard,

If you feel sufficiently involved to say in print what you say in your letter about Pound, I can see to it that it gets printed. I hear that others, including Eliot, are doing the same kind of thing. The real question so far as I can make it out is whether one can say that a poet is more a subject for mercy than other human beings. The forgiveness and mitigation of which you speak has to be for everyone or for anyone or for no one. I think however that what you say ought to be said and printed.

I am serious indeed about Princeton and indeed I am serious in all things, and it has often been said to me that I am too serious: "You are too serious, Delmore," they say. To teach the freshmen about the infinite possibilities of the sentence is interesting and pleasant for a time, but there are many other subjects and too often I have had to stop myself from speaking of them.

I was not supposed to speak of the new difficulty in keeping *PR* going, and I wish you would say nothing about it to anyone because the impression of failure appears to have the wrong effect on everyone who is not concerned. There remain some thirty pages of poetry which must be gotten into print before I can look at your long poem as an editor. On first, second, third and fourth readings, it seems very exciting, but unfinished. In some places, the versification looks rough to me. // But all of this is the fault of the reader and the richness of the poem, and I think you are right in thinking this one of your best pieces. I am going to keep it until I think I know it well and until I can regard it as a poem to be printed, although it is likely enough that I may never arrive at that moment.

Blocks more than sinus or larger keep me from journeying anywhere. I should visit my grandmother, I should buy my first pair of shoes since 1943 and my first suit since 1942, and if I do not soon visit the barber, instead of combing my hair, I will have to beat it like a rug.

Yours,
Delmore

TO ROBERT LOWELL

Dear Cal,

I hope that you come to stay with Jean [Stafford] whenever you like and stay as long as you like. The longer you stay, the longer I will like it. I should in honesty list my shortcomings such as morose silence, but they are boring and obvious. The charming and fey lady at 225 E. 19th St. might be used as an excellent reference, though I prefer the mind of God. At any rate, there are two floors, two typewriters, beautiful pictures, too many books, but in fine, adequate provision for whatever solitude and privacy you and Jean may require. I forgot to say, two studies. I won't be able to get back to my place until the 1st of February, but if you come any time after that, the pleasure and delight will be such that I will play Mozart as a greeting. There are also two stoves and two beds. If you and Jean don't like a studio couch for two, let me know before I depart from New York so that I can take back one of the cots I have here.

My brain pan still throbs in empathy after Jean's story ["The Liberation"?], which there can't be any question of our taking as long as Jean does not mind waiting until some less good stories are published. I think much of the writing is as good as anything else of Jean's and only the death at the end might I think be questioned as not truly prepared for or necessary, but perhaps I am at fault as a reader. //

Your dialogues as projected make me think that with a sufficient amount of indoctrination, no more than that of any medical student, Jean and I might induct you as an apprentice in the black tongue circuit, whose founding fathers are Juvenal, Horace, Dante, Swift, Lear. Jane Austen is a founding aunt. As a beginning or conclusion to the conversations with Allen, I'd like to suggest what may have already occurred to you, a conversation in which Allen exhausts his friends and starts running himself down, and then accuses himself of lack of charity, forbearance, and imaginative sympathy.

'Tis bitter chill and I am sick at heart, for I feel as if I were one thousand years of age. I feel as ugly as yonder shoes. And yet as Lady [Mary Wortley] Montagu said on her deathbed, "It all has been most interesting." But this does not belong in a letter.

Yours affectionately,
Delmore

1. S. was staying at William Van Keuren's apartment.

TO ELIZABETH POLLET

20 Ellery St.
Cambridge, Mass.
January 19, 1946

Dear Elizabeth,

As you may have seen in the newspaper, I narrowly averted death by returning to Cambridge last Saturday instead of yesterday.[1] I am back in my own house and tomorrow I intend to make my own breakfast, which means that existence is as normal again as it has ever been for me. But what a week [it] has been: I drove my tenants from the house, for they had painted the dining room an extraordinary aluminum silver, and the floor of the bedroom an obscene red, for they were newlyweds. And I accused the landlady's husband of treason because he objected to drink in general and my drinking especially when everyone knows I never touch the stuff and the Volstead Act has been repealed. The day after my return Bill [Van Keuren] and Jeremy both went to bed with the flu, but not before I had had interesting conferences with both and begun the *Odyssey* in a free paraphrase as the story of a boy who was looking for his father. But to return to my labors which gave me a feeling of self-reliance proper to New England, I summoned the locksmith, I secured coal from an unwilling dealer, I started the well-known furnace, I bought wood and paint, the well-known Chem-Tone for to take that vulgar silver from the dining room walls. I carried books, on which my tenants had spattered paint, I bought soap, eggs, coffee, crackers, toothpowder, oranges and milk. I visited the sick, greeted the well, and inspected Jeremy's cats. Simplex, named because it was for a time supposed that he was simple, is an ageing tomcat, quite affable, not very clean, and addicted to lost weekends from which he returns wounded and exhausted. Carrie is quite young and a girl, but Simplex is not interested in her, perhaps because of her extreme youth. Both are likeable, but needless to say not in the same class as Riverrun, in whom Jeremiah has expressed no little interest. Simplex has one trait which made me think of poor Pushkin, dead in early youth. He is not interested in the fish in his dish as long as he thinks he has a chance of a handout from the dinner table.

It turns out that the university is still running on a wartime schedule for the educational reason that thus it makes more money. This appears to mean that I will have to teach next summer, but not during the fall term, so that I can again come to New York's cold-water flats for four months. Bill has an excellent apartment which he never uses and to which I now have a key, and I would say that it is only an hour and ten minutes from New York to here except that after yesterday's accident, I don't want anyone to visit me by plane, although I intend to come to New York by plane so that it can be said that I left this life in the cause of literature, hurrying to argue with William and Philip.

Will you tell Will to send my mail and my copies of *Time* here, so that I can keep up with the current falsehoods? And will you take possession of my big orange squeezer, my coffeepot, my electric stove, and my broken turntable, especially the latter, since you can't get a phonograph in Cambridge? Now that you are at leisure, you ought to write me a long letter.

As ever,
Delmore

1. A plane from New York to Boston crashed a week after S had flown back.

TO WILLIAM PHILLIPS

20 Ellery St.
Cambridge, Mass.
Sunday [January 1946?]

Dear William,

I am back in my own establishment after a week of real estate successes which suggest that my mother may have been right to say that I should have followed my father in the real estate game. However, I feel that a year's training in the dialectic with you, illustrious and undefeated veteran of a million arguments, made these provincials easy opponents.[1]

Anthony [George Anthony Palmer] has the books by Beauvoir and will decide this week if he wants to do the translating. I will let you know immediately. The more I think of it, the more I think the French issue ought to be postponed until the summer. Wanning, when I told him about not using his James review, suggested that he make it the basis for an essay on James. I said that I would have to speak to you and Philip, and that my impression was that James had been exhausted. However, he can be put off without difficulty.

Did you tell Philip that I tried to call him? I did not get the books or rather plays by Camus before I left, since Philip forgot to bring them to the office. Tomorrow I will go to the library and look at the new French books. Don't forget that I can do one of the rewriting jobs, if you use Guterman.

I bought a copy of the *Pocket History of the Second World War*, which is awful, but which might be used for a good review by Handlin. How about that?

Would you get one of the girls to put the ledgers of my father's real estate business in a carton and send them here express collect?[2] //

Let me know when to send you a page about Turgenev or Lawrence for Dial, and you might remind Philip that Lawrence was my idea.[3] And let me know immediately by phone or telegram if it is *in the least possible* to substitute my new version of my story in the *P.R.* anthology. It ought not to be too late, this version is much better, and I will pay the expenses involved, if there are any. Both *Accent* and Laughlin have given their authors a chance to make revisions.

My romance is at an end.[4]

If you had to exist among these Gentiles, you would come to see what Will means about the Jews.

The Lowells will be here soon and Jean says that she is getting a bed, so that there will be plenty of room for you, and though I fear a continuous house party, perhaps all will be well. Best to Edna,

Yours,
Delmore

1. Phillips had been in New York during S's sabbatical year.
2. S was negotiating with lawyers over his father's estate, convinced it should have amounted to more.
3. Phillips was co-editing a series on world literary figures, to be published by Dial.
4. S's courtship of Aileen Ward.

TO JEAN STAFFORD

20 Ellery Street
Cambridge, Mass.
Jan. 20, 1946

Dear Jean,

The coal should be here by Monday, that is, January 21, and since I have driven my tenants from the house because of the vulgarity with which they attempted to imitate my painting job and scheme, there is no reason why you and Cal should not come whenever you like, but if you want a definite date, let us say, either Wednesday the 30th of January, or Monday the 4th of February, or any time in the immediate future and the sooner the better. The 1st of February is black Friday because then we read 1500 anticipatory themes in order to permit 4 freshmen to be excused from English A. //

I don't see why you have to bring a ham to Cambridge. // Have you considered that this Lanyon, whether or not he writes from Tokyo, may be your husband, irritated by the other fan letters and determined to surpass them? I feel that there must be some connection (and Whitehead says that everything is connected) between that beard and your report that Cal needs a haircut.

Love,
Delmore

P.S. When you get here, I hope you will feel like accompanying me when I go to choose my cat. I need feminine advice, but Albert says that Frederick Kuh was just an ordinary cat, and though I don't believe him, still this will be my first cat since the age of six and I don't want to make the wrong choice. I must put appearance out of my mind and choose the kitten on the basis of companionship. If it is a male, the name will be Schwartz, if it is a girl, I will call her Oranges.[1]

1. The cat Oranges is immortalized in Lowell's poem, "To Delmore Schwartz," in *Life Studies*: "Your tiger kitten, *Oranges*, / cartwheeled for joy in a ball of snarls . . . "

TO R. P. BLACKMUR

[Cambridge]
January 23, 1946

Dear Richard,

I will consult with the boys, but I doubt the outcome, for, good as your poem is, I am allowed only five pages an issue for poetry, and though I think an exception might be made in this instance, the next issue is French, there are some eighty pages of prose in proof, there is a story fifty pages in length which has been held over for almost a year and which must be used because it won half of third prize in a contest, and there are now more poems accepted than will be used in the fall issue, if there is a fall issue. In my youth I was under the strange impression that the only question for an editor was literary merit, but now I see the abysses of my innocence. Just between us, it was necessary to become angry before any of John's poems were accepted.

I am back in the establishment which has more history than any other place I ever lived in and pleased to be back and glowing with triumph, having overcome my landlady and my tenants [. . .] // However, all is well and behovely now, and if you were but in Cambridge, then it would be possible for me to converse with one literate human being who did not make me uncomfortable because I do not admire his prose or verse. I mean to say, I desire the comfort of admiration, and in Cambridge it is lacking. First thing I see in Cambridge is the elongated being of Theodore Spencer, looking more and more like a depraved Roman senator.

Yet there is also your noble nephew Jeremiah [Jeremy], with whom I conferred last Sunday, immediately after which he went to bed with the flu. He is now my godson in an official sense and I am giving him the *Odyssey* in a free paraphrase as the story of a boy who is looking for his father and a man who just wanted to go home from war. Jeremy appears to be interested, but I suspect that he likes Joyce better, for he responded with a glee his elders have not yet shown to choice sentences from *Finnegans Wake*. When we came upon a passage in one of his books about right and wrong, I asked what they were and he said they were just like good and bad, and when I asked him what good and bad were, he said, I don't know. Neither do I, I remarked, but don't think that that means that there is no good or bad. This left the noble child indifferent, for he thought I was holding out on him.

I am still perplexed that you should find a resemblance in this quarter to Alyosha, especially since the Xmas before last you remarked justly, "I never said that you were not malicious." I suppose I will have to come to Princeton to find out what you meant. I also want to buy on a lend-lease basis or for keeps one of Helen's pictures. What is the price?

As ever,
Delmore

TO WILLIAM BARRETT

[Cambridge]
January 27, 1946

Dear Will,

My letter the other day was probably impatient, but I had written eight letters to New York without getting an answer. Will you tell Elizabeth to send me the electric radiator? It was the electric stove that I told her to keep. //

Here are no bushers, Finnegan, here are unburied corpses, except for the little child about whom you do not seem to feel very much enthusiasm. At the cocktail party I went to last night a youthful captain told me that he thought Fitzgerald was wonderful and Eliot unreadable. A middle-aged matron yearned for [Chaucer scholar George Lyman] Kittredge and wanted to know if Trevelyan ever published the second volume of his biography of Fox. And all were perplexed when I told of how Truman, when headed for Potsdam, exclaimed: "Now I am going to meet all those celebrities!"

However, I am gone back to the little things with an ease which I hardly understand, carrying books, shoving furniture, buying groceries, and the like. It is all very interesting, since I have enough energy. I fixed my radio, though with crude means, and during the last week I've been making myself marriage-forestalling or contra-espousal meals, nothing but the best in cans, money no object. Can it be that I am at last to arrive at adulthood?

I am sure that William & Philip regard you strangely only because they don't have you figured out. If you announce now that you don't intend to translate anything at the last minute, there won't be any difficulty. Now that you are on the masthead the only way in which you can be removed from it is by your own request. However, I will keep as a secret whatever you say about the boys. I don't want to hear what they say about me, since I feel I know what it is in principle and would like to disregard that aspect of reality for a time.

Now I must pause to hear the new symphony by Stravinsky.

It was fairly good.

Now that I've become so much of a housewife, I think I would like to have my trash-can, orange-squeezer, sauce-pan, and whatever other useful objects I left behind me. I've asked Elizabeth to get them and keep them until I come to New York. How do you like 91 Bedford St. now? // Soon I will paint the dining room walls, varnished with great vulgarity by my tenants. Hitler began as a house painter and I will probably end as one. //

Best to Julie,
Yours,
Delmore

TO PHILIP RAHV

20 Ellery St.
Cambridge, Mass.
Jan. 27, 1946

Dear Philip,

I was sorry to have to rush off without saying goodbye to you and Nathalie, but I had a lot of packing to do at the last moment.

Anthony does not want to do the translating of the Simone de Beauvoir, so I am sending back the novel today. If there is no one else available, I can do a part of *Pyrrhus and Cineas*, though I'd prefer not to have to do it. The essay is much simpler French than the novel. Perhaps the girl who did *La Nausée* would do for the novel, which, from the little I've seen of it, is quite interesting. Or perhaps Katherine Hoskins could do it. I don't want to get involved with someone in the French department here who may not write good English.

Will you let me know how many poems remain accepted and not yet published so that I can figure out how much room there will be in the summer issue? And will you get the girl to send up the poetry every week or every two weeks? Blackmur wrote me, asking if I thought his ten-page poem might be printed *next fall*. I told him I would consult with you, but that there was so much unprinted material on hand that the fall issue would be over-crowded if there was a fall issue. //

I've looked in the library for new French material, but apparently it's been impossible to buy anything except magazines. Some of the people here kick because they have not received the new issue yet.

Have you any objection to Berryman's attempting the poetry chronicle? He's more likely to do it, if I ask him far in advance.

Yours,
Delmore

TO ELIZABETH POLLET

[Cambridge]
February 2, 1946

Dear Elizabeth,

Your gloomy letter made me gloomy and not only because of River-run's departure. It's about time, however, that I had some of the burden of your emotions, since you have so often had mine. I will certainly read your manuscript whenever you like,[1] indeed I am eager to see it, but I might be better able to make out what it is like if you sent me a copy instead of waiting until I come to New York. I trust that you are using a carbon because only false bohemians do not. And when I come to New York you know how harried and hurried I am likely to be.

For a time I toyed with the pleasant idea that perhaps Riverrun had left New York to visit me in Cambridge. I soon recognized that this was wishful thinking. But where is he? Can't you look for him? Perhaps he will return in the spring.

Yesterday the school year began with the marking of the freshmen examinations, the most depressing of beginnings, and on Wednesday Cal and Jean arrived, having called to ask if they might arrive sooner because like me they cannot wait for the future. So far all is pleasant. Jean has shown no interest in the furnace, but Cal is fascinated by it and begs to be permitted to take care of it. But I have refused to let him do anything but regard my tending. However, Jean makes dinner, I make lunch, each of us breakfasts alone, and in mid-morning the household resembles either a literary movement or a school for typists. The only unpleasantness is that Jean gets most of the mail.

I visited Jeremy on Tuesday and he wished to hear stories of my childhood. He found them very interesting. The story of the *Odyssey* has been stopped for the moment because Jeremy and Elizabeth want to hear about a Dr. Doolittle who spoke perfect English. It turned out that this fish had escaped from the aquarium in Battery Park and was full of phrases like "Don't Spit," "This Way Out," "Smoking Forbidden." This book was written at the turn of the century, I think, and the unconscious motives of the author [Hugh Lofting] with regard to children would suffice to get him sent to Alcatraz, if he acted upon them.

Most of the time I have been too much involved with the houshold and with a new story to be as aware of my emotions and thoughts as is customary with me, but some kind of nervous exhilaration has taken hold of me, causeless and as much a kind of illness as its counterpart of apathetic depression. Still, one is much to be preferred to the other, unless it is true as it probably is that the two are really a unity.

How about writing me sooner this time and telling me more news and that you are no longer sick?

As ever,
[Unsigned.]

1. *A Family Romance*, a novel which New Directions published in 1950.

TO WILLIAM PHILLIPS

[Cambridge
February 1946]

Dear William,

Surely you can force the issue about giving me a volume. If the series means anything, then you are going to run out of world figures pretty quickly, since Joyce is dead, Mann has been used, Proust is dead, and Eliot will not do anything. Moreover as an editor of the series you ought to have as much to say as [Joseph Wood] Krutch, Van Doren, and Margaret [Greenberg]. I really need the money, literally, and also because I would have to write fifty reviews to make as much money as I might in that way. Moreover, there is an obligation involved in my having suggested the volume of all of Lawrence's stories.

The Lowells have been here for a week and it has been very pleasant so far. // Meanwhile school has begun, but the great institution which drew me back here—the institution of the monthly check—does not arrive until the 1st of next month, so that I need that twenty dollars. By the way, I would make as much from one of the volumes in the series as I do from six months' drudgery at marking one class's papers, and I might be able to stop one of them and thus have more time for my own work in the fall: so don't let me down on something as simple and as important as this.

I wrote to Margaret in place of saying goodbye to her and told her to let me know if she came up here and to my astonishment she and Clem as well declared that they might come in the near future. Since you're so shy about such matters, I will tell her that you ought to get the Melville volume and that Kazin is a psalm-singing peasant. Another possibility which might or might not be sensible would be for you to tell Margaret that you are visiting me and have heard that she might, and would she like to come ajunketing with you. This will not stop me from speaking to her, it will merely change the frankness of my conversation with you while she is here.

I have done some work on the psychoanalytical volume [never published] and there are some problems which I must discuss with you: for example is there any point in the photostats until I am sure of the permissions?

Everyone here seems to like the new issue a lot; I don't mean only Cal and Jean, but just plain subscribers.

I hope you're making sure that you get the right doctor for Edna. A good diagnostician is as rare as a major poet, I hear, and the rest make all kinds of errors.

Yours,
Delmore

TO R. P. BLACKMUR

20 Ellery Street
Cambridge, Mass.
[February 1946?]

Dear Richard,

I like your poem, though I do not like it as much as the long one, and I will forward it to New York this week. I don't think there will be any question of using it, but I must consult the other three. Your other two poems will appear when there is room for them, which will perhaps be in the summer or the fall issue. As for the reasons that your long poem was not used, I do not think poetry is moribund, I prefer not to be able to use it because of length than because I do not like it, and I am distressed by your remarks about length. The essay by Hannah Arendt was supposed to be twelves pages long and when she refused to reduce it, after painful explanations were made to her in the office, it was decided to call her Hannah Arrogance and never commission a piece by her again. As a result of her prolixity, a story held for over three issues by an unpublished boy was omitted for six months more and this morning, arrived a letter of abuse from the hopeful author in which he declared that Philip obviously was never going to print the story. I might remark that both Tate and Ransom have more room and do less with it, that the essay on Stevens and the chronicle by Fitts also represent room for poetry; and in fine I feel that your protest is unfeeling.

Whether I am right or not about your lack of sympathy, this is clearly the appropriate place to ask two graces of you. The first is a desire—no other word is exact—for a Rockefeller grant to help me rewrite my book on Eliot. I've already written it twice, but I'd like to try to write it a third time, undistressed by the temptation of writing short reviews and while I am teaching only one class. Can you tell me how to proceed, when applications must be made, and if you will tell Marshall[1] that I am not as I may seem, but studious, intelligent, and industrious?

The second grace seems less likely to me to seem to you a righteous one, and I will not mind if you say no. What I want to be able to say is that you have told me that you will recommend me as your assistant at Princeton when an assistant is chosen. Since at least a year will pass before such an occasion arises, you don't have to consider such permission binding in the least. While I was in New York the higher composition courses were given to instructors who not only are not instructors in composition, but also have neither the desire nor the ability to teach composition. I intend to insist on the articled privileges of Briggs-

Copelandship and my insisting will be helped if I can say that I might soon go elsewhere. However, as I said, if this will embarrass you, I will seek outside support elsewhere.

Meanwhile Spencer has been given the Boylston chair. He came here to tell me the news with much humility and no little generosity, for he avowed that he would certainly make every effort to keep me here permanently and though I spoke politely of my love of New York and sought to conceal my curling lip, I do not think that either of us was much deceived by the other. What says the ghost of J. Q. Adams?[2]

Cal and Jean, who are very pleasant to live with, have taken to calling me THE BOY. Boy! I fluttered their doves at Corioli! I used to be known as Dub and Del Monte peaches, my former wife called me a Pharisee once, but best of all is the comparison to Alyosha, false but pleasing.

Yours,

Delmore

1. John Marshall, associate director of the Rockefeller Foundation.
2. S is referring to Adams' doctrine of integrity, which Henry Adams, in Blackmur's biography, sees as buried.

TO R. P. BLACKMUR

20 Ellery Street
Cambridge, Mass.
[March 1946?]

Dear Richard:

Many thanks for your effort with Marshall, which came to nothing. Will you keep it a matter of confidence that I asked about a grant? The reason is that the boys may feel I should not have asked, if there is any possibility at all of *PR* getting help. I don't think there is or that there will be. At Christmas you suggested that Barrett might be able to get some aid. He was indifferent at the time, but now that he is having much difficulty with the fiction he really wants to write—for which he gave up his State Department job, and his job at Brown—he needs money. I am enclosing Marshall's letter, on the chance that it may help you to figure just what kind of a project will stand a chance of seeming attractive. //

It is hard for me to believe that you can have any doubt as to my views on $3500 a year. Thanks for mentioning me to [Christian] Gauss. John ought to come first. He is really a wonderful teacher, however difficult elsewhere, and I've always felt that deans are only concerned about getting good teachers for the students. In actual fact I will bet you a case of Scotch that neither John nor I gets the job.

There is room for you and Helen here in June or any other time and at last count there were nine sleeping places in the house, which has made some of my guests wonder at the chastity of my life. The truth is, I sleep with my cat, Oranges Schwartz, a girl, very affectionate, so affable indeed that for a time I thought she was a dumbbell. My relation to her is maternal and this shows that I've always wanted to be a mother. When I bought her two cans of $.52 sardines last week,* Cal and Jean decided that you were right, I was not of this world. When spring comes to Cambridge, I am going to give a cocktail party for Oranges and let Oranges look over some of the better-looking tomcats. Perhaps you can bring Pomfret? Oranges ought to meet a woman of the world.

Yours,
Delmore

*Because I had been waiting too long in the store and was hungry myself, very much of this world.

TO ELIZABETH POLLET

[Cambridge]
March 26, 1946

Dear Elizabeth,

I told Will to tell you that I would write you as soon as I was able to write patiently. I am not yet patient, but it is not at all clear how soon I will be, so I had better write to you now. So much has occurred of late that years will have to pass before I understand what has occurred. The chief external event has been the mantle of assistant professor, which was placed upon my head or is it shoulders, while I was looking elsewhere. This vainglorious title is not as impressive as it sounds, as I will explain to you, but it is meant to be impressive and it is, to those who are interested in status and the mother and not in poems and the child. Anyway, it means that you must stay with the Dicksons or at a hotel when you visit me; unless, as I suggested to Will, you come with the Barretts.

Barbara's [Elizabeth's sister] son appears to be quite fat. I hope he continues to gain weight, but not in the head. You ought to bring your sister not flowers but books. Let her weep about the death of Desdemona and take as an example the wisdom of Portia.

Where is that overrated ingrate Riverrun? Oranges has been in heat, much to her distress and mine. Like her sponsor, she was soothed by catnip. The Lowells have departed, but not before they begged to take Oranges to Maine for a visit. Calvin has gone to a retreat among the Trappist Fathers, desiring silence after hearing what I had to say about the Holy Apostolic Church. And Jean has returned to Maine where there will be silence too. Both are so devoted to me now that I am ashamed.

I see that you have decided about the summer without waiting for me to decide anything. If I were able to write a patient letter, I would explain patiently that you should have been more patient and less independent. It is all right to be independent if you are, but if you are not, it is shadowboxing. Since I too am not independent, I must wait patiently before I know if I can return to New York in September.

The Guermantes Way seemed best to me not because the subject is near to my heart, but because in it is the passage in which Proust understands what his motives are. The rest is revelation and proof, and though the very end is a beautiful statement of his motives, it is mere resolution and besides he had no chance to rewrite most of it. Best of all, I like the death of Bergotte, but the subject really near my heart as you should know is the end of *Finnegans Wake*.

If you are distressed by anything I say or don't say, you ought to ring me. And you ought to send me both your novel and your story, along with the laundry I left at Grove Street. Or better than sending me the laundry, just take possession of it for the time being.

As ever,
Delmore

TO MARK VAN DOREN

20 Ellery St.
Cambridge, Mass.
March 29, 1946

Dear Mark,

Many thanks for sending us the poem, "The Stranger's Tale," which I like very much and which we will use as soon as manuscripts accepted before this have been printed. I wanted long before now to ask you for some verse, but my first two experiences in asking others to give me verse—for a review which the other editors feel, I think rightly, must emphasize topicality—left me so embarrassed by complications that I hesitated. Just between us, I will never get over the effort involved in getting three brief lyrics by John accepted; and part of the difficulty, as you can well imagine, was John, who had submitted eight poems. Since we can't use the poem immediately, I hope you will forgive me for being an interminable literary critic and saying that a few phrases are good enough but perhaps might be much better. In stanza 1, line 5, "lone in the wind" seems to me less effective than you have often been with the same idea in other poems. In stanza 2, line 6, "generous birds" seems to me a transferred idea. In the context, the age and the gods are generous, and the birds are as Yeats would say only self-delighting. In stanza 4, "wild cities" and "high laws" both seem like adjectives which are not as specific as they might be. And in the last stanza, the reference to men as sparrows with providence for watcher, which I take to be a reference to the New Testament phrase about God's marking even the fall of sparrows, is not as explicit about the reference as it could be. But then I may be forcing a reference which is meant to be passing and implicit. In any case, I think the poem is very good as it is. It makes me think of passages in my favorite book, *Finnegans Wake*, when the theme of the age of the gods and the age of men is taken up.

Perhaps these observations are the consequence of earning my living for so long by teaching composition. I was thunderstruck the other day by being made an assistant professor, a meaningless ascent, all connotation, like Swinburne, since the move was made to keep instructors from going elsewhere in hordes and in my own instance meaningless because I will still have to teach freshman composition.

> Yours,
> Delmore

TO ELIZABETH POLLET

> 20 Ellery St.
> Cambridge, Mass.
> March 29, 1946

Dear Elizabeth,

The tone of my letter was the reason I had need of being patient. When I am patient, I remark upon my tone.

I will be in New York next Friday afternoon or on Saturday, the day of the big party, and I will talk to you about your story then. Can I stay at your place while Will's is my official domicile? If so, then would you give Will or Julie a pair of keys so that I don't have to walk about with a suitcase?

If it is not mere rhetoric and you really mean what you say when you say, "I will do anything you want me to do!", then let us have a real though minor trial: will you learn shorthand as soon as possible? It is a skill worth having anyway. //

The city is bitter/beautiful as the country, as Socrates remarks in the *Phaedrus*, and he was no fool.

I can't describe the internal events now, I can't be sure of what they truly are. One of them appears to be an overwhelming desire to compose a musick or biographical poem about the Master of Joy, Doctor of Love. But I must forbear for if I do not correct my themes what will become of my child and grandchild? And I must start now.

As ever,
Delmore

TO JEAN STAFFORD

[Cambridge]
Saturday [Spring 1946]

Dear Jean,

I feel pretty much as you do, and Oranges after two days of looking for your coat or perhaps Cal's went into heat again and started to yowl like a Wagnerian soprano, though I told her that silence was best and ripeness was all. I let her out yesterday to lose her virginity and she was nearly killed for Eros by a passing car. She started again today and the catnip did nothing but bore her and then when the Parkers[1] arrived for to take me out to lunch, she was gone again. The serving lady had let her out because she did not like the yowling. When I returned from lunch and lightened by three martinis, four tomcats had cornered my little girl, but she had chosen the biggest and fattest tomcat of all and I felt as Oedipus' father might have felt when his son punched him at the crossroads when I saw the look in the stout tomcat's face. He had been having difficulties of his own because of the other boys who were trying to horn in. All that Oranges wanted to do was to be alone with the choice of her heart but the other tomcats were getting ready to scratch it out with the victor just as he was being extremely victorious. I decided to desert and return and then a world war started and Oranges was the innocent bystander just about to lose not only her innocence but also her eyes. Consequently, I stepped across the wire fence, started after Oranges, who did not want to come home, drove all the tomcats off, and found myself being yelled at by an old man on whose newly planted garden I was walking. I was tempted to yell right back at Jehovah, but I told him I was only looking for my cat and the soft answer turned away his wrath. He summoned his son, and they found Oranges and returned her to me. She did not want to come back and I don't know what the future will hold, but anyway I will report to you in detail, if you are interested.

I am beginning to think that I don't like experience.

I intend to go through your book [*The Mountain Lion*] today and tomorrow and then send it back Monday or Tuesday.

Love,
[Unsigned carbon.]

1. Mr. and Mrs. Francis Parker. Parker had been a classmate of Lowell's and illustrated many of his dust jackets and frontispieces.

TO WILLIAM BARRETT

[Cambridge]
April 9, 1946

Dear Klip,

On my way back as I looked down from the plane window so that I might say again, *I spit on this life*, it recurred to me that on Saturday night my former life [*sic*] I mean death had replied to, "How are you?" with "O you know, on the brink of suicide every day," while on Sunday apropos of the sunlight or something you remarked that you expected to annihilate yourself in 1210 days. These connected promises or whatever they are suggest the likelihood that the two of you will hold hands at my funeral, as in 1935. Such at least is the general tendency of the effect of such remarks upon my none-too-easy mind. The only safeguard I can think of is to promise you that if you kill yourself, I will attempt to persuade your widow to become my third wife, even if it means marrying a Jew.

From the dingy airport of the provincial capital I went straight to the Dicksons to get back the Princess Oranges, who had won much praise for her intelligence and caught cold, so that when she saw me she sneezed. After being given a detailed discount of her five days of alienation, from which she has not yet recovered, I went upstairs to visit our Socialist King and his sister. He was hiding under the blankets to attract more attention and came out only when it was clear that I enjoyed conversing with his sister who wanted to keep Oranges and was not dissuaded by the logic, obviously socialist, of the fact that the household already possesses two cats. Jeremy emerged from the blankets to add his desire to his sister's, and when I said,

"Jeremiah, what have you been doing?"

"I have been *thinking*," he said with italics.

"What have you been thinking *about*?" I queried.

"I have been thinking about *everything*," he giggled.

"How can you think about everything?" I asked, still under the influence of Sidney Chop [Hook].

"That's *all* there is to think about," replied our growing ruler in triumph.

Long live the King!

Now that we are alone together again, Oranges does not sleep with me, perhaps because I toss about too much, and she has found herself a hiding place somewhere, which appears to be some kind of game of getting me to look for her. And her cold has made her indifferent to the catnip mouse I brought back with me to heal the breach in intra-personal relations.

Let me know if you are coming next Sunday and if you come, bring me Hook's book. As I said, there is something wrong in both of us appearing punitive in the same issue. Well, Al, sin is before us But / All shall be billed, all matter of thinks shall be billed /After the purification of the motive / In the grind of our sublimation, I mean, alienation.

Yours,
Delmore

TO JEAN STAFFORD

[Cambridge]
Thursday, April 11, 1946

Dear Jean,

I am too worn and too near the inevitable slump to write much of a letter, or report the party, or engage in discussions of what I said 2½ weeks before.

I am sorry to hear that you are not feeling well. Oranges has a cold and as you see I am not very well.

The only piece of news that I can consider as absolutely factual and not transformed by my present state is the fact that John Berryman has gone to Sewanee [Tennessee] to see if he wants to be Allen's successor, as editor.

The Parkers did not come to the party which was a pity because some interesting painters were present. The Parkers may not have come because I did not ring as I said I would if I had a chance. But

I had no chance, being bemused by a hangover worthy of the Dionysian revels which must have followed the first performance of *Oedipus Rex.*

Do you mind if I wait until the 1st of the month before paying you what I owe you? All my senseless excursions have left me with little money until the monthly check. The telephone bill arrived again but without a list of the toll charges. The sum is $20.10 and since I made only one call to New York, I doubt that my own part of it is more than $5. Enclosed are the milk, electric and gas bills. I am enclosing them so that you can figure that your own estimate that I owe you $50 is probably right. //

Love,
Delmore

TO ALLEN TATE

20 Ellery St.
Cambridge, Mass.
May 9, 1946

Dear Allen:

Cal stopped by yesterday on his way to Maine and said you had asked him [about] doing *An Introduction to Criticism* for Holt. I hope you won't mind if I push myself forward and say that I've thought of some such book for a long time and I think I could get together one which would be popular as a textbook as well as adequate from a critical point of view. I take it that what you have in mind is something like the Brooks & Warren books on poetry and fiction. If you have anyone else in mind, will you let me know, since I want to try to do something of the sort and tie it up with the teaching I am doing this summer.

Yours,
Delmore

TO R. P. BLACKMUR

Partisan Review
46 Astor Place
New York, New York
July 25, 1946

Dear Richard,

I guess I will go and visit the Lowells who are at Boothbay Harbor wherever that is and write you from there when I get there which will be some time next week. I can't stay away very long from the *PR* office because I am allowed only two weeks' vacation without pay and the thousands of bad stories and poems must be rejected with regularity, consequently my stay with you may be very brief, but I should think you would need rests between guests. I will arrive with liquid provision and if the future again resembles the past you will have to use it all yourself because I won't be able to stand anymore for a time.

You did not say if you wanted to review *Angel in the Forest* and I will assume that you do not unless you write me this week. John said he was going to the Cape this week, but if he arrives when I do, you can put me anywhere because a truly veteran insomniac does not distinguish between beds and abodes. I hope hitchhiking is still possible because I want to pay my chum Jeremy a visit.

Yours,
Delmore

TO MARK VAN DOREN

20 Ellery St.
Cambridge, Mass.
Oct. 22, 1946

Dear Mark,

Last summer I heard that the head of the English Department at Columbia had been here and had asked about me. And now it's occurred to me that perhaps I ought to do something to encourage his interest, since I am extremely eager to get back to New York. I should guess that there might be something suitable for me, since Columbia is giving special attention to the teaching of composition and since I have no desire whatever for the kind of academic advancement which apparently makes a department hesitate to take on anyone new.

On the other hand, I know how uncomfortable-making this kind of query can be to anyone in your position, and I should say that this is a matter of preference and not of necessity. My job here is a perfectly good one, except that it is not in New York, and I hope you won't put yourself out in the least about the whole thing. My main difficulty so far as any place in New York goes is the impression that no one would want to depart from Harvard except for something better, and that was why I thought I had better write you.

Yours,
Delmore

TO MARK VAN DOREN

20 Ellery St.
Cambridge, Mass.
Nov. 12, 1946

Dear Mark:

Many thanks for your letter, which I did not get until today because of a mixup in the mail. The business of getting to New York has a fine irony in it, since I imagine that many would gladly take my place and give me theirs, if only a trade might be managed, as among baseball teams.

I've been working fairly well most of the fall, though not without the feeling that I might again be dissatisfied with what I've been doing after a few months. I think it must come from reading too many books. What I would really like is to get rid of the idea, with which I started, that one *ought* to be productive *all* the time.

Yours,
Delmore

TO MARK VAN DOREN

[Cambridge]
Sunday, Nov. 24, 1946

Dear Mark:

I've been going back and forth between Cambridge and New York so much of late that my mail has been mixed up and I did not get your book [*The Noble Voice*] until the other day and I can't tell if the publisher or you sent it to me. But many thanks, anyway, for the book itself, which is very exciting in many ways, especially, I think, because the comments always add something to the wonderful quotations. I won't try to say more because I have to review it, except that if only more minds were fixed in the direction in which the book goes, I think it would be much easier to write much better poetry.

Yours,
Delmore

[In the spring of 1947 S abruptly left Cambridge for New York. Once he had abandoned Harvard, and was in the midst of literary life in Manhattan, he seemed not to have felt the need to write so many letters. Many of his previous correspondents lived in New York.]

TO JOHN CROWE RANSOM

Partisan Review
45 Astor Place
New York 3, N.Y.
[1948]

Dear John,

Many thanks for your very kind note on my book of stories [*The World Is a Wedding*]. To be able to please you is a wonderful satisfaction. I wish I had something new to send you and when I do, I will.

With best wishes,
Yours,
Delmore Schwartz

TO ROBERT LOWELL

Partisan Review
1545 Broadway
New York 19, N.Y.
Sept. 15 [1948?]

Dear Cal—

Do you have any verse for us at all? We are in desperate need of something good. Please let me know. If things don't improve I'll have to release some of my own poems I am uncertain about.

Also, is it possible for me to remake the records I made in April?[1] There are so many sighs, hesitations and pauses in them I'd like either to remake them or not have them used at all. Do let me know about this too, and if you're in N.Y. and have the time and mood, please ring me. My address is 75 Charles St., and my No. WA 9-8194.

Best,
Delmore

1. At the Library of Congress, where Lowell was Consultant in Poetry, 1947-48, and in charge of a program to record American poets.

TO JAMES LAUGHLIN

[New York City, 1948?]

Dear Jay,

Sorry to say that I spoke too soon and that we won't be able to use either canto [of Pound's] because they just don't seem good enough as poetry to justify the amount of room they would take. Perhaps they will seem different in the context of the other new cantos, but in isolation either of these would seem mostly inchoate incoherence.

Yours,
Delmore

TO ROBERT LOWELL

75 Charles St.
WA 9-8194
Dec. 19, 1948

Dear Cal,

How are your long poems going?[1] We might be able to give over a whole issue to one of them.

I wish you would call me when you're in New York. I'd like your poetic advice on finding myself a new cat.

Yours,
Delmore

1. The long poems Lowell was writing about this time include "The Mills of the Kavanaughs," "David and Bathsheba in the Public Garden," and "Thanksgiving's Over."

TO KARL SHAPIRO

75 Charles Street
New York City 14, N.Y.
Oct. 19, 1949

Dear Karl:

Your essay seems very good to us but in its present form—and quite naturally as a lecture—you use about half your pages in dealing with what is for our small audience theses which we have tended to take for granted—for example, the value of explication. From p. 13 on, however, what you have to say is new and in a way a very eloquent personal testament as well as general analysis. If you could be persuaded to make an essay of this, we would be very eager to use it. Needless to say, our objections are not at all to your essay in its present form, but simply a matter of not discussing again what has been discussed in our pages (though not much elsewhere) often before.

This is a good opportunity to say again that I hope you will let me know when you come to New York.

I was in a state of physical exhaustion when we met last year in Washington and I'm afraid I seemed so.

Yours sincerely,
Delmore Schwartz

TO NELA WALCOTT

75 Charles Street
New York City 14, N.Y.
December 13, 1949

Dear Nela,

I should certainly have answered the very nice letter you wrote me last spring or winter, but I was in an awful fog again, as is my custom and as you know.

First, to answer your questions, for a wedding present I would like an original Breughel as you suspected, but secondly an original Sage or if not that, five snapshots of Sage, Susie, and your version of Paul Bunyan and Gargantua.

If you and Jack [Nela's second husband] do come to New York, we must have some kind of small party with Philip and Tessa. My number is WAtkins 9-8194, and it is no longer in the book because rejected contributors began to call me in the middle of the early morning to make very unpleasant remarks about me as an editor. Indeed, one of them announced that "My hatred of you has turned to pity" just before he hung up, so I decided to get out of the book.

Much has happened since last we met, including [. . .] my brother's departure from wife and children, an event which caused wild jubilation in my mother, who called me to tell me that the boy would have been better off in Buchenwald—she really said that—than married to that woman. I responded to her excitement by announcing my own marriage, which she had not heard about, but I think she feels she is still making out very well because she likes my brother much better than me. //

One new development was that I did stop drinking all summer and returned to an infatuation with ice cream sodas, two at a time, and for weeks I did not understand why.

But I will go into detail when you come down. Meanwhile my best regards to Jack, and the children if they remember me, and the boy-with-the-biggest-balls-ever and to the Dicksons and the Palmers if you see them.

Love,
[Unsigned carbon.]

The 1950's

TO JAMES LAUGHLIN

[New York City, 1950?]

This is Delmore Schwartz's first book of poems since 1943. It is a remarkable book in many ways, but perhaps most of all in its richness of emotion and of subject-matter.

Subjects such as existentialism, famous men, automobiles, promiscuity, marriage and divorce, Hamlet and Iago are the starting point for a profound excursion among the extremes of emotion: hope, joy, suffering, innocence, guilt and forgiveness, sorrow, excitement, and exaltation.

And Mr. Schwartz's style, which moves freely and exactly through the modes of wit, irony, narrative, and analysis, is an extraordinary profusion of colloquial speech, Elizabethan form, the imagery of the theatre, and the conflicting points of view of modern thought.[1]

1. S wrote this as jacket copy for *Vaudeville for a Princess and Other Poems* (1950). It was not used by Laughlin.

TO KARL SHAPIRO

75 Charles Street
New York City, New York
February 25, 1950

Dear Karl:

I was very sorry to miss you and Evalyn, and very sorry to hear that you were sick. I hope we can make it some other time soon.

Everyone was pleased to hear that you were going to edit *Poetry*. I imagine that you'll find it a fascinating experience.

I don't want to review Eliot's new play [*The Cocktail Party*] (which is

quite poor, I think) because it would get in the way, for me, of fitting
it into my book about [him].

Best,
Delmore

P.S. The lyrics you're going to use are from a new book of poems
called *Vaudeville for a Princess*. It will probably come out some time
during the summer.

TO KARL SHAPIRO

75 Charles Street
New York City, N.Y.
March 12, 1950

Dear Karl,
I've been ill, and that's the reason for my not answering you to say
that I wish you would not use any photograph at all. They don't look
like me.[1] I thought of sending my pictures of my cats, since Winters
used his terrier, but probably that's too much of a labored joke.

Also, I must apologize because one of the poems, "Once waiting in
that studied living room," had already been accepted and set up in
proof by the *Kenyon Review*. I've been careless about what poems I
sent out partly through natural laziness and partly through the difficulty of holding down three jobs while not well. I hope you can deduct
the cost of the poem which must be withdrawn from whatever I get.
I know what a dreadful nuisance this will make for you, since it happens
now and then on *P.R.*, so please think of me as guilty and contrite.

Best,
Delmore

1. S was always loathe to have new pictures taken. When *Time* wanted a new
photo in 1948, to run with its review of *The World Is a Wedding*, he refused; the one
they used was twelve years old.

TO WALLACE STEVENS

75 Charles Street
New York City 14, N.Y.
April 1, 1950

Dear Wallace Stevens:
I hope it won't seem wrong for me to tell you how much pleasure

it was to read about your getting the Bollingen Prize. It makes me think poetry itself is victorious, at least some of the time. When I saw and then read Eliot's new play and heard so many intelligent human beings say that it was a masterpiece, I began to think that either something was very wrong with me or—which was what I really thought—something was very wrong with many other people. Which makes me think of Eliot's remark two years ago about great poets: he said that a great poet was one who wrote good poetry at 70. He was thinking of Yeats, I imagine, but I thought then of you.

I meant to thank you before now for your congratulations when I was married. I hope that when you are in New York and in the mood, you will call me. My number, which is not in the Directory, is WAtkins 9-8194, and my wife and I would be very pleased if you felt like visiting us at very short notice.

Yours sincerely,
Delmore Schwartz

TO HOWARD MOSS

Partisan Review
1545 Broadway
New York, N.Y.
June 18, 1950

Dear Howard:

I like several of these poems very much (as well as some of your recent poems elsewhere) and have kept them until now, hoping there would be room for them. But now that PR is a bi-monthly, we can't accept anything new until we've published what we accepted on the basis of 12 instead of 6 issues. Won't you send them in again during the fall, and with more new work. By then we ought to be able to accept more new work.

Regards,
Delmore

TO GEORGE PALMER

RFD #2
Saugerties, NY.[1]
August 2, 1950

Dear George,

I've been teaching at Kenyon and no manuscripts have been sent to me. That's why I've taken so long to write to you. I'm sorry that your story does not seem successful to me. My feeling, for what it is worth, is that it does not draw on enough reality to make the reader accept the initial fantasy. I feel that way about some of Kafka too, so perhaps the defect is in me, and the nighttown scene in *Ulysses* is the example I would use to make clear what I mean by drawing on reality for the sake of satirical fantasy.

I hope you and Marjorie are having a good summer, and that you will let us know when you come to New York. I can't honestly say that I expect to be in Cambridge very soon since the fact is that, if practical needs are not operating, I hardly like to leave the house.

Best,
Delmore

1. The Schwartzes drove up to Woodstock to spend the summer on the Pollet family farm with her father.

TO JAMES LAUGHLIN

RFD #2
Saugerties, New York
September 8, 1950

Dear Jay,

There are about six errors in my book [*Vaudeville for a Princess*], and several of them make a difference in the sense—for example, *though*, on p. 77, is printed as *through*. And at another point, *Not* turns the meaning of a sentence upside down. I suppose it is too late to do anything about this, unless you want to insert a list of errata, which is a lot of trouble, of course. I'll be back in New York by next Wednesday or Thursday, and you can let me know then.—I'm extremely sorry about the errors, and I was quite careful I think. But I can't read proof of my own work as proof should be read, and I guess most proofreaders are not very good with poems.

I should also have done something about a new photograph, just in case someone wants to use one. Old ones taken in the last half of the 14th century, which never looked like me anyway. I have a great one taken on the Kenyon courts just after I took another set from Arthur, but unfortunately I am unshaven. I'll bring it down with me next week, but I suppose it's too late to do anything about this too.

My brother-in-lust Sylvester [Pollet] asks me to tell you that I ought to be billed as Bernie Schwartz.[1] He thinks that this would increase sales. I pass this advice along to you without comment.

I can't make head or tail of the review list for Elizabeth's book [*A Family Romance*] because I don't know much about the many newspapers on the list, or about how you handle novels. There are about eight people who might make some favorable comment, and who are not on the list. Is that what you want?

Best,
Delmore

P.S. On second thought, I'm enclosing the photograph and the list of critics for E's book.

1. The real name of film star Tony Curtis.

TO RANDALL JARRELL

75 Charles St.
New York City 14
Oct. 4, 1950

Dear Randall,

I must get an introduction to Turgenev's *Fathers and Sons* written in eleven days,[1] so this can't be much of an answer to your letter, which I would otherwise want to answer at length. I hope you won't mind if I do answer later what you say about writing for no audience since I think something can be gained, at least by me, by comparing impressions.

We're delighted that you and Michael can come up during Christmas. I'm sure you'll find it pleasant and perhaps, if the dates are right, I can give what I've long wanted to give, a small and carefully considered New Year's Eve party. The ones I've been to in recent years are so crowded, in several ways, that I've had the feeling that I was present at a traffic jam of the lost waiting for the ferry across the Styx.

I spoke to Jay Laughlin after getting your letter and he said that he would very much like to publish you, but that he could not make the first move, given your connection with Harcourt, Brace. He suggested that you write to him with whatever proposals you have in mind. I can't say that New Directions is perfect by any means, not after my own experience of the past 12 years (your problem about getting your book reprinted after it was sold out has occurred more than once for N.D. authors too), but there is a real advantage in having a publisher who is chiefly interested in poetry and criticism, while elsewhere, so far as I know, books of criticism are published as a magnanimous favor and at the publisher's leisure—Harcourt, Brace, for example, won't publish a book of Blackmur's essays until he finishes his book on Adams. However, there are disadvantages about New Directions which may or may not trouble you. If you're interested, I'll write you further; in any case, let me know if you want to make the change.

I read Cal's long poem ["The Mills of the Kavanaughs"] and did not like it at all, though I did not tell him so for several reasons, one of them being that I was in so poor a frame of mind at the time that I did not trust my impressions, and another being Cal's frame of mind which was such that he did not perceive my lack of enthusiasm.

Sylvester has just become an ichthyologist because writing is too hard and he likes fish more than books.

Yours,
Delmore

1. Published as the Introduction to the Harper's Modern Classic edition of the Constance Garnett translation (1951).

TO WALLACE STEVENS

75 Charles Street
New York City 14, N.Y.
October 11, 1950

Dear Wallace:

Many thanks indeed for the copy of your new book [*The Auroras of Autumn*]. I have not yet read it all, and in any case your poems always do take a certain amount of living with. But the initial impact is the same as with all of your books, the feeling as one looks up from the page, that everything has been made very interesting and new and strange and exciting all over again. And then there is the excitement or incitement to start to write oneself, because of the ways in which one's sense of language was awakened and intensified.

I hope you feel like visiting my wife and myself some time when you are in New York—but only, of course, when you feel like making visits (which I say because I often avoid making visits and find my disinclination misunderstood as unfriendliness).

Please don't feel you have to say anything whatever about my book.[1] I'm not particularly pleased with it myself, now that I see it in print, and I don't want my dissatisfaction to become another's embarrassment.

Yours sincerely,
Delmore Schwartz

1. S had sent Stevens a copy of *Vaudeville for a Princess*.

TO JAMES LAUGHLIN

75 Charles St.
New York City 14
May 8, 1951

Dear Jay,

I can't find your last letter at the moment, but will try to answer it from memory.

You mention your poems, but I thought you just gave me one, entitled "Step on His Head." However, if there were two or you have another one you want to publish now, please send it to me at the above address.

Unless I am mistaken, which is likely enough, you may have taken my remarks on money in my last letter as a kind of hint, naturally enough. But I merely meant to report on what preoccupied me, which is the only way I can write letters, and I sincerely yearn for the day when our friendship is so pure that all my royalties can be assigned to some charitable cause such as a society for making it clear to the American people that MacArthur is an unspeakable ham.

I have decided not to be a bank clerk, after all, since I would probably be paralyzed by the conflict between my desire to steal money and my fear of doing so.

It was pleasant to learn that you expected our correspondence to be read in the international salons and boudoirs of the future. Do you think they will be able to distinguish between the obfuscations, mystifications, efforts at humor, and plain statements of fact? Will they recognize my prime feelings as a correspondent—the catacomb from which I write to you, seeking to secure some word from the real world, or at least news of the Far West—and sigh with compassion? Or will they just think that I am nasty, an over-eager clown, gauche, awkward, and bookish? Will they understand that I am always direct, open, friendly, simple and candid to the point of naiveté until the ways of the fiendish world infuriate me and I am forced to be devious, suspicious, calculating, not that it does me any good anyway? And for that matter what will they make of your complex character?

It develops that the jukeboxes in bars now have an item entitled Silence, which costs a nickel, just like Music. This can only lead to drunken disputations between those who want silence and those who will be goddamned if they can't have a little music with the beer.

The Giants, after losing eleven straight and thus preventing me from buying the newspaper for eleven days, defeated Pittsburgh twice in three days, which made me reflect on the fact that I have been a Giant rooter for thirty years: the expense of spirit in a waste of games.

Did you see that MacArthur called his wife "my best soldier" and told the D.A.R. that they were the advance guard of the American society? Maybe you ought to invite him or them to appear in the next New Directions annual?

Probably I've forgotten something you mentioned in your letter, but I'll check up when I locate your letter.

Yours,
Delmore

TO CONRAD AIKEN

RD 1 Box 230
Pittstown, N.J.
January 28, 1952

Dear Conrad,

I was sorry to miss you at Xmas when our disorganized flight to the above address began. It is not yet complete by any means and we live in between three places, Princeton, where Elizabeth has a job, and where I must drive her every day, New York, and the farm from which I am writing you now.[1] I hope that you and Mary can at least stop by on one of your trips to New York. We have a fine guest room though it has more books in it than anything else. There won't be a phone here until April, probably, so please come unannounced or announced by a card: we will certainly be here every week-end. The town nearest to us is Baptistown where the people at the country store can tell you how to find our place. And the nearest big town is Flemington on U.S. 202, eight miles from Baptistown.

I would write at more length if I were not in such a state of frantic hurry; I've been trying to do so many things I don't know how to do that sometimes I pass myself in the mirror and don't recognize myself.

> With best regards to Mary,
> Yours ever,
> Delmore

1. S and his wife bought a three-bedroom farmhouse on six acres of land with a barn for $4500.

TO NELA WALCOTT

> RD 1 Box 230
> Pittstown, New Jersey
> January 28, 1952

Dear Nela,

I have not answered your Xmas card until now because I can't find it. Just before Xmas, Elizabeth and I tried to move to the farm house we bought last summer and from there I am now writing. Elizabeth got a job at the Princeton Art Museum since, for the first time since 1940, I get no wages and am almost penniless. So every day I must rise at six, drive Elizabeth to Princeton, wander about the library until five in the afternoon, and drive Elizabeth the 33 miles back to the farm. I started out as a chauffeur but am concluding as a chauffeur. Among all the incredible things which have happened since the 27th of December, I can't think of any which will seem convincing or likely to you—I would not believe they had occurred myself, if I had not been present. For example, on our very first day Elizabeth was literally almost arrested on Main Street in Flemington: the general idea was that she was a blonde bandit. If the attempted robbery for which she was stopped had occurred a half hour after, we would have been unable to establish our innocence and would have spent the first night in jail.

> [Unsigned carbon.]

TO ALLEN TATE

> RD 1 Box 230
> Pittstown, New Jersey
> February 3, 1951 [1952]

Dear Allen:

We were delighted to get your Xmas card and to know that you liked Minnesota very much. During the past 5 weeks and now too Elizabeth and I have been struggling, with dubious results, to get adjusted to our country place, and to live here, in Princeton (where Elizabeth has a job) and in New York (where I have a cold-water flat). By spring or summer we should be fully installed here in the country and then I hope very much that you and Caroline will honor us with a visit. At the moment I don't know whether we are landed gentry or poor white trash, but I know that right now I can't tell the difference. Probably we are displaced Bohemians and urban emigrés. But you must come to see for yourself.

Yours,
Delmore

TO JOHN CROWE RANSOM

RD 1 Box 230
Pittstown, New Jersey
February 8, 1952

Dear John:

I was very glad to hear from you; though somewhat disturbed by Brooks's note. The single error, "sky-blue parlors," which he finds in my piece, seems entirely picayune (there are a good many of the kind in the book of his I was writing about—for example, a mistake about hedges in Massachusetts—but I did not think they made a serious difference).[1]

I should have written you a long time ago to tell you how much I enjoyed our visit to the School of Letters.[2] Elizabeth did also and she managed to finish her second novel due to the good working conditions provided for her (she had an office for the first time in her life and this delighted her in itself and helped her to get her work done).

I enclose the carbon copy of a story, since you ask for verse or a story for the *Kenyon Review*. Under ordinary circumstances I would not send you a rough carbon which may be trying to read and which I know makes it difficult for an editor. But right now and for the past six weeks, Elizabeth and I have been laboring with all the trials which are inevitable, I suppose, when two city beings have to move to the country. We have also been struggling with a family economic crisis as a result of the fact that there are no longer editorial salaries on *Partisan Review*. This is one of the reasons that we moved to the country in the dead of winter. Another is that Elizabeth has a job in Princeton, which is thirty miles from here, and until she learned to drive the other day, I had to drive her to her job and back five days a week. In addition, I have to go into New York at least once a week for *P.R.* editorial meetings, so you can see that I have not had the leisure to do my own work with much care. All of this is by way of explaining my sending you a carbon instead of getting down to the typewriter and preparing a decent copy. I have some hope of being fairly prosperous by May, but for the time being whatever I do must have some rapid connection with earning the money to pay our mounting bills.

I had half-promised the enclosed story to *P.R.* which is always hard-up for fiction. But I'd prefer to have it appear in *Kenyon* for a number of reasons, including the obvious one that a story in the review of which one is an editor hardly has the prestige of being accepted by another editor of another review. If you can let me know soon if you like it enough to use it soon, then I can afford to spend some time in preparing a good copy. Needless to say, I'd welcome any suggestions you and Phil Rice [an editor of *Kenyon Review*] have to make. I'd especially like to know if you think that using names such as Luciano and Costello is too obvious and facile an irony.[3]

Yours,
Delmore

P.S. Would you return the enclosed letter, and if you have the time, tell me what you think of it. I truly did not know that I was erotic or sometimes too shocking. (I thought [John] O'Hara and Erskine Caldwell took care of the latter.)

1. S's review of Van Wyck Brooks's *New England: Indian Summer*, originally published in 1941, was reprinted in the anthology *The Kenyon Critics* (1952).
2. S had taught at the Kenyon School of Letters, convened in Bloomington, Indiana, the previous summer.
3. The story was "The Fabulous Twenty-Dollar Bill," published in *Kenyon Review*, 19 (Summer 1952). The name "Luciano" was changed to "Tuciano" when the story appeared.

TO VAN WYCK BROOKS

RD 1 Box 230
Pittstown, New Jersey
February 8, 1952

Dear Mr. Brooks:

John Crowe Ransom forwarded to me, the other day, the note you wrote him about the error in [my] piece about *New England: Indian*

Summer, which was reprinted in *The Kenyon Critics*. I am sorry about the error ("sky[-blue] parlors"), but glad to get the note, since I had been thinking of writing you for several reasons, one of them being that I had been reading your new book, *The Confident Years*, in December, and though I had to read my borrowed copy rapidly, I felt very strongly that I had to reexamine what I had said and written about your books.

I hesitated because I had no way of knowing if you felt any interest in any change of mind on my part. The piece to which you refer was written in 1940 and I wrote another of the same in *Partisan Review* (of *The World of Washington Irving*) in 1944. Both pieces were written under personal circumstances which induced a bias of which I hope I am now at least in part free. And I did not know that the piece in the *Kenyon Review* was going to be reprinted, since I was ill when Mr. Ransom asked for permission and my wife was taking care of my correspondence. I have thought, however, of reprinting both pieces in a collection of criticism, but not without adding a third part in which I stated what I thought was wrong with the bias and the point of view from which the previous expressions of opinion had been written. To try to be as brief as possible about what my change of mind is and some of the reasons for it: I was unaware, although I should not have been, of the extent to which Henry James and T. S. Eliot were hideous snobs in their work. I would have [been] less unaware, had I not been living in Cambridge, Massachusetts, and struggling with the unfortunate consequences of an unfortunate marriage. Since that time, I've returned to New York, moved to the country, and gotten married again, all of which has had the effect of making me see with some clarity how one-sided and distorted my own view of literature (and in particular, of the relationship of literature to life in America) had been in certain important respects. I still think that James and Eliot are great authors, but I feel now that the leading social attitudes in their work are vicious and destructive too often. I do not think the same is true of Joyce, however, for he seems to me to be fundamentally affirmative in a way that neither James nor Eliot are. If you happened to have seen any of the criticism I've published during the past four years—particularly my review of *Four Quartets* (the only unfavorable review) and "The Literary Dictatorship of T. S. Eliot" (in *Partisan Review* in 1949)—the nature of the change of mind will be clear to you. What I think now, in short, is that although one cannot condemn a literary work because some of its elements are reactionary and despairing, one must nevertheless recognize and evaluate the effect of those elements upon the reader, no matter how eloquent and powerful the work may be. I did not recognize this was one of the most important things you were doing until I read *The Confident Years* and perceived how much more fruitful as a creative writer I might have been, had I not suffered from too uncritical an admiration of Eliot in particular. For personal reasons which will be obvious to you as well as for principled ones, I think, no authors more than James and Eliot would be likely to create so many feelings of self-distrust and conflict of mind in a person existing in my own social and literary situation.

I hope that I have not been too personal in making this explanation, nor too involved. Someone quoted Metternich's advice recently: "Never explain, never excuse" as [an] example of the European mentality in comparison with the American, which explained and excused all the time. So if I've explained too much, I think I can claim that it is a habit induced by environment, although I know there are other reasons.

Yours sincerely,
Delmore Schwartz

TO JAMES LAUGHLIN

RD 1 Box 230
Pittstown, N.J.
February 10, 1952

Dear Jay,

Your hot communiqué from Pasadena was hilarious. But I had Great Expectations when it arrived and left it unopened, thinking perhaps that in it you announced that you were bringing back not only the bacon, but the prize pig ($, *in hoc signo vincit*). So my joy in the jokes was mixed with letdown and disappointment.

I will obey your command of silence. I do have a tendency to blab when I am not particularly instructed to be silent. But once instructed, I do imitate tombstones and Trappist Monks. Besides, when I blab it is so mixed up with free associations, far-fetched metaphors, and desperate puns that anyone who is attempting to pump me ends up in a state of mystification, if he or she is conceited, and in a state of deception, if they take me too literally and too seriously.

If you feel like passing along a piece of well-meaning advice to King (as you call him: I take it you mean the Prince of Peace), you might tell him that it is my considered opinion, for whatever it is worth, that he will never be made Pope. He might become President of the U.S.A., however, if there is a split in the Democratic Party, as there might very well be in 1956. You remember, it was split in the Republican Party in 1912 which made it possible for college president Woodrow Wilson to become Chief Executive and subsequently to be royally f---ed like Isabel Archer and Daisy Miller when he went to Paris and dealt with those arch-seducers Clemenceau & Lloyd George.

Speaking of Presidents, it does seem as if we may be living through the last days of the great Republic, for if Eisenhower is the megalomaniac some say he is, it will be Julius Caesar all over again, and even if Thomas E. Dewey plays Brutus and assassinates him, and tries to take power himself, one of Eisenhower's nephews, Octavius Augustus Eisenhower (now a student of Blackmur's at Princeton) will win out after Dewey falls madly in love with Lana (Cleopatra) Turner (Topping!).[1] Anyway, history certainly sometimes repeats itself, and existence frequently imitates Shakespeare.

Personally, I think I will vote for Truman if he is senseless enough to run again, on the grounds that a politician who tolerates the petty thieves of mink coats and deep freezes is preferable to any five-star general who has convinced himself that he can do no wrong. That's what Eisenhower said of D-day when the reporters wanted to know what he would have done if Rommel had been permitted to drive him back into the nasty water. He said something like: You can't do something like that (invade Fortress Europe) if you think you might not succeed. The ego-element here, I think, is: "If I want to do something very much, I am bound to succeed," and this is, is it not, a very dangerous view for a President to maintain. First thing you know he may decide that either he or Stalin has to be the first real emperor of the entire globe. I don't like either-or guys because they conclude by saying neither-nor, except for me.

Speaking of Stalin, they have just drafted Willie Mays, which is obviously the result of Stalin's lust for Korea, and the rest of the world, and though they have also drafted Don Newcombe, the Giants' pennant chances are seriously weakened, unless [Leo] Durocher can find an intelligent thought in his head, namely, to put Bobby Thomson back in center, Hank Thompson on third, and get Laraine Day Durocher to find a high yaller girl friend for Hank Thompson—one who will convince that high yallers are the best of two worlds, which they probably are, I am told. The newspapers said that Thompson, who is very gifted, has "personal problems." This can mean only one thing: he must set his bed in order.

I came upon one glitter of hopeful interpretation in your passage reading: "They are wetting down the oubliette for you in a certain Embassy on Connecticut Avenue. The lady you wrote those jokes about is now a Queen." If I interpret this with wild optimism, it may mean: a cradle is being prepared so that Elizabeth can bring a poor chilled into this grave new world. I feel that in such an eventuality, the second Elizabethan period has a chance of surpassing the first.

What does M.F.H. mean after my name on your envelope? My Friend Hershey? My Frantic Henchman?

You say that I was seen without a necktie in the Huntington Library. This is untrue. I was wearing one of my three neckties that day.

It has been a sad week. I wrote a piece of 4200 words in the hope of being paid $.10 a word by *The Reporter*. The only thing I've heard so far is that Phil Horton, to whom I sent it, took sick the day after he received it. No news may be good news, but it is also nervous-making.

> *Messers., faites les jeux!*
> *Nos jeux sont faits!*

P.S.

I better get away from French: it's unlucky. Did I ever tell you my version of the last two lines of *Faust:* "The eternal frau (fiancée, bride) / Can get it up."

P.P.S.

If the former boy wonder thinks that all roads lead to Rome, he is really wrong. Stalin thinks all roads lead to Moscow. He is wrong too. Nor do all roads lead to Washington, though more and more will (e.g. the Jersey Turnpike). All roads, I feel at the moment, go in a vicious or benign circle, since all roads lead nowhere or to Inferno, Paradiso, &/or Purgatorio. Perhaps we can hold a post-mortem on the subject some day in Purgatorio. It is pretty cold in this house and I could do with a little more fire.

P.P.P.S.

If a guest editor will get $2500 for an issue, should you not get $2500 for the pilot issue?[2]

1. Society figure Bob Topping was one of Lana Turner's husbands.
2. Laughlin was to edit *Perspectives USA* for the Ford Foundation.

TO JOHN CROWE RANSOM

RD 1 Box 230
Pittstown, N.J.
March 17, 1952

Dear John:

Enclosed is a revised version of my story. I was delighted that you liked it and in going over it, I thought it was the best piece of fiction I had written in years. The ending is a little augmented, and if you and Phil Rice don't like the addition, which begins with "Would you like a drink, dear?" in the middle of the last page, please cut it.

There are six or seven pages which are pretty untidy, but clear enough, I think, for the printer. Under ordinary circumstances I would retype them or get them typed for me, but I still have a difficult time in getting used to living between New York, Princeton, and the above address: [...] I have a feeling that I know what the life of a travelling salesman must be like.

Would it be possible for me to be paid immediately instead of waiting for publication? I've been without a monthly salary since December for the first time in eleven years, and it does make me feel weird. By next fall, when I start to teach at Princeton,[1] I certainly ought to be less frantic about these matters.

As ever,
Delmore

1. S was to direct the Creative Arts program at Princeton while Blackmur was away as a Fulbright lecturer in the Middle East.

TO JAMES LAUGHLIN

RD 1 Box 230
Pittstown, N.J.
Sept. 10, 1952

Dear Jay,

Joy was unrestrained in this obscure plot of New Jersey when your news arrived.[1] Elizabeth (Barrett Browning Pollet) Schwartz sat up in her sickbed, color rose to her cheeks, and she timidly inquired as to whether we could now purchase the pop-up toaster which has been the apple of her eye for the past eight months.

I won't embarrass you with the clinical details of our difficulties of the last few months—but we're both more grateful to you than you could possibly imagine without knowing the details.

—I've read the piece by E. M. Cioran on Scott Fitzgerald and cannot say that it seems very good to me.[2] There is something dreadfully off-key—at least to me—in writing about Fitzgerald's "Pascalian experience" and thinking about him in terms of Kirkegaard and Dostoyevsky. Nothing that Cioran says is particularly wrong (though much of it is a sumptuous intellectualized paraphrasing of the obvious), but—the point of view is such that the next step would have to be *John O'Hara and St. John of the Cross* or *Walter Winchell and Thomas Aquinas' Doctrine of the Angellic Intelligences*. What Pascal, Kierkegaard, and Dostoyevsky said apply to Fitzgerald, since they spoke of the universal human situation; but the intermediate steps are missing. I may be wrong and I would guess that European readers would not know what is lacking in the piece while Americans probably would not read it at all. Since the typescript is a carbon, I'll send it back to your Ford office.

I wait impatiently for orders to proceed with the digest.[3] I suppose the first one should be ready for the January issue.

I see that the Ford Foundation is tinkering with the [intellectual?] level of Television. This seems to me a profound error to judge by my impressions of the new art form garnered at the village saloon where I irritate the bartender by drinking only Coca-Cola: the dramas on TV have an effect hitherto unknown in any literature or art. Their representation of existence makes existence appear to be so awful, banal, vulgar, and pointless that the "viewer" returns to his own life with a feeling of *escape*. Instead of escaping from life's pain by means of literature and art, we now can enjoy escaping from TV drama into actual existence. To improve TV would be to lose this new and important experience. If Dante were able to revise the *Inferno* he would have the new form of damnation an eternity in which one looked only at TV.

Yours,
Delmore

P.S. Have you listened to the utterances of Adlai [Stevenson]? Perhaps it is time for you to choose between literature and the G.O.P. (War has broken out on *Time* magazine. T. S. Matthews [editor of *Time*] has discovered, after 20 years, that *Time*'s stories are *slanted* (!) (*he* is a Stevenson man.) It is also reported that the Old Possum himself has said that although it would be improper for him to express any view with regard to our domestic problems, if he were an American (!), he would vote for Stevenson.)

266

1. Laughlin offered S a job as a literary consultant to *Perspectives* and reader of manuscripts for New Directions.
2. Cioran's essay, "Physionomie d'un effondrement," on Fitzgerald's *The Crack-up*, appeared in *Profile*, Oct. 1952.
3. Synopses of important articles from literary journals for *Perspectives*.

TO JAMES LAUGHLIN

RD 1 Box 230
Pittstown, N.J.
Sept. 22, 1952

Dear Jay:

Your letter from Frankfurt of Sept. 11 was not typed in New York until the 15th and did not reach here until today. The local postman, essentially a dreamer, delivered it at the home of the other Schwartz of the neighborhood who comes out only on week-ends. I've explained to him that mail from you has an international urgency and he seems adequately impressed, though I would not be surprised if the hole in his consciousness, caused by the cessation of the letters you wrote me from all over the country last winter, has made him unconsciously resentful of mail directed to me. Be this as it may, perhaps you ought to write me directly—with just the few essential sentences of direction—whenever any haste is required, since there is some obviously unavoidable delay in N.Y. I will apply all my forces to being as efficient as a cash register, prompt as an alarm clock, and uncomplicated as a safety pin.

I also wrote you about ten days ago sending the letter air mail to the Paris address you gave me, saying how delighted and grateful I was about the job and reporting a somewhat adverse opinion of Cioran's essay on Fitzgerald: to the effect that a discussion of Fitzgerald in terms of Pascal and Kierkegaard took the reader away from Fitzgerald instead of bringing him closer to the pure product of American life, Princeton and *The Saturday Evening Post*. I added that I might be wrong and that most European readers would not know that there was anything wrong with the essay. To illustrate briefly, no essay on Fitzgerald can explain anything when the author does not know fully what a tycoon, a Yale-Harvard football game, and a Southern belle are. Fitzgerald might have lived his life out and written his books in Bulgar in Cioran's point of view. Still and all, I may make too much of F. as essentially an *American* novelist. But I do know that the French have never been able to read Henry James because no critic tries to explain how American and in what important ways he was. //

Tomorrow I'll confer with Ms. Cox, in accordance with your instructions, about dates and deadlines. I'll also arrange about magazine exchanges with her and I think you're right about keeping the copies in your office there, though I will have to take them home from time to time unless you want me to work at a desk there.

The few months in advance deadline makes no difference to me, but you might reflect on the possibility that some of the journalistic and topical point of the summaries might be blunted by the delay. Perhaps it is of no moment at all, but you would know and I don't. In any case, it is important that you pass on whatever I prepare with ruthless candor before it goes to press, and correct me or suggest revisions.

You had better decide also on how extensive a coverage is desirable. My own feeling is that the more extensive the coverage, the more valuable the digest will be. For example, there are pieces in the philosophical journals, the journals of sociology, history, psychology, art and music which might be more impressive sometimes than essays in the literary quarterlies to the foreign reader. Most of what they print is intramural technicality, but sometimes it is not. Towards the other end of the highbrow, middlebrow, lowbrow and halfbrow spectrum, there are sometimes pieces in *The Atlantic*, *Harper's*, *The New Yorker*, and *Fortune* which would interest the European reader very much—e.g., Lillian Ross's profile of Hemingway in *The New Yorker* and the terrifying discourse on what happens to American business executives' wives in *Fortune*. What do you think? It will make more work for me to cover these too, but I don't mind if it will help make the digest better.

Though I am obviously not an expert on something like sociology, music, or painting, I am sufficiently the ordinary educated reader and aware enough of how to avoid amateurishness to do justice to these things, and I can consult the experts I know to be sure.

If you think complete comprehensive coverage is desirable, I probably need 7 or 8 pages of small-space double column; if not, 4 or 5 ought to be enough. I am judging by the amount of space Eliot used to give to the review of periodicals in *The Criterion* as well as the "abstracts" in journals of psychology and medicine.

The typography and format on the pilot issue of *A Selective Listing of New Books* seemed very nice to me, and I don't see that any change is necessary, unless you feel the need for typographical variety. I enclose a specimen as you request (the jocosity and irony are entirely *pour vous distraire* and will be absolutely absent from the finished product as well as all remarks which might disturb the pride of literary politicians or lead to accusations of bias). This should give you the general idea, I think, and please do not hesitate to tell me immediately if anything is wrong or lacking. The title, *A Review of Reviews*, may seem pretentious, but on the other hand, it may be attractive—it's been used before for the same kind of thing. If you don't like it, call it something else.

I've spent an inordinate amount of energy in composing the notes to contributors for Blackmur's issue. It's an experience like chewing rocks because data is lacking that is required, and you have requested something more than the bare facts. Unless it makes some trouble for you that I can't foresee, wouldn't it be best, as some reviews do, to send out a little printed set of questions to each contributor? And then I could compose the notes by using the answers. For example, it took me days to find out who John Lyndberg is. Another alternative would be for me to communicate with the editor of each issue, since there are bound to be people I know nothing about; but I'd prefer not to seem involved to any official extent since I am not, and corresponding with the editors of issues might suggest that I am to some people.

I hope you are having fun; please keep me informed with regard to the red-headed chick in Hindustan, and if you get a chance, would you purchase for me one of the oriental treatises on sex which Mrs. [Wallis] Simpson is supposed to have studied in Harvard and which Mr. Simpson's daughter Audrey insisted to me explained the over-whelming hold the lady had on the Duke of Windsor. Now that I feel nouveau riche, I think I can afford to pursue my scholarly inclinations in that direction. Audrey appeared to be eager to tell all, but I am as you know very bashful and hence changed the subject to avoid unmanly blushes and conceal my voracious curiosity.

Yours,
Delmore

TO MEYER SCHAPIRO

RD 1 Box 230
Pittstown, N.J.
Dec. 11, 1952

Dear Meyer,

I've put off writing you repeatedly because what I wanted to say was that I've been sunk for months in the worst part of the manic-de-pressive disorder which does not show much on the surface, but makes it an ordeal for me to see anyone. Every time I've tried to tell anyone about this, to explain my easily misunderstood behavior, I merely succeed in causing embarrassment, but I'm sure you'll forgive me for mentioning something so vivid inside of me and invisible to almost everyone else.

During the last few days I've begun to break out of the longest depressed period I can remember—or at least I hope I have—and I hope I can get to see you and Lillian sometime during Xmas week.

Long before my turn as a guest editor of *Perspectives* comes along, I imagine some other guest editor will want to use your wonderful piece on the Armory Show, but if not, I hope I can use it. Needless to say, I would like to have anything else of yours; and since one of my (many and nebulous) functions on *Perspectives* is to suggest pieces to guest editors, please let me know if there is anything you want to print or to have reprinted.

With best regards from Elizabeth,

Yours always,
Delmore

TO JAMES LAUGHLIN

RD 1 Box 230
Pittstown, N.J.
December 21, 1952

Dear Jay:

Enclosed is a revised carbon copy of my digest. I left a clean proof-read copy with Carruth on the 15th as requested.[1] There are 41 new items and I could have made it 80, since I read more than 400 articles for the piece. I was much surprised that you were not entirely satisfied by my first effort since I tried it out on a number of people in Princeton, and in addition Blackmur, who did not know I had done it and who was sent a copy as the editor of the issue, said that it was very good. However, I can make it whatever you want it to be, as soon as I know exactly what you want. It is much easier to do an index than a commentary, obviously, but the problem, I think, is that it will then not be particularly interesting; and there is an *International Index of Periodicals*. As soon as possible I will send you specimens of the magazine digest in European periodicals so you can see what Europeans want or rather so you can see what I modelled myself upon.

Carruth will send the good copy to the printer as soon as he hears from you. I have many other matters to tell you about but can't write much of a letter today since Elizabeth is ill again. I should be able to write you during the week and I hope very much that you can spare me two or three hours of your time as soon as you return. Perhaps we can set up a rapid system of communication: that would help a lot, I think.

The first issue of *Perspectives* was a big hit in Princeton and even Edmund Wilson expressed approval and a desire to write for it. But he wanted to give an essay on Sartre's book on Genet which *The New Yorker* would not print because it was too "scabrous," so I put him off until I could find out what your policy is. This is one of the things I mean by the helpfulness of rapid communication. Which reminds me that one of the sentences in my piece is a quotation from Tate on Hart Crane as "an extreme example of the unwilling homosexual." Please advise on this and let me know when you are coming back.

Yours,
Delmore

P.S. I sent a carbon to England. No one was sure of just where you would be.

1. Hayden Carruth also worked for Laughlin on *Perspectives*, from an office in the Pierre Hotel.

TO JOHN CROWE RANSOM

RD 1 Box 230
Pittstown, N.J.
Jan. 31, 1953

Dear John,

I'm afraid that due to circumstances I could not have foreseen, when I wrote you, I can't get my review of Wilson's book [*The Shores of Light*] done for this issue. One of the circumstances arises from Jay Laughlin's return from Europe and a lot of unexpected work to be done for *Perspectives USA*, which is now my main source of livelihood, as you may know.

Do you want the piece on Wilson for your next issue? I had planned to make it more of an essay than a review and to point out the respects in which Wilson's *kind* of criticism has been neglected by those of the new critics who follow Eliot and [William] Empson too mechanically.

I'm disappointed about not being able to make the deadline as I promised. I had counted on the interval between terms at Princeton for the leisure to write it and to finish a story about the niece of Uncle Sam, a millionaire, who is courted by a general of industry and by a melancholy witty lawyer. The general tells her she will have no problems if she marries him, and the lawyer courts her by telling her that marriage is no panacea and she will have many problems, since there are always problems. Naturally she decides to marry the general, but four years after she divorces him and marries the lawyer. Long live Adlai!

The new issue of the *Kenyon* has just arrived and it looks very exciting, especially Warren and Jarrell. If you print long poems, I think perhaps more good long poems will be written.

As ever,

Delmore

P.S. If you have the time, I wish you would tell me what you think of my piece in the current *P.R.*, "The Duchess' Red Shoes."[1] I've heard nothing but surprising praise and I can't think unanimity is ever accurate or just.

1. A controversial two-part essay in which S answered Lionel Trilling's critique of "the liberal imagination" as set forth in his essay "Manners, Morals and the Novel." The resulting correspondence between S and Trilling is in the Columbia University Lionel Trilling collection.

TO ALLEN TATE

RD 1 Box 230
Pittstown, N.J.
Feb. 11, 1953

Dear Allen,

I was delighted to hear from Philip [Rahv] that you approve, at least in part, of my piece on Trilling *et al.* In fact, I meant to write and ask your advice about it as an authority on manners and devout dogmatism (in the best sense). Which leads me to say how much I've been illuminated by your recent criticism (which I mention in the next issue of *Perspectives*, in the periodical chronicle), and how wonderful I think the new part of your long poem ["The Swimmers"] in *Hudson* is. (I've not yet seen the current *Sewanee*.)

We still hope to get [you] out here to the farm or see you and Caroline in Princeton. With our best to both of you,

Yours as ever,
Delmore

TO VAN WYCK BROOKS

RD 1 Box 230
Pittstown, N.J.
Feb. 27, 1953

Dear Mr. Brooks:

The deepest thanks to you and the committee of the American Academy for your award.[1] Coming as it does at a time of much stress and strain, it is like a benediction. I'll look forward very much to being present on the 27th of May and to meeting you again.

Yours sincerely,
Delmore Schwartz

1. S was awarded a one-thousand dollar grant by the American Academy and Institute of Arts and Letters. Formal presentation was in May.

TO JAMES LAUGHLIN

Princeton University
Princeton, New Jersey
Friday, March 27, 1953

Dear Jay:

The Wilson review is OK with Wilson. In fact, he was flattered that you wanted it. //

How about going with Elizabeth and me to the opening game? It has been observed that anyone who has not seen me at the Polo Grounds has not seen me.

All the editors of *Diogenes* ought to get free bathtubs as honorariums.[1]

Delmore

1. A journal published by the International Council for Philosophy and Humanistic Studies. S's name appeared on the masthead.

TO RICHARD S. BURTON[1]

[Pittstown?
April 1953?]

[Portion of Author Information Sheet prepared for New Directions]

HOBBIES & INTERESTS:
New York Giants (since 1921) and cats and comic strips (Pogo).

WHAT GROUPS MIGHT BE INTERESTED IN KNOWING ABOUT YOUR BOOKS:
All the colleges where I have taught and I was told that Adlai Stevenson said to a reporter during the campaign that he was particularly interested in my work as a poet, storyteller, and critic.

ANY NOTEWORTHY OR ANECDOTAL EVENT IN YOUR PAST LIFE THAT MIGHT BE OF INTEREST?
At the age of 3½, I admired a streetcar which passed the apartment house where I lived and at the window I watched it. A pretty lady came to call on my parents and kissed me and I called her a streetcar. I was applauded for this poetic metaphor so much that I decided to become a poet.

I was named Delmore instead of Joseph because both my grandfathers were named Joseph and one of them was still alive and thought that to have a grandchild named after him would be unlucky. I have never been able to make out whether I was lucky or not...

1. Member of the publicity staff, New Directions.

TO JAMES LAUGHLIN

RD 1 Box 230
Pittstown, N.J.
May 22, 1953

Dear Jay:
As a result of deliberations in which everyone was consulted except the College of Cardinals, the Supreme Court, the Board of Health and Oscar Williams, Princeton has decided that I would be a valuable addition to the faculty. The proposal, which was unanimously affirmed by the full professors, the Dean, and President Dodds is as follows:

I am to be appointed resident lecturer for three years and my duties are limited to teaching a course of my own, Advanced Composition, and acting as a preceptor in three departmental courses, which makes a total of six hours a week, and which should not interfere with what

I have to do for *Diogenes* and *Perspectives*. In return for these efforts I am to receive $5000 a year which Princeton would like the Ford Foundation to pay, although it was indicated quite clearly that if anyone else wants to do so, that will do quite as well. In addition, Princeton would like the Ford Foundation to pay $300 more a year to cover my annuity, but if there is any question as to this additional sum, Princeton will be delighted to show how desirable a teacher I am by paying the annuity from the university funds. The procedure, or protocol, or whatever it is, which must be followed is that the Ford Foundation communicate its willingness to pay my salary to President Dodds. If this could be done quickly, it would be helpful indeed to everyone, and I would be overjoyed. The limitation of the appointment to three years is a mere formality, since "the presumption" is that the appointment will be renewed every three years, provided that I do not commit "moral turpitude," which I would have to commit on Nassau Street during Alumni Week, to judge by various episodes which I will not dwell upon now.

The advantages to you as publisher of Intercultural Publications are fairly clear, I think, particularly in connection with *Diogenes* where, in dealing with professors, I will certainly be better able to correct the style of the learned gentry and speak with authority if I am part of a university faculty. In addition, it is quite likely that this kind of a permanent job would help me be more efficient in regard to *Diogenes* and *Perspectives* by lessening the anxiety about money which has crippled me in recent years. And then there is the further possibility, in which I am not sure that you are passionately interested, that our hurly-burly friendship might achieve exalted regions of disinterested benignity which death alone will surpass.

There is a further link between Princeton's proposal and the Ford Foundation which I am not sure ought to be dealt with right now, and about which I would like to write to Hutchins[1] in detail, if that is all right with you. I don't think that this link is necessary, and in view of all that will have to be done when I become active on *Diogenes*, it would obviously be wiser to postpone anything which would increase the amount of work I have to do immediately.

However, if a further tie-up with the purposes and objectives of the Ford Foundation is necessary, and since you said the money would probably be forthcoming from the Fund for the Advancement of Education, my course could be used as a kind of research into the reasons that so many intelligent and trained human beings write English so poorly, and misunderstand or are baffled by serious literature. Since it is my own course, and it is a course in composition, I can direct it partly toward getting some concrete data on this truly important problem, in which I am interested, anyway. You remember, this was the official reason given for the Rockefeller Foundation's paying of I. A. Richards' salary at Harvard for more than ten years, and had much to do with two of Richards' most influential books, *Practical Criticism* and *Interpretation of Teaching*. And the Rockefeller Foundation has supported Blackmur, and F. L. Leavis, for doing things of a similar kind at Princeton and at Cambridge.

I won't try to outline the project in full now, particularly since I'd like to write Hutchins some sort of prospectus, and also because I don't want to embark on it during the coming year, unless I have to, in order to get the Ford Foundation's support, which is all I need for the job. But the general project can be illustrated by some of the key problems:

1) Why do intelligent human beings have so much difficulty in reading and in writing intelligently?

2) Why do people who can speak very well write lifeless and hackneyed prose?

3) What are the effects of mass culture—the radio, the newspapers, and the films—upon the intelligent reading and writing of English?

4) Why are advertisements written so crudely and directions so inefficiently?

5) What is the effect of a training in the classics, and in logic, upon the reading and writing of English?

And the like, of which these questions are only a sample. There have been any number of efforts to explain the semi-illiteracy which prevails, but they all seem superficial or wrong to me. For example, the secondary-school teaching of English is blamed, but this merely begs the question as to why the high-school teachers of English have been so poorly trained themselves. And then it is said that if only Greek and Latin were required subjects, people would read and write as well as they once did. But this is foolish too, since Greek and Latin teachers also write poorly, as most scholars do, and there is no significant difference between students trained in the classics and those who are not, when it comes to any real skill in reading and writing.

This is a rough and abbreviated formulation of what would be, I think, a very useful project about which I could write the kind of report or reports which Foundations seem to love.

As a special supplement, I would gladly deal with the fascinating topic: the strange English of Dwight D. Eisenhower; and advance reasons or hypotheses to explain such as his pronunciation as *Career* when he is speaking of *Korea*, and his virtually unfailing inaccuracy in the use of demonstrative pronouns—for example, "these Republicans" he said recently, speaking of the Republican party.

Seriously, however, will you let me know as soon as possible how matters go forward and if you think it would be proper for me to write to Hutchins directly, since, as you said, Princeton's proposal is not within your ordinary field of operations?[2]

Yours,
Delmore

P.S. Rereading what I wrote on the second page, it looks a little too general. To try to be more concrete, what I mean is the kind of thing encountered when a student who spoke fluently in answering a question suddenly became tongue-tied—halting, choppy, and wobbling in delivery—as soon as he was asked to read a passage of prose aloud. Or students who wrote beautifully and lucidly about some subjects [but] wrote very poorly about other subjects. And the like, but I won't try to say any more than the whole situation can be made quite vivid by using all the instances I accumulated during my long years in the vineyards of English freshman composition.

P.P.S. Please don't mind my sending this to you special delivery; it won't get to you any sooner, but nevertheless special delivery expresses my feelings.

P.P.P.S. If the toils and travails of the Ford Foundation seem trying, you might find much solace and reassurance in Allan Nevins' new biography of John D. Rockefeller. There is a full account in the second volume of what happened during the first years of the Rockefeller Foundation—which is to say, it has all happened before.//

1. Robert Hutchins, associate director of the Ford Foundation.
2. S was plotting to gain a tenured position at Princeton University, after which he expected the Ford Foundation to underwrite an endowed chair in the English Department, to which he would be the first appointee. He was not successful.

TO ROBERT HUTCHINS

RD 1 Box 230
Pittstown, New Jersey
May 29, 1953

Dear Dr. Hutchins:

I have just heard from Jay of your initial reaction to my proposal about Princeton. In his letter Jay said that you were "not at all optimistic," which left me perplexed as to whether or not you meant to submit the proposal, though doubtful as to the outcome. However, since the entire matter was broached to you on the phone, I wonder whether it would be possible for me to see you soon and tell you about it a little more fully, as, in fact, I would have tried to do soon after meeting you last month, if you had not gone to Europe. When I asked Jay this morning about seeing you and suggested going to Pasadena, he said that you would be in Chicago fairly soon, and perhaps you would have the time to see me then. In any case, I would be very grateful for the chance to talk to you either in Pasadena or in Chicago, feeling as I do that the entire matter will appear in a different light more than it can have in the immediacy and meagerness of a telephone call. For one thing, there is what I interpret as a good deal of precedent in the support which the Rockefeller Foundation gave for years to I. A. Richards, R. P. Blackmur, and others for the same kind of thing at Harvard and at Princeton, which I mention because Jay reported you as saying that "questions of precedent would probably be involved." And there are various other good—very good, I think—reasons for supposing that this would not be merely help for me, but would lead to useful results of the kind the Ford Foundation is interested in.

What has happened so far may amuse you as a veteran of the academic life. After a brief talk with the chairman of the English department, I wrote to Jay asking him if he and you could help me, and assuming quite wrongly that help would be understood as financial support. Probably my own warped view of academic propriety, protocol, and indirection made me think that it would be coarse to specify help as money, and my misunderstanding was magnified by my notion of the largesse of foundations; while Jay for his part apparently assumed that help meant merely a letter of recommendation. On the basis of this double misunderstanding, everything went forward at Princeton: my character, competence, heterosexuality, and the like were submitted to the labyrinthine gauntlet with which you must be very familiar, and I emerged as entirely acceptable to the full professors, the deans, and the President, and finally as the delighted object of much unofficial congratulation. Since all my experience and all that

I was told made me suppose that the truly difficult obstacle was Princeton itself, Jay's message naturally left me with the feeling that I might suddenly turn out to be a new Captain Cook or a 1953 species of confidence man.

At any rate, you can understand my eagerness to see you, as I hoped to, anyway, without any such question involved. I would go on at greater length if Jay had not told me that you dislike long letters.

Yours sincerely,
[Unsigned carbon.]

TO SAUL BELLOW[1]

RD 1 Box 230
Pittstown, N.J.
Oct. 9, 1953

Cher frère, mon frère, handsome & Creative Writing Associate,

I'm still virus-groggy, also Ford-Foundation groggy and things appear to have taken a new as yet inconclusive turn.

I take it you would like to have Anthony West's head broken in. I will. Before I'm through West will be East. It has become a family feud—his mama [Rebecca] said my uncle James J. Bloom was no gentleman and had no taste. Will also break several other heads, if there is room. I want to say something about Augie's relation to American humor, Gatsby, Huck Finn, Daisy Miller, Captain Ahab, Emerson, Clem Greenberg, Hank Greenberg, Leo Durocher and Red Grange. Try not to let the reviews disturb you (not that I could)—they're really favorable at their worst in the spread of attention and awareness. Did you expect to work a masterpiece [*The Adventures of Augie March*] and also be *understood*?

I don't think I'd better decide right now about when we can meet about the textbook[2] (the virus gets me down one day and lets me up the next). But I'll write or call you about a definite date by next Monday or Tuesday. Let me know if there is any rush.

We both want to visit you, but not immediately since E is just getting her new book underway and also we want to pay several respects on households on the same trip. //

Hang the Kaiser,
Delmore

1. S had brought Bellow to Princeton to serve as his assistant during Blackmur's absence.

2. S planned to collaborate with Bellow on a textbook, *What the Great Novelists Say About Writing the Novel.* It was never completed.

TO CONRAD AIKEN

RD 1 Box 230
Pittstown, N.J.
Oct. 16, 1953

Dear Conrad,

I am much ashamed and mortified about the manuscripts for which we have looked everywhere and which are not the only ones I misplaced during the extremely crowded days of last spring when I was involved with four different places of publication in addition to teaching. We'll continue to look but meanwhile perhaps there is some way in which I can make up for the loss—pay for the typing, for example. Please let me know.

I was delighted to get a copy of your *Collected Poems* which arrived at about the same time as *The New Republic* asked me to review it.[1] Yesterday I finished my fourth version—the only real difficulty was having a great deal more to say than could possibly be said in the thousand words allowed me. I had more than enough for an essay, which I am going to write sooner or later. Anyway, I hope you like the review, and I think you will because Elizabeth does, and she is your very devout admirer as well as a very severe critic of criticism.

Please forgive me about the manuscripts. I was truly bogged down in more unrelated editorial jobs than I've ever been before, or than anyone else I've heard of—so much bogged down that I've had to be released of most of them.

We can't possibly do any travelling now, and even New York is difficult most of the time, but we'll certainly come to town when you do. With love to Mary and you from both of us,

Delmore

1. "The Self Against the Sky," *New Republic*, Nov. 2, 1953

TO MEYER SCHAPIRO

RD 1 Box 230
Pittstown, N.J.
Oct. 27, 1953

Dear Meyer,

Many thanks for your note and invitation. I have not been coming to the city very often, and right now I'm all tied up in a textbook for creative writing courses which I'm doing with Saul Bellow and for which a first draft has to be ready very soon if we are to get the advance we both need very much. It's proving more difficult than either of us expected and until it's done I can't afford an evening in New York: but it should be done within the next two weeks and then I'll be free to call you.

As you may have heard, everything to do with *Diogenes* is entirely up in the air and may come to nothing. The same is true of *Perspectives* which is the reason for my unexpected and sudden financial problem and the textbook.

If you don't have a copy of Saul's novel, I have an extra one which I've been meaning to give you for some time. With our best to you and Lillian,

Yours,
Delmore

TO CATHARINE CARVER[1]

Sisyphus, New Jersey
Thursday, Dec. 15 [1953]

Dear Katie,

Since my proof corrections and additions are more messy than even I can bear, I'll print out the two long ones: please excuse me, and if you have any trouble call me. The parenthetical insertion of William Dean Howells is based on James's using Howells as a model for Strether and Trilling's using Howells as an excuse for philistinism. //

Thanks for your sympathy—this jaundice is quite unserious, it is a wholly mediocre disorder which invites boredom and irritation. *Impeach Eisenhower.*

Yours,
Peter Rocky Sisyphus

P.S. I may be better next week, so will you let me know if there is a meeting?

1. Managing Editor of *Partisan Review.*

TO ARTHUR MIZENER

RD 1 Box 230
Pittstown, N.J.
Dec. 30, 1953

Dear Arthur,

The reason I've not written you before now is that everything has been so unsettled—as it continues to be. But my issue [as guest editor] of *Perspectives* is settled, though the date is not set, and so I hope you still feel like doing an essay on American fiction between 1920 and 1940. If you don't or there is something else you'd rather write about, please let me know. I was much taken with your story in *K.R.*; but as things are on the Ford Foundation—which is one of the unbelievable but real problems—it might make difficulties if I tried to use it: My last stricture from that old captain of the avant-garde, Jay, was: "You *must* make your issue as *conservative* as possible." I can't pretend to know what a conservative issue is, but I must proceed by vague negative intuition, sensing what is not desirable even though I do not know what is. Anyway, let me know soon what you can be persuaded to do—you can, of course, publish your piece elsewhere too, though then you often have to divide the quite considerable loot.

I wish you and Rosemary could be persuaded down to the old plantation on one of your visits to Princeton, or any other occasion. Please give my love to Rosemary and tell her that I know now she was [right] about that story of Hemingway's, and happy New Year from both of us.

Yours,
Delmore

TO ARTHUR MIZENER

RD 1 Box 230
Pittstown, N.J.
January 15, 1954

Dear Arthur:

I'm delighted that you feel like doing the essay. Can you keep it to 5000 words? It's impossible to get anything straight from Jay (who has just left for Rome after having become so conservative that he thought he had better get married again—: but apparently has not, uncertain as to whether marriage is conservative), hence I am not sure about how many pages *P* issues will have during the next year. However, it now again appears, for the moment, as if *Diogenes* will come along sooner or later, in which case I won't have to confine anyone to a mere 5000 words. The deadline is the 1st of June.

I couldn't have come to Cornell this fall, as I should have written you long before this. I would certainly have liked to, however, and many thanks for thinking of me.

I've not seen *The New Republic* for weeks, but am very pleased to be a classic, which I should have suspected for some time, in view of the fact that a classic is what no one reads. //

The countryside is imitating Bruegel and something is wrong with the plumbing for the 10th time, so I had better get to work. Love from both of us to Rosemary.

Best,
Delmore

TO JOHN CROWE RANSOM

RD 1 Box 230
Pittstown, N.J.
February 2, 1954

Dear John:

I've put off answering your letter about the *Perspectives'* payment for my story because I hoped (as I wrote you in December) to get one or two essays or a longish poem done by your January 31st deadline. But I've not been able to pull the essays together properly as yet— partly because they began as lectures and the transposition is always difficult for me—and at the moment the poem looks quite awful. In any case, neither essay is particularly timely, since one is about Dostoyevsky, Freud and God (!) and the other about Joyce's use of language as exorcism (of his resentment of Ireland), so there is no particular hurry.

The two matters of an essay and the payment are inseparable in my mind because as I was trying to get them into the proper shape I could hardly help but think that the *K.R.* was one of the two places where I could write on an uninhibitedly serious level, and there is almost always more room in the *K.R.* than in *P.R.* Moreover, you and the *K.R.* have always been so generous and hospitable that my diffidence is bound to be quite intense.

However, since I wrote you the summer before last that I thought *Perspectives'* payments ought to be divided between the author and the periodical, I've heard the other side's argument which is first that this kind of reprint does not compete directly with the periodical as anthologies, etc., do, and second that the Ford Foundation, however modestly, does help magazines like the *K.R.* and *P.R.* by buying copies. Hence the policy adopted by every periodical of which I know—*P.R.*, *New Directions*, *The Atlantic*, *The New Yorker*, and I gather, the scholarly journals, has been to give the author the entire amount.

And then—which is beside the point of principle, of course—my very handsome job with the Ford Foundation was suspended or terminated—it is not clear which—last August, and since then Elizabeth and I have been more hard-up than ever before and I've had to borrow continually, and to an extent which can't continue, to keep going through the year, having had, so far, no luck with getting a teaching job or hackwork.

On the other hand, as I said but should say again, I feel devoted and obliged to the *K.R.* as a matter of the seldom-mentioned civil liberty, the freedom of the intelligence to speak in its own terms, so I would want to be the last one to object to any course which might help to sustain the *K.R.*

I'm sure that it's needless to say that the decision is entirely yours for a variety of reasons, including the fact that you can decide about the whole matter from the point of view of the *K.R*'s interests, which I know about only by analogy with *P.R.* But I hope you can let me know very soon what you do decide (without troubling to go into detail about the *K.R.*'s specific problems).

With best regards, and please forgive me for writing about my personal economic problem,

Yours always,
Delmore

TO HOWARD MOSS

5536 Dorchester
Chicago 37, Ill.[1]
March 10, 1954

Dear Howard,

Many thanks for sending me a copy of your new book [*The Toy Fair*]. I've gotten a lot of continuous pleasure reading it and your poems—at least to me—are much more impressive collected and next to each other than when encountered separately. I'm not sure but it does seem better that this should be the case than the reverse. Moreover I like some of the poems by themselves very much also.

Yours,
Delmore

1. S had an appointment at the University of Chicago for the spring quarter.

TO WILLIAM COLE[1]

RD 1 Box 230
Pittstown, N.J.
March 23, 1954

Dear Bill:

I would have written you before now if I had not been under the weather to say thanks for Kafka and Jarrell's book, and to explain that two flat tires stopped my wife and me on our way to the Book Award shindig.

I was particularly pleased to get *The Castle*. As for Randall's book [*Pictures from an Institution*], I enjoyed a lot but for the wrong reasons, so I'm afraid I can't say anything about it that would be useful. It's not a novel, at least to me, and there's a peculiar sexlessness about the characters which makes them unreal to me even though I've known some of them for fifteen years. It's quite beside the point, but I feel baffled by a satire upon a recognizable lady novelist [Mary McCarthy] who is partly satirized because she writes satirical fiction about recognizable people. But I'm being naive, I suppose.

I'm going out to the University of Chicago to teach until the middle of June, but I hope we can spend an evening together some time soon after I get back.

Yours,
Delmore

1. Cole was in the publicity department of Alfred A. Knopf.

TO PASCAL COVICI[1]

RD 1 Box 230
Pittstown, N.J.
March 23, 1954

Dear Mr. Covici:

I'd like to have the first installment of my advance (for the book

I'm doing with Saul) now. I've not seen him, but I've been getting some of my part of the work blocked out. I feel more and more that it will be something which really sells.

It was very pleasant to meet you—at last, after all these years—and I'm only sorry that we missed connection way back in 1937: I'm sure I would have been better off.

// With best wishes,

Yours sincerely,

Delmore Schwartz

1. Editor at Viking Press who had contracted for the fiction textbook with S and Bellow.

TO SAUL BELLOW

5536 Dorchester
Chicago
March 31, 1954

Dear Saul,

I thought we would be driving out here and would stop by and accost you at Bard en route: but we decided at the last minute to come by train and save working time. Before that, I was working well for the first time in months and afraid to break the spell by moving about— I've been to New York only once since February.

Thanks for the addresses of friends. At the moment I'm so burdened with students, classes, the faculty, and the desire to keep working, while I can, that I'd rather put off any encounters I can avoid: I'll assume it makes no difference to you unless I hear otherwise.

How about you and Sandra spending the summer (or whenever you get back from Reno) in the fair fields of New Jersey near us? In addition to the pleasure of your and the beautiful young lady's society, we could probably get the main part of the textbook pulled together in half the time it would take under other conditions.—The neighborhood is hot in the summer but otherwise fine for sustained work and you could get a pleasant place for a modest rent.

I'm delighted you liked those poems. In the midst of teaching the creative writing class the other day, I had to ask myself once again: If it is so easy, why do I quite often find it so difficult? It is either easy or impossible.

Have composed a weird excursion called "The Yogurt and the Halivah," which takes up the well-supported view that Dwight is a cigarstore Indian, Bowdoin [sic] Broadwater[1] and Lionel Abel are

English gentlemen, and Clem's secret aim in life is to open a shoe store on Staten Island. It also deals with Troilus and [Arthur] Koestler and Elliott Cohen [editor of *Commentary*] (used together, they are at ease in Zionism)! You can judge by this as to my particular mood.

Chicago is, as you know, terrific, and it's very strange, after two years, to be living day in and out in a big city: roller skates scraping the sidewalk sound exotic.

I trust you are well under way in a new book—if only so that I could have something worth reading. (I reread parts of *Augie March* after you protested—I hope with some insincerity—in being compared favorably to *Huck Finn*.[2] All I can say is that it is quite possible that you don't know how good it is, because you're still too close to it.)

Impeach Eisenhower.

Love from both of us to both of you,

> Yours,
> Delmore

1. Bowden Broadwater was a Cambridge dandy and Mary McCarthy's husband.
2. In S's review of the novel, *Partisan Review*, 21 (Jan.–Feb. 1954).

TO JAMES LAUGHLIN

> RD 1 Box 230
> Pittstown, N.J.
> August 6, 1954

Dear Jay,

I had already written several gingerly pages on Dos Passos' novel [*Most Likely to Succeed*], and avoided the political theme disingenuously and awkwardly. But you're undoubtedly right to suggest that it would be best to ignore the book and concentrate upon Faulkner's [*A Fable*] (who has been dreadfully misrepresented in all the reviews I've seen). In addition to the politics in Dos Passos, the book is very bad as a novel and only worth attention in the context of Dos Passos' career. It is also libellous and has been withdrawn for changes which could not possibly make any difference other than a legal one.

Agreed then that the Dos Passos is junked. I trust I can have a few more days—until the 25th of August instead of the 20th—because I will now have to begin all over again (I had been comparing Faulkner's and Dos Passos' careers in terms of the effect of the Depression and their reputation and their development, since the Depression helped Dos Passos and kept Faulkner from adequate recognition). I probably won't need the extra time, but I'll do a better job if I don't feel rushed.

Faulkner also requires the exercise of some tact since it is, in one respect, an anti-war book (but only in one respect) and Faulkner's general is Petain (not Foch, as some reviews said). He is called Bidet in the book, a possibly interesting transposition, and F. is thinking of Petain as the head of the Vichy regime as well as the general who stopped the mutiny on the Western Front in 1917. However, I will touch on these connections quite briefly and in such a way that if necesary you can simply delete any paragraphs which might be misunderstood as adopting a political view.[1]

For the time being I must postpone remarking upon your desire to become a Giant fan. Willie Mays has been going steady with Miss Bronze America, but I think she may be playing around with Jackie Robinson, Roy Campanella, and Junior Gilliam because Willie goes to bed so early in the evening. Anyway, she has been telling him that it is rude to say to the pitcher as he rounds third after hitting a homer, "Excuse me." She thinks, like most, that Willie is a simple spontaneous child of nature and Willie is too brilliant to undeceive her.

Last month while wandering over the green fields of my little plantation in search of uranium, I came upon what may be the spiritual equivalent of it. If tests still to be performed prove that I am not deluded, I will need a collaborator, and after much thought I've concluded that you may be the lucky chap, a choice in which my gentle wife-in-law concurs. It is too soon by several weeks to say more, but perhaps I should immediately assure you that your participation will not require the expenditure of a bronze cent on your part, although it will require your knowledge, experience, and time, and in addition a new pseudonym: William Candlewood and Hiram Handspring will not serve the purpose for a variety of reasons. I will not keep you in the dark any longer than necessary if only because I am impatient myself.

Yours,
Delmore

P.S. The contents of my guest issue of *Perspectives USA* are complete, with two exceptions. Let me know if you would like a list of them. I hope you can manage to schedule it for this year because otherwise I'll have to go to the bank again and borrow to pay interest on the expectation.

Does the enclosed comic strip, which please return, impinge upon your sensibility as it does upon mine?

P.P.S. In rereading my last paragraph, I see that it may seem merely a jest, which does not matter, at present. But, to coin a phrase, I was never more serious in my life. The Kingdoms of the Spirit and of high culture may be on the verge of an unimagined transformation.

1. The piece was published as "Faulkner's *A Fable*," in *Perspectives USA*, No. 10 (Winter 1955).

TO JAMES LAUGHLIN

RD 1 Box 230
Pittstown, N.J.
August 27, 1954

Dear Jay:

Many and profound apologies for the lateness of the enclosed, which was due to unforeseeable and unavoidable causes. The chief of them was the virus which overtakes first Elizabeth and [then] myself nearly every August, which I suspect is due to the drought and use of rainwater. In addition, both typewriters broke down just as a Woodstock undid another scoundrel, Alger Hiss; and the character of provincial life, which undid Madame Bovary, caused an absence of onion-skin paper, in our province. And finally the shakiness of the virus was intensified by a desire to assassinate Durocher for trying to prove (in seven games which were lost) what a great genius he is by not walking the batter who came up before the pitcher with the winning run on the bases (yesterday again, in Chicago).

I am aware that the review is about eight or more pages than you requested. I have not only cut it down from sixty pages in the first draft (which I would like you to read some time) but omitted many excursions—which at the time seemed quite original—on the relation of Faulkner to Schweitzer, Bergson, Malraux, Uncle Tom, Gandhi, Tolstoy, Erich Maria Remarque & Marlene Dietrich, to say nothing of the extent to which I had to forbid myself to discuss the great novelist's view of the Negro and the attitude he is likely to adopt when he hears how much Willie Mays is paid in 1956.

// As you know, it is very hard to write this kind of review, since it means forgoing self-expression and sticking to the book itself very closely. I did so because the reviews are all so stupid, the book is wonderful, and everyone around here says that they can't read it (everyone of the Indian tribe resident in Bucks County and named the Martinis, but I gather the same is true elsewhere): the enclosed clipping is further evidence.

If you've read the book, I don't think you'll want to cut the review at all. And if other changes are necessary, please summon me and I'll arise from the melancholy of middle age and journey to Babylon on a moment's notice, despite the fact that the twenty-seven days' toil over the review is twenty-five days longer than I have ever before given to any review.

Yours,
Delmore

TO KARL SHAPIRO

RD 1 Box 230
Pittstown, N.J.
August 30, 1954

Dear Karl,

I've kept putting off an answer to your two notes for several reasons. One of the reasons was that you wrote me at *P.R.* and the letters were opened by one of the girls in the office (the excuse is usually that my mail may contain mss. But often enough I'm afraid curiosity as a Bohemian privilege is involved). So I was quite embarrassed, when I finally got the forwarded notes, to see that you had quite rightly adjured gossip. Anyway, I was delighted that *Poetry* was going on and you are going on with it—everyone I know thinks you've been doing very well with it, not only better than previous editors, but better than most.

I also postponed writing you because I wanted to ask you for some new poems for my guest issue of *Perspectives USA.* and everything has been unclear about my issue, so that I was not sure I could ask you for as many as four poems—new ones if possible, and if not, four already published which I wish you would either choose yourself or let me choose as being, so to speak, "representative" (for Europe). The financial setup may have changed but you would probably get more money for unpublished poems—or perhaps have to divide up some of the money with your publisher—but in any case, you will be paid quite well and better than anywhere else.

I've been irritated, probably more than you have, by some of the reviews of your last book [*Poems 1940-1953*]—all favorable and admiring, but I think insensitive too. One of them had an invidious comparison of your work to mine which is entirely false unless I've lost my mind and another—Louise Bogan's—had you pigeonholed as a satirical poet. I hope you don't take these remarks seriously and I only suppose that you might because I often do—but anyway, my own conviction, for what it is worth, is that you are far more than a satirical poet and mostly not a satirical poet at all unless Dante was a satirical poet too because he attacked what he detested. I couldn't write the last sentence without thinking of my tending to make uncalled-for remarks of every kind: but I won't suppose you'll be annoyed by my comment if you're not by the remarks which prompted me.

I think I mentioned in sending you my piece on Eliot that I had better see proof—to be able to put in two footnotes (I returned to the Bohemianism of youth when I wrote it and made no carbon, so I don't know exactly where they belong).

My gentle wife-in-law and I enjoyed seeing something of you and Evelyn at last and I hope we'll be able to see both of you for a longer time henceforth, though it does seem unlikely right now.

Do let me know fairly soon about the poems, and the best from both of us.

Yours,
Delmore

P.S. Please give my regards to Isabella[1] and her husband; and forgive the difficulty of my handwriting: I've just had a mild virus infection and my typewriter an apoplectic fit. I don't think the makers of typewriters have heard of what happens when one revises, erases, revises, and wonders why one began in the first place.

1. Isabella Gardner, then married to Robert McCormick, helped Shapiro edit *Poetry*.

TO KARL SHAPIRO

RD 1 Box 230
Pittstown, N.J.
Sept. 13, 1954

Dear Karl:

There is a job every year at Princeton in the Creative Arts project, the rotating one which Jarrell, Berryman, and I have had. It pays only $4500 and there's not much left after the rent, but it might serve as a good springboard if you're resigned to a permanent teaching post, and it would also keep you near enough to New York to see what else might be possible outside of teaching. I'm sure Blackmur would be delighted to have you, but if you are interested you'd better write him as soon as possible: I'll speak to him when I see him, too. It's quite a pleasant job and you're more likely to hear of teaching possibilities elsewhere while there.

Speaking as a veteran of the entire situation, I've been trying to get away from teaching for eight years now, but without any real success, so that I'll be looking myself at the end of the year. The trouble with everything but teaching is that one spends so much time thinking of making money and making it only in makeshifts that one is more distracted than ever, and I imagine you would have more reason for anxiety than I do because of your children. In any case you can't get to be a prostitute any more in Hollywood or New York by free-lance writing or the like unless you change your name and grow a beard: you're typed as a poet and they don't want to deal with anyone they might have to treat with respect.

I'll choose your poems and let you know: if you do write something new, which you can give me, please do: you'll get more money that way.

Yours,
Delmore

P.S. Perhaps you feel like writing a piece on the situation of a poet—it's a depressing subject but you'd get at least $500 for it. Or if you have any other articles in mind, do let me know.

TO KARL SHAPIRO

RD 1 Box 230
Pittstown, N.J.
Sept. 25, 1954

Dear Karl:

The article you have in mind sounds wonderful, but I couldn't get it into *Perspectives*—which has as its primary purpose not only to show the most admirable aspects of life and culture in America, but also to play down those aspects which Europe admires and are not highbrow. For example, an article on jazz was knocked out of one editor's issue, and a fine piece on mass culture was dumped into *Diogenes* when the author made a fuss.

I had in mind another—and inferior—kind of piece but at the moment it seems pointless to speak of it since it's quite possible that

292

Perspectives won't be continued long enough for me to get my issue published. On the other hand, I may be taking a rumor all too seriously and if so, I'll write you about the other piece. You wouldn't get paid until publication.

But the kind of piece you've suggested would be welcomed by *P.R.* and elsewhere too, I suppose—it's subjective in the best (and Kierkegaardian) sense. Your feelings at 18 have at least the merit of being related to reality. I myself was under the impression that to be a Jew and have a Jewish name was a wonderful advantage! At least for a poet. And it was inconceivable that anyone would want to be anything else. How I managed to keep this benign idea isolated from some of the cracks in my favorite modern poet, Uncle Tom [T. S. Eliot], is something I have as yet been unable to fathom.

But I do hope that you feel moved to write your piece, and I'll write you again whenever the future of *Perspectives* is clarified.—If you saw Malcolm Cowley's piece in *The Saturday Review* this week, you saw that we're all in the same overcrowded boat so far as making a living goes; which reminds me that I had better get back to the hackwork which just barely keeps us going out here.

Best,
Delmore

TO KARL SHAPIRO

RD 1 Box 230
Pittstown, N.J.
Sept. 27, 1954

Dear Karl:

I'm extremely sorry to have to say that I can't consent to the cutting of my piece: how an essay of seventeen pages could be reduced to three hundred words is, under the circumstances, a mystery to me which, however, is beside the point. The point is that I consulted you about the length of the essay before writing, spoke to Joost also, worked at it for two weeks, and counted on payment for it as part of the extremely small living by means of which Elizabeth and I are trying to get through the present year without the interruptions of teaching. I would hesitate to make my own personal problems part of the point, even though they clearly are, were it not that I can't place the piece anywhere else now, having contracted to write similar pieces for all the other reviews open to me, during the next nine months as the only way of making a living. Our recent exchanges were marked, I think, by references to this effort on my part.

There are other considerations too, which would make me feel that your suggestion that I cooperate in this way is quite unreasonable, apart from my own financial problems. For example, you have had the essay for more than three months, and if, during that time, you had expressed misgivings about its merits, or some other difficulty, I would have withdrawn it and been able to publish it elsewhere, even though it is written to some extent in a way it would not have been written for a review not devoted entirely to poetry. But I don't want to go on, at further length; as a question of principle, there can hardly be any doubt that a change of policy is not supposed to be retroactive to the extent of months, and in the twenty years I've written for reviews I've not heard of anything of the sort: but the contrary is the case, articles are paid for, though a magazine suspends publication, and commissioned pieces are paid for even when they prove unusable.

The one consideration on the other side would be your own personal difficulty as an editor with the finances of *Poetry*, or something of the same kind. But at present I am in no position to regard a literary review's financial problems as having a prior claim to my own problems, which are such that I've been on the verge of asking for payment several times and have not, but only because I supposed that I would be paid within a few weeks. If you like, I'll waive the question of publication, though with acute disappointment. But I can't waive the question of payment in full, which, as you must know, is customary practice. So will you please decide about publishing the essay—which I regretfully make a matter of your option—and however you decide in that regard, see that I receive the payment in full on which I've counted for months, or if that is too difficult, let me know when I can expect it.

With best wishes,
Delmore

TO ARTHUR MIZENER

RD 1 Box 230
Pittstown, N.J.
Oct. 27, 1954

Dear Arthur,

You would have heard [from] me about how much I liked your piece, which was indeed very much, except that I thought you were going to be full and bright in Europe for a whole year. I certainly don't want to give it up, but you can, if you like, publish it elsewhere first—my guest issue may be any one of the next three or nine. I think you'd lose some of the filthy lucre—but on the other hand, you might not, since the amount keeps increasing and, the greater the delay, the more the piece will make. This was brought home to me with all the delightfulness of the unexpected when I received $600 for a 15-page review of *A Fable*, that sum being merely a first payment. A year ago it would have been $250 at the most.

I am glad to hear about your liking England, though I trust it won't go so far as literal departure. We ourselves are more and more pleased to be where we are, despite a slight poverty. To think that I was full of contempt for country folk! And we feel more convinced than ever after the spring quarter at Chicago, which was very nice, up to a point—reached after the first four weeks.

I'll be writing you again soon about other matters. At the moment I am in the midst of prolonged throes which resulted in dislocating my typewriter, my shoulder, slightly (hence this sloppiness, for I'm using Elizabeth's), and other forms of excitement. With the best from both of us to Rosemary and you,

As ever,
Delmore

TO KARL SHAPIRO

RD 1 Box 230
Pittstown, N.J.
November 2, 1954

Dear Karl:

I'm glad to hear about your job [U. of California, Berkeley]: you sound satisfied with it, and it also sounds like fun, at least for a year.

I don't see why you don't keep on with *Poetry* indefinitely, or at least until you've found a permanent place. I should imagine that moving it, or at least part of it to California, might, among other desirable things, provide fresh sources of the benefits of the income tax, benefactors, etc. There is no one I know would take the job (and at the same time be capable of handling it adequately) without getting closer to a living wage through it (directly). You doubtless know, but it is worth saying anyway, that no one who is good enough to do the job will not also want to do his own work as a poet and/or critic.

If I should think of someone as a possibility, I'll write you: I know people with an income and people who might be good editors, but at the moment I can't think of anyone who belongs to both categories.

I'm much relieved that the business about my piece is all straightened out. If I sounded too piqued, it was because I get sick of having to write and do so many other things for money, when I want to write poems and stories, a feeling you must know as well as I do.

When there is a definite date set for my issue of *Perspectives*, I'll be after you; I'm sure *P.R.* will be glad to get the other piece. With the best to Evalyn and you from both of us,

As ever,
Delmore

TO MEYER SCHAPIRO

RD 1 Box 230
Pittstown, N.J.
December 9, 1954

Dear Meyer,

You would have heard from me long before now, had I not been under the impression that you were still in Europe. And in fact I started to write you last spring when in Chicago the paintings at the Art Institute made me think of all the very illuminating things you had said about Seurat and the Impressionists.[1]

I come to New York as little as possible—once in every three weeks—and stay for as short a time as I can manage, for a variety of reasons, emotional as well as economic: but I will call you next time I come in. We both want you and Lillian to visit us either for a week-end or a Sunday as soon as the annual gathering of Elizabeth's clan is over. We keep becoming more and more attached to our post-Bohemian, post-urban establishment and now it is beginning to be difficult to imagine how anyone can bear to live in a big city. With the best from us to you and Lillian,

Yours always,
Delmore

1. Which resulted in S's best late poem, "Seurat's Sunday Afternoon Along the Seine," dedicated to Schapiro and his wife.

TO JOHN CROWE RANSOM

RD 1 Box 230
Pittstown, N.J.
December 10, 1954

Dear John:

The enclosed poem is part of a longer one, but I am sure self-contained enough to appear by itself.[1] It's the first verse I've sent you (and almost anyone else) in over five years, and I hope you won't mind my saying that I feel, at the moment at any rate, that it's as good as the best lyric I've written, "Starlight like Intuition Pierced the Twelve," which you published ten years ago last summer. I've never felt this kind of confidence before, but I am even more confident that you will know far better than I if my feeling is justified entirely or to some degree. I hope that you can write me about it before Xmas, since I've been asked for new poems by several others, and in fact, I think that it was Phil Rice who last asked me to send him new verse for the *K.R.*, so perhaps I ought to address this note to him too.

Elizabeth and I continue to enjoy country living and country knowledge as, I suppose, only two over-urbanized human beings can. We have some faint hope of some time getting you to visit us, however briefly, if you are in transit to Princeton, Philadelphia, or some such nearby place; and we have a hope less faint that we will at least see you again somewhere before too long—perhaps in New York.

Our country knowledge moved into a new dimension, I think, during the past few weeks, when a cat decided that our two cats were living well here (as they are, compared to the farmers' half-starved ones) and kept coming in tenaciously whenever he could. At first I thought he was merely a glutton and then merely a parvenu, but his patience has changed his appearance from that of a marauder to that of an immigrant. It's too long a story to be detailed, but the conclusion I've reached is that all political problems—and perhaps all problems—are insoluble. Perhaps I should have found this out before now, and I only found it now when I realized that the question was not economic, nor even social, for no matter how prosperous I was, I could not have the emotional capacity for more than two cats; while it's clear that the outsider himself can see no justifiable basis for our caring for our two native cats and excluding him. As I said, it all may be obvious to others, but it's never been to me, and makes me for the first time entertain a respect for the politics of royalism (as fixing status once and for all), a feeling that also is encouraged by my sad efforts to persuade the farmers around here that Adlai belongs in the White House and Dwight at Remington Rand.

I've several other matters to write you about, but I don't want to be too voluble after a long silence and they can wait a few weeks.

Yours always,
Delmore

1. "The First Morning of the Second World," published in *Kenyon Review*, 17 (Fall 1955).

TO SAUL BELLOW

RD 1 Box 230
Pittstown, N.J.
Dec. 10, 1954

Dear Saul,

Is it all right if we don't make up our minds about coming to your masked ball—since it's presumably a big party, etc.? If I don't hear from you, I'll assume that it's all right to leave it tentative. You mustn't conclude that you don't see me more often because I don't love you and the beautiful Sandra, but because I lose my momentum, elán and concentration in my work for several days every time I come to New York. This ought not to be true, but it is. And at present I lack the strength to aspire to the classic ideal.

Please tell Sandra that I've read her review and would be delighted to have her write my reviews for me at the usual rates.

I trust that I will be permitted not only to dance at your wedding but will be appointed beast [*sic*] man—or bib [*sic*] man—or something. I'll give myself away.

It does seem as if the New York International Style is winning out. A leading review in the *London Times Literary Supplement* (of a biography of Gladstone) begins, "What a sorry mishmash..." etc.

I've read *Augie March* again—for the 4th time—as a result of an admirer of the book saying to me my review praised it too much, which was not good for you. (I told him reviews were meant for readers, not authors.) And rereading it made me feel that it was not only better than I thought and said but better than you think (to judge by your own protest, which was like the admirer's).

—Call me Mishmash.

Best,
Delmore

298

TO CATHERINE CARVER

RD 1 Box 230
Pittstown, N.J.
December 27, 1954

Dear Katy,

I've read through the copy of [William] Gaddis' novel [*The Recognitions*] you sent me. If anyone else had sent it to me I would not feel moved to comment at all, but I've always admired your efforts on behalf of new writers, and perhaps, if the book irritated as many people for the wrong reasons as I think it may, this letter may be of some use. It's unlikely, I suppose, that anyone will buy a book because I say the writer is very gifted—as Gaddis obviously is—but my experience as a scout for Laughlin made me aware of how some publishers are influenced by the comments of other writers, even if they are only letters.

Anyway, my impression, for what it is worth, is that Gaddis has real genius, but that his novel reads at times as if Ronald Firbank and Thomas Wolfe were Siamese twins who had written a novel to prove that Truman Capote and William Faulkner ought to become converted to Catholicism. This may be too personal a way of putting it: the point is that Gaddis is very often wholly uncritical of his primary attitudes towards his characters—uncritical or unaware, it's hard to be sure. I think that his way of taking hold of Catholicism (he knows a lot more about sleeping pills than about the Church, despite the allusions) gets involved as an obstruction, so that he does not know the difference between genuine desperation and melodramatic attitudinizing (there are pages which would justify a suit for the affecting of alienation).

However, he is so gifted a writer, and so likely to mobilize the inferiority complexes of the Orville Prescotts [a reviewer] who are born every minute that I think it ought to be said also that he might very well become a great writer after he gets rid of the adolescent junk and old maid resentments which he cultivates. The important point is that he may have to write several books as the only way of getting purged.

I also may be quite cockeyed, as, at the moment, I am literally lopsided, having an infected jaw which makes me look like a sagging pigskin. Since I don't know anything about Harcourt, Brace, I don't know whether this or like comments can be of any use, though I do know that they may be disastrous in some publishing offices. In any case, you decide if this letter can help or ought to be destroyed immediately. And if you don't get enough good comments from other readers, let me know if you think I can help: though it means perjuring my immortal soul, I imagine that I can manage a Jesuitical comment for publication, saying how gifted I think Gaddis is without saying that the book is good.

> Yours,
> [Unsigned carbon.]

TO KARL SHAPIRO

> RD 1 Box 230
> Pittstown, N.J.
> January 20, 1955

Dear Karl:

I was disappointed that my footnotes, which took a good deal of two days' time, were left out of my piece.[1] (I've not yet got a copy), and a little perplexed as to how any money matters were involved, since other people are on the staff. But it's not really important, I should have sent in complete copy to begin with, and though I'd be more than disappointed if it were almost anyone except you, I now feel that we are spiritual kin (I hope you don't mind) (or tell anyone) in a special way having nothing to do with our earthly forebears. It occurred to me after seeing you again in Chicago that you were just as much an underground character—in Dostoyevsky's sense—as I am, though you handle it with far more grace and tact.

In any case, I can't afford to be annoyed since I must beg you for a poem, if possible, and soon, for *The New Republic*, of which I've just become poetry editor and several other things too. Can't you get a special dispensation from *The New Yorker*? I'd be extremely grateful since I want to make a good showing from the start. I intend to ask Isabella too, but observe an order of precedence: you might however tell her to send me a poem now if she has anything new. The *N.R.* does not pay much, but does have 40,000 readers and the (perhaps) advantage of literate serious readers who are not poetry-cultists or new critics. I expect to have a far freer hand than on *P.R.*—if I can be said to have had any kind at all there. Best from both of us to Evlayn and you,

> Yours always,
> Delmore

1. "T. S. Eliot's Voice and His Voices," *Poetry*, 85 (Dec. 1954).

TO CONRAD AIKEN

RD 1 Box 230
Pittstown, N.J.
January 24, 1955

Dear Conrad,

You've not seen or heard from me (since that beautiful party where I become so talkative) for the usual infernal reasons—which you understand, as most do not, so, as there is no need to detail them to you, it's pointless to tell them to most others.

However. I've just become poetry editor of *The New Republic* and would be very grateful indeed for a new poem of yours. The one I liked so much in the *T.L.S.* would be fine if that issue had not been so much around. At any rate, I won't have any of the difficulties I've had on *P.R.*—some unavoidable in a literary review like that, some unjustifiable, but all making for a paralysis of initiative on my part. I suppose I'm too optimistic about the *N.R.*—there'll be new difficulties, as there always are—but despite a veto power in reserve, I ought to be able to be at least unembarrassed for the first time since beginning with *P.R.* //

Yours always,
Delmore

P.S. My guest issue (along with all others) of *Perspectives* was called off—and that's why you've not heard from me about that.

TO ROBERT LOWELL

RD 1 Box 230
Pittstown, NJ.
January 27, 1955

Dear Cal,

I've just become poetry editor of *The New Republic* (as well as engaging to write a column twice a month for them) and naturally would be very grateful for a new poem from you. It would be a considerable favor in itself in helping me to make a good showing at the start, and it would help me in dealing with your imitators, who have already appeared in the unsolicited mail. Maybe you remember my theory and subsequent counter-theory about imitators—the first one was the notion that real poetic establishment showed itself in the sincerity of imitation. This had to be discarded when I thought of Kipling and watched Auden, and in place I decided that what was necessary were good imitators, who became genuinely original, as Yeats's have (as in some of Allen's poems). And then a third theory had to be invented because I remembered how Shakespeare made good poets bad when they imitated him. I could go on, indefinitely, but what I started out to say is that some of your imitators are turning out very well and one of them will appear sometime soon in the *N.R.*

I don't know whether Katie Carver told Lizzie [Elizabeth Hardwick]—had the chance to, that is—how much I liked her new novel [*The Simple Truth*] and how I did not think it would be entirely desirable for more than one of the *P.R.* circle (sickle?) to appear in jacket comments. Assuming that Philip would say something, I told Katie to decide the matter, and let me know if a word from me would be of use, in which case I would of course have been delighted to pontificate. Anyway, I not only liked the novel very much as Elizabeth did, but thought it was the book everyone ought to read after *Crime and Punishment*, which I had just previously been rereading in the new Penguin translation.

You would be surprised, perhaps, at what a country boy I have become. And a West Jersey localist, intensified recently when I learned that N.J. was the first New Caesarea. In fact, it's too long a story to tell but a stray cat almost made me a royalist in December, as I wrote John Ransom who appeared to have had the same feelings. Anyway, at present, I am entirely, for the remainder of January, a royalist in literature, a classicist in politics (e.g., the Athenian Republic), and an Anglo-Catholic in all questions of lyric poetry. As for religion, I am seriously a theist who wants to write poems to the King of All Hearts, but when disheartened I think I ought to believe in everything: it's safer that way.

However. This is late afternoon which somehow makes me facetious. Do let me know and soon if possible about new verse, and I'd be delighted to hear from you about other things, though I know you don't or didn't like to write letters. Best from both of us to Lizzie and you,

Yours,
Delmore

TO WILLIAM COLE

RD 1 Box 230
Pittstown, N.J.
April 22, 1955

Dear Bill:

Gilbert Harrison [Editor of *N.R.*] has asked me to write to Albert

Camus and try to persuade him to do a Paris letter for *The New Republic*. Since I've met Camus only once, very briefly, and since he may know nothing about *The New Republic*, it occurred to me that you or whoever handles his books in America for Knopf might be far more persuasive. The general idea would be five or six letters a year, and in addition to being fairly well-paid for, the letters would have some value—I don't really pretend to know how much, or how little—in keeping up an interest in Camus' books. At least that appears to have been one of the chief reasons that writers like Mann and Eliot wrote for *The Dial* thirty years ago, but now I should think there would be the additional argument that *The New Republic* represents a point of view pretty close to Camus', particularly since he would not have to restrict himself to the French literary scene. I won't go into further detail now, and I hope this won't be any particular trouble. I can of course write to Camus directly.

I thought you were a novelist rather than a poet, and I still retain the initial impression, with the addition, but would be delighted to see poems of yours for the *N.R.* As I think you more or less predicted in February, a poetry editor's task is not an easy one—the one solid result of three months' activity is a new example of what I think of —a little pretentiously—as Schwartz's paradoxes: "There are more poets than poems," which follows upon, "There are more good book clubs than good books." This must sound dismal, but may reflect only the emotion of a disturbed Giant fan—which I was long before getting involved with the higher forms of culture.

Best,
Delmore

TO JOHN CROWE RANSOM

RD 1 Box 230
Pittstown, N.J.
June 11, 1955

Dear John:

I'm truly sorry to be the cause of so much trouble about something which should have been quite mechanical. The enclosed new copy is not perfect either, but I think it is clear enough for the printer's purposes. I would keep typing until I had a perfect copy, but the result would be an irresistible urge to augment and revise. The outpouring of which this poem ["The First Morning of the Second World"] was an early product has continued and I've written a good deal more—

very little, however, which leaves me so little troubled by doubt, but then nothing else in years has—and, in short, the tendency to elaborate is naturally much abetted by what I've written since. But I have, apart from four lines, resisted all additions, and this new copy will look longer only because I followed your instructions exactly in making indentations and margins consistent. It seems to me now, as it did not when I typed the first copy, that the way in which these kinds of lines are set is not important and that the context suffices to set the pace, phrasing, and overflow; but if there is anything wrong or difficult, any alterations of yours will be fine.

I thought the last issue of *K.R.* was particularly good, so good that as I read through, I forgot my disappointment—which was of course entirely unreasonable—that my poem was not in print. But I had better put off for a while the remarks I meant to make about that issue and several other things that would interest you, but aren't urgent. I have the feeling, which may be foolish, that the *K.R.* may be near enough to going to press to make a day or two's delay a further hindrance.

As a temporary substitute for the more serious matters I want to write you about fairly soon, I'll list a few sentences which I call somewhat pretentiously Schwartz's Paradoxes—I don't know what some of them mean, but they certainly bear the marks of emotion: There are more scapegoats than goats. There are more good book clubs than good books. There are more poems than trees. There are more poets than poems (and the converse is also true, at times). The world is a great success precisely because it is at once a prairie oyster, a white elephant, and a gift horse (and much else). These seem less worth setting down that I thought, so I'll stop. Elizabeth sends her best regards, yours,

Delmore

TO GILBERT HARRISON

RD 1 Box 230
Pittstown, N.J.
July 29, 1955

Dear Gil:

I have been thinking and making inquiries about both a writer on TV and on psychiatric trends. I feel a little more certain about the latter problem as a result of the experience I had—which I may have mentioned to you—when I was commissioned to do a psychoanalytical anthology in collaboration with a psychiatrist: the idea was partly to have me see that the articles were not too technical for the general public and it all fell through because every single pro with whom I conferred—there must have been twenty before I gave [up]—couldn't abide most of his colleagues: when they did not sound like Stalinists—as of 15 years ago—discussing Trotskyites or vice versa, they sounded like poets at their worst. Though the difficulty can't be so great when it's just a question of an article which is a survey (and there is a wonderful doctor named Max Gruenthal [S's psychiatrist] who would be fine if he could be persuaded to write: I've tried in the past for *P.R.* and given him books to review, to no avail), it might be a good idea to experiment with two literary people. I've mentioned Robert Gorham Davis to you several times, but I doubt that I said that he knows as much about psychiatry as most professionals and keeps up with the technical journals: he did write one comparatively weak piece for *P.R.* called "Art and Neurosis," 1945, and I'll see if I can't find a copy in the attic if it ever gets cool enough to go up there without taking a chance of bursting into flames. Davis writes well and naturally has no axe to grind, and he is the sort of writer who responds best when given the kind of editorial guidance which I'm sure you'll provide (when he writes for the *Times*, he gets involved in a kind of double talk which is entirely unnecessary, and only if you know him and Cambridge, Mass., do you know what he is really saying). The other possibility, a less promising one, but worth one try at least, is Lillian Blumberg, who did work as a research assistant for a time for a psychiatrist and who wrote an excellent piece for *Commentary* (which I'll also try to find and send you) on the differences of the schools. She kept away from all the intramural quarrelling which makes every difference into a feud. I don't have have her address but can get it out of the N.Y.C. directory: Davis, though he may still be at Salzburg, can be reached c/o Smith College, and I think that in any case it would be good to use him for all sorts of things, of a very different kind; it's worth repeating that he needs editorial support to be as first rate as he can be: he's stuck his neck out with a good deal of courage several times (on the New Criticism, e.g.) and then did not get backed up as he should have been, for example, by *P.R.* And you can be sure that you won't have to be anxious, as of course you might be with any professional, that you'd get a piece too technical and internal for the lay reader. Among the professionals, in addition to Gruenthal, there is Franz Alexander (I may be all mixed up about his being still alive!): he has been a sort of diplomat and dean, mediating among the feuding evangels of peace of mind, but he certainly would be in touch with developments in matters like medicine and its relation to psychiatric developments, something which the most competent outsider naturally can't take into account. There is also [Harry] Murray at Harvard as another possibility, and Arnold Cooper, who is quite young, particularly for a psychiatrist, but who may not work as well as he talks.

The problem of TV criticism is a lot more difficult, as you indicate; I thought the piece in this week's *N.R.* was quite feeble, though it seemed possibly so because of self-consciousness, etc. I don't see the bright young fry as I used to when I lived in the Village, but it's from that group, I imagine, that the most likely candidate may come; and I imagine that it might be best to give the most rope to a young writer, since of course you not only want good lively writing, but a young writer is so much more likely to see TV from the point of view of the *N.R.* reader, while anyone who works inside is likely to forget that point of view. I have the feeling that the problem is made more complicated by the fact that one trial is likely enough to be misleadingly promising, or the reverse, while on the other hand you can't really be expected to hold a prolonged series of trials. Everyone I know in N.Y. appears to be on the Cape right now, but I should be able to ask about more after Labor Day. One trouble, for me, is that I don't glance at the periodicals as I used to, since it involves driving 30 miles to Princeton instead of walking across Washington Square Park to the N.Y.U. Library: *Commentary, The New Leader,* and sometimes even *The Hudson Review* have turned up new writers, in their book reviews, from time to time; and that's a more reliable way of course of unearthing candidates than asking people or talking to people who are recommended. But I'll make a point of spending a few afternoons in either the Princeton Library periodical room, or in New York, and perhaps have more specific possibilities to mention.

˙ I've been noting down books I thought might be reviewed: one is the new book on the Dreyfus Case; Hannah Arendt would be excellent on it, though she's written at such length on the subject in her book on totalitarianism that she might naturally not want to deal with it: but Niebuhr might be even better and less likely to miss the human situation involved: no one that I know has ever given the credit and honor due to Picquart, as heroic in his way as Gandhi—and not even Proust (who would be the best reviewer of all if he were but available) says anything about the nobility *and* the cunning with which he broke open the whole affair, knowing very well that he was throwing away a brilliant military career and actually risking his life.

I'm not surprised to hear that Angus Wilson is being slow; it's what has happened so often whenever transatlantic reviewing occurs; I'd guess that he will come through, but if he does not, there are several other people who might be almost as good: one is Noel Annan who has written a first-rate book on Leslie Stephen, but may be too much of an intellectual historian to be in touch with literary London, and the other is MacNeice.

You and your wife must have the same feeling as we do about vacations: it's so much more trouble to go and install oneself than just to stay at home. With the best to both of you from Elizabeth and myself,

Yours,
Delmore

P.S. I've several other novel new suggestions which I'll save for my next letter. I can't remember if I mentioned that Silone might welcome the chance to do an Italian letter.

TO PASCAL COVICI

RD 1 Box 230
Pittstown, N.J.
Aug. 20, 1955

Dear Pascal:

Saul is right in saying you are like a father but he ought to add like a Santa Claus too. I'd not merely be enthusiastic but overjoyed to do a *Portable Heine* and there would be a good many respects in which it would be as if you were publishing a new European—this will sound *too* enthusiastic to be true, but the fact is that Heine is one of the most known and loved and translated of poets (which makes that part of the editing simple: the numerous translations I mean) and yet most people are hardly aware that he wrote prose too and very good prose and even when they know this, they don't feel drawn to reading his prose writing, perhaps understandably enough because if there have been translations in America since the Bohn's Library one, they are out of print. And I think I could write a very lively and interesting introduction—biographical more than critical perhaps or both combined, since that is, as you probably feel too, the only possible right introduction to so lively and interesting a human being, one capable of saying when he was dying and in much pain that God will forgive me "*C'est son métier!*" And the introduction might attract attention to the volume—though I gather that the Portables are immensely successful—in presenting Heine the poet as not only a wise guy like Ogden

Nash, and he certainly was that, in part—but he [was] also and in the same poem sometimes a poet like Baudelaire too; but most translators are so charmed by the Ogden Nash that they try to get that quality instead of the Nash-*cum*-Baudelaire quality which makes him really serious. I'll go into further detail in the volume itself—and one special, interesting, but perhaps unnecessarily trouble-making and awkward topic which perhaps should be included or avoided, the comic and tragic farce of Heine in the Third Reich. And perhaps I had better mention one new idea, which may or may not be wacky, since you mention the untranslatability of his best poems: to print these in German with the kind of word for word prose version in English that one gets in the ponies which schoolboys use for Virgil. I myself always found I had come closer to the spirit from looking at these (not for school, but after) and since in addition so many readers know a little German, or some Yiddish, they may be advised to read the poems that way (this kind of bilinguality has become so widespread and marked that a scholar has recently written a very learned analysis for one of the most learned journals (I'm assuming you don't see it unless you enjoy being bored from within), which is on nothing more or less than a new language which he calls Yinglish and which he finds being spoken by radio comedians, movie stars—in and out of the movies, and written by people like Damon Runyon. The fact is, that Saul sometimes writes in that new lingo too, which is natural enough—but when I saw last fall a London *Times Literary Supplement* leading article, a review of the diplomacy of the British Foreign Office between the two wars, beginning: "What a sorry *mishmash* these documents make, etc." I realized that there was another reason for believing Saul will be a great novelist—the triumph of Yinglish as an acceptable lingo some of the time).

As for my own novel, that's quite a complicated matter, but it may be easy enough to resolve the complications. I've been at work on it for years and it's very long by now but it has one completely self-sustained and independent whole of 350 pages, which needs only to be typed in a clean copy (the whole work is called as a working title: *The American Dream*, with the sub-title, *A History of the Boys and the Girls*, and each part is how a boy or girl lived in relation to an American Dream): but I'd better say no more right now since it must be a matter of confidence for the moment. I have no contractual obligation to New Directions for any novel, but I do get a small stipend for reading mss. which has become a sinecure since no books can be accepted—and if Laughlin finds out that someone else wants me, he'll fire me for the tenth time. But I'd like very much to sign up with Viking and have the benefit of your tutelage as Saul did, and it's worth the loss of the stipend-handout if you and Viking are definitely interested.—By which I mean, not an advance—I don't want any more advances: they're demoralizing and useless, since they neither pay the bills nor help the work to get done. I don't want any for the Heine if that goes through until I've delivered the goods—but merely a contract which would be a good deal but not entirely a formality since of course I would hardly want my book on which I've worked so long and will work longer to be put out by a publisher who was not enthusiastic, at least mildly so, as a beginning, for a long work.[1]

Well: I hope you don't mind long letters, because if all goes well, you'll be getting them from this direction; and when I hear from you, I think I'd better come and talk to you (whenever is right for you), particularly about the novel. (I can come at any time but prefer the middle of the day.) With many thanks,

> Yours,
> Delmore

P.S. Please excuse the sloppy letter with the carbon copy on the wrong paper and all, but I've got a fearful deadline with the Sunday *Times Magazine* section, after which years as a poet, critic, and fiction writer, I am now a specialist on Marilyn Monroe![2]

1. Neither project was ever realized.
2. S had written on Marilyn Monroe for the August 8, 1955 *New Republic*. This article appeared as "Survey of Our National Phenomena," *The New York Times Magazine*, April 15, 1956. After his death an unpublished poem, "Love and Marilyn Monroe," was found in his papers. It was published in *Partisan Review*, XLIII, 3 (1976).

TO PASCAL COVICI

> RD 1 Box 230
> Pittstown, N.J.
> December 15, 1955

Dear Pat,

Many thanks for the book about Hogarth, which just came today. [Peter] Quennell is always interesting and sometimes more than that, so I'm delighted to get the book.

I'll answer your last letter in the detail necessary when I see you, which should be as soon as I get everything organized for a return to New York during the winter. But meanwhile I had better say that I am making steady progress with the Heine (I am going to use the "Dr. Faustus," which is quite short), though unable to do much else save for my piece every other week for *The New Republic* and other things that I have to do for them.

You're certainly going to get the book Saul and I planned under other circumstances. If necessary, which I doubt, I'll do it all myself. As a next-to-last resort I'll write an extra chapter on How to Make Women, based on all my many failures, and if this does not bring back Saul from Nevada to add his wealth of experience to the writing of fiction, then I misunderstand Saul entirely. Joking aside, I am counting on the $500 advance I'm to get, so there is every reason, including the desire to use all that I've accumulated as a teacher and critic, for me to get the book done. I have an unorthodox and perhaps weird or *verboten* scheme for making you even more certain, which is to regard the $500 already paid me as the first half of what is due for the Heine (and then give it back to me when the other book is delivered). This sounds strange even to me, but the reason for proposing it is that advances put one in an impossible position and I intend to accept no more of them and I would not have taken the money you gave me if I had known that so long a delay was at all likely.

There are several important questions involved in giving Viking my novel or rather the first self-contained volume of it, and though it is too soon to try to deal with most of them, since I won't have a chance to get to work on a good script until the Heine is done, perhaps I had better mention the most important of them. I am now entirely free of Laughlin and New Directions insofar as I want to be, except for my book on T. S. Eliot and the advance he gave me for it, which can be taken care of, if necessary, by giving him the complete manuscript as it now stands. The reason I have not is that the advance was based on Eliot's just having won the Nobel Prize and written a Broadway hit; now and for the past two years, it's unlikely that the book will make back the advance, as it would have in 1950 and may in the future. I also secured and forgot all about a release on whatever fiction I wrote, so the trouble I feared in that respect is gone. But the question for me, before any other one, is whether Viking will be willing to publish my poetry and criticism too. Several other publishers would do so, thanks to, I think, the results Knopf has had with Randall Jarrell, and I can still get anything I want published by New Directions, undesirable though that is in every way except that I don't have to wait or implore anyone. But once I give my novel to Viking, there is bound to be some difficulty with any publisher except the New Directions kind for the perfectly good reason, which you must be quite familiar with, that no one particularly likes to get the skimmed milk and not the cream. I'd rather be with Viking because of you, and what Saul has said and other reasons, including the lady who handled [Harvey] Swados' book and was so deft in getting me to say something about it when I did not want to. However, you'll understand and sympathize, I think, with my reluctance to be in a position where I have to find myself a publisher whenever I get a book of verse or criticism done. All this is premature, but not academic, since I have a good deal of both accumulated and it is seven years since I published a book of poems. But we can talk more about the problem when I see you. Perhaps I should add that nothing short of a contractual assurance would mean very much, since most publishers—not you, but all the ones I know about—make sincere promises when they are prospering and sincerely forget them when they are not. The only way you resemble the other publishers is, to judge by Saul's as well as my own impressions, in expecting me to do everything all at once, an expectation which I myself sometimes have with the worst results.

My wife is in Woodstock now because her mother and sister are ill and she has to tend to her sister's three children:[1] otherwise I would try to get you out here to meet her and see how we live before we return to the big town. I think I told you that she is a novelist too and that her first novel sold more than 300,000 copies as a Signet paperback. Since she is dissatisfied more than I am with New Directions, and can leave any time another publisher offers an advance higher than New Directions, it may be that she is the more desirable novelist of the family. Someone told me that it was not a particularly good idea for a husband and wife to have the same publisher and I can see why, but at any rate she might be a future possibility in another two years—she has not gotten very far with her new novel yet—and I can't see how anyone who has a paperback sale like that is a risk at all.

I should not go into all these future matters now, since Heinrich has to be sorted out and there is so much that is good that I keep changing my mind about the selections: the deadline will put an end to all hesitation, however. I have enough material for several introductions too, but I think I'll concentrate on the biographical and the history of his reputation as most likely to make a poet in another language—even one who is as much a wise guy as Heinrich—interesting to the readers.

There will be a piece of mine in the Sunday *Times Magazine* soon—at least, I think soon—which I hope you read for, among other reasons, to see if I have succeeded in writing so that the ads and the photographs don't entirely keep the great public from reading what I have to say to the end.

Best,
Delmore

1. According to Atlas, Elizabeth Pollet had left him in the late autumn and S was living alone again. They were reconciled for a brief period in the spring.

TO KARL SHAPIRO

Hotel Marlton[1]
5 West 8th St.
New York City, NY
[1956]

Dear Karl,

I was delighted to hear from you and then to read your reply to Graves. In addition to the nobility of attitude throughout, it deals with such complex matters as Pound's poetry far better than anyone else has, so far as I know. My own effort[2] was full of pulled punches for various reasons, among them the important one that I might, as poetry editor, be assumed to have accepted or assented to the publication of Graves's articles. I was told about them, but did not see them until they appeared in print, something which happens a good deal of the time because I am delinquent in writing letters or being at all efficient as an editor of a weekly journal.

Elizabeth and I have been in New York since January, attempting to cope with various problems, economic, medical and the like, with little success, so that Nebraska, or at least New Jersey, sounds fine at the moment and a permanent job wonderful. The one direct relation to literature I have right now is the task of making a Viking Portable of Heine's prose and poetry which would be fun if I were able to do my own work too. But by summer we ought to be back on the farm again and if you and Evalyn do come East at all, you must let us know.

With best regards from both of us.

Yours,
Delmore

P.S. One of the best things in your reply involves Eliot and what you say is strengthened by Eliot's actions with regard to Pound. He not only tried to get Pound to become an Italian citizen in 1939 or 1940, but Laughlin told me that he made a good many inquiries before the Bollingen Award as to whether it would have any undesirable effect upon Pound's status.

1. In January 1956 S gave up his New Jersey farm and moved to the Hotel Marlton. He was to return to the farm later that year.
2. "Graves in Dock: The Case for Modern Poetry," *The New Republic*, March 19, 1956.

TO GILBERT HARRISON

Hotel Marlton
5 West 8th Street
New York City 11, N.Y.
[1956]

Dear Gil,

I think it might be a good idea to write you in detail about some of the matters which have interfered with my functioning adequately as a part of *The New Republic*. Then when I see you next week we can spend the evening, or most of it, without being concerned about matters which have to do with editing.

The basic problem so far as my own relationship to the *N.R.* is involved is an economic one. To do justice to the obligations I am supposed to fulfill would require at least three days a week, and often more. Perhaps someone else would be quicker about these things, but I doubt it. But since for quite private reasons I can't get along on less than $500 dollars a month—and this was true in January 1955 when you first wrote me—$150 a month is not a living wage. I've tried quite unsuccessfully to make up the difference since January 1955 by doing some of the writing I did before then. The result has been increasingly futile to me and I imagine to you. Thus during this month and last I have had to do a Viking *Portable* for which I am paid $1000 and this is the kind of thing which I can get several times a year as a means of livelihood, if past experience prior to January 1955 is any guide, while at the same time having enough time for my own work, the poetry and fiction which [are] more important to me than anything else. But when I try to do justice to my duties on the *N.R.*, and to matters like the Viking *Portable*, the result is, and has been for the past year and four months, unsatisfactory all around and I am unable to do any of my own work at all, to say nothing of the illness from overwork which occurs off and on. Hence, much as I would like to continue to be on the *N.R.* it is a luxury which I cannot afford at present so far as I can see and the problem is one which cannot be helped by any temporary aid, at least as things are now and as they are likely to be for some time to come. As you know, I am extremely grateful for all your patience and kindness, and I would guess that you have problems with the *N.R.* which make it impossible to make any decisive and lasting change in my relationship to the *N.R.*, although I have thought of several possible changes which would put matters on a basis less difficult for me, as well as for you. There is no need, so far as I know, for any immediate decision on your part or mine, but the chief problem, the fact that $150 a month is not a living wage—nor was it twenty and thirty years ago when the *N.R.* was at the peak of its position in the literary world, though everyone had less economic pressure—remains quite insoluble. There are other problems too, but they could be worked out gradually, I think, if this problem were not in the way.

I must add that the entire situation is my own fault, in that I should have known, when I began and if I had not been unduly optimistic about my own capacities, that I could not be adequate to more work than I already had. And it would certainly be foolish to expect you to know what I myself overlooked.

Best,
Delmore

TO J. M. KAPLAN

81 West 12th St
New York City
March 30, 1956

Dear Mr. Kaplan:

Meyer Schapiro told me that you and your wife had been the source of the grant given me last week by the New School, and he told me that it would be entirely proper to thank you myself.[1]

The aid came after months of extreme difficulty and thus was far more helpful and important than much larger sums would have been at any time during the past twenty years. And I doubt very much that I will have any such difficulty in the future.

The enclosed poem is part of a new book of poems which I am trying to complete, and I should like to inscribe it to you, if you do not think that to do so would be in any way embarrassing or inappropriate.[2] Please do not hesitate to tell me if it is. I myself have sometimes been embarrassed in this way. With many thanks again,

Yours sincerely,
Delmore Schwartz

1. Meyer Schapiro had arranged for the grant.
2. The poem "Abraham" was dedicated to Kaplan, a philanthropist.

TO JAMES LAUGHLIN

Gambier, Ohio[1]
Sunday, July 23, 1956

Dear Jay,

I'm in the doldrums deep, so the enclosed is the best I can do. Sorry not to be able to be more helpful and hope to see you soon as we get back.

Yours,
Delmore

P.S. Have you ever thought of reprinting in the New Classics Kenneth Burke's *Towards a Better Life*? It's a wonderful piece of eloquence (somewhat like [Djuna Barnes's] *Nightwood*) and Burke has an unpublished short synopsis of the narrative situation which would add a good deal to it. It came out in 1932 when everyone was too bewildered to pay attention to it, but now a reprint might get the recognition which the book deserves.

1. S was teaching at Kenyon College School of Letters.

TO SAUL BELLOW

RD 1 Box 230
Pittstown, N.J.
Nov. 11, 1956

Dear Saul,

Pat sent me a copy of *Caesar's Day* [*Seize the Day*] and I not only could not put it down, but I could not stand up, not even to get a fresh pack of cigarettes, the hypnosis of attention was so intense. This is not only true success, I think, but shows that you are a wholesome author and good for the reader's health. I will tell Van Wyck Brooks if you will tell Pat that Balzac and Dickens have been dead for some time now and both might have lived longer and written better books if they had hurried a little less.

If you like I'll tell you more of my impressions of [Thornton Wilder's] *The Ides of March* (which are shared by Elizabeth and Josie Herbst[1]) when I see you. Right now I must return to work since it has literally become a question of eating-money from week to week, so I will limit myself to one among many impressions, that you have a special genius for minute particulars (as you doubtless know)—for example, the ticket in the windshield wiper which turns out to be an ad and not a ticket. There is a lot more to say, but nothing that you don't know unless it is that (don't get irritated) you may not know how good you are, at least not all the time.

However, no one asked me. And I started this note to tell you that I have a lot done for the textbook, but must get the Heine portable done, or put it aside for a few weeks, before I organize my material for your examination. However, I can send you a tentative list of contents if you like and I wish you would send me yours and Sandra's.

Best,
Delmore

1. Josephine Herbst, the novelist, who lived across the Delaware River in Bucks County, Pa.

TO ELIZABETH AMES

RD 1 Box 230
Pittstown, N.J.
November 15, 1956

Dear Elizabeth:

I don't know if I can be of much use in helping you to prepare a guest list this year, since I have had so little to do for some time with young writers. Even as poetry editor of *The New Republic* (which I no longer am), I found so few new poets worth printing that I hardly thought the effort of going through manuscripts worth the trouble.

However, I myself would like to come, at long last—it's something I've thought about again and again and always put off asking you in the hope that it would be more fun after finishing some piece of work or before beginning a new one. My belief that there would be such a time has gradually deteriorated with each year. I'll wait until you've taken up the question of my coming with the Committee before telling you when I would like to come and asking if it would fit in with your plans. I certainly look forward to coming and to seeing you again. My visit seventeen years ago was not only very pleasant in itself but memorable for all sorts of other reasons and when I left at Christmas and went to the Modern Language convention in search of a teaching job (which I was unfortunate enough to get), my own badge of identification said Yaddo where others had the name of a university, and I've been reminded of this time and again when I meet someone who has been to Yaddo too, since it is an old school tie in the best sense of the word.

It's possible that I may be in New York City more often during December and see more of young writers than is likely here in the country, and if I see someone promising, I'll certainly tell them to write you.

With best wishes,
Delmore

TO CONRAD AIKEN

RD 1 Box 230
Pittstown, N.J.
November 30, 1956

[No salutation.]

Since I failed to write even a lobster and orange blossom note of thanks to Mary last June, I would feel embarrassed to break the silence with the request for a favor were it not that the cause of silence is different this time—external problems of extreme vulgarity instead of the usual internal difficulties which kept me from communicating with everyone. When I went to New York last week to explain why I had not yet finished the Viking *Portable Heine* which was supposed to be done last March, I saw Malcolm Cowley and asked him about the grants to Rome, particularly the poet-in-residence fellowship.[1] Malcolm told me that I had a friend on the committee and that it would not be unbecoming to write you about how much I would rejoice in a grant. He said also that you were not the only voice on the committee and added that on the other hand I probably did not know of how favorably you regarded my "Work" (my quotation marks), which not only gave me much pleasure and made me aware that I was not entirely beyond being pleased, but what is more, provided a banquet of thought of various subjects—so many that I had better wait until I see you to mention them.

Though I would be delighted with a grant, I should say that there are other altenatives available and though they all lead back to the classroom, they would suffice to terminate the external problems and permit me to concentrate on the far more interesting internal ones. So the most I can say in my own favor is the somewhat ambiguous possibility that a year in the eternal city might enable me to finish "Dear Pope," the poem in overly heroic—not to say megalomaniacal—couplets, in which I advise [Eugenio] Pacelli [Pius XII] on the character of modern life, courting the favor of His Holiness by remarks about how Dostoyevsky's characterization of the Grand Inquisitor was not entirely accurate and Saturday night in Boston is not the only evidence of the moral authority of the Holy Church. It all began when I read of a Bible Belt's greeting to the Holy Father—"Any friend of God's is a friend of mine," and if Rome might induce me to destroy it, it might also make it all the more tactless.

Since it is a matter of preferring one rather than several other possibly more practical ways of coping with acute need, I had better admit that some candidate more interested in the visible world might make more of the grant, so please don't regard this as more than a reminder. Elizabeth says to ask you to think of us also if you have not sublet your New York apartment; she has recently made her start as an art critic for *Arts* and thinks that she has to go to New York to see the shows before writing about them, so we will have to be in New York for this and other reasons during the winter, a prospect which would be entirely unattractive to me except for my morbid curiosity about what art circles say and feel when they become aware of the voice of a point of view which combines the vision of Louisa May Alcott and Dostoyevsky in a Russo-American alliance which proves that reality is wilder than the most unhampered fantasies.

Don't trouble to answer if you've already disposed of your place or are using it, but please do let us know if you are in New York or en route to Washington. I hope it will be some time before we leave West Jersey—and particularly since we may not be here again for a protracted period very soon. Among the other things we must tell you about there are our impressions of the performance of "Mr. Arcularis"[1] we watched on TV, including immense pleasure, despite alterations of the original and a dim sense, which proved true, that some of the beautiful sentences would blight our dear evening addiction for weeks to come [...]

Yours,
Delmore

1. The American Academy and Institute of Arts and Letters Rome Fellowships in Literature.
2. Dramatization of an Aiken short story.

TO JOHN CROWE RANSOM

RD 1 Box 230
Pittstown, N.J.
December 26, 1956

Dear John:

I put off answering your note immediately first of all because I wanted to see if I could not begin the grant [Kenyon Fellowship] in July and I did not know, as I now do, that it would be simple to set aside most of the things I had promised to do during the next few months. Apart from a lecture and a certain amount of proofreading, I am free to accept it, beginning with the first of the year and put it to the uses for which it was quite rightly intended. I also delayed because I wanted, as a concrete expression of gratitude, to say something about my own observations not only of myself but of other poets which make an entirely free year a special blessing. I'll go into detail when the holiday season is over—I doubt that any of the things I have to say are unknown to you, or for that matter to John Marshall, but they were unknown to other poets and myself until recently and concern the effect of teaching and other fascinating skills upon anyone who wants to write poetry first of all and how misleading the truth that there is no such thing as a professional poet can be.

However, I must not run on right now, except to say that I must also explain some of the prose enclosures I sent along with my application, and add, along with our deepest thanks, a poem (!) for the season and in reply to the Xmas card you and Mrs. Ransom sent us.

Poems are writ by chaps like me,
But mankind made the Xmas tree.

This was not inspired by Joyce Kilmer, the holiday, or our brave Hungarian world,[1] but by our sibylline cat Dame Aethyl Pollet Schwartz [...]

Best as always,
Delmore

1. Reference to the Hungarian revolt of 1956.

TO DWIGHT MACDONALD

RD 1 Box 230
Pittstown, N.J.
December 26, 1956

Dear Dwight,

It is so long since I last wrote you that the act itself seems a little like a class reunion, particularly since I used to write you quite often, as you may not remember—my impression was and is that you wrote others quite often too but I did not—Anyway, to get to a new sentence and before explaining the reasons why we did not meet before your departure for the Old World, as I believe it is called, I'd better dispose of the fiscal-literary matter which I hope you can do something about. I sent *Encounter* two poems just about this time two years ago and heard from Stephen Spender to the effect that they would soon appear. I would write him about the poems except that I have the impression, based on Harvey Breit's column [*New York Times Book Review*] (my only source of direct communication with this brave Hungarian world) that he is somewhere in America. So would you mind arranging for the payment, for the poems. I can wait for publication indefinitely with a patience learned as a poetry editor, but we have been and are quite hard up for the time being and will be until next fall and if you were not protected by the Atlantic, I would accept the offer of the twenty bucks you made in March of 1939 or perhaps it was early in the fourteenth century. The poems are good, I think, and this is not always, alas, the way I feel about anything I write after two years' time, and their names are "Hölderlin" and "The Fulfillment," but it is the money that I want, and though the sum seems small, it is all relative or comparative as I did not know quite as intimately as I thought until this fall. I mean, I am perforce entirely crass and mercenary for the time being and will be glad to supply two other poems in any verse form desired to take the place of the ones accepted two years ago if they do not seem attractive enough any longer.

Money is life: why did you not acquaint me with this truth in my first youth? Instead of wasting your time and my hearing aid in impassioned defenses of Clement Greenberg, champion bullthrower?

I will immediately terminate the crimination: it is entirely nostalgia, as I learned from a Miss Catherine Carver who had removed or should say absconded with all the letters we exchanged from the files of America's best literary review, God help us all, having decided that they belonged to the ages, or at least were an invaluable record of the period. My remarks to you, she said, were "fresh," very often, and yours were preemptory and dictatorial, particularly when the bone of contention, on the surface, was an article by old Rahv, in two parts, in which I wished and you refused to distinguish between prose style and perception. To judge by her account (she refused to let me read the letters for fear I would alter them), I was perfectly willing to admit—with the reasonableness which has always been characteristic of me—that the style resembled an effort to park a Rolls-Royce on a window seat, but you insisted that style and analysis were inseparable and besides the essay was much too long.

I can't remember precisely what kept me from attempting to arrange a meeting with you and your fair bride [Gloria, his second wife] before you left either for Chicago or Europe, but it was my third attempt and you had to see your mother the second time and both of us, I think, were somewhat overbooked, or whatever it was that we were.

We may meet again sooner than I would have thought until recently, if I should get a Fulbright, in which case Elizabeth and I will try to start for Europe a month ahead of time and stop in England if only to ascertain with our own ears whether or not you have acquired an English accent. I am also very eager to visit Westminster Abbey and hold a seance with Matthew Arnold, on the subject of Lionel Trilling, and finally I would be grateful if you could arrange a meeting for me with Major General J.F.C. Fuller,[1] the only human being, to my knowledge, who avows candidly, what so many others believe and conceal, that everyone else is always wrong and he is always right. Since I may never arrive at all, and your opportunities of conferring with him are greater, perhaps I had better tell you one of the major topics I am eager to discuss with the General: he professes to be mystified by the Japanese strategic intention which led to the Battle of Midway Island and suggests only that it may have been an effort to lure an American task force into a trap, or to capture the Island of Oahu and thus sever the line of communications between America and Australia. In my view (ho, ho!), it is perfectly obvious that Midway, though small, would have provided the best possible air base for attacks on Hawaii. Your low view of my talents as a military strategist, which is not unknown elsewhere, and the General's low view of all other minds ought not to make impossible a statement of the reasons for believing that I am wrong again. The fact is that anyone who has ever succeeded in getting *P.R.* to print a piece which old Rahv did not want printed has had an experience of strategy and tactics which makes all warfare as simple as checkers.

It is so long since I saw you that I could run on indefinitely and feel a strong inclination to communicate news, news, all the news, but if I do, it may—or may not—make you feel you must answer at the same length and thus keep you from answering promptly. So I will save most of the rest until I hear from you, which is I hope as soon as it usually used to be. I doubt that any of my news will seem at all as fascinating to you as it does to me. For example, after you polished off that great thinker Wilson, *The Reporter* published a deliverance of his with much pride. And thus and so, apart from the comments of my cat Dame Aethyl Pollet Schwartz on the national campaign—"I like I.Q.," and "The White House has become a hospital," and "I never speculate about the locomotives of others," a sentence inspired by the press conference at which Eisenhower told the newsmen that "As you know, I never speculate about the motives of others." There are more but this letter is already longer than any letter that I myself would be likely to read at present at one sitting.

Best from both of us,
Delmore

1. Author of *The Second World War 1939-1945* (1948) and *A Military History of the Western World*, 3 Vols. (1954-56).

TO HENRY RAGO

RD 1 Box 230
Pittstown, N.J.
January 21, 1957

Dear Henry,

Many thanks indeed for your note. I would have written a piece for you on Graves's book [*The Greek Myths*] long before now, had the past year not been extremely difficult, so difficult that the Kenyon Fellowship was a kind of melodramatic thing which I kept thinking of as a ransom, for otherwise I would have been looking for any kind of teaching job whatever in the middle of the academic year. The reason for the trouble was, for once, not a matter of my own ineptness: we were supposed to go to one of the small colleges of the University of California [Santa Barbara] for a year, at an extremely good salary, and then, in the middle of summer the chairman called the whole thing off and explained that it was not his fault if the man I was to substitute for had changed his mind about taking a sabbatical. It turned out that the hero in question was Hugh Kenner, who, you may remember, feels rather strongly about my work. As a result of his stand, a fracas developed and Kenner ended up as chairman, which is all quite flattering to me in a peculiar way.[1]

322

As long as there is, as you say, no urgency, I'd like to keep the Graves and send you a fairly longish piece immediately that I have the time. The book is extremely bad and it would not be worth writing about if Graves were not so gifted a poet and taken seriously in whatever he writes, so seriously that the Penguin people were willing to let him do the book even though their standards are quite high. Under the circumstances, however, I think something ought to be said about how this and Graves's book on modern poetry [*The Crowning Privilege*] (which I commented on last spring in *The New Republic*) constitute an object lesson in the corruption of fame. Graves's interpretation of the Oedipus story is typical: it is a decadent version of the overthrow of a matriarchy devoted to the White Goddess!

I also have some poems which I would like to send you fairly soon, if I can bring myself to stop working at them. I have not seen *Poetry* in several months but when I last did I thought you were doing an extremely good job under conditions which, I imagine, continue to be as difficult as they were for Karl. With my best to your wife and to you,

Yours,
Delmore

1. Kenner, who had cruelly reviewed *Vaudeville for a Princess* in *Poetry*, was out of the country for the year and, according to Atlas, knew nothing of S's appointment.

TO ELIZABETH AMES

RD 1 Box 230
Pittstown, N.J.
March 9, 1957

Dear Elizabeth:

It is very kind and patient of you to suggest keeping a time open for me at some point during the spring and summer, and I would be grateful if you could without too much inconvenience. I began to write to you several times before getting your note to explain what had occurred which made it difficult for me to leave here and failed to finish each attempt because my explanation seemed unduly complicated, so I had better be as brief as possible. Since I last wrote you I have gotten a Fulbright for next year,[1] and a fellowship the year after makes it seem likely that my wife and I will be in Europe for two years and I was eager to get various publishing projects finished before going away and expected, foolishly enough, to be able to do so before visiting Yaddo, for it would be quite difficult to try to get them done in Yaddo, let alone abroad. In addition, my wife was going to write to you to ask if she might come at the same time I did—she is, as you may know, a novelist—and when she took on the job of writing monthly art reviews of current shows in New York, there was an additional reason for not being sure when I would be able to come.

I should be able to get some of the work done fairly soon, although you know how uncertain such things are, and it would be wonderful to have a visit to Yaddo to look forward to, particularly since it will be so long before another visit is possible.

One of the jobs which has caused uncertainty is a textbook and the other a Viking Portable selection of Heine's prose and poetry and I need to be fairly near a big library to work at both, and both have proved far more difficult to conclude than I expected. I'll assume, unless I hear otherwise from you, that when I get them both out of the way, my wife and I can write you.[2] With many thanks,

Yours always,
Delmore

1. To teach at the Free University of Berlin in the fall. S cancelled the fellowship when Elizabeth left him shortly before they were to depart, triggering a psychotic episode.
2. The Schwartzes spent the summer at Yaddo.

TO PASCAL COVICI

RD 1 Box 230
Pittstown, N.J.
March 25, 1957

Dear Pat:

Many thanks for Zabel's book [*Craft and Character in Modern Fiction*]. I can't say very much about it without being pointlessly unkind to Morton, and ungrateful too, since he has often been very nice to me.

I meant to write you before the book came and I have not simply because, although I have gotten a good deal of work done on my novel since last talking to you on the phone, I am not sure whether it is progress or merely increase. The less said about this the better, too, except to assure you that I am going to continue to work on the novel and refuse every other thing for the time being, now that I am free for the first time in years—and possibly the last for years—of immediate financial pressure. I think I had better stay away from New York as much as possible, but I will let you know when I do come in and we can discuss some sort of arrangement about the novel when it is finished and possibly before then. I have also spent several hours of each week on the Heine, and the task of correcting the existing translations, which is the main trouble, is painless now that the immediate pressure is off and I am spending most of my time doing what I want to do.

Best,
Delmore

TO ROY P. BASLER[1]

RD 1 Box 230
Pittstown, N.J.
May 28, 1957

Dear Mr. Basler:

Many thanks indeed for your invitation to lecture at the Library of Congress next January. I'm delighted to accept it. The subject you propose is not only an important one, but one which seldom gets the right kind of direct and explicit attention. I have, as I think you know, been living intimately, for almost twenty years, with the problems which modern American poetry involves, and although I've accumulated material for a series of lectures or a book, there has almost never been any occasion to deal with modern American poetry directly, and concretely.

As it happens, I am going to be a Fulbright lecturer at the University of Free Ideas [sic] in Berlin from next September until May 1958, but this post requires only two lectures a week and there is a recess of seven weeks beginning at Christmas. This will mean of course a good deal of travelling on my part and greatly reduce the fee for the lecture. But even if the drawbacks were far more serious, I would feel that I had to accept an invitation which is both an honor and an opportunity, and one which seldom occurs.

Your letter was not forwarded to the above address immediately and hence I am hurrying to answer you today. Some time soon I'd like to write to you again to indicate the various areas which I might attempt to cover. Since the lectures are to be published as a brochure, the overlapping which you anticipate might be somewhat reduced if each of the lecturers[2] had some broad idea of what the others would be talking about, although insofar as the overlapping is agreement, I imagine it has a value of its own which is quite desirable. With many thanks again,

Yours sincerely,
[Unsigned carbon.]

1. Director, Reference Department, Library of Congress.
2. The other lecturers were John Crowe Ransom and John Hall Wheelock.

TO STEPHEN SPENDER

Hotel Chelsea
222 West 23rd St.
New York City 11, NY
August 8, 1957

Dear Stephen:

Many thanks indeed for your letter which, under the circumstances, is very kind. My own letter was written in extreme haste; and as a result of practical and personal problems, was hardly very temperate or clear. I would have to go into much detail about these immediate problems to be clear now and perhaps I will be able to do so when I see you, although the problems are familiar enough to poets and to other unmetered human beings.

Let me say something briefly about one of the practical problems which made me write as I did. I have been trying to get my new publishers[1] to print a book of new and old poems, and they are inclined, as most publishers in America, to be so interested in fiction, even my own fiction, that they have been insisting (the unfortunate word in my letter to you is one which I have had to hear and then use for the first time in my life) that they must have the finished script of my novel before they will agree to publish my book of poems, though they promise to do so a year—so to speak—after the novel appears. I could make other arrangements with ease, since there are now several good publishing houses in New York which do not insist—the same old word—that a poet write a novel to get a book of poems published. The catch is that this might mean the cessation of advances which I have been given for my novel, which is the chief source of my livelihood at present. Since I intend to be in Europe for most of the next two years, I felt that I had to get the entire matter settled before leaving the country; it would be difficult if not impossible to do so by air mail: it is difficult enough as it is.

All of this has, of course, no direct connection with your problems in editing *Encounter.* This is the reason that I did not speak of it, except in the most general terms, when I wrote you. But the fact that I had used the acceptance of my poems as an arguing point seemed to make some impression, and though I doubt that the publishers would notice the appearance of the poems except briefly, and though their failure to appear would hardly be likely to be remarked, nevertheless the fact that they appeared in an international review which is much read and admired in New York might very well help me very much. There is a good deal more involved, including pressure to finish my novel, but I imagine that you are familiar in one or another way with this kind of situation. I hope that English publishers are not quite as convinced that a novelist ought to operate with the efficiency of a cash register and I know that they do not believe that the best of all books is the bankbook and the writing of poems a self-indulgent hobby. But your autobiographical book [*World Within World*], and other of your writings in prose, indicates that you know the problems of getting publishers to regard books of poems in a rational light.

At any rate, I hope this will make clear one of the causes for the character of my letter: it is, I mean, an emotional explanation, at least, which is not to say that I do not regret having written as I did to someone I have admired very much for many years, for reasons which have to do with literature and are, I think, essentially unrelated to publishing.

I am delighted that you still like my poems and whether or not their publication serves any purpose in relation to my own work (it may very well, to judge by the experience of others) their appearance will be, needless to say, an honor and a pleasure in itself.[2]

Finally, I had better say something about what was on my mind when I used that unfortunate word "insist." I'm not sure just what you had taken me to mean when I used the word, but what I had in mind were experiences of an editorial kind for almost twenty years— with *Partisan Review, New Directions,* and *The New Republic,* when, as an editor, I was continually embarrassed by the postponement of publication of poems I had accepted and the indignation of poets, which usually occurred within a few days after a new issue had appeared of those periodicals or the New Directions anthology. If Dwight is around, he will tell you of some of the most trying experiences of the same or a like kind, particularly on *Partisan Review,* and involving poems, stories and reviews. The point, in general, is that once a piece of work has been accepted, there is a commitment to publication on the part of the editor, even if he has changed his mind about the merits of the piece and even if, as with reviews, he has every reason to believe that the review was personal, etc. in a way which he had no way of knowing in advance. When it is a matter of poetry and of all fiction (unless it is libellous), no question of malice or personal motives exists, of course, so that even if an editor has changed his mind about the worth of a poem, the most that I have ever tried to do as an editor is to point out to the poet that he might regret the appearance of the poem (a Sisyphean point if there ever was one) and might feel like Cocteau that he would gladly sell his soul to remove his bad works from existence. As an editor, I never persuaded any poet and some of them spoke with assurance of the approval of Posterity, a period about which it is difficult to argue. However, on every such occasion, an accepted poem was published.

[Unsigned carbon.]

1. He may have been counting on a contract with Farrar, Straus & Cudahy at this time.
2. No poems of S appeared in *Encounter*.

TO WILLIAM PHILLIPS

[New York City?][1]
Monday [January 1958?]

Dear William,

The enclosed story[2] can be cut by at least twenty pages with ease, as you will see, and cut even further at certain points by substituting a few transitional sentences. I don't think that cutting will improve it particularly, but it won't interfere with it as a portrait of a purely American *luft-mensch*, and one which, I think, is authentic and comic at the same time.

However. As you know, it is a question of money and nothing else right now, and to have money which was earned, not borrowed, would be a refreshing experience, so I hope that you can let me know soon. I hardly have to add that I'll make any changes of any kind to make the story usable.

See you on Friday.

Yours,
Delmore

1. S had retrieved his belongings from the New Jersey farm and rented an apartment in the Village in November, 1957.
2. Probably "The Hartford Innocents," which was unpublished until included in *Successful Love and Other Stories* (1961).

TO HOWARD MOSS

81 West 12th St.
New York City 11, NY
February 11, 1958

Dear Howard:

The enclosed poems, which are the first I have ever sent to *The New Yorker* (although I was invited to do so a long time ago), have been chosen from a good deal of verse in manuscript and typed hurriedly— as you will see—since I am trying to earn some money as quickly as possible by means of my battered typewriter. So I hope you can let me know if they can be used in a short time. I myself was so dilatory a poetry editor that I would refrain from asking any other poetry editor to let me hear from him as quickly as possible, under ordinary circumstances. But I have been having a hard time financially.

That's the reason I'm sending you six poems too. Needless to say, I don't expect all of them to be usable, though I would be delighted if they were.[1]

Yours sincerely,
Delmore Schwartz

1. Moss accepted "Dark and Falling Summer," "Vivaldi," and "During December's Death."

TO DWIGHT MACDONALD

81 West 12 Street
New York City 11
March 10, 1958

Dear Dwight:

Here's another story for your inspection, at your leisure, of course. One thing is certain: the typescript is much better. But I'm afraid it's too long, too full of sex, and even too eggheadian. I've started to rewrite the story we discussed last week but it's going very slowly, probably because of the memories involved.

However.

I enjoyed lunch far more than you did. I'll call you on Thursday about lunch on Friday. Perhaps by then I will be less stricken with comeback fatigue.

Best,
Delmore

TO JOHN CROWE RANSOM

81 W. 12th St.
New York City 11, N.Y.
March 12, 1958

Dear John:

You would have heard from me long before now if I had not had all sorts of trouble, personal, unpleasant, lurid and implausible. All the enclosed poems were written during the period when I was, thanks to your kindness, a Kenyon Fellow in poetry. But as a result of choices I not only did not make but did not hear about, I did not enjoy the leisure and freedom which the fellowship would have provided under ordinary circumstances.

I need not say that sending you so much verse is not the sort of thing I'd ordinarily do, not after being a poetry editor myself. The reason for sending so many poems is a need of money. Perhaps you can take a few of them on a tentative basis and give me an advance which I can earn some time during the next few months, either through the poems, or a story, or a critical piece.[1] You may remember that we had an arrangement of this sort in the winter of 1951 when I sent you the first draft of "The Fabulous Twenty Dollar Bill." I have a good deal of fiction and criticism in first draft now if that would serve the purpose of making possible an advance.

I followed you at the Library of Congress last January and heard the most impressive accounts of your lecture from Randall and from others who are less critical. *Newsweek* apparently set up a whole article on the three lectures ["American Poetry at Mid-Century"], yours, mine, and Wheelock's, and then decided that the week had passed.

My copy of the new *Kenyon* did not come until yesterday and I have only had a chance to turn the pages and look at the table of contents, but this sufficed to remind me that the best of all poetry periodicals was being published in the middle of Ohio. Here in my native city the theme of meter is usually thought to be a reference to parking meters, gas meters, and speedometers. Nevertheless all conversations occur, unknowingly, in meter, here as elsewhere.

As ever,
Delmore

1. Ransom generously accepted six poems: "O Child, When You Go Down to Sleep," "Secession," "Sequel," "Once and for All," "At a Solemn Musick," "The Foggy, Foggy Playboy," and "Sonnet: The World Was Warm and White When I Was Born."

330

81 West 12th St
New York, N.Y.
March 22, 1958

Dear John:

Many thanks indeed for your letter, particularly for its preachment, which, as on other occasions in the past, is scriptural in the best sense, for what you say makes me conscious of the direction in which I am and have been trying to go. This was true of your comments about my long poem ["The First Morning of the Second World"] in the *K.R.* in the fall of 1955 and the discussions of meter which occurred subsequently and are, I see, still continuing in the current issue, and which I think you first began to discuss in print when you wrote about pure poetry and idea poetry and sensuous poetry sometime in 1934. The whole problem of the place of ideas—and of the "ideas of the age"—in the writing of poetry is of course insoluble in any final sense, and the most one can expect is a lucid interval between the exposure and destruction of one set of abstractions and the emergence of a new set of enchanting concepts. And it is so difficult to remember how inadequate the old and used-up ideas of the past were while in a state of infatuation with a new set of ideas. But my feeling now is that any set of ideas ought to be regarded just as one regards a set of dishes: they are meant to be used and used up and all of them will be broken sooner or later by the inexhaustible demands of "experience," which in itself of course is an idea and only an idea to most writers of fiction in America, and most critics. The real trouble, I imagine, is that one has to be so defensive about the intellect, about being an intellectual, and about eggheadism because modern poetry is so often attacked as being "cerebral." You remember how Degas went to Mallarmé with a newly written batch of sonnets, was told that they were worthless, and complained in disappointment that he had put such good ideas in the sonnets, and was told by Mallarmé that poems were made with words, not with ideas. This is the instance which always makes me think of how complicated and insoluble, in principle, the problem is. For Mallarmé made his poems with genuinely metaphysical ideas as well as with genuinely recondite words which he found in Larousse, so that his answer, in terms of his practice, should have been, Poems are made with words and with ideas: the words lead the poet to the ideas, the ideas help the poet to recognize the words at the right time: but one can never be sure that one has the right words and ideas until one has the blessing of another authoritative sensibility.

And most of the authorities are undependable, at times, also: One of the most hilarious experiences I have ever had occurred when I was reading Mallarmé and Valéry two winters ago and consulting Larousse for the more difficult French words: I came upon a brief biographical description of Mallarmé who was characterized, roughly speaking, as a poet who was obscure to such an extent that he was virtually meaningless. This defined a theoretical limit of some sort, for not only would the poems Mallarmé wrote not have been what they were if not for Larousse, but they would remain meaningless to an important degree if it were not for the labors of Larousse.

However, I must not run on at such length, particularly since these are matters more adequately expressed in conversation than in any other form, and perhaps we can talk about them when you come to New York again: I imagine that the remaining months of your editorship are likely to be too crowded to allow you to do much travelling, so when you do come to New York, please don't hesitate to let me know even though it is a matter of an hour's notice. I would guess that the conclusion of nineteen years of editorship would be [an] enjoyable prospect to you[1]—I've always thought that Eliot's poem "The Difficulties of a Statesman" was inspired by the difficulties of editing the *Criterion*—but to those who have been writing for you it means one more uncertainty in an ever-more uncertain future: no matter how good your choice of a successor, he can't begin by being experienced, since experience isn't, after all, an idea.

When I saw Randall and he told me that you were not continuing and that you had thought of Peter Taylor as the next *K.R.* editor, I wondered, silently, about what the effect of editing would be upon both Peter and Randall: neither of them would ever be the same again, although I'd guess that each would change very differently.

The check for the poems arrived this morning and the batch of poems you sent back arrived yesterday and included one of the poems you had listed as held for publication ("O child when you go down to sleep, etc."), so I am enclosing it again. The poems you took are exactly the ones I would have restricted my batch to, if financial need had not made me think it best to send you as large a batch as possible for selection. With many thanks again and all best wishes,

Yours always,
Delmore

1. Ransom retired as editor of *Kenyon Review* with the issue for Autumn 1959.

TO ROY P. BASLER

> 81 W. 12 St.
> New York City 11, N.Y.
> March 30, 1958

Dear Mr. Basler:

Enclosed is the form you sent me to sign the other day.

I should have written you long before now to thank you for your hospitality and to say something about the speed—the undue speed—of my lecture.[1] I did not do so because of several matters which I hoped I might not have to mention at all. As you probably have heard, I had been under a considerable strain for several months and this has taken various forms. The only one I need mention to you is the attempt made by Conrad Aiken, indirectly, through uninformed and innocent persons, to suggest that I would be unable to appear for the lecture. Since the letter you wrote to my wife and addressed to me was written in September and the lecture was not to occur until the 21st of January, the mere number of months intervening is enough to indicate that slander and libel were intended, although certainly not by you or probably not by your informant. However, since Aiken made a point of boasting on a number of occasions that he had seen to it that my lecture was cancelled, there is no doubt of what occurred, and how incapable he is of distinguishing between the expression of personal rancor (and unprovoked rancor, at that), and interfering with a fee which, like a job, is a means of livelihood. I hoped it would be unnecessary to speak of this to you, particularly since you were entirely innocent of what was going on; but I have been advised to tell you now, simply as a matter of making less likely that others whom Aiken singles out (and there have been a good many during the twenty years I have known him) will be distressed.

In a variety of ways, this kind of misrepresentation continued and made me nervous as I was during my lecture, and as I ordinarily am not. I may be coming down to Washington in May and I hope it will be possible to meet you again then, and also Mr. [L. Quincy] Mumford and your other colleagues. I saw a handsome tribute to you in a new collection of Edmund Wilson's essays [*A Piece of My Mind*] the other day. I myself have read about Lincoln a good deal, though in a dilettante and erratic way and written several long lyrics about him.[2]

With best wishes,

> Yours sincerely,
> [Unsigned carbon.]

P.S. If it is not too much trouble, I'd like a copy of my lecture in its final form.[3] I promise that I won't make any changes, unless you think them necessary.

1. S's speech at the Library of Congress on January 20, 1958—like his reading there at the National Poetry Festival on October 22, 1962—was delivered in a rapid manner which alarmed some listeners.
2. See "Lincoln" in *Summer Knowledge*.
3. "The Present State of Poetry," in *American Poetry at Mid-Century*, Library of Congress, 1958.

TO WILLIAM STANLEY BRAITHWAITE

[New York City, 1958]

Every American poet is indebted to you for your devotion, through the years, to the art of poetry.[1]
With very best wishes to William Stanley Braithwaite on the occasion of his 80th birthday,

Delmore Schwartz

1. Braithwaite, a black poet, compiled for many years *The Anthology of Magazine Verse and Yearbook of American Poetry*.

TO DWIGHT MACDONALD

[New York City]
April 2, 1958

Dwight—
The enclosed prose parodies, if they are parodies, were rejected by *The New Yorker* in 1949; "The Passionate Shepherd," "The Spoils of Joy," and the Shakespearian sonnet appeared in *P.R.* Although I was the only editor to vote for them (I imagine). "O Susanna" was rejected by *The New Yorker* and is at present being regarded by *Esquire*. Etc. Etc. I'll send you "The Foggy, Foggy Playboy" as soon as I type a clean copy.[1]
I meant to say to Mike with avuncular pride that I knew him before he was born, but all undergraduates are embarrassed by the "historicism" of the middleaged (all over 30).
Isaac Rosenfeld once translated "The Love Song of J. Alfred Prufrock" into Yiddish—it's a wonderful parody and could be translated

334

back into Yinglish (the language of Jack Benny and Milton Berle) by Will Barrett.

See you Thurs.
Delmore

1. Macdonald was compiling his *Parodies: An Anthology from Chaucer to Beerbohm— and After* (1960).

TO ROY P. BASLER

81 West 12th Street
New York 11, N.Y.
April 18, 1958

Dear Roy:

Many thanks for your letter. I certainly do not feel that you acted in any way other than you had to act under the circumstances which prevailed last summer: it would be foolish of me indeed, to suppose that your informant was not also acting in good faith entirely under the circumstances in which it was probably impossible to be fully informed. The culprits in this instance were in New York City and I had been the object of illegal arrest and illegal detention.[1] The purpose, as I have been advised to say, was literally to terrify me. I won't go into further details. The real point so far as you go is to assure you that I have no doubt whatever as to your innocence in the whole matter; and secondly to express the hope that you will communicate these facts to your informant so that I will not have to do so myself.

I have been aware of all these things since October and as I said in my last letter [and] to you personally when I came down to Washington to give my lecture. The reason for breaking a silence I would much prefer to have maintained is that there seems to be no other way at present to vindicate myself and to avoid the necessity of appealing to the law.

I look forward very much to seeing you when I am next in Washington and perhaps by then the entire matter can be disregarded as an unpleasant thing of the past.

With best wishes and many thanks again, Yours sincerely,

[Unsigned carbon.]

1. In 1957 S was handcuffed, put in an ambulance, and committed to Bellevue Hospital after harassing Hilton Kramer (whom he falsely accused of having an affair with Elizabeth) and police officers.

TO WILLIAM MAXWELL

725 Greenwich Street
New York 14, N.Y.
April 29, 1958

Dear Mr. Maxwell,

Dwight Macdonald suggested that I send you some more stories. The enclosed story[1] is but one of many which I have in first, second, or almost final draft and I am sending you this one rather than some of the others immediately because it is the only one of which I have a clean typescript. I would be glad to make any cuts or changes which would make it suitable for publication and I have made a few in the enclosed ms.

This is a good opportunity to say that I have found your comments on my stories, as Dwight communicated them to me, quite illuminating. The remark you made about "A Colossal Fortune" seemed to me very much the kind of observation at which I could never have arrived myself. What Dwight said, if I remember, was that the story moved from point to point purely in terms of concepts. This is true of most of my work until the past two years and I do not feel certain even now that I am anything other than an egghead who becomes all the more so, the more he becomes aware of the limitations of being an intellectual.

I'll send you some more stories soon and perhaps we can meet and talk about fiction and other matters.

Sincerely,
Delmore Schwartz

Mr. William Maxwell
The New Yorker
25 West 43rd Street
New York 17, N.Y.

1. "The Track Meet," published in the Feb. 28, 1959 issue of *The New Yorker*.

TO EMILY SCARLETT[1]

725 Greenwich St.
New York City 14
May 10, 1958

Dear Emily,

I am sorry indeed to have to send the enclosed to you and to ask

336

you to see that it is served.[2] I don't think that you are likely to do so unless you consult a competent lawyer. I would also suggest that you consult Dr. Gruenthal and anyone outside your family circle as to the wisdom of doing so. Since you have already testified in writing again and again as to the literal truth of what has occurred during the past year and many other years, you are an unequivocal witness, no matter what you may say and think or desire now, or in the future.

May the future have mercy on all of us: or at least may we recognize how often we are deceived about the actuality of justice and love.

Honestly,
[Unsigned carbon.]

1. Elizabeth Pollet's stepmother.
2. Possibly one of S's affidavits in the "Case of Delmore Schwartz versus Hilton Kramer, Elizabeth Pollet, James Laughlin, Marshall Best, Saul Bellow, The Living Theatre, William Styron, Perry Miller, Harry Levin" in consequence of his detention at Bellevue.

TO WILLIAM MAXWELL

725 Greenwich St.
New York 14
May 31, 1958

Dear Mr. Maxwell:

After writing the pages which I sent you the other day, I made the following summary of "The Track Meet." It suggested, as you will see, the possibility of introducing a direct and explicit formulation of the theme of the story at one or another point, or of rewriting several passages so that the ending would not seem to the reader as surprising, at first, as it does now.

When the narrator goes to an actual baseball game with the first visiting Englishman, it is difficult for him to explain the game to the Englishman and the latter doubts that the fans are, in fact, rooting for the home team with genuine seriousness and passionate intensity, or that they mean what they say when they call out to the umpire in great anger. The narrator tells the Englishman that umpires have actually been hit by pop bottles and suffered serious concussions, but the Englishman thinks that he must be joking.

In a like way, the narrator at the track meet attempts to discount or deny whatever disturbs or shocks him by supposing that the incidents are merely part of a dream. And when he sees his brothers shot, he attempts to deny the horror which he has been watching by asserting that it is just a dream and trying to run away from the track. It is then that the second Englishman knocks him down—an action which at once prevents him from escaping from the brutality and cruelty he has just witnessed and is at the same time another instance of it. Thus when the Englishman answers his assertion that this is only a dream by saying: "What difference does it make whether it is or is not a dream," what he means would be explicit in an argumentative and expository sense, if he added, "It makes no difference whether or not the incidents which have shocked you so much are part of a dream or have occurred in actuality, since what occurs in actuality is very often of the same character as those incidents: the cruelty, brutality, ruthless competitiveness, estrangement and conflict of those incidents are merely an exaggerated dramatization of what occurs in reality. You were disturbed by the news stories which actually occurred in the same way as you were disturbed by what occurred on the track; your attempt to discount the news stories as a one-sided and hence inaccurate version of experience is the same kind of evasion as your effort to dismiss the incidents on the playing field as *only* a dream. Yet the news stories were if anything far more shocking than anything which occurred on the field. Furthermore, if what occurred in the dream were merely imaginary and had no resemblance to the reality of experience, then your plight would be far worse, although you think that the contrary is true. For if what occurred in your dream were merely your own private hallucination, then the evil which has terrified you would be rooted solely in your own mind and heart, and your plight would be precisely like that of a drunkard in the throes of delirium tremens: when he suffers from the hallucination that he has encountered a tiger or a snake, his plight is far worse than it would be if he encountered a real tiger or snake: for his delusion as to the nature of what threatens him makes him entirely helpless: in reality, he would have at the very least a fighting chance or a chance to escape from what threatens him. Reality is dangerous enough, but it is impossible to cope with it at all once its dangers are denied or unrecognized."

This is surely too didactic, except as a summary; and if you think that the additional pages are too indirect an explication, I will be glad to rewrite one or another passage before the conclusion so that the theme will be the subject of a direct statement. For example, the discussion of the news could certainly be made intense enough to lead to an explicit formulation of the theme and the same is true of the discussion of Kierkegaard which will have to be revised in any case. My own feeling at the moment, which I do not trust very much, is that the new conclusion makes the point sufficiently clear by referring to one of the supposedly outlandish incidents which have preceded the conclusion and thus, I hope, making the reader recall the other incidents. It would be simple enough to introduce other actual news stories to make [the] point more emphatic and to support the reference to the Second World War. But it's probably best not to go into detail about these and other possible elaborations—for which there is ample narrative justification—until you've read the new conclusion.

The process of going over the story has made the past week delightful, partly because I had to try to think of how I felt when I first wrote the story eight years ago and partly because I felt like a young writer again: it is certainly a far more pleasant experience than actually being a young writer, and I am not thinking of myself alone.

Yours sincerely,
Delmore Schwartz

TO DWIGHT MACDONALD

725 Greenwich St.
New York City 14
June 24, 1958

Dear Dwight (and Gloria),

I'm afraid that the coming weekend has to be called off—for reasons too painful to discuss at the moment. Perhaps when I get back from teaching at Syracuse,[1] you'll be able to ask me again and I'll be able to be a house-guest.

Best,
Delmore

1. A conference in the summer school program at Syracuse University.

TO ROY P. BASLER

725 Greenwich St.
New York City 14, N.Y.
September 9, 1958

Dear Roy:

Enclosed is the corrected copy of my lecture. You have edited it very well indeed and it must have been a trying task. I also enclose a list of the names of people I would like copies to be sent to; if it is possible to send more than twenty-five copies I wish you would let me know: and if it is a question of the Library's budget I would be glad to pay for the additional copies. As you doubtless know, this is the practise of a good many literary reviews.

I am sorry to have to say that I will almost certainly have to make use of the letter you wrote me last September, about my being able to lecture in January. I would prefer of course to forget about everything that happened, including your letter, but it is impossible at present to do so. I am sure that you acted not only in all innocence and in natural concern about your program; nevertheless, the incident is important for a variety of reasons on which I will not dwell except to say what is relevant to your letter of inquiry concerning my health. It had not occurred to me when I last wrote you that it would have been possible to find out if I had lost my mental health in a good many ways other than that of writing a letter, the envelope of which was addressed to me—so that I would be certain to get it—but the body of which was addressed to my former wife. You will understand my feelings about the matter if I tell you, as I may [have], in part, before now, that I was the object of illegal arrest and detention in Bellevue for seven days, during which, as a result of improper treatment and false information, I had a heart attack on the fourth day and was put in a straitjacket and came close to dying. I did not know of this until last spring when I had a chance to examine the medical records. Your own letter was but one incident—there were a good many others—in which persons of great wealth, having involved themselves in a criminal conspiracy of the most serious kind—attempted to make it impossible for me to protect myself by preventing me from getting any financial help. Use was made of others as innocent of what was going on as you were and also of persons as unscrupulous as Conrad Aiken. During the past year I have repeatedly found that the defamation and the stigma consequent upon it have had serious consequences which I cannot do very much about personally, either through my work or by an explanation which sounds lurid and implausible to anyone who does not know the personas involved. I make this explanation to you with the same feeling that, although I owe it to you as someone who honored me by inviting me to lecture, it will nevertheless fail to be entirely convincing. This is one instance in which there is only one side of the story.

Sincerely,
[Unsigned carbon.]

TO WILLIAM MAXWELL

725 Greenwich St.
New York 14
September 16, 1958

Dear Mr. Maxwell:

I hope that the typing and revisions in longhand of the enclosed piece ["The Gift"?] won't be too trying. I have tried on several occasions to use the incidents on which the piece is based as the subject matter of a story and once as part of a long narrative poem. At the moment it seems to me that my dissatisfaction with previous attempts and comparative satisfaction now may very well be because the material ought to be dealt with as a memoir or autobiographical essay, since it is, as you will see, essentially personal in ways in which fiction and poetry are or ought not to be. I hope you won't hesitate to tell me if sending you copy so untidy makes any difficulty for you; if it does, I'll certainly send you good typescripts henceforward.

Since you told me on the phone about a month ago that you were eager to see more ficiton, I've been going over several stories and blocking out first drafts of stories and other pieces like the enclosed one, and I think I ought to be able to send them to you fairly soon. But in any case, I hope you can let me know soon, perhaps by phone, if this piece seems usable, either as it is, or revised. The editing of the story which you accepted last spring improved it more than I realized before I reread the first version the other day and saw how the omissions, which I at first regretted, made it more of a story and less personal or special.

Yours sincerely,
Delmore Schwartz

TO WILLIAM MAXWELL

725 Greenwich Street
New York City 14
September 21, 1958

Dear Mr. Maxwell:

This is one of the stories which I mentioned when I wrote you last week. The others are quite different and I am sending this one along first solely because it was the shortest and thus the one I could get from longhand to typescript in the shortest period of time. I'll almost certainly send you several more within the next few weeks, so that if you'd prefer to wait and choose among them, you might prefer to put off reading the enclosed story for the time being.

Yours sincerely,
Delmore Schwartz

TO WILLIAM MAXWELL

725 Greenwich Street
New York City 14
September 27, 1958

Dear Mr. Maxwell:

Here is another story. I hope that I am not mistaken in taking you literally about sending you material continually. When we last spoke on the phone, you urged me to do so, I think, saying that *The New Yorker* as a weekly was always in need of more pieces than most periodicals. I have several more stories which I'd like to send along soon.

The typescript is even more untidy than what I sent you two weeks ago, and the reason is that when I type out anything of my own, my inclination to revise continually and indefinitely, like that of most writers, I imagine, keeps interfering with the mechanical process. The present story has been rewritten several times and the typing is worse each time around. I am also enclosing a story published five years ago which is the first in the series to which the present story belongs on the chance that I may, among other things, be taking something too much for granted in this story, failing to define the characters sufficiently for an independent piece of fiction, or the like.

Yours sincerely,
Delmore Schwartz

TO HENRY RAGO

725 Greenwich Street
New York City 14
September 27, 1958

Dear Henry,

Many thanks indeed for your rapid and very helpful answer. As you doubtless know, the praise of another poet is far more gratifying than that of several other more easily pleased readers. I'm sending you the enclosed batch of poems as quickly as possible: I don't expect, needless to say, that you can use all of them, but since I do have an abundance—my only abundance—you might like a variety out of which to choose. "Summer Knowledge" is probably going to be the title poem of my new book of poems,[1] and it was, originally, a part of "The Kingdom of Poetry," of which I am sending one more complete poem—there is a good deal more and you might like other passages and poems more than the "Swift." But my typescript of most of "The Kingdom of Poetry" is marked with four years' revisions. Excuse me for not sending tidier copy right now, among the enclosed poems: If I do the typing, the poems keep changing and I can't get anyone else for the time being.

Don't hesitate to send all the poems back if they seem not sufficiently sustained.[2] But in any case I'll look forward to hearing from you within two weeks and getting paid on acceptance—both are very real kindnesses, which I hope I may not have to accept in six months' time. And I'll be glad to review Roethke's new book.[3] Many, many thanks again,

Yours,
Delmore

1. A collection of new and selected poems accepted for publication by Doubleday in April.
2. Rago accepted four poems: "Summer Knowledge," "Mounting Summer, Brilliant and Ominous," "Swift," and "The River Was the Emblem of All Beauty: All."
3. *Words for the Wind.* S's review appeared in the June 1959 issue of *Poetry.*

TO HOWARD MOSS

725 Greenwich St.
New York City 14
October 1, 1958

Dear Howard,

I am sending you the enclosed batch of poems for pretty much the same reason as when I sent you a 1st last March. I hope you won't mind if I send you another batch tomorrow. Poems are the one thing I have in abundance, so much abundance that I find myself indifferent or oblivious to rejection, a state of mind which would have been inconceivable to me ten years ago.

You have not heard from me all this time simply because my personal difficulties have continued, although I expected them to be at least partially terminated long before now, and expected that I would get title to my house and by selling it to be rid of that kind of economic pressure which is something I've never known before this year and which leaves me too demoralized much of the time to see friends.[1]

I must say—you probably have been aware of it for some time—that to appear with a poem in *The New Yorker* attracts more pleasant attention than an appearance anywhere else. Even though my little poem "Dark and Falling Summer" was printed on p. 121, it immediately resulted in compliments, congratulations, invitations from three little magazines, and in general appears to have been read and liked by more readers than six poems last summer in the *Kenyon*, one in *P.R.*, and my last volume of verse in 1951.

I'll assume unless I hear otherwise from you that you don't mind getting poems in quantity; and I hope that you'll take it for granted that I don't expect you to comment or even to write me when you reject them.[2] If it's simpler to call than to write about any question of revision or the like—I always preferred to use the phone—then I wish you would, at any time. My number is in the book and I gave it to you I think, but I'll write it again: ORegon 5-4482.

Best,
Delmore

P.S. I'd very much like to have a printed copy of "Vivaldi," if it's not too much trouble. I found the quotation from Goethe[3] in a novel by George Dahamel—which still leaves its accuracy out of reach.

1. Dwight Macdonald was arranging for the sale of the farm.
2. The last poem Moss accepted was "A Little Morning Music."
3. One of three epigraphs to the poem.

TO BRUCE ELLIOTT

725 Greenwich St.
New York City 14, N.Y.
October 8, 1958

Dear Mr. Elliott:

Since this is an unsolicited manuscript, perhaps I should say something of my work. My poems and stories have appeared or will soon appear in *The New York Times*, *The New Yorker*, *Commentary*, *Partisan Review*, *Playboy*, *Playboy* annual, etc., and Doubleday is going to publish a volume of my poetry early next year and a book of my stories next summer or fall: the enclosed story is part of the latter book.[1]

344

Looking at copies of *The Dude*, it occurred to me that the present story might be too long for periodical publication: I'd be glad to make any cuts or changes which would help to make the story usable. I hope, in any case, that I will hear from you soon, since I would like to send the story elsewhere and see it in some publication before my book of stories appears.

Yours sincerely,
Delmore Schwartz

1. Doubleday did not publish *Successful Love* in 1960. Corinth Books brought it out a year later.

TO WILLIAM MAXWELL

725 Greenwich Street
New York City 14
October 11, 1958

Dear Mr. Maxwell,

Many thanks indeed for your letter about the work I sent you last month. I think you're right about both the story and the memoirs. I'd like to try the genre of the memoir again fairly soon: I think that if I deal with later experience, I'm more likely to get beyond the overly personal and subjective, and I've already blocked out several pages about being a critic, editor, and particularly a teacher of English composition for seven years.

Both of the enclosed pieces of fiction may seem usable to you, although "The Hartford Innocents" in particular is too long in its present state. I began it several years ago, thinking of it as a long story, and it could certainly be reworked in several ways for periodical publication: it could be shortened, for example, and I think that the entire third chapter might be better as third-person narrative instead of a letter in the first person.[1]

I'm grateful indeed for your assurance that I won't be trying your editorial patience if I send in a good deal of work at once. I've accumulated a great deal of fiction in first draft, and if I can get it typed, I'll send it along fairly soon. Most of these stories have remained in first draft largely because something more pressing, such as teaching or editing, had to be done, and this was the case with the story which you accepted last spring too, which had remained in first draft from 1950 until last April.

Perhaps it is unnecessary to say that rejections don't distress me for various reasons: one of them is that some of my fiction many years ago was not only published but reprinted, although it was poor or no good at all. The editors who printed the work suffered from the same poor judgement as I did—or the same preoccupations—but I am still embarrassed that the work was printed, particularly since occasional requests for permission to reprint a story create a hopeless dilemma, a choice between offending someone else or permitting work I know is not good to be used again.

It may also be needless to say that sending you so much work, in such a state of untidiness and haste, is economic. During the past six months I have had more prose and verse accepted for publication than at any other time and more than I would in the past have thought either possible or desirable; but the amount I was paid by *The New Yorker* for two poems and a story exceeds all the others combined.

I very much liked what you said about Virginia Woolf in this week's *New Yorker*. She has certainly never gotten the attention she deserved as a critic, perhaps because her kind of criticism is not fashionable. Although, as you say, she is better on books of the past than on Lawrence and also Joyce, she sometimes was amazingly perceptive, as I discovered several years ago while writing a piece about Ring Lardner:[2] probably she did not know the difference between a double play and a double-header and yet she understood how good Lardner was when American critics were dismissing him as someone who wrote about baseball.

I did not mean this letter to be so long and I hope you won't feel that you have to answer in kind or even to say very much at all if the enclosed fiction doesn't seem to be right for *The New Yorker*.

> Yours sincerely,
> Delmore Schwartz

1. S did not change it.
2. "Ring Lardner: Highbrow in Hiding," *The Reporter*, August 9, 1956.

TO HOWARD MOSS

> 725 Greenwich St.
> New York City 14, NY
> October 12, 1958

Dear Howard,

Here are some more poems. There are a lot more and I'll keep sending them unless I am using up too much of your time. Don't trouble to comment on them unless you feel like [it] or you think they can be improved.

Best,
Delmore

TO GILBERT HARRISON

725 Greenwich Street
New York City 14, N.Y.
November 12, 1959 [1958]

Dear Gil,

Many thanks indeed for your note, which I was delighted to get for its own sake as well as for the very nice things you say about "Kilroy's Carnival."[1] As you perhaps guessed I began it when I was writing film reviews, and it's the sort of thing I've always wanted to do, so perhaps the future will be less difficult than the past.

Best,
Delmore

1. Published in *The New Republic*, Dec. 1, 1958.

TO DWIGHT MACDONALD

House of Mirth
The Crack of Dawn
December 14, 1958

Dear Dwight,

Events are in the saddle, as Emerson rather pallidly remarked 100 years ago. But before burdening you with what has occurred since Saturday at 3, I must tell you that I can't use your check until I hear from *Art News* [see next item] and immediately add that this letter is *not* a new attempt of Laughing Boy to ask you for more financial aid. You've been more generous in all ways than anyone else, by far, and this sentence is, to be plethorically emphatic, sincere, candid, unequivocal, literal, etc.

However.

On Saturday night two hoodlums called on me at 2:30 A.M. and stayed until 5, trying to get me into a fight. When they left—partly because I had begun to ask them to stay—I went to the police station where the desk cop wrote my complaint into his intimate journals. He was rather impressed that one of my friends had taken a few dollars out of my pants pocket, and had been so dedicated to the task of throwing all my belongings on the floor (he was, he said, trying to find out whether I had what he called spunk) that he dropped his draft-board card amid the chaos of books and paper. The desk cop seemed to be delighted by this evidence that I had not been dreaming, but his delight was pure disinterested joy, for he has not sent a detective around, as he said that he would.

Last night my well-wishers and would-be friends, whoever they are, were tired or compassionate, for they restricted their courtesies to ringing the downstairs doorbell every hour from one to five.

The only reason I report this to you is the desire to do so. When I started the letter, I intended to describe a joint project called "Eggshells," but now that the dawn's mauve light has become a cotton pallor, I don't feel like writing about it. It is a serious project, however. But there is no hurry whatever.

Best,
Delmore

TO DWIGHT MACDONALD

[New York City
December 1958]

I.O.U. $105.09 of the amount I get paid by *Art News* for the poem accepted by *A.N.* payable immediately upon *Art News's* paying me.

Delmore Schwartz

TO J. M. KAPLAN

725 Greenwich St.
New York City 14
December 26, 1958

Dear Mr. Kaplan:

When I wrote you last spring to thank you for your generous help, I was confident that I would not have to appeal to you or anyone else ever again. This confidence was based partly on the fact that I had never before made such an appeal, partly on the expectation that I would be able to sell the house and farm which I own in New Jersey,

348

and finally on the feeling that I would get a good deal of writing done in a short time.

Although I have gotten even more work done than I thought I would, I cannot, at present, sell my house. I won't burden you with a detailed account of the situation which has left me deprived of all resources, despite twenty-three years of writing and teaching. I'd be quite glad to make all the facts known to you or anyone who assists you in these matters, and the only reason I do not do so now is that most of the facts may not be of interest or relevance.

I won't be in the least offended if you think it best to disregard this letter entirely. Before writing you, I asked Meyer Schapiro whether or not it would be proper to do so, and although he did not say so in so many words, I think that he thought I ought not to; he said only that he was doubtful and that you might send someone to interview me. Ordinarily I would not disregard even an implicit suggestion on Professor Schapiro's part, for I have admired him very much for many years. But at present I feel that I must. And, unless I am wrong in assuming that Professor Schapiro's impression that I would dread, rather than welcome, any interview or inquiry, he too has been misinformed as to the actual facts involved. I said as little as possible about these facts, which are matters of health as well as much else, until last March when I discovered that silence had been used as the most effective and insidious lie of all and combined with clever expressions of pity for my situation and admiration of my work.

I just say again that I really hope you will disregard this appeal if it seems at all unjustified. While writing, I kept thinking of a proverb I read last summer: "If you don't have a dog, you must do your own barking." With best wishes,

Yours sincerely,
Delmore Schwartz

TO DWIGHT MACDONALD

725 Greenwich Street
New York City, N.Y.
December 26, 1958

Dear Dwight,

Would you mind holding my check for a few weeks more? The money is in the bank, but that's all there is there. However, if you feel for any reason whatever that you have to cash it, go ahead: no explanations are necessary, and you don't even have to tell me. Four editors who promised to pay me by now were either joking, boycotting the post office, or have become, like all my friends, jurists without portfolio. I don't know why I always believe what people say.

I am now going into a retreat until I shut up. Seldom have so many people had so little money: I know: by the evidence of my senses: not even at "the height of the depression" (as a student once wrote) has money been so scarce and credit so tight.

Silence is the most insidious of lies. But let the cagy beware: they will conclude in a cage. T.S.K.

Best,
Delmore

P.S. I'll let you know as soon as [I] do get paid. But please do as you like.

TO GILBERT HARRISON

725 Greenwich Street
New York City 14, N.Y.
January 5, 1959

Dear Gil,

Do you have any books that I could review for the *N.R.*? The reason I ask you instead of Bob [Linscott] is that it really is a matter of acute hardship, rather than a purely literary matter, and the situation in which I've been involved for the past year and a half, and more, seems likely to continue for another year at least. I'd be only too glad to tell you and your wife about the situation in detail—(since it was the real cause, although I did not know it then, of the troubled relations between you and me)—but both you and Mrs. Harrison might not want to hear so degrading a matter.

In any case, I hope you can let me know soon; and I won't be offended at all if you have nothing for me to review.

Best,
Delmore

TO GORDON CAIRNIE[1]

725 Greenwich Street
New York, N.Y.
January 14, 1959

Dear Gordon,

Many thanks for writing me about Bill.[2] Your letter did not get here until today, Wednesday, and its effect was one which I need hardly describe since you felt the same way. I wish you were in New York or I was in Cambridge—solitary grief is as miserable as most forms of solitude. I wish you would drop me a line at the above address, giving me Betty's address and telling me whether or not it is too soon to write her. The only thing I could add to what others say is that Bill was one of the unluckiest and most unfortunate human beings I have ever known and that she did a great deal more than most wives do to make his life less painful throughout their marriage. However, this may not be the time to say this and perhaps it ought not to be said at all. As you know, Bill was extremely reticent about his own intimate feelings to most people. But when I last saw him, he spoke of how Betty had kept him alive when he was most in need of help, usually because of drinking.

I may be able to come to Cambridge in the next few months, and I'll let you know beforehand. The Grolier Bookshop always was a second home to me and to a lot of others. In addition to myself and Bill. And it was not the books but the proprietor who made us feel that way.

Best, as always, to you, dear Gordon,
Delmore

1. Founder of the Grolier Bookshop in Cambridge.
2. William Van Keuren. He had just shot himself.

TO GEORGE PALMER

725 Greenwich St.
New York City 14
February 23, 1959

Dear George,

Many thanks for all the very nice things you say about my new poems: praise from you is and has always been praise indeed. You sound very happy which is just what one expects of the bridegroom when the bride is Phoebe. I did not know that you had married Phoebe until your letter came; but now that I know I will try to celebrate the occasion in verse as soon as possible.

I hoped that I would be able to come to Cambridge this winter or spring, after the termination of the degrading mess which has been continually exhausting me for the past two years. Please give my love to Rose and Wallace and tell them—*sotto voce* of course—that nothing has occurred during the past thirteen years to alter my political views, past, present, and future.

Best, as always,
Delmore

P.S. If you see Nela and Jack before I do, please give them my best regards.

TO HENRY RAGO

725 Greenwich Street
New York City 14
March 5, 1959

Dear Henry,

Enclosed is the first half of my review of Roethke. I'll send along the rest in a few days. The point I am trying to make, as you will see from the enclosed, is that Roethke and Yeats use almost the same words and style to come to extremely different conclusions. You can cut the review or do whatever you think best.

I hoped to get proof of the poems you accepted last fall by now: can you see that it is sent along soon? I hope I don't sound impatient. The pressures which existed when I last wrote you are over, for the time being at least, so don't feel that I should get any extra consideration.[1] You've been very generous and helpful in every way.

Merry primavera to you and your wife and *Poetry*.

Best,
Delmore

P.S. I've been thinking of doing a piece on *Dr. Zhivago* as a poet's novel: do you think you could use it?

1. A friend from the White Horse Tavern, Marshall Allen, was helping to finance S in the spring of 1959.

TO WILLIAM MAXWELL

725 Greenwich Street
New York City 14
March 6, 1959

Dear Mr. Maxwell,

Here is the last page of the story which I left with you when I last saw you. I've made other changes in previous pages, and I am not sure the enclosed conclusion is not too lyrical or too literary. But I'll wait to hear from you before sending you the revisions. The appearance of "The Track Meet" and my reading of it has convinced me of something which I would have doubted very much in the past—that a story can be much improved by careful editing. Perhaps the chief reason for my thinking that this was not true was that I was unwilling to do it myself as an editor, although I was sometimes asked to suggest changes. I felt that I was bound to get involved, in one or another way which was undesirable, with the writer.

I've been going over a set of connected stories which I wrote at about the same time as I wrote "The Track Meet," and I hope to be able to send some of them along to you soon. Meanwhile, with many thanks indeed for your critical help,

Yours, sincerely,
Delmore Schwartz

TO HENRY RAGO

725 Greenwich Street
New York City 14
March 21, 1959

Dear Henry,

Many thanks for your very nice note about my review. I think I can do the same thing with *Dr. Zhivago*, although the result will certainly be one of the most one-sided of reviews. If I concentrate on one phrase, "the stars in the trees looked like daisies"—and if it is true, as I am not sure, that the Russian word for daisies does not have the same etymological root as in English (you remember, in *Lycidas*, how Milton writes "day's eyes")—then it ought to be possible to do justice to Pasternak's genius for experience and language. If not, I'll write a longer piece and you can cut it and print it when it is best for you.

I wish I knew what my permanent address was going to be: in any case, I'll be here for the next few months, I think. If I had any real choice in the matter, I'd move to Brooklyn. Please let me know if you're going to be in New York. Letter-writing is an inferior form of friendship, at least for me.

Best,
Delmore

TO GEORGE PALMER

725 Greenwich St.
New York City 14
April 9, 1959

Dear George,

Would it be possible for you, or for you and Wallace, to lend me two hundred and fifty dollars for, at most, a period of three months? I feel ashamed to have to ask you, but I'm sure you'll understand that I would not do so if it were not a matter of acute hardship, which is part of the mess I mentioned in my last letter. I am certain that I will be able to repay you within three months, since my house in the country is going to be sold at last.[1] Until now, my right to the house has been made a part of the mess, but just this week a mutual friend [Macdonald] has been given title and I imagine it will be sold fairly soon. I have been publishing so much of my work during the last year merely in order to keep going, but you know how remunerative poetry is. //

Best,
Delmore

1. Elizabeth Pollet had filed for divorce two years earlier.

TO ROBERT LOWELL

725 Greenwich St.
New York City 14
April 12, 1959

Dear Cal,

Many thanks indeed for the money and for the very nice things you say about my new work. Under ordinary circumstances, as you know, I prefer to put off publication as long as possible, but I have been publishing so much and writing so much (I can hardly believe the amount myself) for the same reason that I called and asked for help. Since the situation looks as if it might continue for some time, I suppose that production will have to continue at the same rate until I seem to become not a writer but an industry.

It was very pleasant to speak to Liz—I think the last time I saw you two was in the pages of *Life*—and I hope you will let me know when you're in New York again, so that we can spend an evening together. I liked all of your new poems [*Life Studies*] very much and was quite touched and flattered by the poem to me, and meant again and again to write and tell you so. The stuffed duck belonged to Bill Van Keuren and he shot it—I've never shot anything but pool—and although it was not his first kill, his last occurred a few months ago: he shot himself, something I was afraid would occur for some time, for he was one of the most unfortunate and unhappy beings I have ever known.

Your new poems in the winter *P.R.* are as good as anything you've written and they have that peculiar honesty which Eliot speaks of in Blake and which he says other human beings often find unpleasant. In your poems the courage to be so open and subjective, in the best sense of the latter word, makes your writing have a new quality of intensity, an intensity so moving that it is heartbreaking.

Please do try to see me when you're in New York again: it's been too long, and I thought of you very often, and there's so much to talk about. Love to Liz,

As ever,
Delmore

P.S. I must add one other note of detail about Cambridge in 1946. What I said then, as I know from the anthology I read and wrote in, was: "We poets in our youth begin in sadness
But thereof come, for some, exaltation,
ascendency and gladness."[1]

1. Lowell misquoted S as having said: "We poets in our youth begin in sadness: / thereof in the end come despondency and madness."

TO DWIGHT MACDONALD

725 Greenwich St.
New York City 14
April 13, 1959

Dear Dwight:

I hereby authorize you to sell my house for the sum of $12,000. I will also be glad to sign any waivers which your lawyer thinks necessary to protect you from any attempt on my part to reopen the matter subsequently. This authorization is not made under duress of any kind, except in eagerness, which has existed for some time, to have the use of my books.

Best,
Delmore
(Delmore Schwartz)

TO DWIGHT MACDONALD

[New York City]
April 15, 1959

Received from Dwight Macdonald this day $150.00 as a loan. I promise to repay this on or before December 31, 1959. If my house in Flemington, N.J. which I own jointly with Elizabeth Schwartz is sold at any time, before or after that date, I hereby authorize Dwight Macdonald to deduct this $150.00 from the proceeds of the sale and to keep it for his very own forever, in perpetuum, and permanently.

(signed)
Delmore Schwartz

TO HOWARD MOSS

Hotel Marlton
5 W. 8 St.
New York City 11, N.Y.
September 15, 1959

Dear Howard,

Needless to say, you certainly may use my name in your Guggenheim application. I've been moving about from pillar to post again,[1] and no mail has been forwarded: otherwise you would have heard from me long before now. I'm also going to nominate you for the new Ford grant for poets working in collaboration with a theatre. However, I imagine that my recommendation is far more likely to be of use so far as the Guggenheim goes.

Call me when you feel like lunch or dinner after you come back to the city: the above address is likely to be my pillar and post for some time to come.

Best,
Delmore

1. S was evicted from his Greenwich Street apartment in the spring of 1959 for nonpayment of rent.

The 1960's

TO ALLEN TATE

The Hotel Earle
Washington Square, N.W.
New York 11, N.Y.
January 20, 1960

Dear Allen,

Many thanks indeed for your note [about *Summer Knowledge*]. As you may know, some of the poems—the ones I like best—are directly influenced by your poetry again and again. I say, "As you *may* know" because I did not always recognize the influence of your work until I saw my poems in print.

I was delighted to see the very intelligent comment on your criticism in *Time* a few weeks ago.

I'll be at the above address for the next few months, so I hope you and Isabella [Gardner] and I can have lunch or dinner when you are in New York.

Affectionately,
Delmore

TO ARTHUR MIZENER

The Hotel Earle
Washington Square, N.W.
New York 11, N.Y.
January 26, 1960

Dear Arthur,

I kept putting off writing to you because I hoped to find your very nice letter.[1] I must have misplaced it in the disorderly process of moving from the lowly Hotel Marlton to the present establishment, which is a slight improvement but not enough to keep me from saying, when I awake, not "Rise and shine" but "*Ce bordel où tenons notre chat*" and "*Il faut tenter de vivre.*"

359

The phone number here is OR 7-8150 but you probably have as little or less time for visiting when in New York as I did when I was away from the city. In any case, I'd like to read my poems in Cornell and thus subsidize a visit with you and Rosemary. I'm a much better reader aloud than I used to be, and I can even read a story pretty well. Can you arrange an invitation? I don't lack for invitations of this kind, but most of them are to places where there are no old friends. Do let me know soon, if you can, because I have to decide among the invitations I've already gotten.

I liked your piece in the new *Kenyon* very much and the job you did for the *Times* on that fascinating monster, John (Scarlett) O'Hara. Best to Rosemary,

Yours,
Delmore

1. Richard Farina, a young novelist, recently had seen S, was appalled by his appearance, and entreated S's old friend Mizener to write him.

TO ALLEN TATE

The Hotel Earle
Washington Square, N.W.
New York 11, N.Y.
December 7, 1960

Dear Allen:

I'd very much like to read my poems or give a lecture at the University of Minnesota next January or some later month. I hope it's not too ungracious to say I've become quite good at both in recent years and it would be very pleasant to make the trip.

Perhaps I should add that the extremely nervous state I was in when I saw you last year was quite temporary.

In any case, will you let me know, since I want to ask elsewhere, and I hope very much that when you and Isabella are in New York next, you will have time to have dinner or lunch with me. With my best to Isabella,

As ever,
Delmore

TO ALLEN TATE

The Hotel Earle
Washington Square, N.W.
New York 11, N.Y.
December 14, 1960

Dear Allen,

Many thanks for your letter. I hesitate to trouble you again, particularly during the holiday season when there are so many distractions, but I'd like to take your suggestion that I "get Betty Kray [Academy of American Poets] to book (me) for nearby colleges." The trouble is that I don't know who Betty Kray is, though perhaps I should. Would you mind letting me know how I can get in touch with her as soon as possible, since there will be a problem about getting dates in late February and/or early March.

In any case, I'll look forward very much to seeing you then. One lecture subject I'd like to deal with is "Twentieth Century Poetry and Criticism"—there is an obvious unity of the two, which would in itself be worth discussing—and I'll mention other subjects I've been making notes on, if you like—e.g., "Life As a Criticism of Literature"—but I'd also like to read my own poems. Perhaps I can do both on the same visit.

I have been working at new poems, but in a state of so much distraction—since I have to do so much I don't like doing to pay the bills—that I would be quite surprised if they were even good beginnings. I've also thought again of making a selection of my criticism—but I doubt that I can get a publisher. No prize seems to mean much if your books don't sell.[1]

However, I've been too fortunate in many ways to be justifiably aggrieved. And the last few years, however trying, prove the proverb is true: "A rolling stone gathers no remorse." Merry Xmas to you and Isabella,

Yours ever,
Delmore

1. S recently had won the Bollingen Prize for *Summer Knowledge*.

TO HOWARD MOSS

289 W. 12th Street
CH-2-3615
[1961]

Dear Howard—

I sent you another batch the other day, but perhaps to the wrong address, since the enclosed came back when sent to 36 W. 12th. Hope to see you as soon as I get domesticated at the above address.

Best,
Delmore

TO ROBERT GIROUX

The Hotel Earle
Washington Square, N.W.
August 8, 1961

Dear Bob:

Your letter and [Bernard] Malamud's new book [*A New Life*] did not get to me until last Monday, and it may be that my joy in being home after six weeks in Southern California [teaching at U.C.L.A.] makes me overestimate the new novel. But in any case, I'm sure Malamud is first rate, so I think I'll try to get the book for review, perhaps in the *Times*. This ought to be more helpful than a statement, if that's what you wanted. Let me know, however, if you'd prefer the latter.

I hope you won't mind if I add—in the interest of candid friendship, and friendly candor—that I felt fascinated and flattered to have you and Roger [Straus] send me the book. The feeling of being flattered was based solely on what may be a mistaken or true assumption—the hypothesis that you and Roger believed me capable of keeping separate things separate. Our last two professional meetings were pointless pantomimes which would not have taken place, had I not assumed that you and Roger—but Roger even more so, because he is financially independent—were capable, also, of keeping separate things separate.

Please forgive me for being explicit, and certainly I may be unjust or ignorant about the editorial decisions [not to publish *Successful Love*] you made twice in 1959. It was the last sentence of your letter which made me feel I ought to refer to the past at all, since it was the kind of sentence I used to write when I felt embarrassed, as a *P.R.* editor; you wrote: "Justified praise from you would help the book enormously." I know that, sooner or later, justified justice is going to help me. And I could hardly expect unjustified justice or engage in unjustified praise.

Yours sincerely,
Delmore Schwartz

TO DR. MAX GRUENTHAL

The Hotel Earle
Washington Square, N.W.
New York 11, N.Y.
August 23, 1961

Dear Dr. Gruenthal:

I doubt whether seeing you now would serve any purpose—I thought it might when I called you, but it's pretty obvious now that not even you can convince the defense attorneys that nothing except a trial by jury will—after four years of conspiracy and worse on the part of too many people—satisfy me. With best wishes,

Yours sincerely,
Delmore Schwartz

TO VICTORIA BAY[1]

[September 1961?]

Dear Vic,

I was in L.A. on Wednesday to see the Yankees play (something you can do whenever you want, although somehow I doubt if you take advantage of it). Anyway, while I was there I noticed, among other things, that you weren't.

Inasmuch as it would be particularly silly for me to try to talk you out of something you've already done, rest assured that such is not the purpose of this letter.

The purpose of it is, actually, because I kind of wanted to talk to you, and since (a) I don't know your phone number, if you have one, and (b) it's cheaper to write, I'm writing. What I wanted to say is that I'm a little concerned about you—not that you can't "take care of yourself" at twenty or nineteen or whatever you are (what are you, anyway?), but mainly because I imagine it's kind of lonely in so grubby a pit as New York gets to be after anything longer than a few weeks at the most. It will also, shortly, get particularly cold, although as you read this you probably don't believe that.

Anyway, if you need anything, like money, for example, let me know, care of The Monarch of the Dailies (Mer will tell you how I can be reached) and whatever I can do will be forthcoming.

Proceeding on the theory that you are at least mildly interested in the effect your departure and letter had on your father, I'll tell you the effect these things had on him. He was, of course, in more than a mild tizzy—mostly from worry—when you seemed to have left. Then your letter arrived about the same time I did, at five in the morning. It had, by the way, at least one missing page, and was about five days in transit from New York, and apparently, had been delivered to the wrong apartment, hence it was placed outside #7 on the floor at five in the morning by someone who must have arrived home at that hour (the man downstairs is dead, but maybe it was his ghost...) Anyway, I more or less grasped what you were trying to say, and Victor did too, to a lesser extent. However, your plans weren't included in it (perhaps those were the missing pages: it ended in the middle of a sentence). So when he finds out what your plans are (from you, presumably), and what you're currently doing, I think he'll be more amenable to the whole thing than you probably at first guessed. At the very least, I'm sure an airline ticket will be forthcoming if and when you decide you want to come home.

Meanwhile, it would be to your advantage to write to him requesting such information as: Blue Cross number, insurance policies, etc., in case you need any of these things. Other than that, it seems to be your ball game, so play it as you see fit.

In any event, I too would like to hear from you, despite the well-known fact that you, in turn, may not necessarily hear from me, as sitting down to write a letter is generally about as tasteful to me as Sunday afternoons with Marsha Toy's boyfriend's children[2] used to be.

The main point of this whole abortive letter, I guess, is to inform you that I do care if you're still alive and what you're doing, and would appreciate occasional information on these points.

Love,
D.

1. A student of S's at U.C.L.A. the past summer. She followed him to New York and later to Syracuse. Atlas, in his biography, says she was seventeen when S met her.
2. Apparently mutual friends of S and Victoria in Los Angeles.

TO HOWARD MOSS

289 West 12 St.,
New York City 14, N.Y.
Ch 2-3615
[1961]

Dear Howard,
The enclosed poem is typical, I'm afraid, of all that I have written

in verse for more than a year, so I will spare you the other examples of the results of complete chastity. I just thought I ought to send you something since you asked me and since I've suggested (to my surprise) that two poets I met in the West send their work to you.

Don't do anything but send it back: the others are all more extreme and would be unsuitable until *The New Yorker* and *Playboy* change roles.

I've just moved into the above address and I'll call you when I get all moved in. The palm trees in California are not really dead giraffes that have lost their poise: they are used tobacco cleaners brown with smog.

If I sound a little hectic, I am; last week I almost was killed a second time, at Bellevue, just like four years ago. But it's impossible to exaggerate, so I will be silent.[1]

Yours,
Delmore

P.S. I don't have need at all of money as when I started sending you poems three years ago.

1. S was arrested one night for smashing every window in his apartment. He was taken to Bellevue in handcuffs.

TO VIRGINIA L. DAVIS[1]

[New York City]
October 4, 1961

Dear Jenny,

Come back if you can and feel you can run the Living Theatre all by yourself: the apes have begun to run, send me presents, yell that they are not afraid of me, after another attempt to kill me at Bellevue.

If you're too involved, call me anyway collect and let me know which spire you were on when you said you'd tell me about M's corned beef hash. This left me bewildered for weeks.

The Trojan War has taken place once again!

More & more,
Delmore

1. English professor at Tulane University.

TO ROBIE MACAULEY

289 W. 12th Street
New York City, N.Y.
October 7, 1961

Dear Robie:

The enclosed[1] is sent you more by way of greeting than any desire to appear in print (and instead of letter). The week I spent with you and Andrew Lytle was the last and only pleasant occurrence of the summer.

Yours,
Delmore

Call me at CH 2-3615 if you can when in N.Y.

1. "Journey of a Poem Compared to All the Sad Variety of Travel." The poem appeared in *Kenyon Review*, now edited by Macauley, in the spring of 1962.

TO JOSEPH LANGLAND[1]

Hotel Carteret
208 W. 23rd Street
New York 11, N.Y.
February 12, 1962

Dear Mr. Langland:

I am sorry you had so much trouble reaching me. The poem I like most is the last poem in *Summer Knowledge*, the volume of selected poems published in 1959 by Doubleday, and called "Starlight Like Intuition Pierced the Twelve." Since it was written in 1943 and since I am very much preoccupied, I hope you find it possible to wait a few weeks before I write a short comment about the reasons for my choice. Do let me know if this is possible, and many thanks, in any case, for asking me.

Yours sincerely,
Delmore Schwartz

1. Langland was preparing an anthology, with Paul Engle, to be titled *Poet's Choice*, in which poets were asked to choose a favorite of their own and give the reasons why.

TO JOSEPH LANGLAND

Hotel Albert
23 East 10th Street
New York 3, New York
April 1, 1962

Dear Mr. Langland:
I hope that the enclosed is satisfactory, and I must apologize for having taken so much time to get it to you. Many thanks for inviting me to participate in the anthology.

With best wishes,
Yours sincerely,
Delmore Schwartz

"Starlight like Intuition Pierced the Twelve" was written in 1943, and after so many years it is difficult for me to remember the reasons that caused the poem to be written with a spontaneity and delight which astonished me. But I do remember that, for several years before, I had been reading the *New Testament* again and again, using a text with a very detailed Victorian commentary, and the text combined constantly with the commentary to make me think of modern poems I admired very much—particularly "Dover Beach," Hardy's "The Oxen," Valéry's "Le Cimetière Marin" and Wallace Stevens' "Sunday Morning"—which were explicitly concerned with the decline of Christian belief or the impossibility of any belief whatever. So I think now that perhaps the chief reason the poem pleases me just as much as when I first wrote it is the way in which it dramatizes attitudes which accept Christianity as a reality while at the same time dismissing the question of literal belief as, at most, irrelevant. Thus stated, this is, I know, regarded as a recurrent doctrinal heresy by various Christian theologians. But the poem continues to give me a genuine emotional satisfaction partly despite and partly because of the literal claims of institutional Christianity.

Delmore Schwartz

TO DONALD A. DIKE[1]

18 Bank Street
New York 14, N.Y.
June 3, 1962

Dear Donald:
I was delighted to get your letter and to hear, before that, from

Meyer Schapiro of the efforts you were exerting on my behalf. This is the first really serious job I've been offered in more than five years (apart from Fulbrights of all sorts, and a six-week summer job at the University of Southern California, which is where I spent six strange weeks last summer) and thus it pleased me very much in itself. I was also very glad to hear—or so, I suppose, interpret your remarks—that you and Kate were so much more pleased to be at Syracuse than you seemed to be when I last saw you in 1958 or for that matter in July, 1957, when we were all dissatisfied and I was making all sorts of remarks about having Fulbright's disease without knowing how right I was.

I won't try to go into all the strange things that have happened since then and which I hope I can someday forget. The point right now is that I would be very pleased and honored to accept a visiting professorship either for next fall or for 1963, and I am sure I have sufficiently recovered from what has occurred during the past five years to do a good job. Meyer Schapiro mentioned an additional possibility if the funds are not available for next fall—a reading tour (I've been on several during the past two years), and this would be very helpful since the strain of pursuing the Almighty Dollar continually increases.

In any case, without going into further detail, I think you can take this letter as a definite commitment on my part. I would have written you immediately upon getting your letter except that I was waiting to have a phone installed. My number is WAtkins 4-3059, and I hope you can let me know immediately of any developments or if there is any further question I can answer or clarify. And however matters turn out, I assume that the question of funds makes any eventuality possible, I am sure that you must know how grateful I feel for your efforts.

With the best to you and to Kate,
Delmore

1. Chairman of the creative-writing program at Syracuse University. He offered S a visiting professorship and eventually they shared an office.

TO HOWARD MOSS

18 Bank Street
New York City 14, N.Y.
June 5, 1962

Dear Howard:
Sorry about the last typescript of a poem which you received: I still

don't know how it came to be sent to you in that form—I myself would have trouble in figuring out what it meant—except that, in all likelihood, it was mailed by my-then typist who was herself burdened with a sick baby, a new cold-water apartment, a husband who had left for Asia and a boyfriend who was on his way to Russia.

The enclosed typescript is none too good, but it is, at any rate, legible.

Best,
Delmore

TO MEYER SCHAPIRO

18 Bank Street
New York City, NY
July 5, 1962

Dear Meyer,

Please excuse me for not answering you immediately. I was waiting to hear from Donald Dike as to whether a Syracuse bank could advance me enough to pay the loan and get through the summer with less difficulty. I did get the job, which is a good one, at [...] a year[1]—but no credit is possible until I start teaching. Meanwhile, J.L. is away and Marshall Allen is in Europe, so I have no recourse but to ask you to pay the amount which I will pay back as soon as I get my pay check. I'm really sorry to be the cause of so much unforeseen trouble.

Vicky sends her love to Lillian and you,

Best,
Delmore

1. At the request of Syracuse University, I have deleted the actual salary paid S.

TO MEYER SCHAPIRO

18 Bank Street
New York City 14
July 22, 1962

Dear Meyer,

I am returning the hundred dollars you sent me the week before last. I deposited your check in my own account, then sent a check to the First National Bank, but it was returned because it was addressed to the wrong post office box. Then, after you called me, I went to the First National Bank in the mistaken belief that the loan could be renegotiated immediately, on the basis of my job at Syracuse. They refused to do so. Then I went, as you suggested, to the League for Mutual Aid and was refused a loan because of my inability to find two cosigners. I think the best way of handling the situation is for you to ignore any requests made upon you. Then, when I am at Syracuse, I will repay the loan.

I am sorry that I have caused you so much trouble, but I had no way of foreseeing that it would be so difficult to borrow money or find cosigners. If Marshall Allen should return from Europe before the fall term begins at Syracuse, then I think it is quite likely that he will advance me the money to terminate the whole mess.

With my best to Lillian and you,

Yours,
Delmore

TO DONALD A. DIKE

18 Bank Street
New York 14, New York
August 1, 1962

Dear Donald,

I'd like to come up and stay with you for a few days next week while looking for a place to stay in Syracuse. If this is all right with you and Kate, don't trouble to answer me. I'll come up and send you a wire before I start next Monday or Tuesday, unless I hear otherwise from you.

Best,
Delmore

TO MRS. ODELL

907 Harrison Street
Syracuse 10, N.Y.
August 20, 1964

Dear Mrs. Odell:

I intend to continue to pay one hundred and ten dollars a month rent and to stay in this apartment as long as it suits my convenience, or more precisely my immediate needs. If you believe that you are justified in raising the rent by ninety dollars a month—and thus one thousand and eighty dollars a year—I am sure that it would be wise to consult an attorney and go through the customary legal procedures of New York State when a landlord wishes to raise the rent or persuade a tenant to depart. As you may know, you will be wasting time and money; but if you do not know that this is true, it might be worth finding out for the sake of other such occasions.

The only reason you give for your incredible demands, "excessive damages," has no basis in fact whatever. There are no excessive damages whatever: there are no damages. One mattress, which was very old and torn when I moved here in August 1963, became entirely useless as mattresses invariably do. As I told you in June, I meant to buy a new one myself as soon as my teaching and writing permitted me the leisure. Even if the mattress's obsolescence had been hastened by me, to suppose that it justifies an increase of over one thousand dollars a year, or [is] a threat to the other facilities in any way at all, is so completely fantastic that it is difficult to believe that it is more than a pretext: only a severe lack of relation to reality could make anyone entertain the supposition seriously. The literal truth is that, since I never cook or entertain, I make almost no use of the facilities and furnishings outside of the bedroom and bathroom.

I must say again—though you may know this very well and imagine that I do not—there is an established legal procedure through which a landlord can seek to raise the rent or secure a tenant's departure, and this is not only a perfectly effective recourse based upon many landlord-tenant relationships, it is also the only way in which my plans at present can be altered. I would probably prefer to get another apartment and avoid this very unpleasant letter and to conclude by asking you not to write any more letters to me, but use a lawyer or friend for whatever communications may be necessary. I have already had twelve months of letters characterized by gratuitous and insulting advice, lengthy analyses of character and habits of an intimate nature which a close friend would hesitate to make, and in general an insensitivity, insolence, tactlessness and wholly unprovoked hostility.

In any case, I will not open any further communications from you, but if you do consult a lawyer, I will be glad to provide him, at his request, with copies of letters you have written me.

Yours sincerely,
Delmore Schwartz

P.S. There is a limit beyond which forbearance becomes encouragement—your obvious compulsion to bully, patronize and insult anyone you [becomes illegible and crossed-over].

TO DR. EUGENE N. BOUDREAU[1]

1009 Madison Street
Syracuse 10, New York
October 18, 1965

Dear Dr. Boudreau,

I have not been able to resume monthly payments to you because I have no income at all. This has occurred despite my own wishes and those of the English Department, which recommended unanimously that I be given tenure last fall. The approval of the administration, which has been all that was necessary to give me a lifetime appointment is, as you may know, usually a formality. But the administration preserved an unbroken silence, answering none of my inquiries. There is no point in going into further detail, except to say that my teaching, which has been better here than ever in the past, has of course nothing to do with the remarkable sequence of unanimous recommendation and perfect silence. I think you know quite well the reason these things—and far worse—occur.

As soon as I have a regular job again, or have had some of my recent writing accepted and paid for, I will of course resume payment every month.[2] With best wishes,

Yours sincerely,
Delmore Schwartz

P.S. I must mention one of the far worse things. Last winter I made an appointment with a Syracuse physician for an examination; when the examination occurred, several days later, the doctor, in an extremely sorry voice which I suppose did him credit of a sort, told me my blood pressure was very high and that I might have a coronary at any moment. Since doctors twice before, during the past eight years, have misinformed me in a way meant to frighten me a great deal, I immediately visited another doctor and learned that my blood pressure was perfectly normal and nothing was wrong with my heart. This is but one of a good many instances of the same kind.[3]

[Unsigned. Never sent.]

1. Medical Director, Twin Elms Hospital in Syracuse, where S received extensive treatment.

2. S had nearly four thousand dollars in his bank account at this time.

3. S left Syracuse for the last time in January 1966. He returned to New York City, where he checked into the Hotel Dixie (now the Hotel Carter) on Times Square. On July 11, 1966, he had a heart attack in the Columbia Hotel, while taking out the garbage, and died in an ambulance on the way to Bellevue. His body lay unclaimed in the hospital morgue for three days.

INDEX

Note: Schwartz's works are indexed individually by title.

375

380

384